THOMSON
COURSE TECHNOLOGY

Professional ■ Trade ■ Reference

ADOBE® AUDITION™ IGNITE!

By Eric Grebler

ISBN: 1-59200-429-6

Library of Congress Catalog Card Number: 2004103481

Printed in the United States of America

04 05 06 07 08 BH 10 9 8 7 6 5 4 3 2 1

Thomson Course Technology PTR, a division of Thomson Course Technology
25 Thomson Place
Boston, MA 02210
http://www.courseptr.com

SVP, Thomson Course Technology PTR:
Andy Shafran

Publisher:
Stacy L. Hiquet

Senior Marketing Manager:
Sarah O'Donnell

Marketing Manager:
Heather Hurley

Manager of Editorial Services:
Heather Talbot

Acquisitions Editor:
Todd Jensen

Senior Editor:
Mark Garvey

Associate Marketing Managers:
Kristin Eisenzopf and Sarah Dubois

Project Editor:
Jenny Davidson

Technical Reviewer:
Ron Grebler

Thomson Course Technology PTR Market Coordinator:
Amanda Weaver

Interior Layout Tech:
Shawn Morningstar

Cover Designer:
Nancy Goulet

Indexer:
Sharon Shock

Proofreader:
Sara Gullion

Acknowledgments

Putting together a book like this is always a group effort, and I want to thank the entire Muska & Lipman team for their continued support. In particular I'd like to point out the efforts of Todd Jensen and Jenny Davidson.

Special thanks go to Ron Grebler, who diligently acted as technical editor and was always happy to point out my oversights. Thanks to the people at Adobe, in particular Daniel Brown and Jason Levine, for making a variety of resources available to me.

Thanks to my family and friends and to my loving wife Kara for all of her support and dedication.

About the Author

Eric Grebler is an IT professional, an author, and a certified trainer who has demystified the world of computers for thousands of people. Originally from Ottawa, he currently resides in Toronto, Canada. Eric has published a variety of books on a wide range of technical topics, including desktop publishing, digital audio sequencing, graphics, and operating systems.

When he's not in boot camp, Eric can be found tending to his lawn or running the hardest twenty. His pastimes include raising his heart rate over 170, eating less than 300 calories a meal, and flexing in front of the mirror.

Contents at a Glance

Contents

Introduction

This Ignite! book from Muska & Lipman will help you understand, use, and unleash the power of Adobe Audition, a powerful digital music editing application. Audition is Adobe's incarnation of Cool Edit, a program that was created by Syntrillium Software. When Adobe first acquired Cool Edit, they repackaged it with a few changes and called it Adobe Audition 1.0. This book concentrates on the latest release, Adobe Audition 1.5. Even if you have a previous version of Audition or Cool Edit, you will find much value in this book, as many of the features remain consistent.

While Audition does have some MIDI and video capabilities, its main strength lies in editing wave audio files. It has myriad effects and editing and mixing capabilities that will satisfy everyone from the home musician just getting started to the seasoned sound engineer.

There isn't a book on the market that can teach you everything there is to know about an entire application. The goal of this book is to give you a solid foundation in Audition so that you can further explore and embrace its full potential.

This series is designed for ease of use. It offers step-by-step instructions and provides many illustrations to help you on your way. In addition to the step-by-step instructions provided in this book, you'll notice that there are two other elements designed to help you:

TIP

Tips provide you with quick ways or shortcuts to perform certain tasks.

NOTE

Notes provide you with additional information or background on a particular topic.

1

Exploring Adobe Audition

Several years ago I enrolled in a woodworking course at a local community college. It was a ten-week course and upon arrival on the first day, I was excited to dive right in, start using some power tools, and let sawdust fly! To my dismay, the first two weeks of the course involved nothing but taking tools out of the cabinet and putting them back. This brain-numbing exercise was actually valuable in the long run because it made the process of finding and accessing tools and materials extremely fast when it came time to work on our project. That is the same type of approach you should take with Adobe Audition. Understanding where the tools are and how they can be accessed will help you create your projects faster and easier.

In this chapter, you'll learn how to:

- Change view modes
- Access menu items
- Work with toolbars
- Manipulate screen elements

Views

The user interface (a fancy name for what you see on the screen when the program is running) for Adobe Audition has a split personality. There are two completely different user interfaces depending on what type of view (Multitrack or Edit) you select. Everything from the available menus, buttons, and options will change depending on the type of workspace you have selected. In a nutshell, Multitrack view allows you to view and layout the tracks in your session, whereas Edit view allows you to view and manipulate one waveform at a time.

1. Click on the **Edit Waveform View button**. The view will change to Edit view. If you are already in Edit mode, you can click the Multitrack View button, which is just to its right. The view will change to Multitrack view.

> **TIP**
>
> By pressing the F12 key on your keyboard, you can toggle between the two different views.

Menu Bar

Across the top of almost every Windows application is a menu bar. This bar provides you with a list of most of the commands within the application. The menus are categorized into logical groups, making accessing commands easier. The number and type of menu options will change depending on whether you are in Edit or Multitrack view. Regardless of which view you have selected, the way in which you access menu commands remains the same.

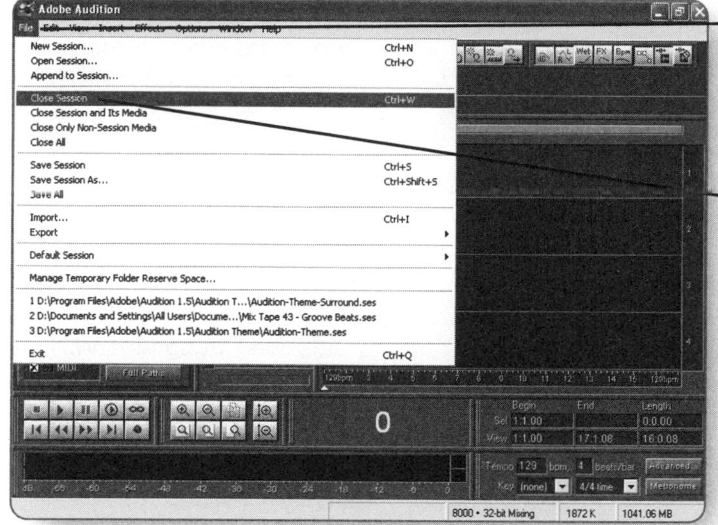

1. Click on the **menu category** you would like to select. The menu associated with that category will appear.

2. Click on the desired **command**. The command you have selected will be executed.

You will find symbols next to some of the menu items. Each symbol has a different meaning.

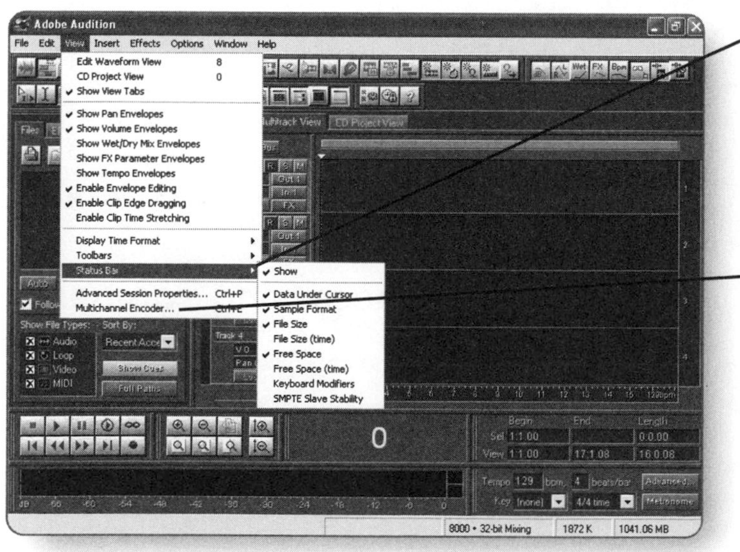

- **Arrow.** An arrow indicates that there is a submenu to that menu command. If you click on or simply hover your mouse over that menu item, the submenu will appear.
- **Three Dots.** Three dots after a menu item indicate that a dialog box will open when you select that menu item.

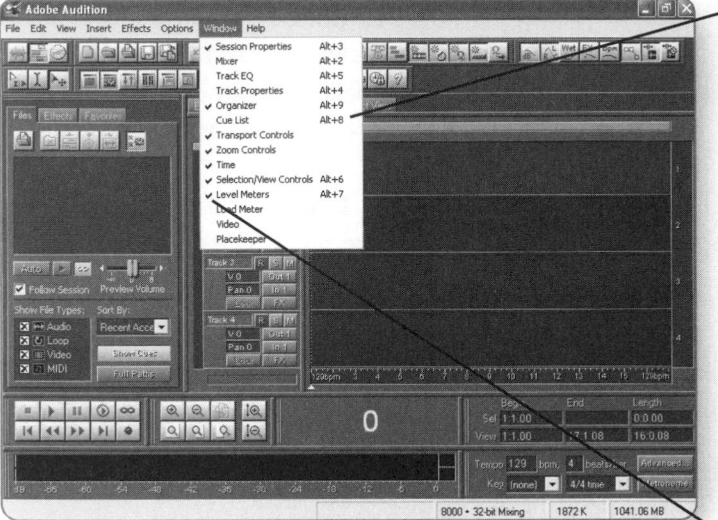

- **Keyboard Shortcut**. Beside some of the menu items, you will find a series of keyboard shortcuts. These indicate the combination of keyboard buttons that will initiate this command. For example, under the Edit menu you will find the keyboard shortcut Ctrl + X beside the Cut command. This means that if you press the Crtl key and the X key at the same time, the Cut command will be initiated.
- **Checkmark**. A checkmark beside a menu item indicates that this option is activated.

Toolbars

Underneath the menu bar, there is a row of toolbars. As with the menu bar, the number and type of toolbars and buttons will change depending on the view you are in, but their functionality remains the same.

Accessing Toolbars

You can open and close toolbars by right-clicking on them with your mouse.

1. **Right-click** anywhere on a **toolbar**. A toolbar drop-down menu will appear. The toolbars that are open will appear with a checkmark next to them.

2. Click on the desired **toolbar** to open or close. The toolbar you selected will either open or close.

Creating Additional Toolbar Rows

Because there is only so much space available for toolbar buttons, if you open too many toolbars, the buttons will appear off-screen. To avoid this, you can add additional toolbar rows. Additional rows can only be added when the first row of toolbars is full.

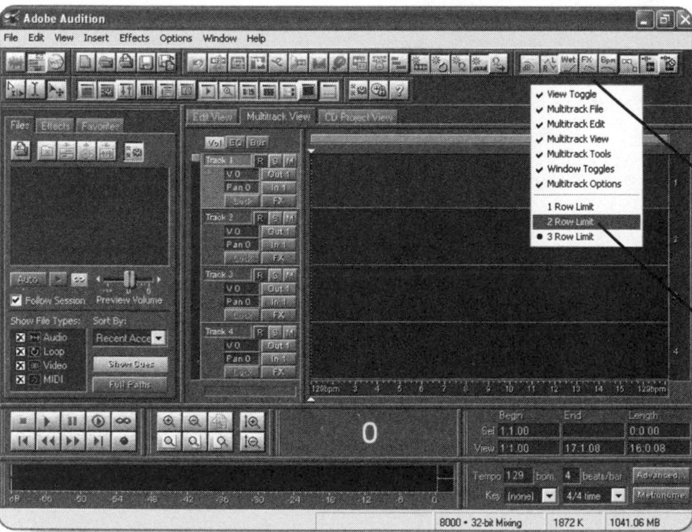

1. Right-click anywhere on an existing **toolbar**. A toolbar drop-down menu will appear.

2. Click the desired **row limit**. Any buttons that had spilled over the screen will now appear on the additional row.

Zooming

Being able to zoom in and out of information on the screen becomes vitally important when it comes time to edit your tracks. By zooming in and out you can obtain much greater detail when creating selections. This is of critical importance when you are cutting or pasting data. Adobe Audition provides you with many tools for zooming in and out of your data.

Zooming with Buttons

You can utilize the buttons to quickly zoom in and out of areas of your screen.

1. Click on the **Zoom In Horizontally button**. This will horizontally zoom in on your data and it will appear as though the information is being stretched horizontally across the screen. When you click on the Zoom In Horizontally button, the time scale of the ruler becomes shorter.

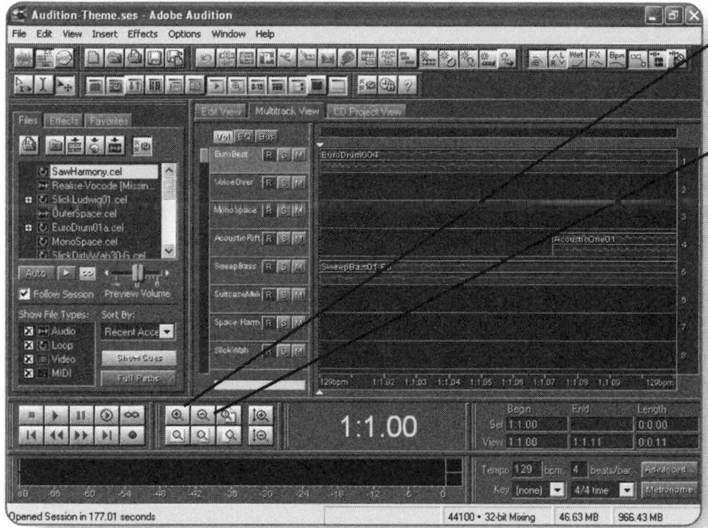

2. Repeat Step 1 until the desired zoom level is achieved.

3. Click on the **Zoom Out Horizontally button**. This will horizontally zoom out of your data and it will appear as though the information is being condensed. This is actually increasing the time scale that appears on the screen.

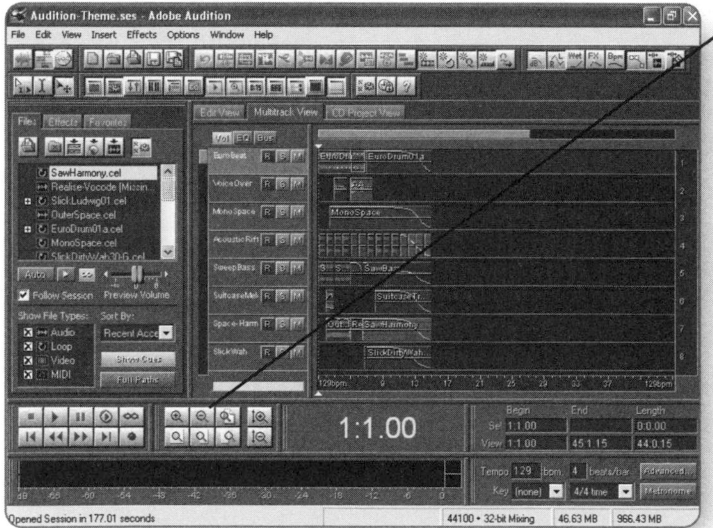

4. Repeat Step 3 until the desired zoom level is achieved.

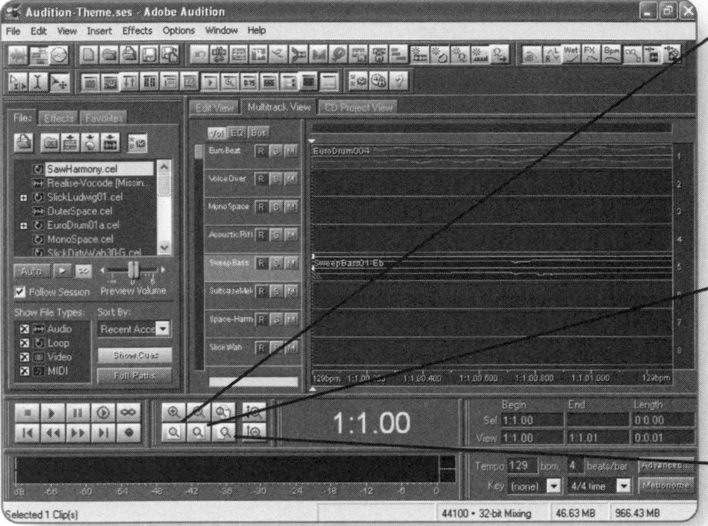

5. **Click** on the **Zoom In to Selection button** to zoom into an area that you have selected. Selections will be covered in the section titled "Making Selections" in the next chapter.

6. **Click** on the **Zoom In to Left Edge of Selection button**. This will zoom you to the left edge of the selection.

7. **Click** on the **Zoom In to Right Edge of Selection button**. This will zoom into the right edge of your selection.

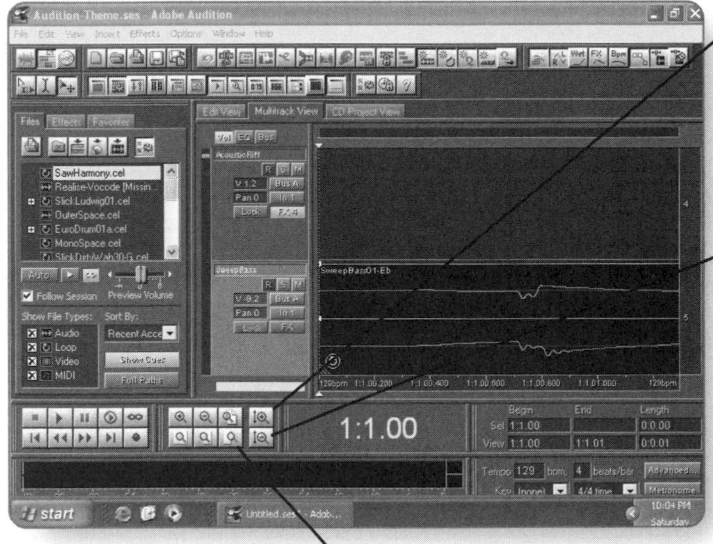

8. **Click** on the **Zoom In Vertically button** to expand the view of the data vertically. This will allow you to see fewer tracks.

9. **Click** on the **Zoom Out Vertically button**. This will increase the number of tracks you can see on the screen.

10. **Click** on the **Zoom Out Full Both Axis button.** This will zoom out so that the contents of all axes can be seen.

Zooming with the Mouse

Using the mouse in conjunction with the rulers, you can quickly zoom into audio that falls within a specific time segment.

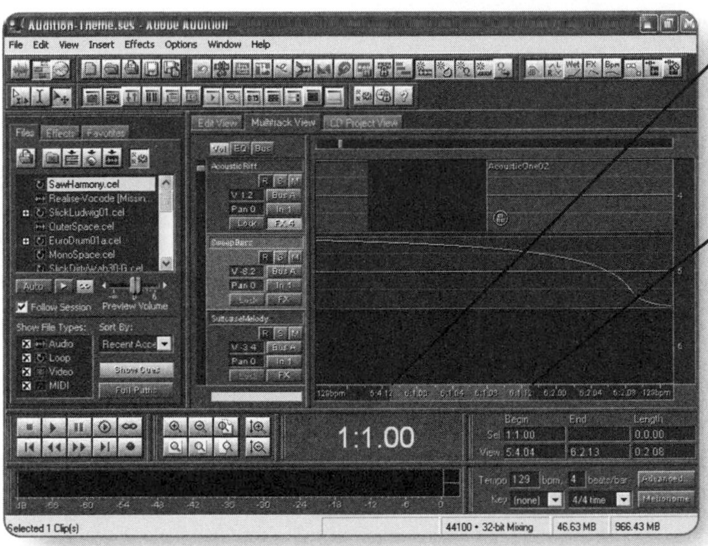

1. Position your **mouse pointer** over the horizontal or vertical time ruler. The mouse pointer will turn into a hand.

2. Right-click and drag to the **left or right or up or down**. As you drag, a segment of the ruler will be highlighted. The highlighted area indicates the timeline that will be zoomed in on.

3. Release the **mouse button**. You will zoom in on the area that was highlighted in Step 2.

Panning

Unlike most Windows applications, Adobe Audition does not have scroll buttons or bars that allow you to move up and down through your document (it uses portion bars instead—see the following section). Within Audition you must pan up or down to move through your file.

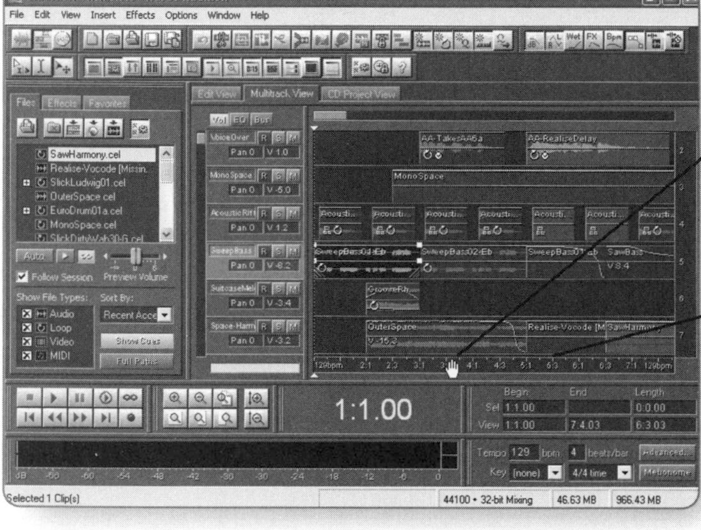

1. **Position** the **mouse pointer** on the horizontal or vertical ruler. The mouse pointer will change into a hand.

2. **Click and drag** to the **left or right or up or down**, depending on whether you are over the horizontal or vertical rulers. The screen will move in the direction you pan.

Portion Bars

The portion bars work like traditional scroll boxes and allow you to scroll through your file.

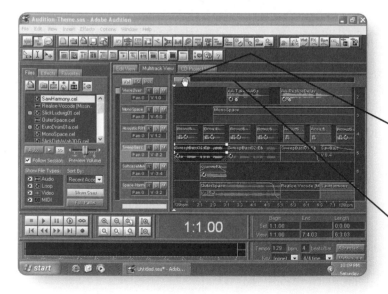

1. **Position** the **mouse pointer** over the horizontal or vertical portion bar. The mouse pointer will change into a hand.

2. **Click and drag** to the **left or right or up or down**, depending on whether you are over the horizontal or vertical portion bar. The screen will move in the direction you pan.

Changing Views with the View Controls

In Edit view there is a set of view controls that allow you to manually set the zoom level. You can set a start and end point for how much of the waveform will be seen in the wave display.

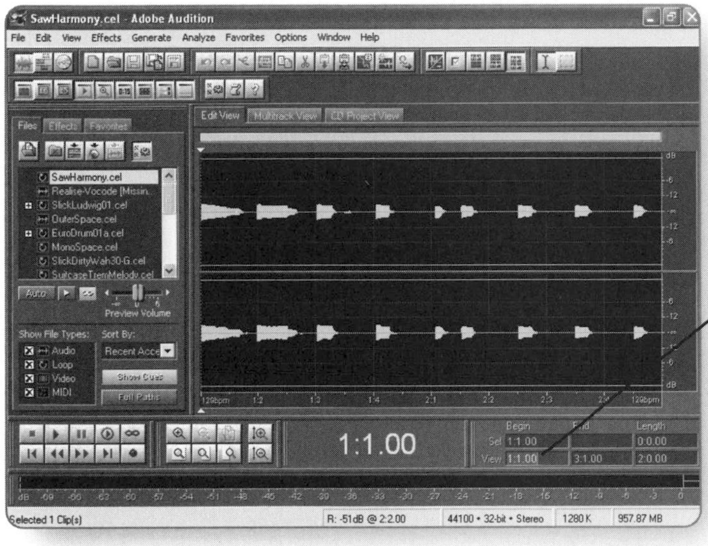

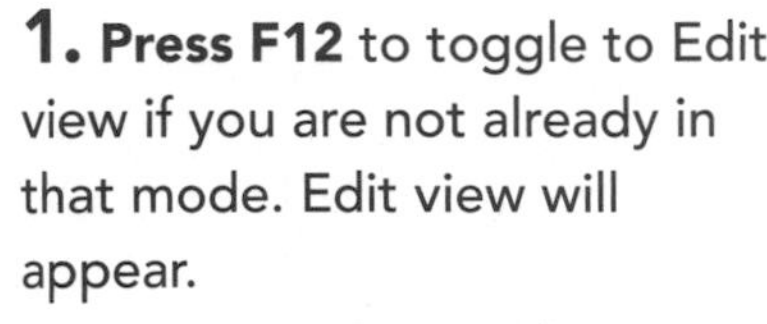

1. **Press F12** to toggle to Edit view if you are not already in that mode. Edit view will appear.

2. **Click once** in any area of the **Begin column** of the View row. The number will become highlighted.

3. **Type** a **number** for the begin time. The number will appear.

4. **Press** the **Tab key** on your keyboard. The number in the End column of the View row will become highlighted.

5. **Type** a **number** for the end time. The end time will be displayed.

6. **Press Enter**. The wave display will change to the parameters that you have set.

Screen Divider

The user interface for Adobe Audition is basically split in half. The left half contains windows that allow you to manipulate data, and the right half gives you a visual representation of your audio information. Depending on the task you are completing, you may want to expand or retract one of these halves to make it easier to work with.

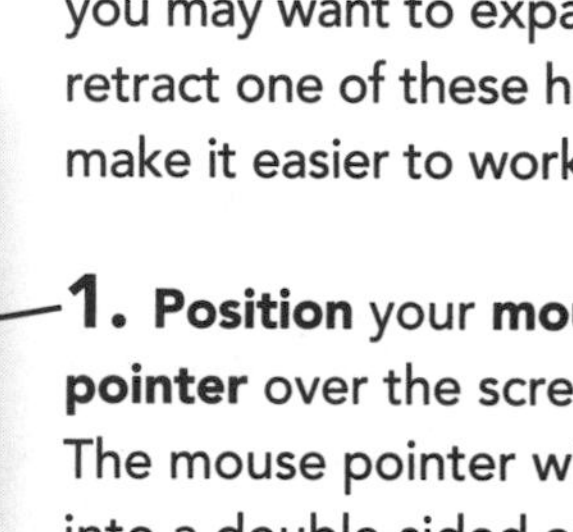

1. Position your **mouse pointer** over the screen divider. The mouse pointer will change into a double-sided arrow.

2. Click and drag to the **left** or the **right**. As you drag, the proportion of one of the halves will change.

3. Release the **mouse button**. The screen proportions will be set.

Moving Screen Elements

We all have different preferences about how we like to work. Some people can only be productive when their desks are spotless, whereas others need complete chaos in order to get anything done. Adobe Audition allows you to move and resize certain elements of the user interface to match your working style.

1. Position the **mouse pointer** over the double gray bars. Only those windows that have two gray vertical bars can be repositioned and resized. The mouse pointer will turn into a four-sided arrow.

2. Click and drag the **window** to its new location.

3. Release the **mouse button**. The window will now be in its new location.

4. Position the **mouse pointer** over an edge of the window. The mouse pointer will become a double arrow.

5. Click and drag in **any direction** to resize the window. As you drag the window will resize.

6. Release the **mouse button**. The window will be resized.

Showing and Hiding Screen Elements

There are certain elements of the user interface that you will use all the time, and there are others that you will use rarely, if at all. Adobe Audition allows you to hide parts of the user interface to help maximize screen real estate.

1. Position your **mouse pointer** over any of the Hide/Show buttons in the toolbar. These buttons all have icons with a blue rectangle at the top. When you have your mouse pointer over one of the buttons longer than a second, a tool tip will appear describing what that button will show/hide.

2. Click on the desired **button**. The button will appear depressed and the screen element that it corresponds to will be hidden. In this example we are hiding the Time window.

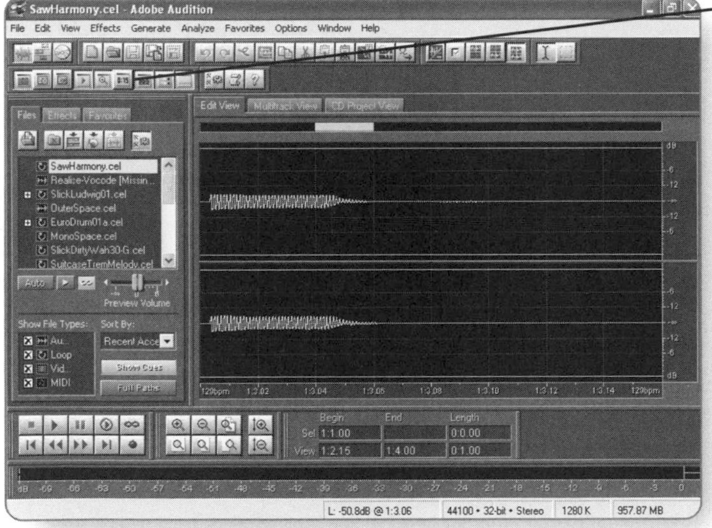

3. Repeat Step 2 to unhide the screen element.

2

Basic Training

The goal of army basic training is to break you down and then build you up again. Don't worry, to learn the basics of Adobe Audition there will be no hills to climb, no push ups, and of course, no drill sergeant screaming commands down the back of your neck. No, in fact, your experience with learning the basics will be a breeze.

In this chapter, you'll learn how to:

- Create a new session
- Open and save sessions
- Append to a session
- Use the transport buttons

Creating a New Session

The projects that you create in Adobe Audition are called sessions. Your session file includes all of the audio files that are contained within your project. You have the option of either starting a new session from scratch or opening an existing session. When you create a new session, you'll have to set the sample rate, channels, and resolution.

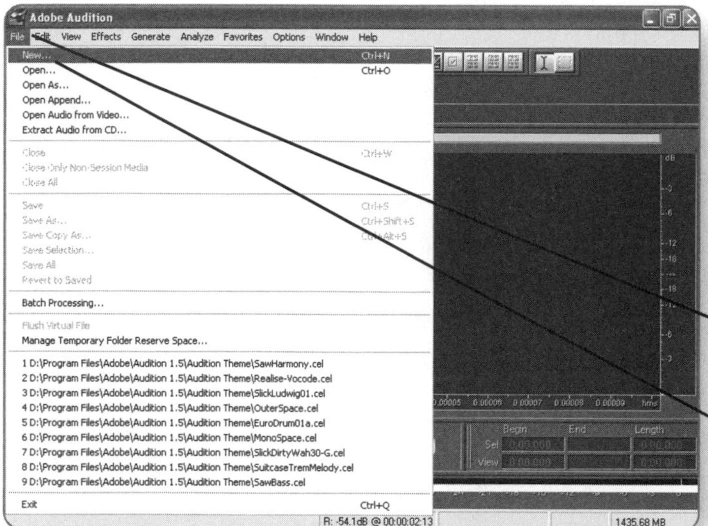

1. **Click** on **File**. The File menu will appear.

2. **Click** on **New**. The New Session dialog box will appear.

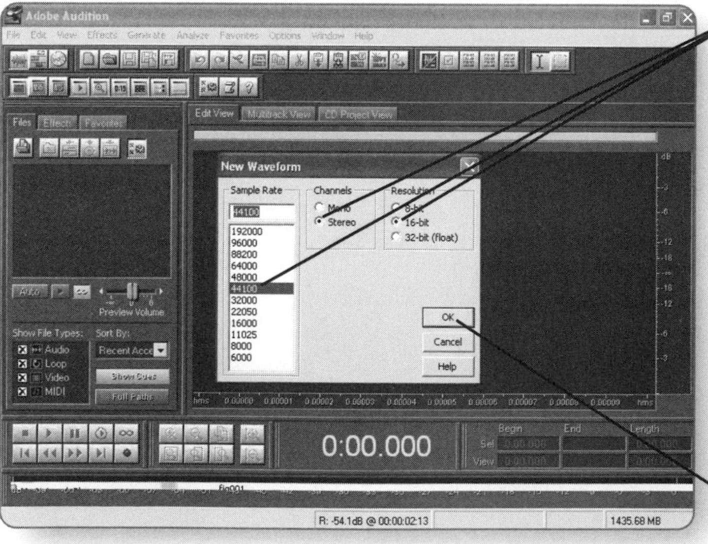

3. **Click** on the desired **sample rate, channels, and resolution**. The options you pick will be selected.

> **TIP**
>
> If you are planning on recording your sessions onto CD, set the sample rate to 44100 samples per second.

4. **Click** on **OK**. The session will be created with the criteria you set.

> **NOTE**
>
> Any audio files that you import within a session will need to have the same sample rate and resolution that you specified when creating the session.

Saving

It's happened to all of us. You're halfway finished working on a file and the computer crashes, or there is a blackout, or the cat chews through the power cord and you lose all of your unsaved work. We all know it's a good idea to save our work periodically, and here's how you go about doing it in Adobe Audition.

Save As

The first time you save a session, you should use the Save As command. This command allows you to name your session and select the folder in which it will be stored. You must have at least one audio file open in your session to save it.

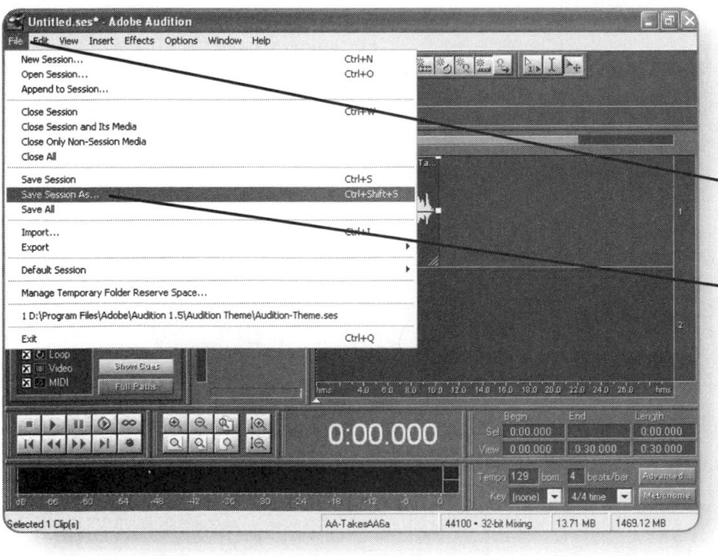

1. **Click** on **File**. The File menu will appear.

2. **Click** on **Save Session As**. The Save Session As dialog box will appear.

3. Type a **name** for your file. It's a good idea to give your session a descriptive name so that you'll be able to recognize it later when sifting through files. Names like Session1 and Session2 make it difficult to figure out the contents of the file without opening it.

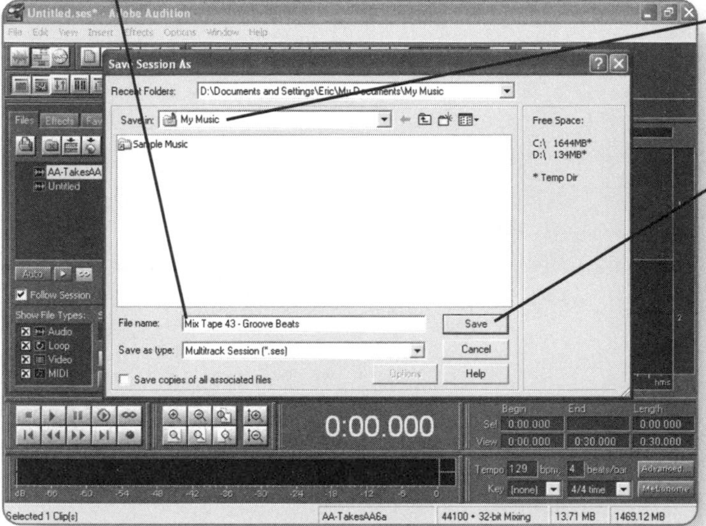

4. Choose a **folder** on your computer's hard drive in which to save the session.

5. Click on **OK**. The session will be saved with the name you have assigned it.

> **TIP**
>
> You can use the Save As command at any time to save your session with a new name.

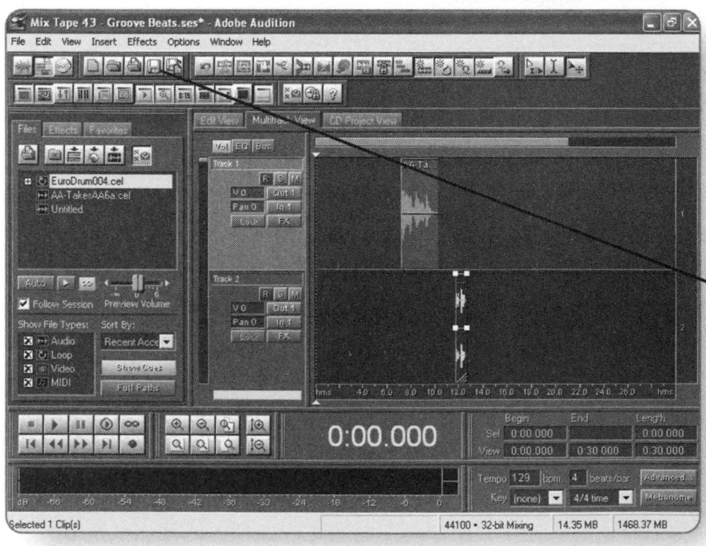

Using the Save Command

Once you have saved a file with a name, subsequent saves become much easier.

1. Click on the **Save the Multitrack Session button**. Any changes that you have made to the file since you last saved will be saved.

Opening an Existing Session

Once you have saved a session, it can be accessed at any time using the Open command.

1. **Click** on the **Open a Multitrack Session button**. The Open dialog box will appear.

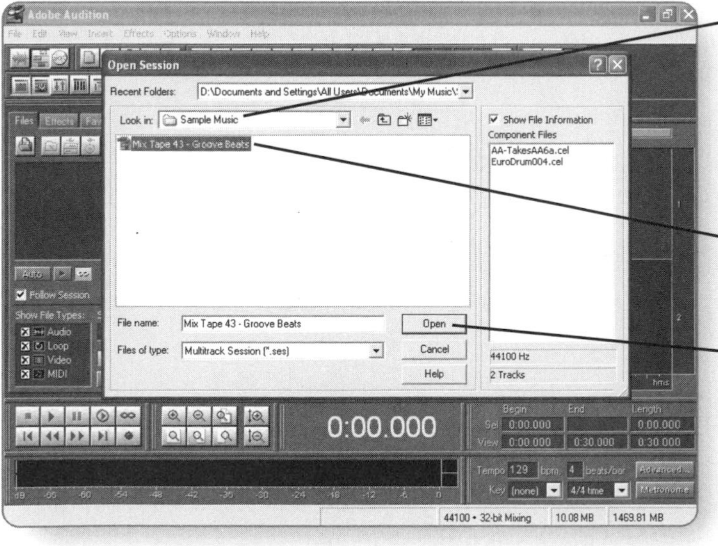

2. **Navigate** to the **folder** that contains the session file that you would like to open. Adobe Audition session files have the extension .ses.

3. **Click** on the desired **file**. It will appear highlighted.

4. **Click** on **Open**. The session, including all of the audio files contained within, will open.

Making Selections

You may want to preview certain parts of your composition, edit specific areas, or move specific clips of audio. In order to accomplish any of these tasks, you must first make a selection. A selection identifies and isolates a specific area for editing. When you make a selection, the area that you select will become highlighted to indicate that it will be affected by any editing, whereas the non-selected areas remain protected against changes. Adobe Audition provides many different ways to create a selection. The selection method that you choose will vary on what you are trying to accomplish and what view mode you are in.

Selecting in Multitrack View

While in Multitrack view, you can select all tracks within a specific timeline, individual clips of audio, or all clips within the session.

Selecting All Audio within a Specific Time Range

Adobe Audition provides you with two ways of selecting all of the audio that falls within a certain time frame.

Click and Drag Selecting

Clicking and dragging, perhaps the fastest method for creating selections, allows you to quickly select audio within a specific time range, using your mouse.

1. **Position** the **mouse pointer** at the left edge of the time range that you would like to select. Alternatively, you can start on the right; you will just have to drag to the left in step 2.

2. **Click and drag diagonally** to the **right**. As you drag, a marquee will appear. The areas the marquee touches will be selected.

3. **Release** the **mouse button**. All of the audio that falls within the time range you have dragged across will now be selected.

Selecting Using the Selection Controls

Although clicking and dragging can be very quick, it isn't necessarily an accurate method for creating selections. Accuracy can be of utmost importance when editing your audio files, therefore Audition provides you with a method to create precise selections.

1. **Click once** in any **area** of the Begin column of the Sel row. The number will be highlighted.

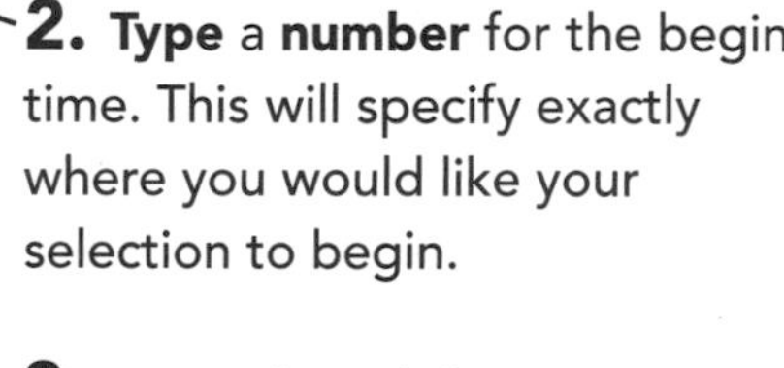

2. **Type** a **number** for the begin time. This will specify exactly where you would like your selection to begin.

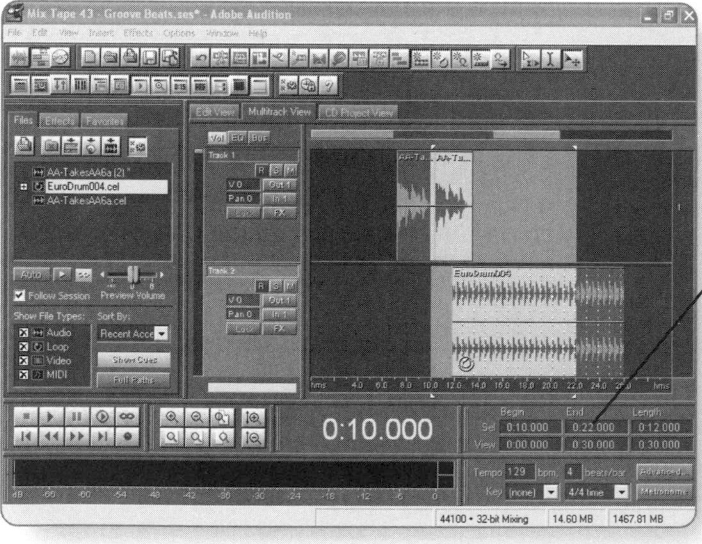

3. **Press** the **Tab key** on your keyboard. The number in the End column of the Sel row will be highlighted.

4. **Type** a **number** for the end time that you would like to be displayed.

5. **Press Enter**. The selection will be made based on the data that you have entered.

Adjusting Time Range Selections

Once you have created a time range selection, it can easily be adjusted.

1. Position the **mouse pointer** over any of the yellow triangles that border the corners of your selection. The mouse pointer will become a hand.

2. Click and drag to the **left or right** to adjust the selection. As you drag, you will see the selection change.

3. Release the **mouse button**. The selection will be adjusted.

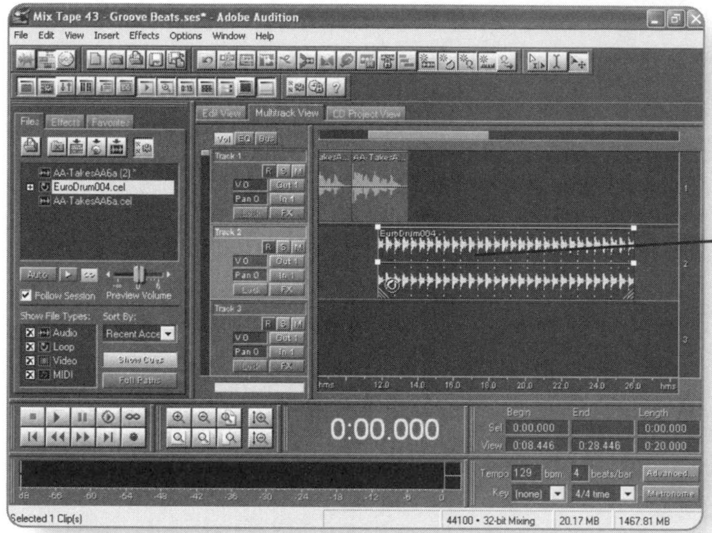

Selecting Individual Clips

You can select individual clips of audio by simply clicking on them.

1. Click on the **clip** that you would like to select. It will become highlighted to indicate that it is selected.

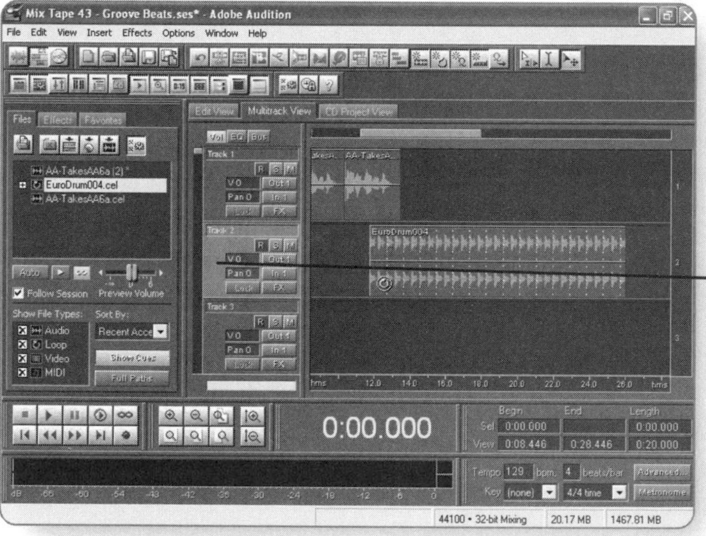

Selecting All Clips within a Track

Adobe Audition gives you the ability to quickly select all the audio within a specific track.

1. Click once in any **blank area** of the Track Control window of the track that contains the audio clips that you would like to select. The track background color will change to a light gray.

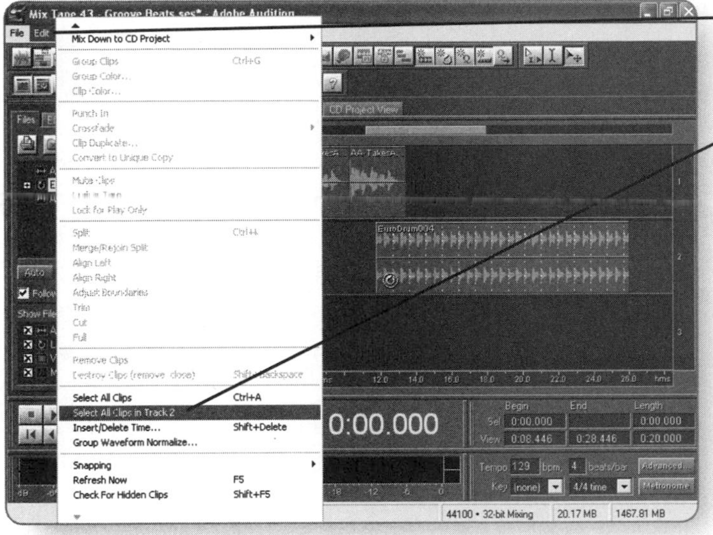

2. Click on **Edit**. The Edit menu will appear.

3. Click on **Select All Clips in Track (Name of Track).** All the clips in the track that you selected in Step 1 will be highlighted.

> **TIP**
>
> To select all of the audio clips within the entire session, press Ctrl + A.

Deselecting

So you've made your selection, completed your editing, and now you want to get rid of the selection. It's a breeze; it just takes one click of the mouse.

1. Click once in any **blank area** of the Session display and the selection will be removed.

Selecting in Waveform View

Many of the same selection methods used in the Multitrack view will also work in the Waveform view. In addition, there is a selection method that allows you to select the portion of the waveform that is in the current window. The Select View command will automatically select everything that is within the current view of the wave display. The fastest way to select all of the audio that is within the current view is to use the mouse button.

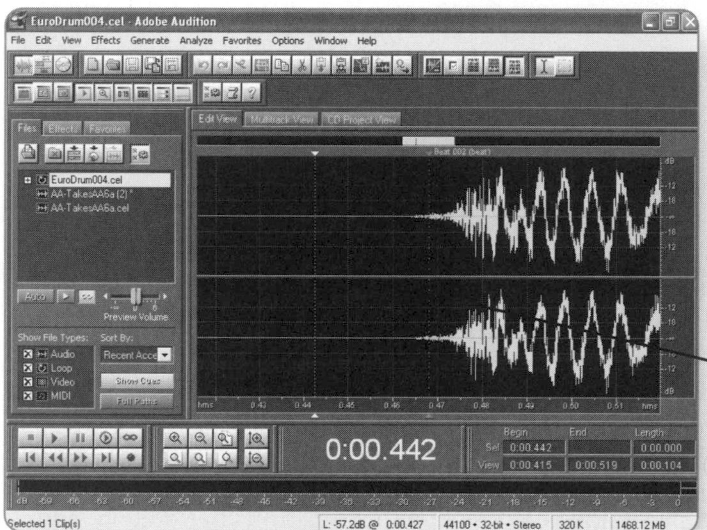

1. **Double-click** anywhere within the **wave display**. All audio within the current display will be selected.

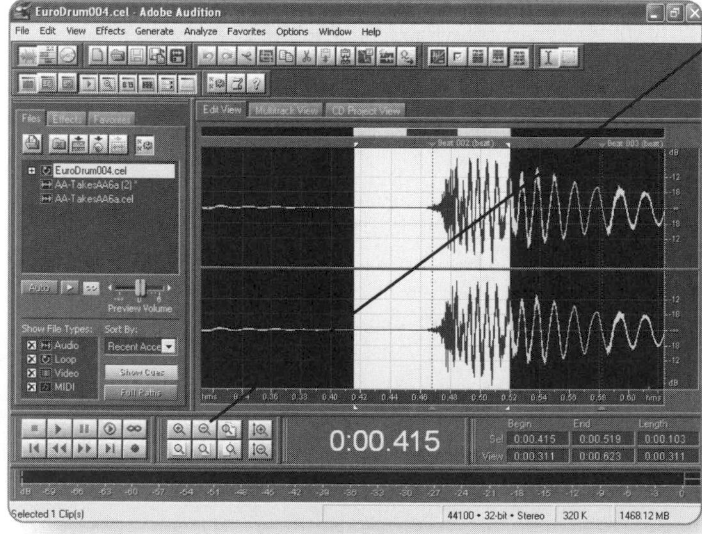

2. **Click** on the **Zoom Out Horizontally button**. You will see that everything that was in your former view was selected.

Playing and Controlling Music

The transport controls in Adobe Audition are very similar to just about every CD player on the market. Once you have a session open, you simply have to click on the appropriate control button and it will activate that command. There are only a couple of buttons that you may not be familiar with if you've never used the program. Whether you are in Edit view or Multitrack view, the controls work in a similar way.

Basic Transport Controls

Once you have a session open, you can playback the entire session or specific waveforms using the transport controls. You'll probably be able to figure out the following on your own, but just in case, here you go:

1. **Click** on the **Play button**. All tracks within your session will be played if you are in Multitrack view. If you are in Edit view, the entire wavelength will play.

2. **Click** on the **Pause button**. The Pause button will turn yellow.

3. **Click** on the **Pause button** again to resume play.

4. **Click** on the **Stop button**. The playback will stop.

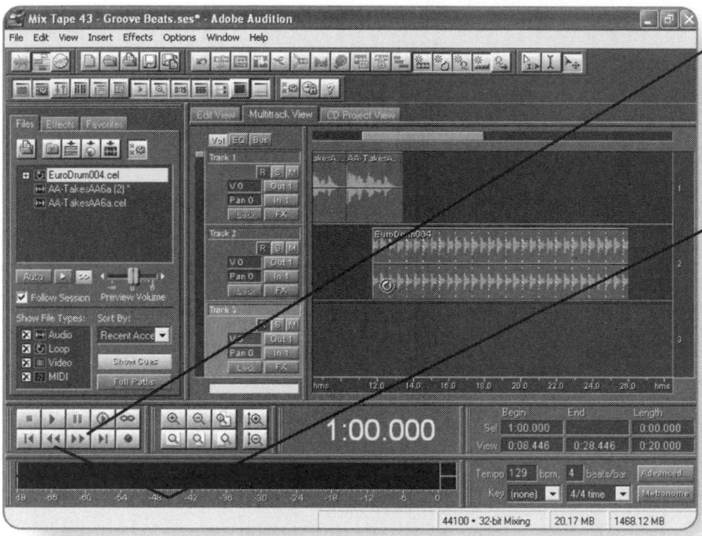

5. Click and hold the **Fast Forward button**. This will move you forward in your session until you release the mouse button.

6. Click and hold the **Rewind button**. This will take you backward in your sequence until you release the mouse button.

Adjusting the Fast Forward and Rewind Speeds

As you click and hold the Fast Forward or Rewind button, you are advanced or taken backwards at a certain speed. You can adjust this speed by right-clicking on either button.

1. Right-click on the **Fast Forward button**. A menu will appear allowing you to change the fast forward speed.

2. Click on the desired **speed**. The speed will be selected. Whenever you hold down the Fast Forward button, you will advance at the speed that you have selected.

3. Repeat Steps 1 and 2 for the Rewind button.

Other Transport Controls

Some of the other, not so basic, transport controls are dependent on a selection having first been made.

1. **Create** a **selection** using one of the many selection methods.

2. **Click** on the **Play button**. Only the audio that is selected will be played.

3. **Click** on the **Play to End button**. The audio will begin playing from the start of your selection and will continue playing until it reaches the end of the session. In other words, using Play to End will bypass the end of the selection.

4. **Click** on the **Play Looped button**. The audio within the selection will play over and over until you pause or stop.

5. **Click** on the **Stop button**. The playback will stop.

Cues

Think of a cue as a bookmark. It allows you to quickly jump to a specific point in your musical sequence. Cues are particularly useful when you are working with a large file. They allow you to access specific locations within your files at the touch of a button. Cues are managed from the Cue List window.

Opening the Cue List Window

The Cue window can be accessed from the menu bar.

1. **Click** on **Window**. The Window menu will appear.

2. **Click** on **Cue List**. The Cue List window will open.

Creating Cues

There are many different cues that you can create. The most common is a point cue, which allows you to reference a specific point within your file. Later using the transport controls, you can quickly jump to the position of the point cue.

1. **Click and drag** the **triangle** in the Session display or in any area of the wave display, where you would like to create a point cue. A yellow dotted line will appear to indicate the position within the timeline. Alternatively, you can create a selection and a cue will be created from the selection.

2. **Click** on the **Add button** in the Cue List window. A cue will be created at the current position. A red triangle representing the cue will appear at the bottom and top of the window with the label Cue 1. The cue is indicated visually through the track by a blue and red dotted vertical line between the red triangles. Each subsequent cue that you create will be numbered in successive order (Cue 2, Cue 3, and so on).

3. **Repeat Steps 1 to 3** until you have added cues to your heart's desire.

Editing Cues

You can rename, delete, or move any of the cues that you have created.

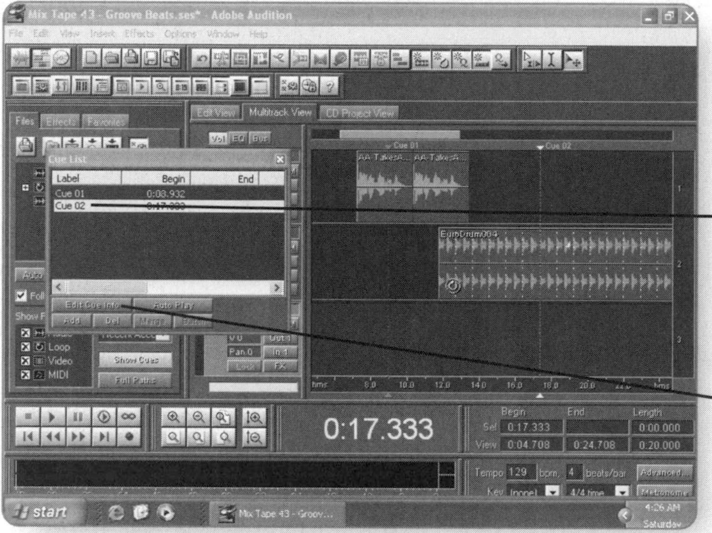

Moving Cues

You can move an existing cue to a precise location using the Cue List window.

1. **Click** on the **name of the cue** that you would like to move. It will become highlighted to indicate it is selected.

2. **Click** on the **Edit Cue Info button**. The window will split in half and specific information about the cue will appear in the bottom half of the window.

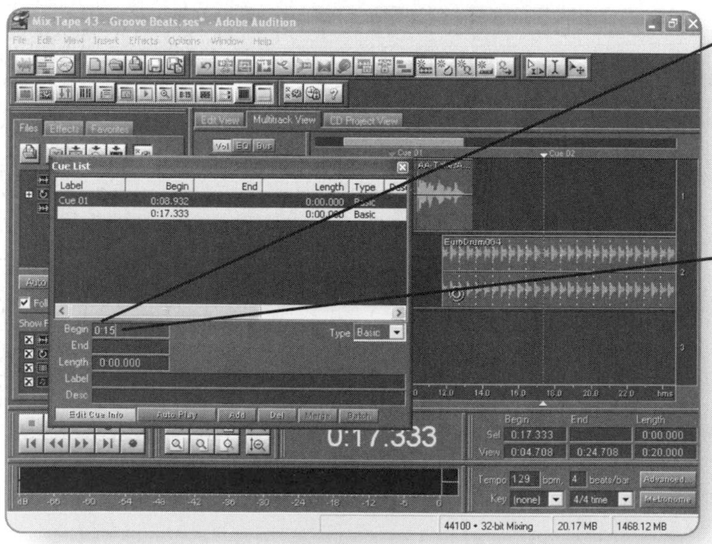

3. **Click once** in the **Begin box**. The number in the box will become highlighted. This number represents the position of the cue.

4. **Type** a new **number** for the location of the cue. It will appear as you type.

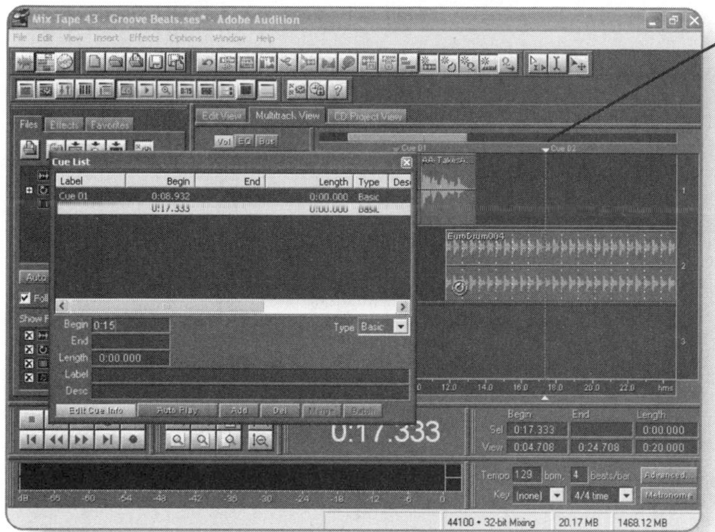

5. **Press Enter**. The cue will be moved to the location that you have specified.

The fastest way to move a cue is to simply click and drag it using your mouse.

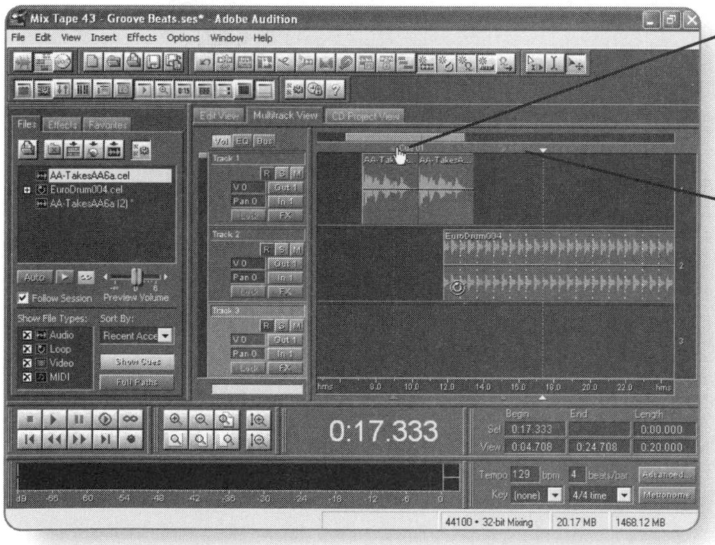

1. **Position** the **mouse pointer** over the cue that you would like to move. The pointer will change into a hand.
2. **Click and drag** the **cue** to the desired location. The cue will move as you drag.

3. Release the **mouse button**. The cue will be in its new location.

Renaming Cues

Whereas names like Cue 1, Cue 2, and Cue 3 may be okay for the amateur digital audiophile, you, the professional, know that it makes much more sense to give your cues specific names. It will save you a lot of time in the long run. Not only can you change the name of your cue, you can also add a detailed description of why you created it.

1. **Click** on the **cue** that you would like to rename. It will appear highlighted.
2. **Click** on the **Edit Cue Info button**. The window will split in half and specific information about the cue will appear in the bottom half of the window.

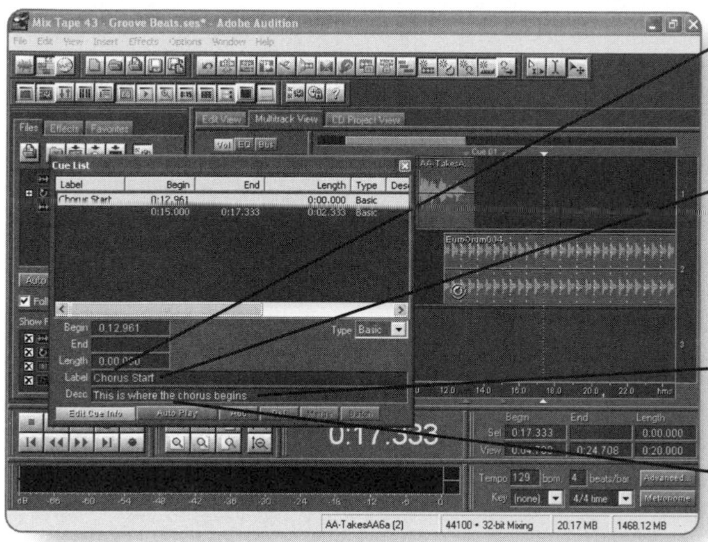

3. **Click once** in the **Label box**. The contents of the Label box will become highlighted.

4. **Type** a **new name** for your cue. It's like having a pet goldfish; you can give it any name you like.

5. **Click once** in the **Desc box**. The box will become highlighted.

6. **Type** a **description** for your cue. It will appear as you type.

Removing Cues

If you no longer require a cue, you can quickly remove it using the Delete command.

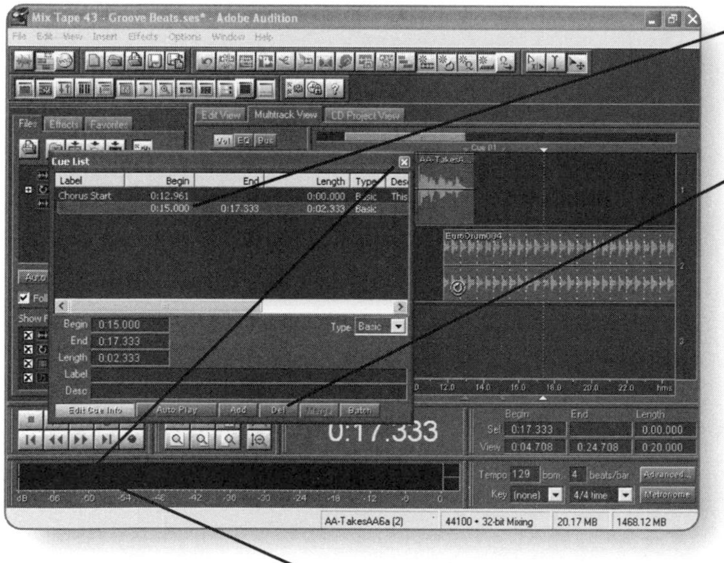

1. **Click** on the **cue** that you would like to remove. It will become highlighted.

2. **Click** on the **Del button**. The cue will be deleted.

3. **Click** on the **X** in the top-right corner of the Cue List window. The Cue List window will close.

Accessing Cues

The transport controls allow you to quickly jump to your point cues.

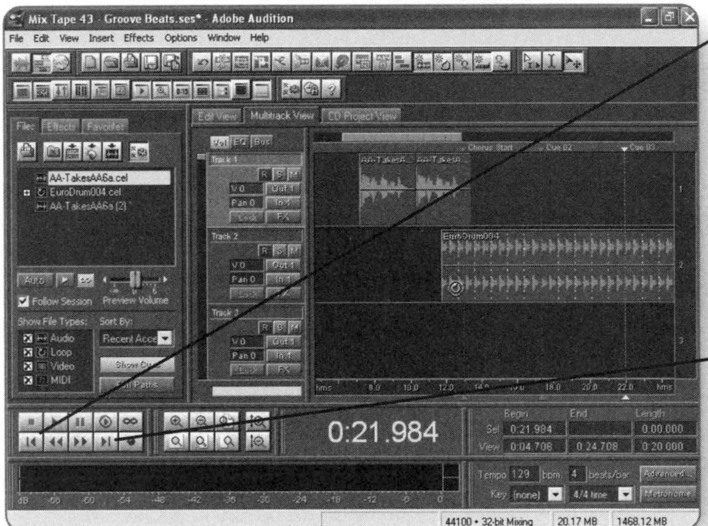

1. Click on the **Go to Beginning or Previous Cue button**. As the button name suggests, this will take you to the previous cue, or, if there are no previous cues, it will take you to the beginning of your session.

2. Click on the **Go to End or Next Cue button**. This will take you to the next cue. If there is no next cue, it will take you to the end of your session.

Time Formats

By default, the unit of display appears in seconds. If you prefer to work in other units, you can quickly change the type of display with a click on the mouse button. The types of different time displays include decimal, compact disc, SMPTE, samples, bars and beats, and custom time code frame rates.

1. **Position** the **mouse pointer** anywhere over the Waveform ruler. The mouse pointer will change into a hand.

2. **Double-click** on the **ruler**. The units in the time display will change.

3. **Repeat Step 2** until you reach the desired time display.

3

Standard Recording

The real joy of digital audio editing is creating and editing your own music. Before you can edit audio however, you'll need to either create it from scratch, record existing music, or import existing digital audio files. There are many different ways you can record your music into Adobe Audition. Once you have the appropriate hardware set up and configured, Audition makes it easy to record your music into editable form. This chapter covers recording waveforms using the Edit view. With this method you create individual audio files that can later be placed into your session.

In this chapter, you'll learn how to:

- Record vocals
- Record from a CD
- Record from a turntable
- Save and name recordings

Recording Vocals

All those years of karaoke at the local bar are finally going to pay off. You can now sing directly into Adobe Audition and it will record your voice and digitize it so that it can be edited. Before you start belting out the tunes, you'll need to first adjust your hardware and make sure that the settings on your computer are correct.

Microphone Setup

Once you have your microphone plugged into the soundcard of your computer, you will need to adjust its settings for it to work properly. By default, the microphone is automatically muted on most computers so you will have to activate it and adjust the volume settings to hear yourself as you sing.

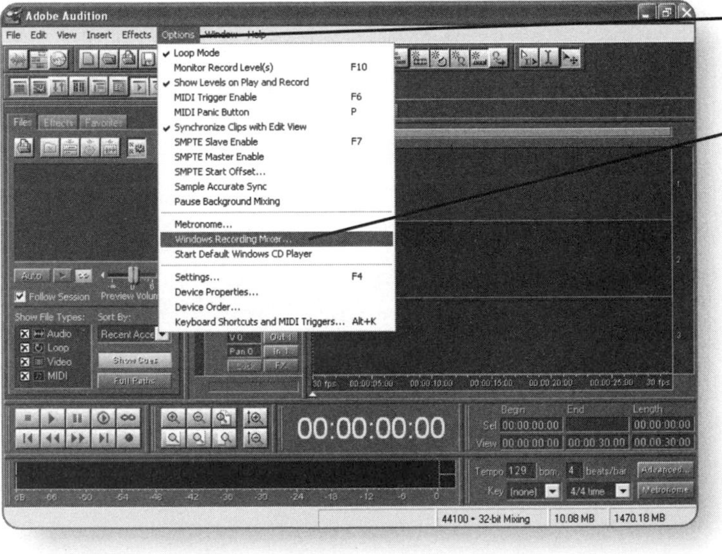

1. **Click** on **Options**. The Options menu will appear.

2. **Click** on **Windows Recording Mixer**. The Master Record window will open.

3. Click on **Options**. The Options menu will appear.

4. Click on **Properties**. A dialog box will open in which you can select the properties for certain audio devices.

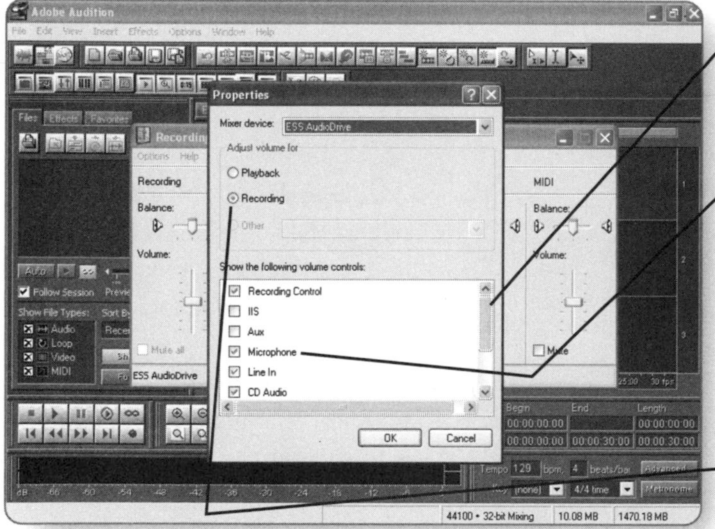

5. Click on the **down scroll button** until you see the word "Mic."

6. Click in the **check box** beside Mic or Microphone (this will vary depending on the operating system you are using) if it is not already checked. This will activate the microphone controls.

7. Click on the **circle** next to Recording. This will adjust the volume for recording.

8. Click on **OK**. The microphone volume controls will now appear.

9. **Click** in the **Mute box** to remove the checkmark. (If there is no checkmark in the Mute box, disregard this step.) This will allow you to hear yourself through the computer speakers when you speak into the microphone.

NOTE

Depending on the sound card installed on your computer, the options you see may appear slightly different. Rather than having a Mute check box, some sound cards have a Select check box. If this is the case for you, click the Select check box for those channels that you want to activate.

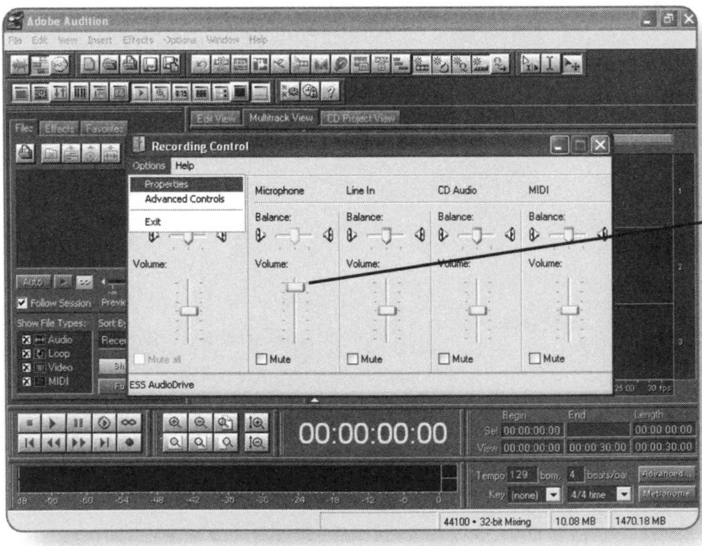

10. **Speak** into the **microphone** to test the volume levels. You will hear your voice coming out of the computer speakers.

11. **Click and drag** the **volume level** for the microphone until it is at the desired level.

12. Click on **Options**. The Options menu will appear.

13. Click on **Properties**. A dialog box will open from which you can select the properties for certain audio devices.

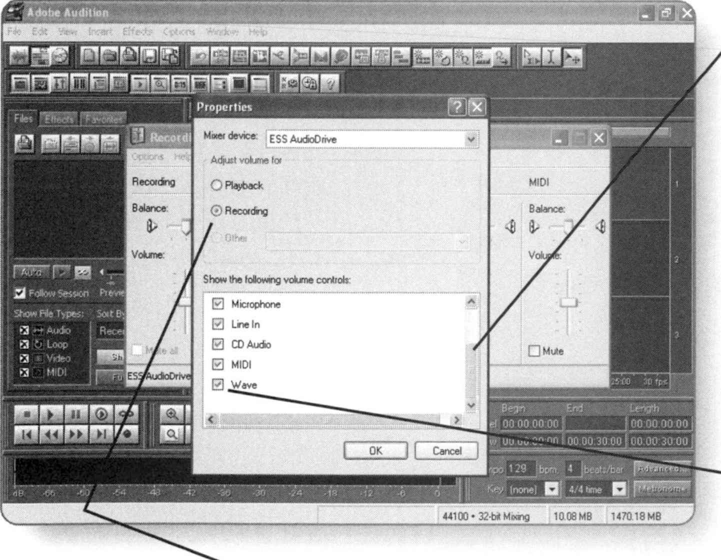

14. Click on the **down scroll button** until you see the word "Wave."

15. Click in the **Wave check box**. This will activate the Wave controls.

16. Click on the **circle** next to Recording. This will adjust the volume for recording.

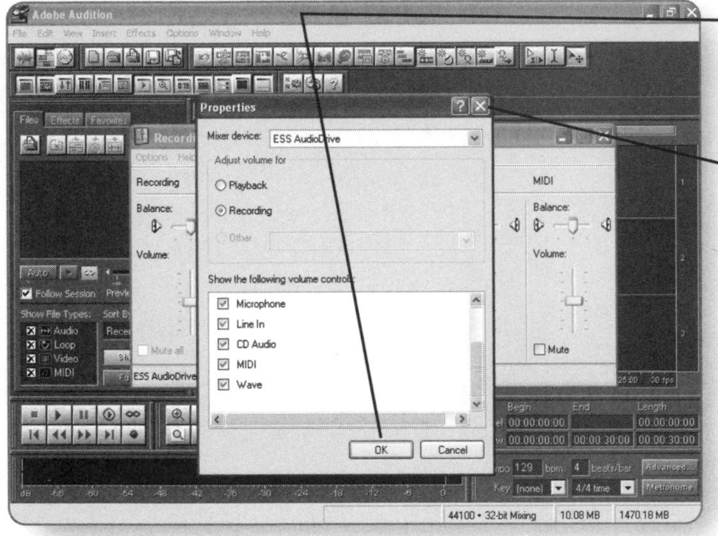

17. Click on **OK**. The microphone volume controls will now appear.

18. Click on the **X** in the top-right corner to accept the changes and close the window.

Recording from the Microphone

When you record from the microphone, you will be creating a waveform file that can later be edited and inserted into your musical sequence.

1. Click on the **Edit Waveform View button** if you are not already in Edit view. Edit Waveform view will appear.

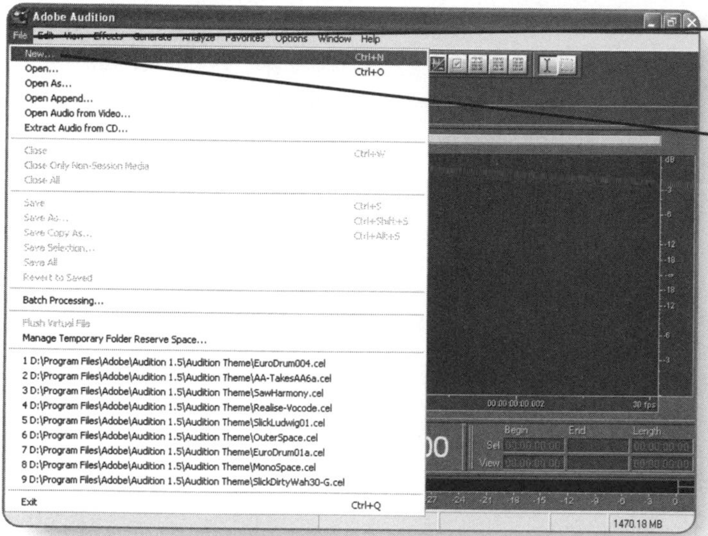

2. Click on **File**. The File menu will appear.

3. Click on **New**. The Waveform display will be clear and you will now be prompted to set the properties for your new waveform.

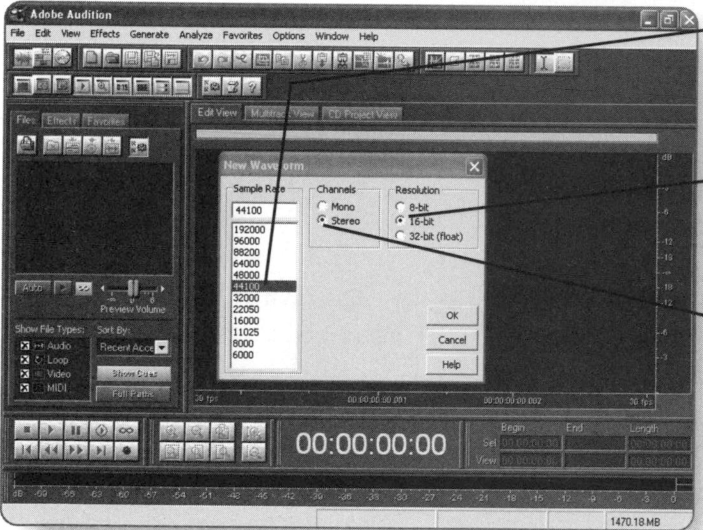

4. Click on the desired **sample rate**. It will be highlighted to indicate it is selected.

5. Click on the **circle** beside the desired resolution. The circle will appear filled in once selected.

6. Click on the **circle** beside the desired channel. Again, the circle will appear filled in once selected.

7. Click on **OK**. You will now be ready to record your audio.

TIP

If your final destination for this waveform will be a CD, set the sample rate to 44100—the channel should be stereo and the resolution should be 16-bit.

8. Double-click anywhere on the **level meters**. This will activate the meters so you can check your levels.

9. Speak into the **microphone**. The levels will dance up and down as you speak.

10. Click on the **Record button**. It will appear bright red once activated.

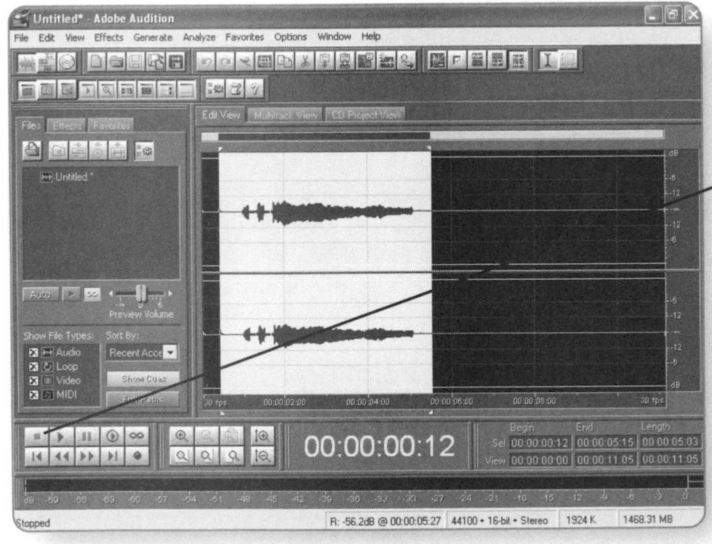

11. Sing into the **microphone**. You will see a waveform being created on the screen.

12. Click on the **Stop button**. Your voice has now been successfully recorded and a waveform file has been created. See the section entitled "Naming and Saving Your Waveform."

Recording from CD

There are two ways to record audio from an existing CD, and the method that you choose will depend on the hardware that you have. If you happen to have an older CD-ROM drive that does not support digital extraction, you have to use the analog method. Otherwise you can use the digital ripping method.

Analog Method

Basically, the analog method of recording from a CD works like this: Your computer plays the CD and Audition records what it hears. This does not give you as much clarity as when digitally ripping CDs, but it's your only alternative if you have outdated hardware. You can always tidy up the recording later in the editing process.

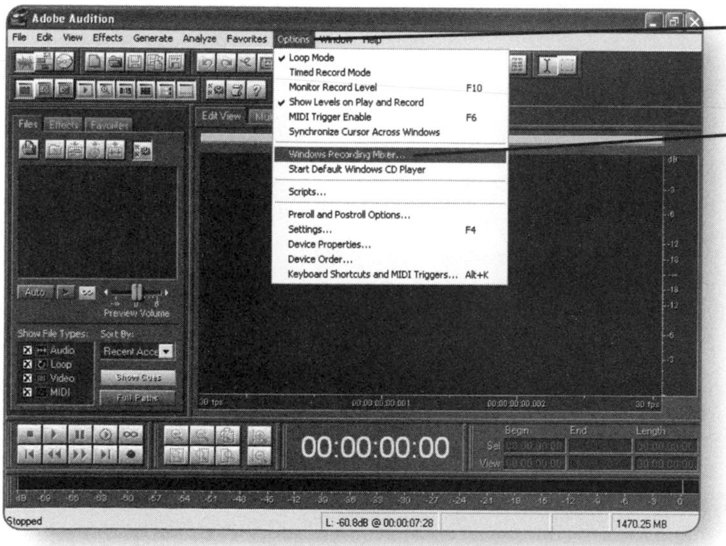

1. **Click** on **Options**. The Options menu will appear.

2. **Click** on **Windows Recording Mixer**. The Master Record or Recording Control window will open.

3. **Click** on **Options**. The Options menu will appear.

4. **Click** on **Properties**. The Properties window will open, allowing you to adjust your audio properties.

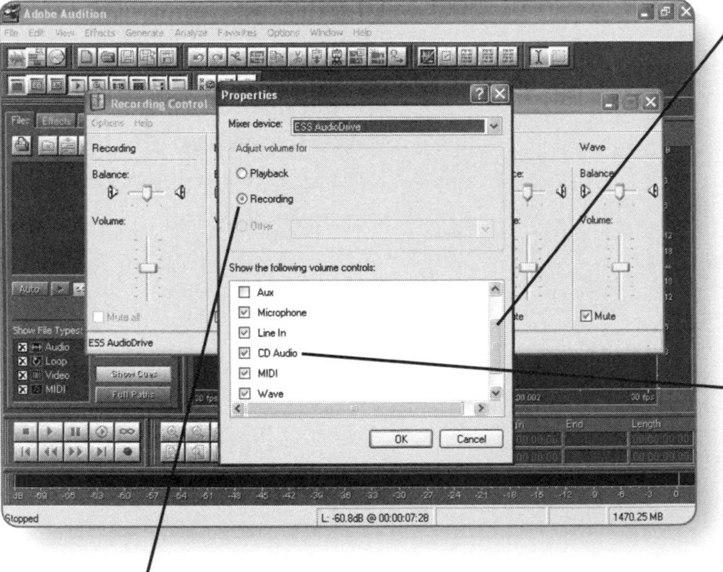

5. **Click** on the **scroll button** until you come to CD or CD Audio.

6. **Click** in the **check box** beside CD or CD Audio if there is not already a checkmark in the box.

7. **Click** on the **circle** next to Recording if it is not already selected. This will adjust the volume for recording.

8. Click on **OK**. The dialog box will close.

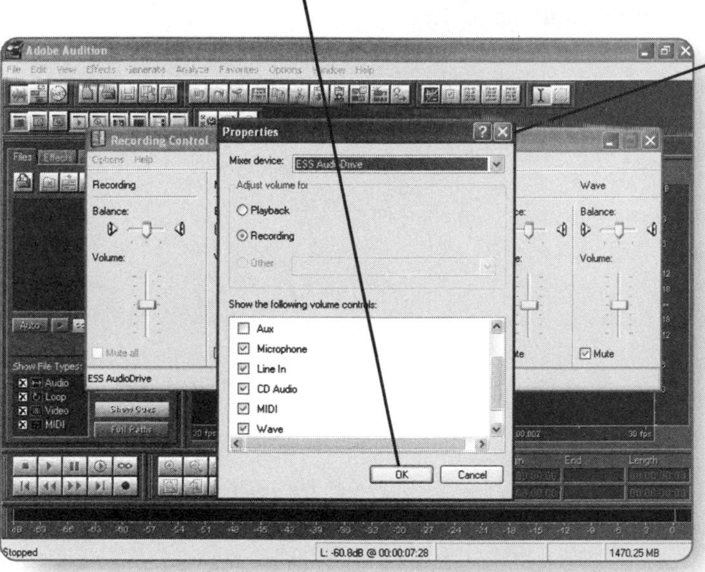

9. Click on the **X** in the top-right corner to close the Master Record or Recording Control window. The window will close.

10. Press F12 to switch to Edit view if you are not already there. Edit view will appear.

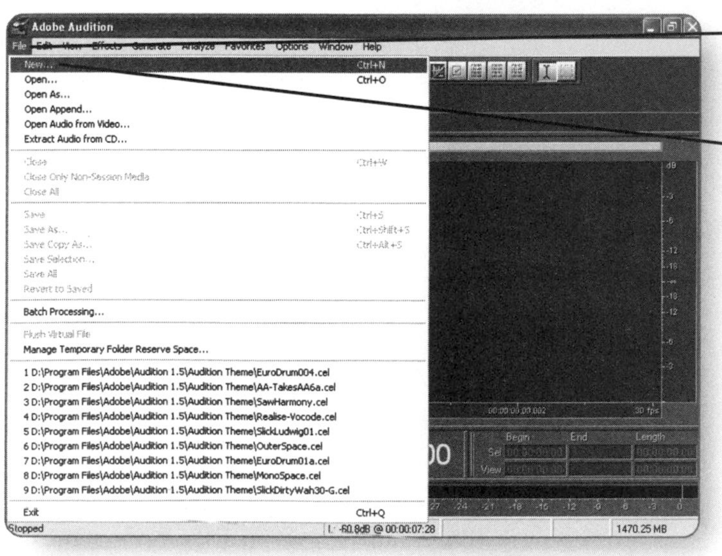

11. Click on **File**. The File menu will appear.

12. Click on **New**. The waveform display will be clear and you will now be prompted to set the properties for your new waveform.

13. **Click** on the desired **sample rate**. It will be highlighted to indicate it is selected.

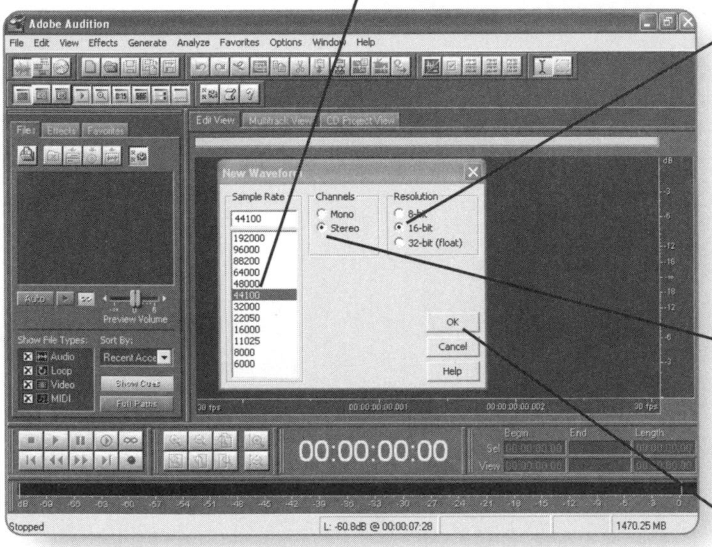

14. **Click** on the **circle** beside the desired resolution. The circle will appear filled in once selected.

15. **Click** on the **circle** beside the desired channel. Again, the circle will appear filled in once selected.

16. **Click** on **OK**. You will now be ready to record your audio.

17. **Insert** the **CD** into your CD-ROM drive. Depending on the configuration of your computer, a CD player program may automatically launch. If this is the case, skip to Step 23.

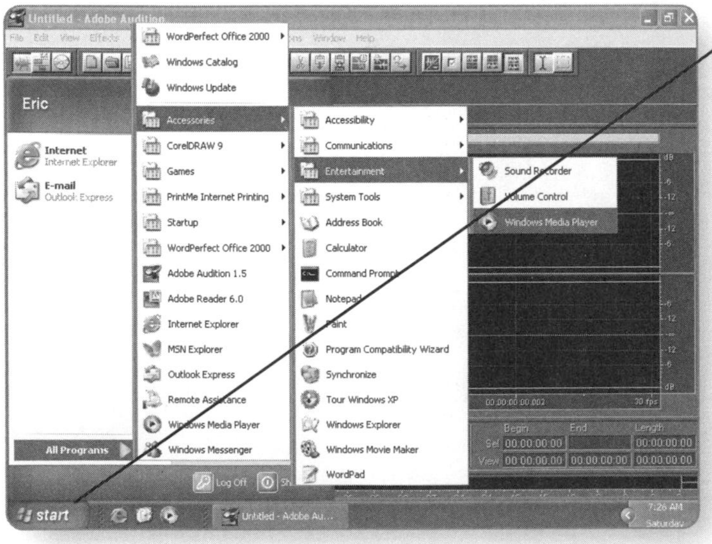

18. **Click** on **Start**. The Windows Start menu will appear.

19. **Click** on **Programs or All Programs** depending on which version of Windows you are running. A submenu will appear.

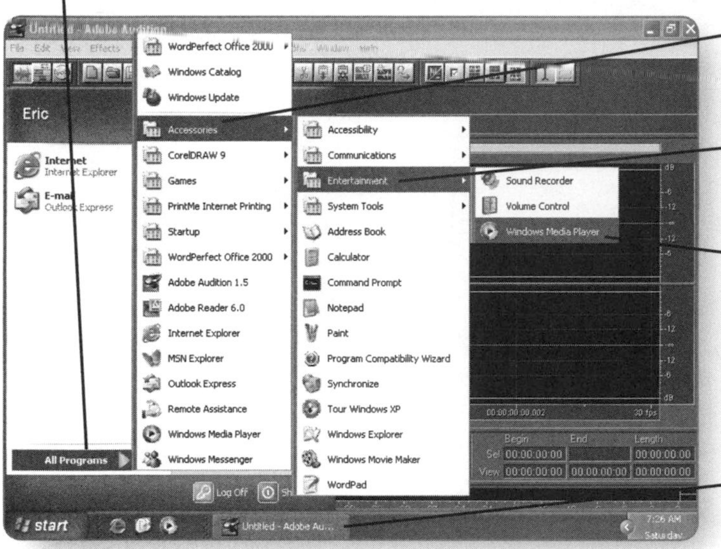

20. **Click** on **Accessories**. A submenu of options will appear.

21. **Click** on **Entertainment**. Another submenu will appear.

22. **Click** on **CD Player**. Alternatively, you can select **Windows Media Player** or any other software that will play a CD.

23. **Click** on the **Adobe Audition icon** in the Windows taskbar to switch back to Adobe Audition.

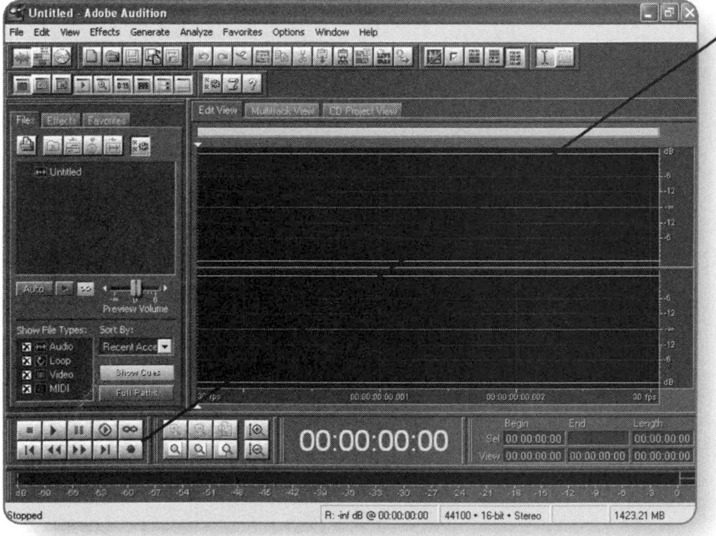

24. **Click** on the **Record button**. Audition will begin recording. You will now have to switch back to the CD player program and begin playing the desired track that you would like to record.

25. Click on the **Window Media Player** or **CD Player icon** in the Windows taskbar to switch to the CD player.

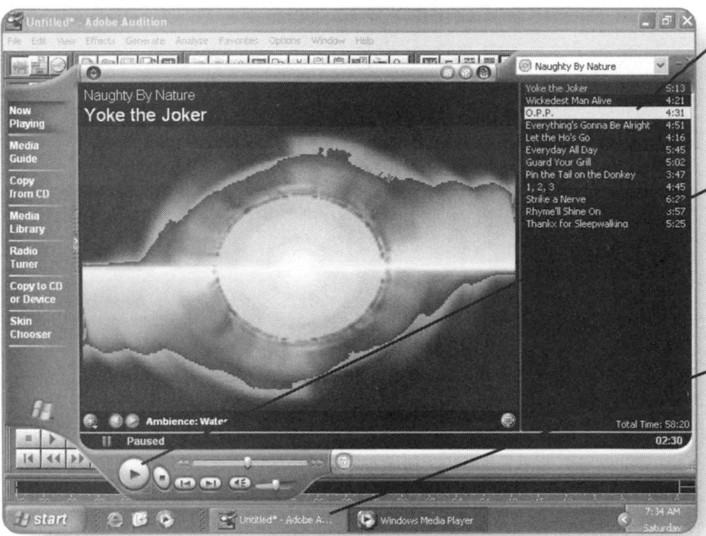

26. Click on the desired **track** from the list. The track will appear highlighted.

27. Click on the **Play button**. The track will begin to play. As it plays, it is being recorded in Audition.

28. Click on the **Adobe Audition icon** in the Windows taskbar to switch back to Adobe Audition. You will see wavelength being created as the track is being recorded.

29. Click on the **Stop button** once the track has finished playing. The CD track is now recorded. The section "Saving and Naming Your Recording" will show you the steps to store the recording.

Ripping Tracks from CD

Digitally extracting audio from a CD is called ripping. Nowadays, most CD players support this type of conversion, which gives you the best quality sound. Adobe Audition makes it quite easy to rip your favorite tracks from CD.

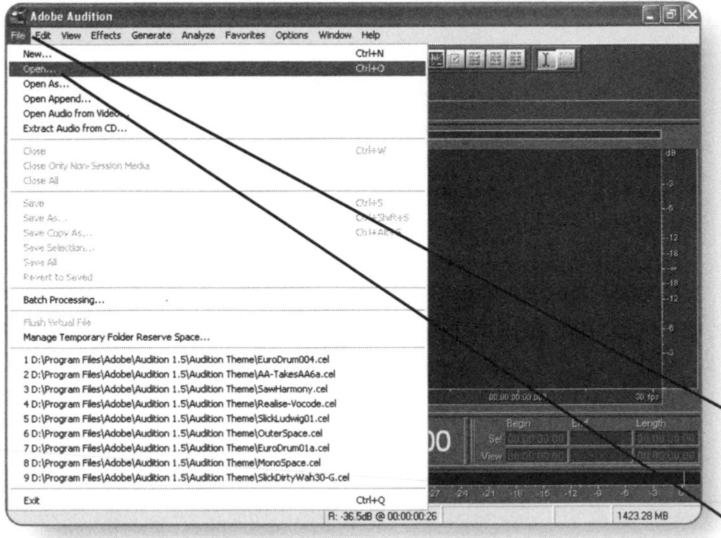

1. **Insert** the **CD** into the CD-ROM drive. If CD software launches when you put the CD in the drive, simply close that software.

2. **Press F12** to switch to Edit view if you are not already in that view mode. Edit view will appear.

3. **Click** on **File**. The File menu will open.

4. **Click** on **Open**. The Open a Waveform dialog box will appear, allowing you to select a track.

5. **Click** on the **down arrow** beside Files of type. A list of different file types will appear.

6. **Click** on the **CD Digital Audio (*.cda) file type**. It will be selected.

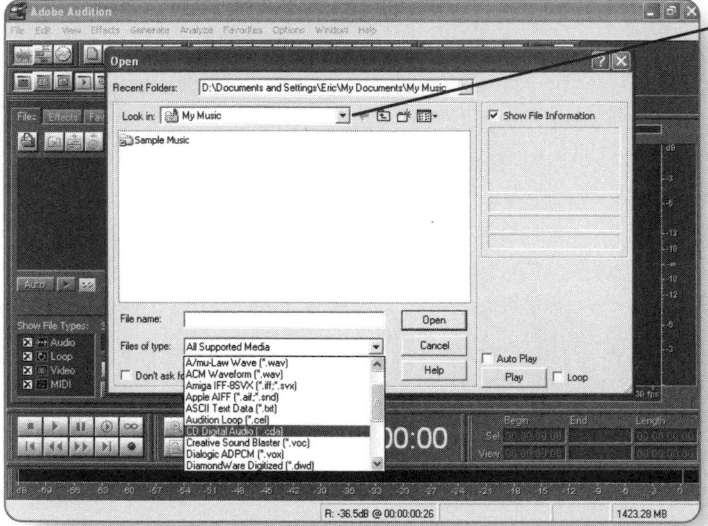

7. **Click** on the **down arrow** beside Look In. A list of drives and folders on your computer will appear.

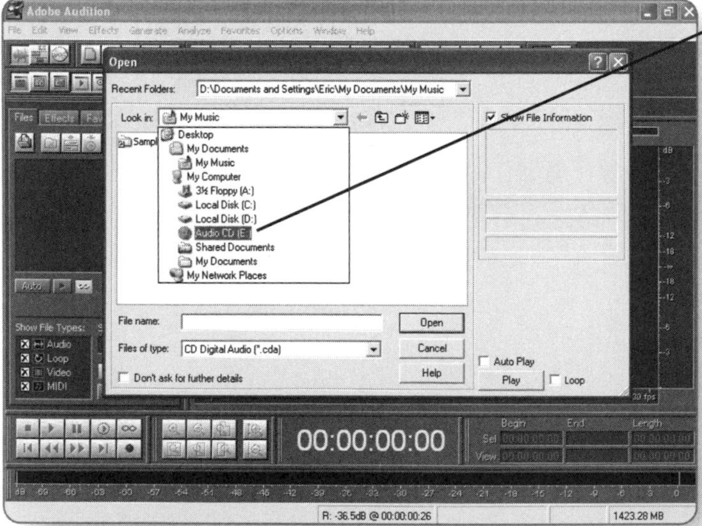

8. **Click** on the **drive name** that contains the CD that you would like to rip. It will be selected and a list of tracks that are on the CD will appear.

9. **Click** on the desired **track** that you would like to digitize. It will be highlighted.

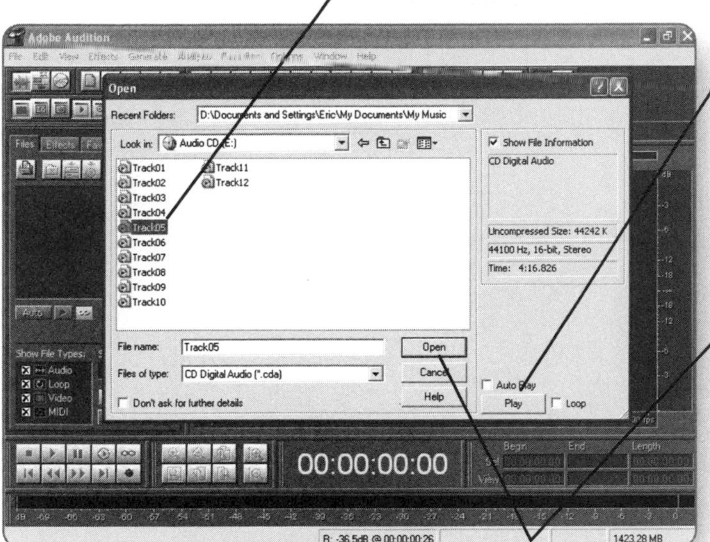

10. **Click** on the **Play button**, if you would like to audition the track. The Play button will turn into a Stop button once pressed, and can be used to stop the playback.

11. **Click** on the **Open button**. A dialog box will appear, showing the status of the conversion. Once the conversion is complete, your track will appear as a wavelength. The section "Saving and Naming Your Recording" will show you the steps to store the recording.

Recording from a Turntable

Go to the basement, dust off your old turntable, and find your old vinyl records, because you can turn those oldies into digitally remastered works of art. Your turntable will need to be connected to a receiver and the receiver in turn will need to be connected to your computer. The Line Out jack on your computer is 1/8 of an inch and your receiver outlets are RCA. There is an RCA-to-miniplug adapter that you can purchase at retailers like RadioShack that will allow you to plug your receiver directly to your computer through the Line Out jack. Once it is connected and powered on, you must adjust some settings in Adobe Audition to enable recording.

1. **Click** on **Options**. The Options menu will appear.

2. **Click** on **Windows Recording Mixer**. The Master Record window will open.

3. **Click** on **Options**. The Options menu will appear.

4. **Click** on **Properties**. The Properties window will open.

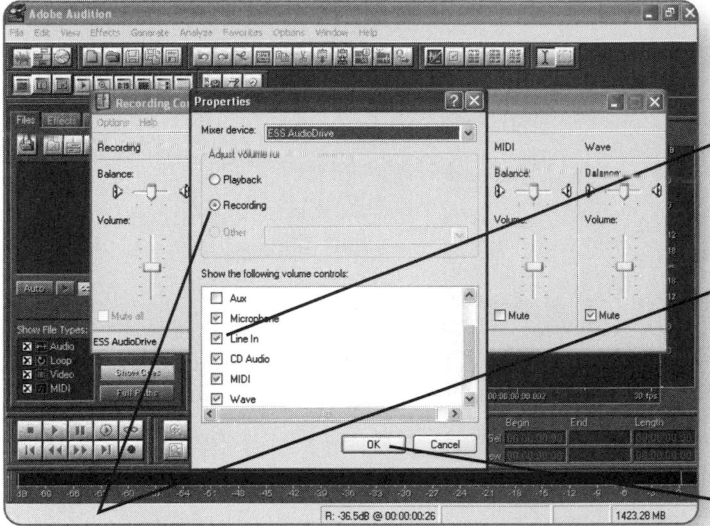

5. Click on the **scroll buttons** until you see the Line In option.

6. Click on the **Line In check box** to display the volume settings for the Line Out.

7. Click on the **circle** next to Recording, if it is not already selected. The circle will appear filled in to indicate that it is selected.

8. Click on **OK**. The Properties dialog box will close.

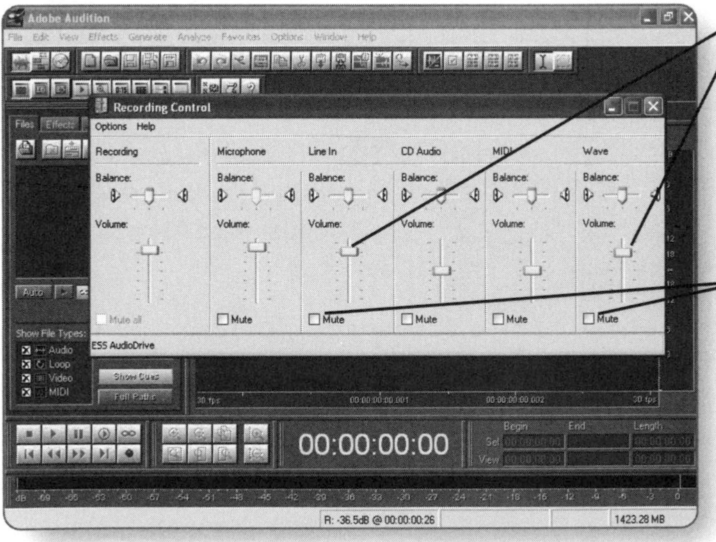

9. Click and drag the **volume setting** for both Wave and Line In. They should be at about three quarters or higher.

10. Click to **uncheck** the **Mute box** in both Line In and Wave, if required.

11. Click the **X** in the top-right corner of the Master Record window. The window will close.

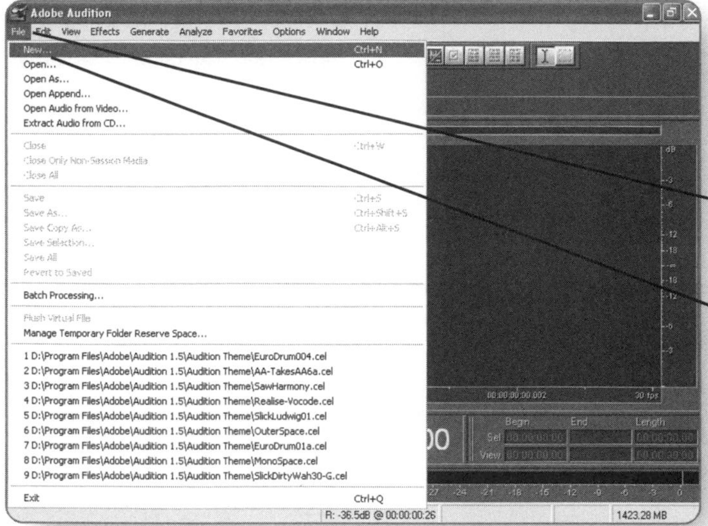

12. Press F12 to toggle to Edit view if you are not already in that mode. Edit view will appear.

13. Click on **File**. The File menu will appear.

14. Click on **New**. The waveform display will be clear and you will now be prompted to set the properties for your new waveform.

15. Click on the desired **sample rate**. It will be highlighted to indicate it is selected.

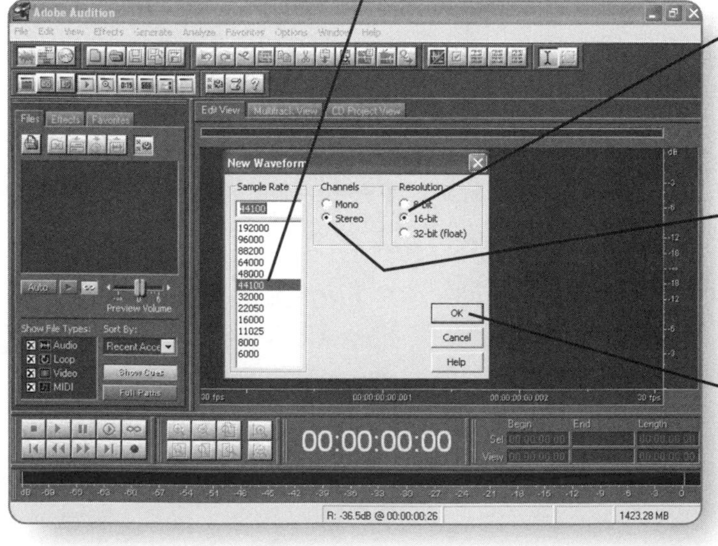

16. Click on the **circle** beside the desired resolution. The circle will appear filled in once selected.

17. Click on the **circle** beside the desired channel. Again, the circle will appear filled in once selected.

18. Click on **OK**. You will now be ready to record your audio.

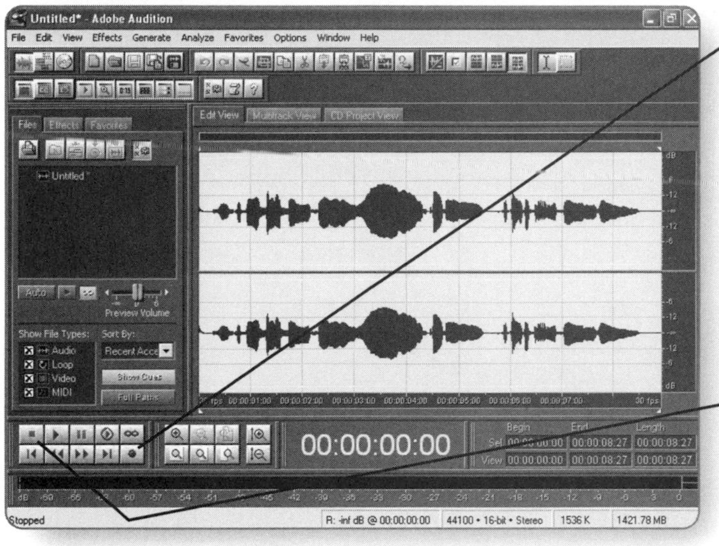

19. Click on the **Record button**. It will turn bright red to indicate it is recording.

20. Drop the **needle** on the record and begin spinning the vinyl. As the record plays, a waveform will appear indicating that it is being recorded.

21. Click on the **Stop button**. The record track is now recorded. The section "Saving and Naming Your Recording" will show you the steps to store the recording.

Saving and Naming Your Recording

When you record a waveform into Adobe Audition, it is given the name "Untitled" until you save it and give it a name. Seeing as how each session that you create could have hundreds of different waveforms, it's a good idea to save your waveforms with descriptive names as you create them.

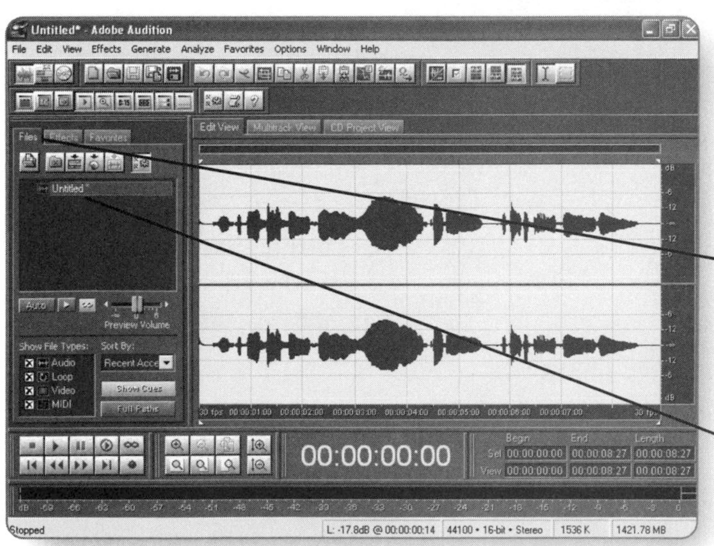

1. Click on the **Files tab** of the Organizer window, if it is not already selected. The Files tab will come forward.

2. Click on the **untitled waveform** that you have just recorded. It will be highlighted to indicate it is selected.

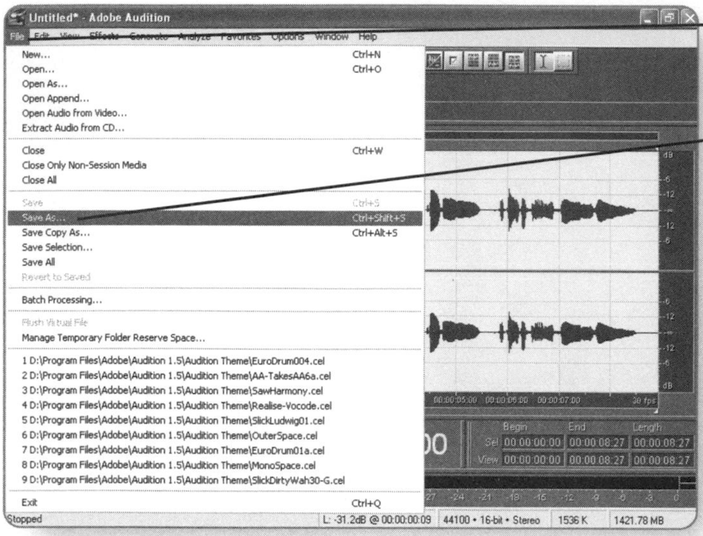

3. **Click** on **File**. The File menu will appear.

4. **Click** on **Save As**. A dialog box will appear from which you can select the name and location

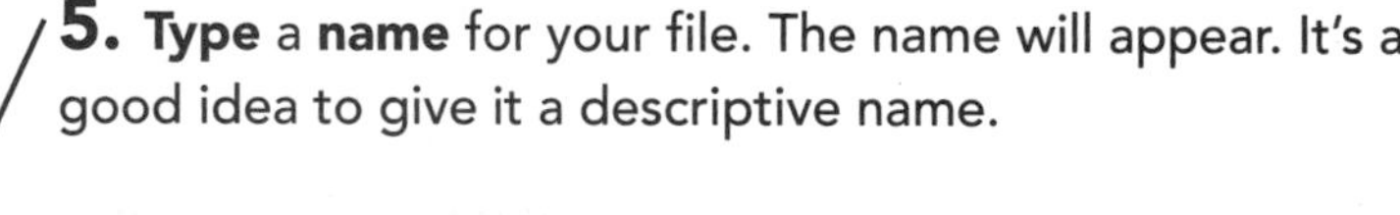

5. **Type** a **name** for your file. The name will appear. It's a good idea to give it a descriptive name.

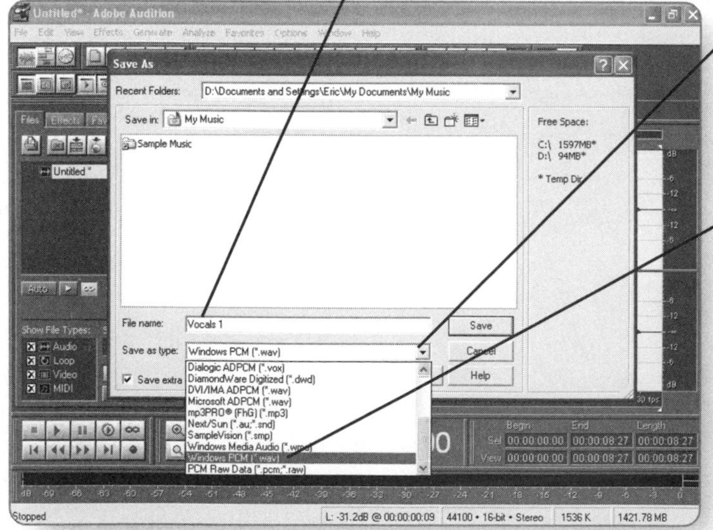

6. **Click** on the **down arrow** beside Save As type. A list of many different audio file types will appear.

7. **Click** on the desired **file type**. It will be selected.

8. **Click** on **Save**. The file will be saved with the name and type that you have specified.

4 Advanced Recording

The recording capabilities of Adobe Audition allow you to do so much more than just simply record from standard audio devices. It is built to meet the needs of even the most demanding digital audio producers. Among other things, you can create your own digital music from scratch, you can select where and when to record, and you can record on multiple channels at once. Adobe Audition also allows you to record music directly from MIDI instruments.

In this chapter, you'll learn how to:

- Make music from scratch
- Record from MIDI devices
- Create punch-in recordings
- Create timed recordings
- Import recordings

Recording Directly to a Track

In Chapter 3, you learned to create waveform files that could later be placed within a track. In this section you will learn how to record directly to a track. The process is pretty much the same as any other recording with the exception of selecting a track and enabling recording to that track.

1. Press F12 to toggle to Multitrack view, if you are not already there. Multitrack view will appear.

2. Click on the **R button** in the track that you would like to record to. Recording will now be enabled on that track.

> **TIP**
>
> You can record onto multiple tracks at the same time by clicking the red R button, which makes the tracks record enabled. Anything that you record will appear on all record-enabled tracks.

3. Click and drag the **yellow triangle** to indicate where in the timeline you would like your recording to begin. A dotted yellow line will appear.

4. Click on the **Record button**. The button will turn bright red and recording will begin.

5. Record your **audio** using any one of the methods described in Chapter 3, "Standard Recording." As you record, the block of audio will appear in the track.

6. Click on the **Stop button**. Recording will end.

7. Click on the **R button** to disable recording on that track. Recording will be disabled.

Creating Music from Scratch

This section could've been named "Creating Noise from Scratch," but the difference between music and noise is all in the ear of the beholder. In actuality, Adobe Audition allows you to create two types of sounds from scratch—noise and tones. What's the difference between a noise and a tone? Read on.

Creating Noise

I picture toddlers hammering together pots and pans when anyone brings up the subject of making noise, but not to worry, the noise that you can create in Adobe Audition isn't the migraine-inducing variety. Noise is defined as sound that contains equal proportions of all frequencies. There are three different types of noises that you can create in Adobe Audition, including white noise, pink noise, and brown noise. Why go through the trouble of creating noise? You can add special effects to the noise that you create to make it sound like realistic natural sounds, including waves, the wind, and rain.

1. Press F12 to toggle to Edit view, if you are not already there. Edit view will appear.

2. Click on **Generate**. The Generate menu will appear.

3. Click on **Noise**. The Generate Noise dialog box will appear.

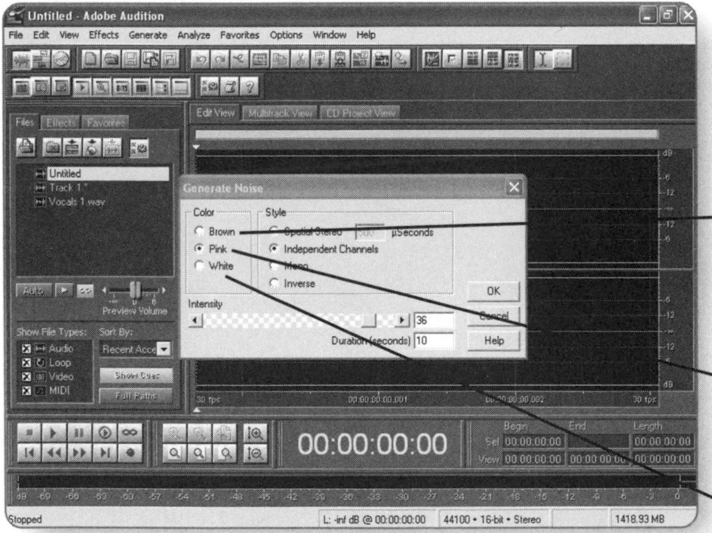

4. Click on the **circle** beside the desired color of noise. A dot will appear in the circle. There are three different types of noise you can select:

- **Brown Noise.** Brown noise is filtered so that the sound appears to have a lower frequency.
- **Pink Noise**. With pink noise the loudness of the higher frequencies is removed.
- **White Noise**. This type of noise produces sound with every frequency in the same amount.

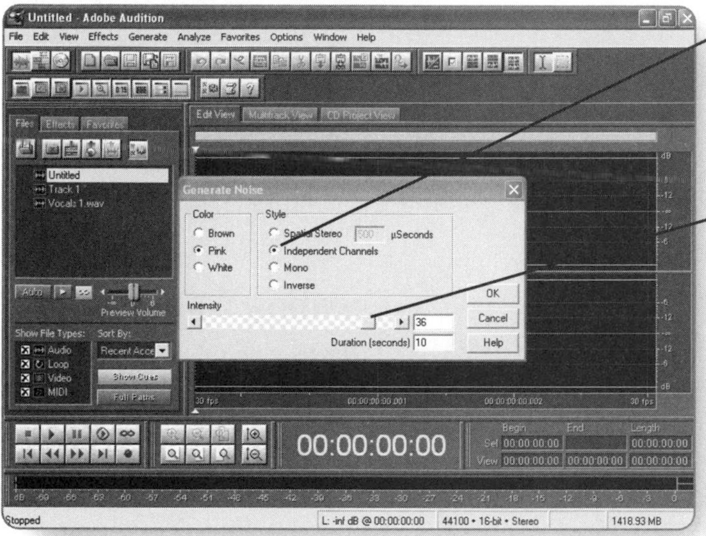

5. Click on the **circle** beside the desired style of noise. A dot will appear in the circle to indicate that it is selected.

6. Position your **mouse pointer** over the intensity box and **click and drag** it to the **left or right** to decrease or increase the intensity. As you drag, the intensity number will change.

7. Release the **mouse button**. The new intensity will be set.

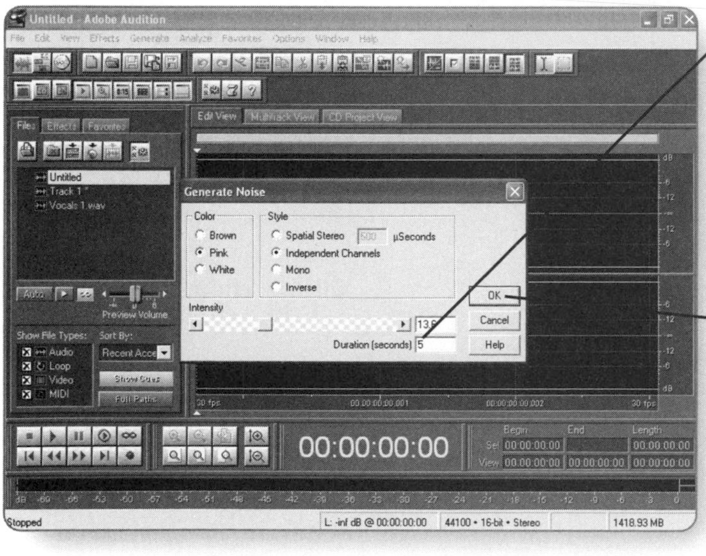

8. Double-click in the **duration box**. The box will appear highlighted.

9. Type the **number** of seconds for your noise to last. The number will appear as you type.

10. Click on **OK**. The noise that you have created will appear as a waveform in the Edit view.

Creating Tones

In addition to noise, Adobe Audition also allows you to create and edit tones. Once you have a tone created, you can apply a variety of different effects to it to create useable audio. You can adjust the amplitude and frequency of the tone that you create.

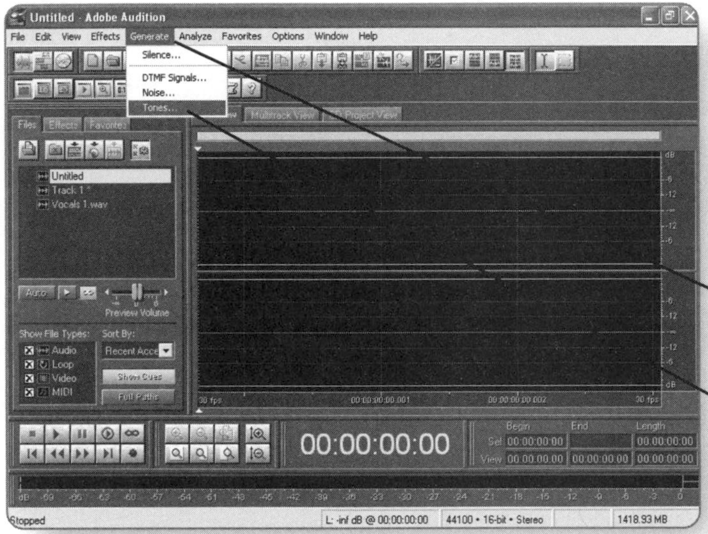

Creating Constant Tones

A constant tone is one whose overtones and base frequency does not vary from its beginning point to its end point.

1. **Click** on **Generate**. The Generate menu will open.
2. **Click** on **Tones**. The Tones dialog box will open, allowing you to create the selections for your tone.

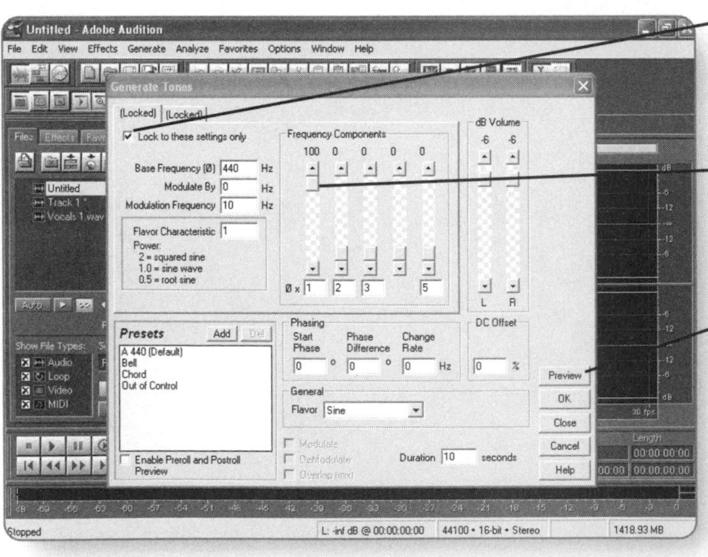

3. **Click** in the **Lock to these settings only check box**, if the box is not already checked.
4. **Click and drag** the **sliders** and **enter values** for the different options.
5. **Click** on the **Preview button** to test the tone that you have made. You will hear the result.

6. **Readjust** any of the **settings**. The preview will react in real time, so you'll be able to hear the effects of the changes that you make, as you make them.

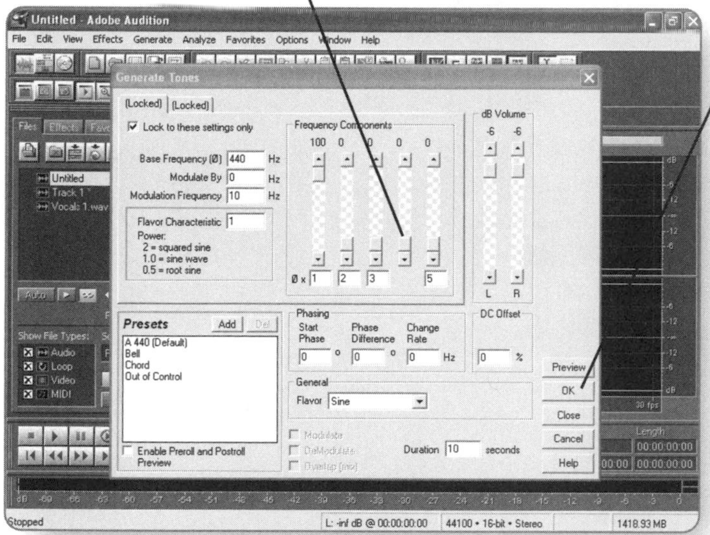

7. **Click** on **OK**. The tone will be created and will appear in the Edit window.

> **TIP**
>
> It's a good idea to experiment with the different settings in this dialog box. You can create a huge range of sounds, from a motorcycle starting up to an alien spaceship landing on the moon.

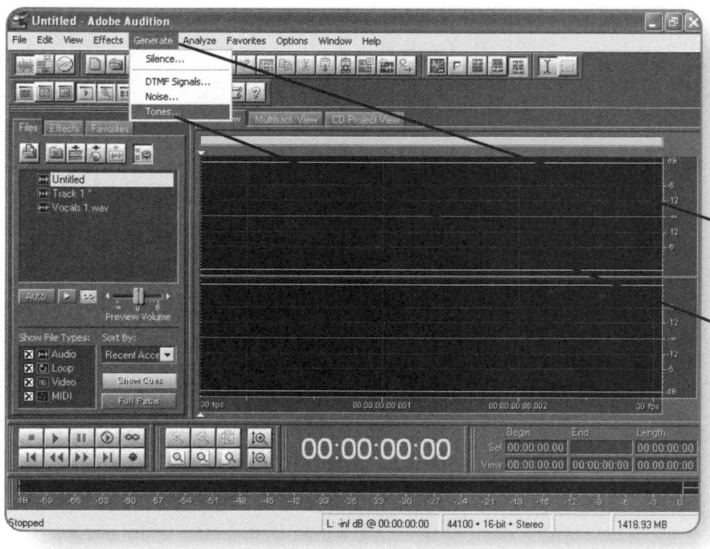

Creating Varying Tones

A varying tone is one whose overtones, frequency, and modulation change over time.

1. **Click** on **Generate**. The Generate menu will open.

2. **Click** on **Tones**. The Tones dialog box will open, allowing you to create the selections for your tone.

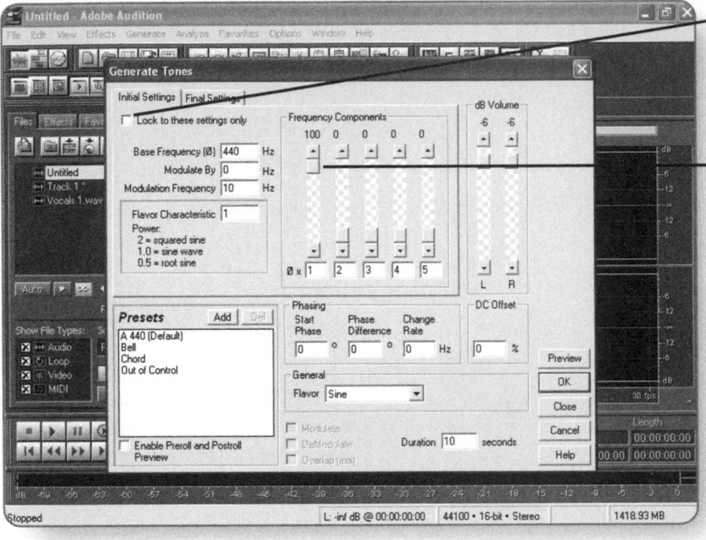

3. Uncheck the **Lock to these settings only check box**, if the box is not already unchecked.

4. Click and drag the **sliders** and **enter values** for the different options.

5. Click the **Final Settings tab**. The Final Settings tab will come to the front. This will allow you to adjust the end points for the tone.

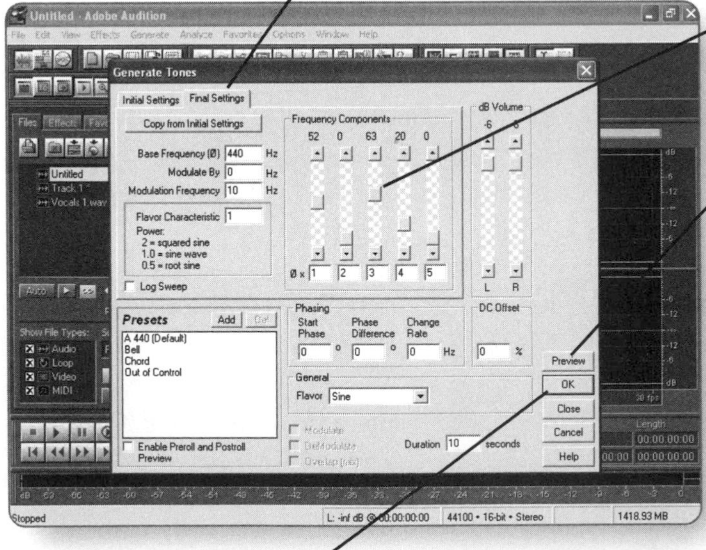

6. Click and drag the **sliders** and **enter values** for the different options.

7. Click the **Preview button** to test the tone that you have made.

8. Readjust any of the **settings**. The preview will react in real time, so you'll be able to hear the effects of the changes that you make, as you make them.

9. Click on **OK**. The tone will be created and will appear in the Edit window.

Importing Recordings

When it comes to bringing audio files into Adobe Audition, you really have two choices. The first is to import the file directly into a track in the Multitrack view. The other option is to import the audio into the Files section of the Organizer window. This method stores the file as part of the session and allows you to place it in a track or edit it at any time. The method that you select will depend upon what you are trying to accomplish.

Importing Directly to a Track

When importing directly to a track, you simply have to determine which track will get the audio. From there you select the track from its location on your computer, and presto, it's part of your session.

1. Press F12 to toggle to Multitrack view, if you are not already there. Multitrack view will appear.

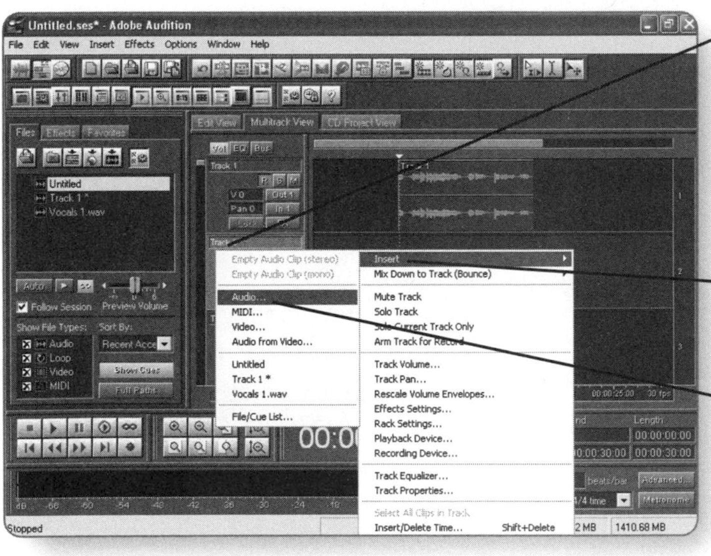

2. Position your **mouse pointer** over the track that will receive the audio file.

3. Right-click anywhere in the track. A menu will appear.

4. Click on **Insert**. A submenu will appear.

5. Click on the **file type** that you would like to insert. A dialog box will open from which you can select the file.

NOTE

If you choose to import a MIDI file, it will appear in the track as a series of little lines, rather than a wavelength. Adobe Audition does not allow you to manipulate MIDI files in Edit view unless they are first converted to waveform.

6. Click on the desired **file type** to import. Adobe supports many different file types.

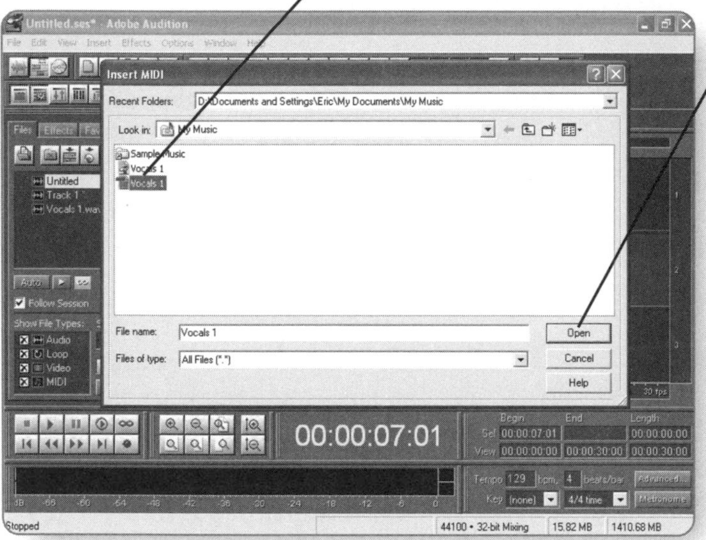

7. Click on **OK**. The audio file will be imported directly to the selected track.

NOTE

If the file you are importing does not have the same audio properties as your current session, you will be prompted to have it converted as it is imported.

NOTE

A copy of the audio file that you have imported will appear in the Files section of the Organizer window. You can now place copies of that audio file in other tracks, or you can edit it in the Edit view.

Importing Files to the Organizer Window

Within the Organizer window, there is a section called files which contains all the audio files that are within your session. Think of this files section as a library of music that you can borrow from to add to your session. You can also take individual files from this "library" and edit them in the Edit view. Adding audio files to this library is simply a matter of importing them.

1. **Click** on the **Files tab** of the Organizer window, if it is not already selected. It doesn't matter whether you are in Edit view or Multitrack view. The Files tab will come to the front.

2. **Click** on the **Open button**. A dialog box will appear from which you can select a file.

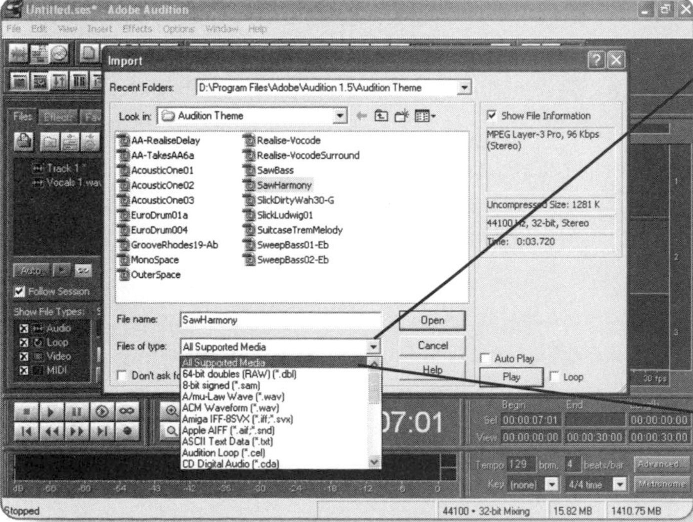

3. **Click** on the **down arrow** to expand the different file types. A list of types will appear.

4. **Click** on the desired **file type**. It will be selected.

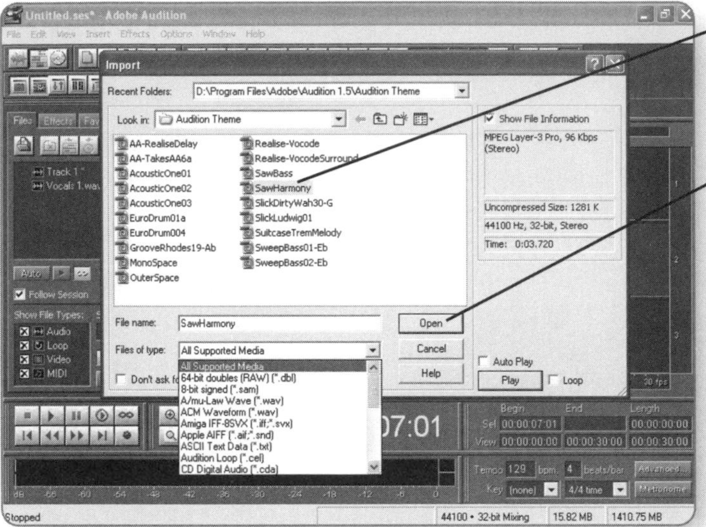

5. **Click** on the **file** that you would like to import. It will be highlighted.

6. **Click** on **Open**. The file will be imported and added to the files list in the Organizer window.

> **NOTE**
>
> If the file you are importing does not have the same audio properties as your current session, you will be prompted to have it converted as it is imported.

Punch-In Recording

If you've ever watched a movie being made, you'll know that it's a very rare occasion when the actors get everything right on the first take. If highly paid actors don't have to be perfect, then why should you? We're all human, we make mistakes, and that is just what punch recording is for. Let's say you've played or sung a piece almost flawlessly, but just want to re-record a portion of the audio. Using punch-in recording, you can specify a time within an audio block for recording to start and stop. You can then record several takes and decide which one sounds the best. Technically speaking, punch-in is the term used when the recording starts and punch-out is used for when the recording stops, but for our purposes, we'll just call the whole thing punch-in recording.

1. Press F12 to toggle to Multitrack view, if you are not already there. Multitrack view will appear.

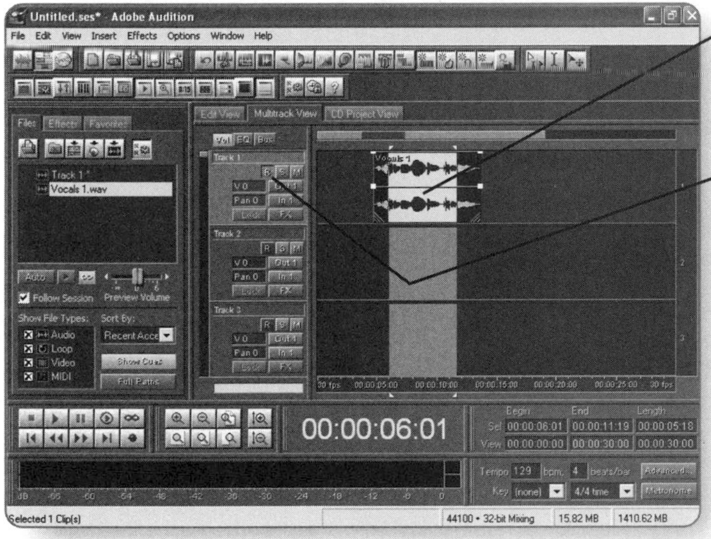

2. Create a **selection** using any of the selection methods. The area will now be highlighted.

3. Click on the **red R button** to enable recording on the desired track. It will turn bright red.

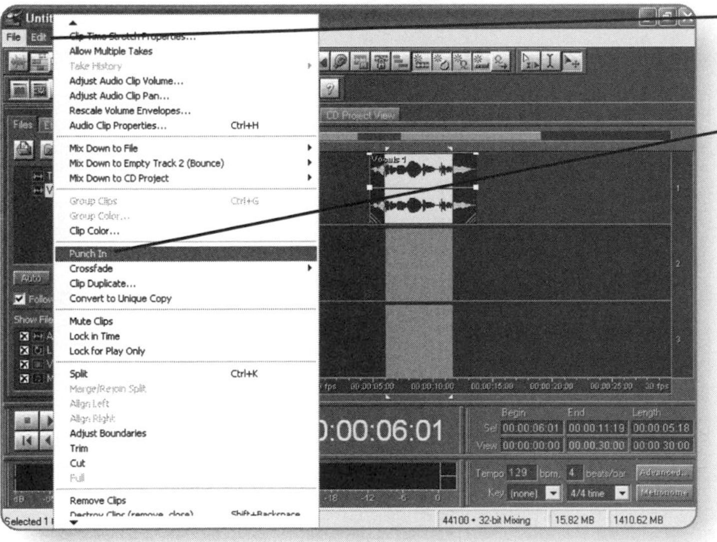

4. Click on **Edit**. The Edit menu will appear.

5. Click on **Punch In**. The highlighted area of the block will now turn a reddish color to indicate that punch-in recording is enabled.

6. Click on the **Record button**. The recording sequence will begin, but actual recording will only occur when the position indicator is within the punch-in area. You can use any of the recording methods covered in Chapter 3, "Standard Recording."

7. Click on the **Stop button**. The recording will be complete, but only the area that was highlighted will be overdubbed.

8. Repeat Steps 6 and 7 as desired. You can record over the area as many times as you like.

> **TIP**
>
> When using punch-in recording, every time you record over an area, the audio you've created is saved as a take. You can create multiple takes and later choose from the one you like best.

Take History

After you've created multiple takes, you can use the Take History task to choose between the multiple takes. You can listen to your session with different takes and then choose the one you like best. Once you've selected your favorite, you can merge it with the audio block.

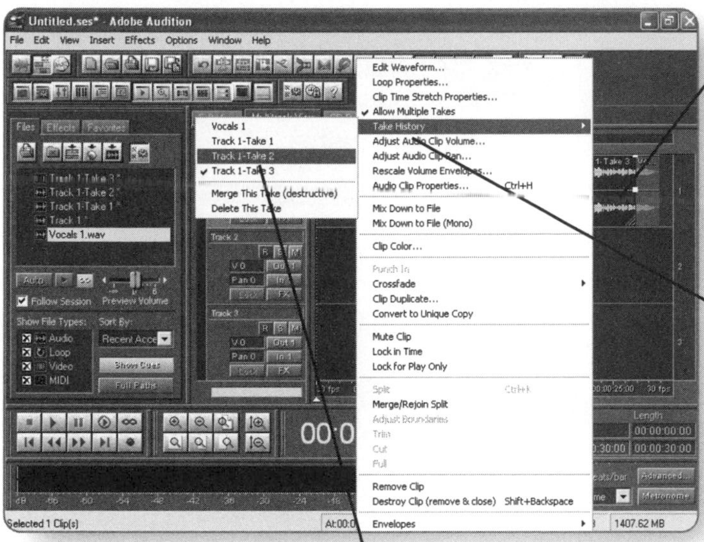

1. Right-click on the **audio block** where you used punch-in recording (the default color for this type of block is red). A menu will appear.

2. Click on **Take History**. A submenu will appear with a list of the different takes that you have created. The take that is currently selected will have a checkmark beside it.

3. Click on the desired **take**. It will be inserted into the audio block.

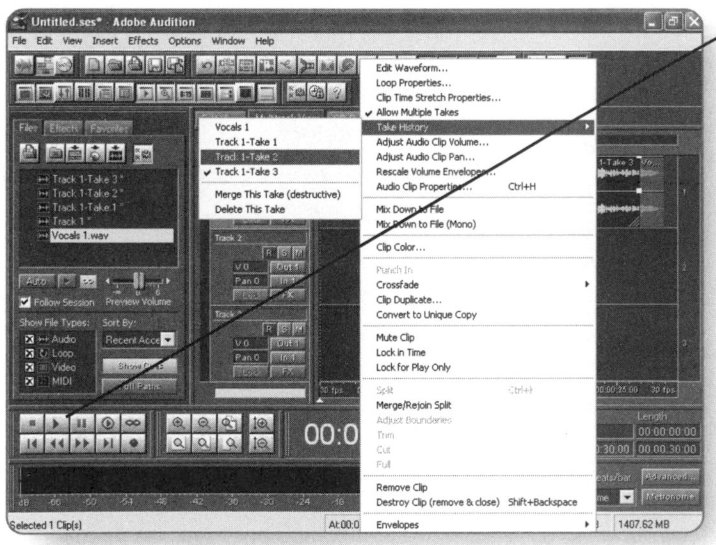

4. Click on **Play** to listen to the session. You can now listen to this take to see if it is the one that you want to use.

5. Repeat Steps 1-4 until you have selected the take you want to go with.

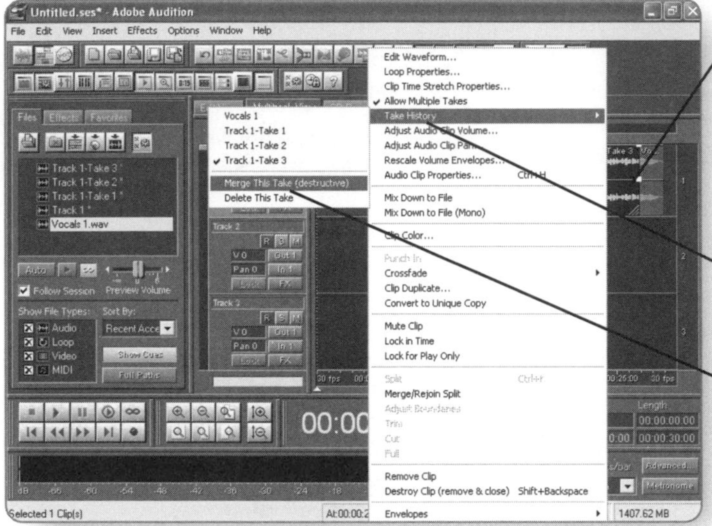

6. **Right-click** again on the **audio block** where you used punch-in recording. A menu will appear.

7. **Click** on **Take History**. A submenu will appear.

8. **Click** on **Merge This Take (destructive)**. A dialog box will appear confirming that you want to have this take merged with the existing audio block. This will permanently delete the other takes and keep this one as final.

9. **Click** on **OK**. The dialog box will close and the take that you have selected will now be merged with the block of audio.

Timed Recordings

There is an option in Edit view called Timed Recording which will allow you to set a specific time to start and stop recording, and choose a specific length of time for recording. You can use this feature to give yourself time to set up audio playback in other software on your computer and to enter precise lengths for recordings so you don't go over a specific amount of time. You can start by opening an existing audio file or creating a new one.

1. **Press F12** to toggle to Edit view if you are not already there. Edit view will appear.

2. **Click** on **Options**. The Options menu will appear.

3. **Click** on **Timed Record Mode**. A checkmark will appear in the check box. The timed Record mode will now be enabled.

4. **Click** on the **Record button**. A dialog box will appear.

5. **Click** on the **circle** beside Recording Length, if you want to set a specific length of time for your recording.

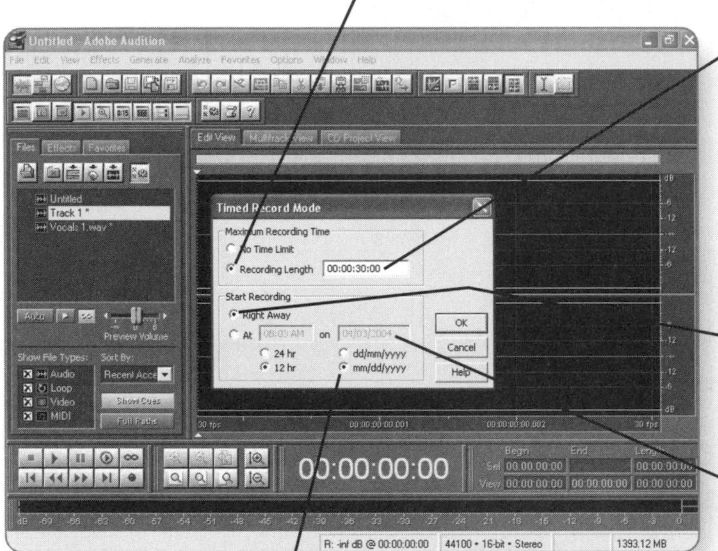

6. **Double-click** on the **numbers** in the Recording Length box. They will now be highlighted.

7. **Type** a **time** for the length of recording that you would like to set. It will appear as you type.

8. **Click** on the **circle** beside At if you want to set a specific time for recording to begin.

9. **Type** the desired **start time** and **date** in the boxes provided.

10. **Click** on the **circle** beside the desired time and date format.

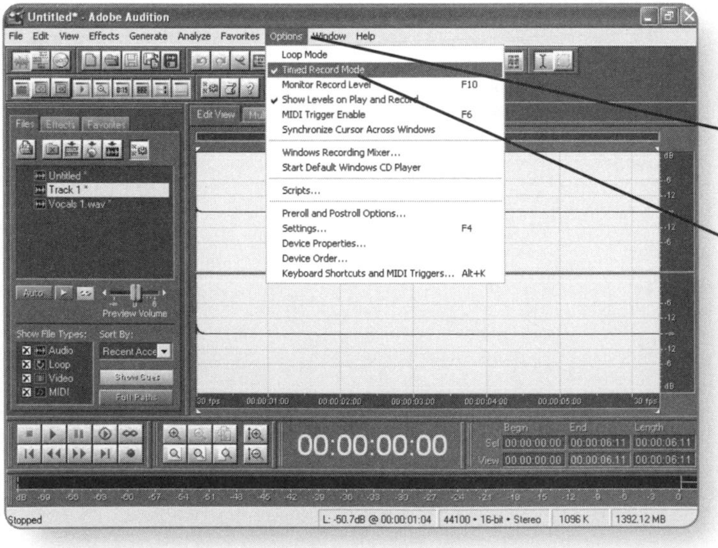

11. **Click** on **OK**. The settings will now take effect.

12. **Click** on **Options**. The Options menu will appear.

13. **Click** on **Timed Record Mode**. This will turn the feature off when you are finished using it.

5

Edit View Editing

The Edit view acts as the operating table for your waveforms. Everything from minor face lifts to major overhauls can be done in this window. By giving you a visual representation of your sound file, you can carefully manipulate the audio until you've achieved your desired results.

In this chapter, you'll learn how to:

- Trim unwanted audio
- Copy and paste
- Use clipboards
- Create crossfades
- Normalize waveforms

Trimming Audio

Probably the most common task in audio editing is removing unwanted data. Whether it's silence at the beginning or end of a track or simply a chunk of audio you don't want, trimming waveforms is made easy in Audition. One primary task you should be familiar with before setting out to trim your audio is making selections. Because you must select the desired data before you delete it, it might be a good idea to review the "Making Selections" section of Chapter 2.

1. **Select** the **data** that you would like to keep, using one of the selection methods. The data will appear highlighted to indicate that it is selected.

2. **Right-click** anywhere in the **window**. A menu will appear.

3. **Click** on **Trim**. The Trim function will trim the data.

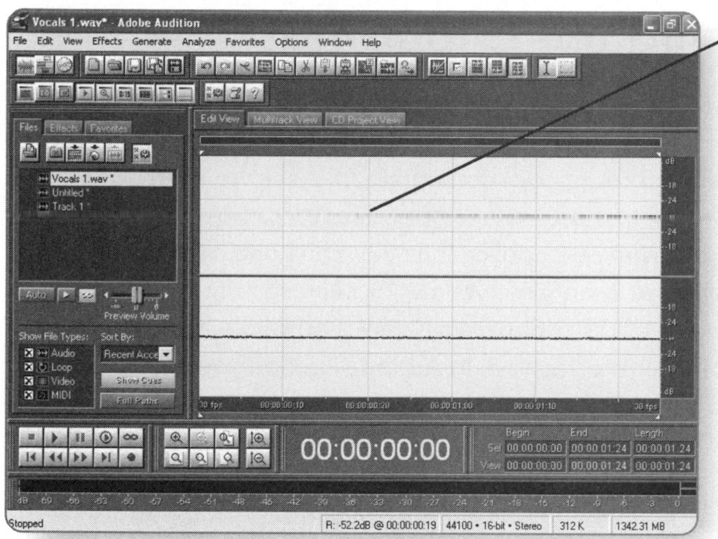

4. Observe the **waveform**. Everything except for the area that was selected will be removed.

Deleting

Like trimming, deleting removes unwanted data, but in the opposite manner. With deleting you select the area that you would like to remove rather than the area that you would like to keep.

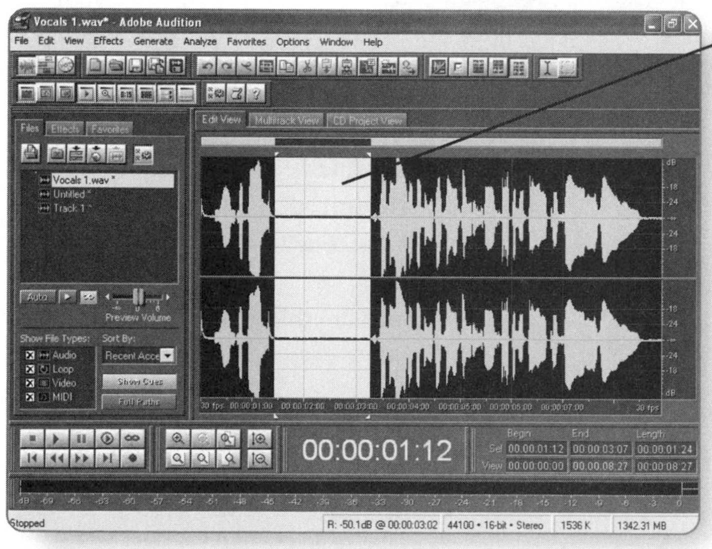

1. Select the **data** that you would like to remove, using one of the selection methods. The data will appear highlighted to indicate that it is selected.

2. Press the **Del key** on your keyboard. The selected area will be deleted.

Using the Clipboards

In later sections in this chapter you'll learn all about cutting and copying data from the selections that you have made. When you cut or copy something, it is sent to a virtual clipboard that acts as a temporary storage area for the data. In most Windows applications you have one clipboard, which means that every time you cut or copy something, the current contents of the clipboard get replaced with whatever data you have cut or copied. In Adobe Audition you actually have six different clipboards that you can work with, meaning you can have multiple items temporarily stored. You simply have to select which clipboard you'd like to use at any given time. There are five Audition clipboards and one Windows clipboard. The Windows clipboard can be used whenever you want to cut or copy data that will be pasted in other applications. Once you have a clipboard selected, you can use any of the copy, cut, and paste techniques described later in this chapter.

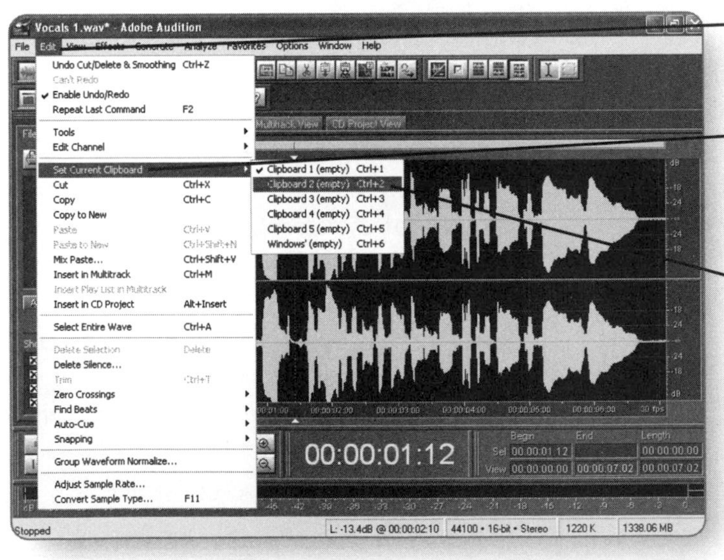

1. **Click** on **Edit**. The Edit menu will appear.

2. **Click** on **Set Current Clipboard**. A submenu will appear.

3. **Click** on the desired **clipboard**. It will now be selected. Anything you cut or copy will go to this clipboard, and anything you paste will come from this clipboard.

> **TIP**
>
> You can use the Ctrl key to toggle between the different clipboards. Ctrl + 1 will select the first clipboard, Ctrl + 2 will select the second, and so on until Ctrl + 6, which will select the Windows clipboard.

Cutting Audio

Similar to trimming, cutting audio will remove any selected portion of the waveform. The only difference is that the audio is not gone for good as it with trimming. When you cut a waveform, the data is cut to a clipboard that stores the information so that it can later be pasted. See the "Pasting" section later in this chapter for more information on what you can do with audio once it is on the clipboard.

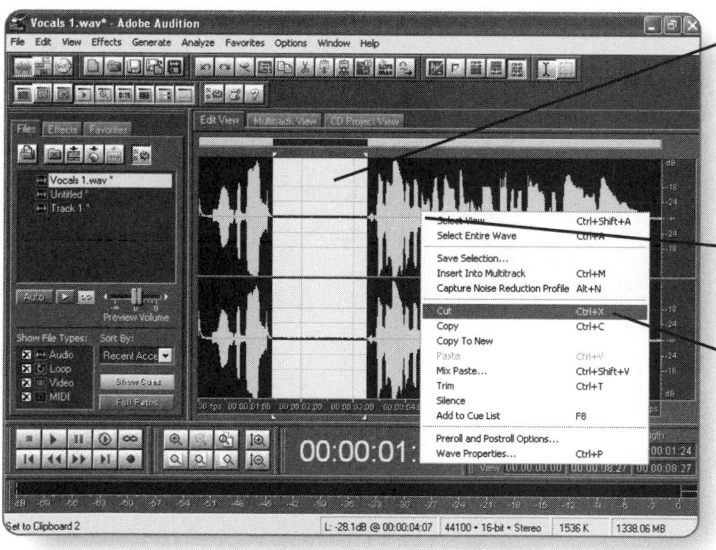

1. **Select** the **data** that you would like to remove, using one of the selection methods. The data will appear highlighted to indicate that it is selected.

2. **Right-click** anywhere in the **window**. A menu will appear.

3. **Click** on **Cut**. The selected data will be removed.

4. Observe the **waveform**. It will be rejoined at the point where the audio was deleted.

> **TIP**
>
> The keyboard shortcut for cutting data is Ctrl + X.

Copying Audio

Copying is a non-destructive way to get information from your current waveform onto the virtual clipboard.

1. Create a **selection** of the data you want to copy.

2. Press Ctrl + C. The data will be copied to the clipboard and the current waveform will remain in tact.

3. Click once anywhere in the **waveform** to deselect the area. The playback cursor will appear at that location.

Copying to New

You can automatically create a new waveform from a selection by using the Copy to New command. Once you have a new waveform created, do the following:

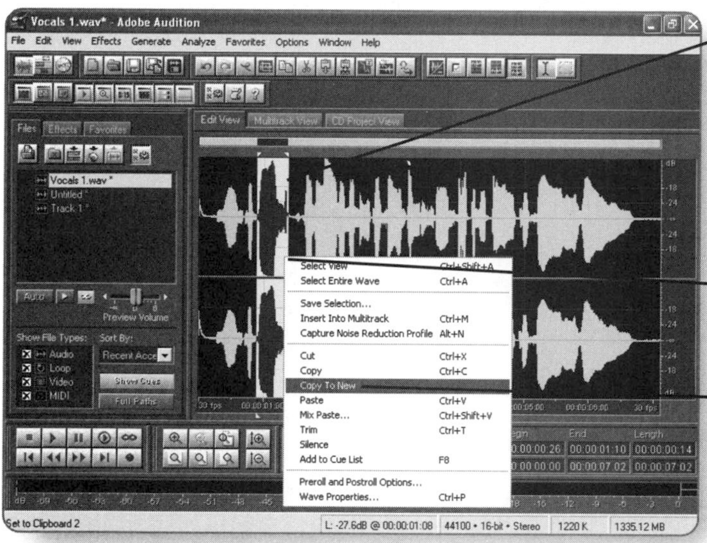

1. Select the **data** from which you would like to create a new waveform, using one of the selection methods. The data will appear highlighted to indicate that it is selected.

2. Right-click anywhere in the **window**. A menu will appear.

3. Click on **Copy to New**. The selected area will now appear as its own waveform.

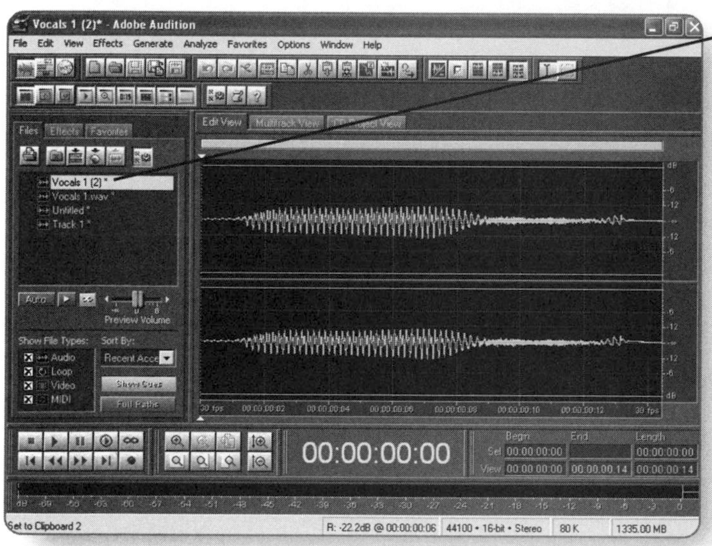

4. Observe the **Files area**. The new waveform you've created has been given a default name based on the file that it was created from.

Pasting

Once you have data on the clipboard, to use it elsewhere you must use a Paste command. There are several different paste methods that control how the data is placed back into the waveform.

Regular Pasting

The typical method for pasting is to select where you would like to place the data and then simply insert it using the Paste command.

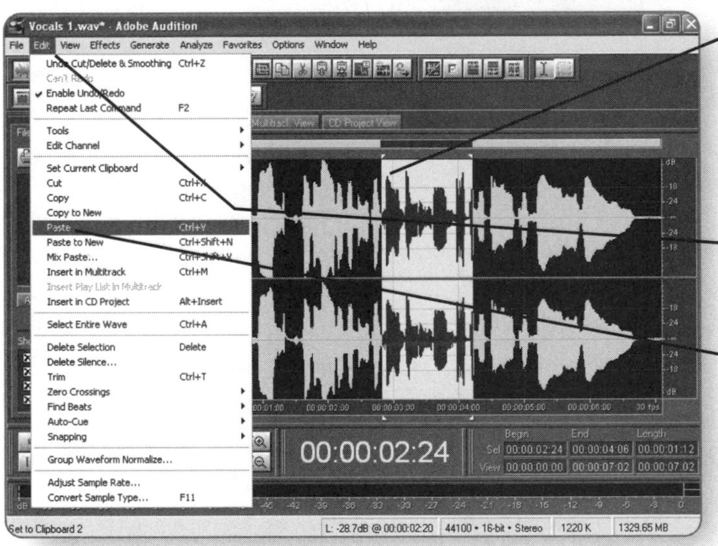

1. **Click once** where you would like to **insert** the data that you have on the clipboard. The playback cursor will appear where you have clicked.
2. **Click** on **Edit**. The Edit menu will appear.
3. **Click** on **Paste**. The data from the clipboard will be inserted at the point of the playback cursor.

Selection Pasting

You can remove specific audio and replace it with the contents of the clipboard all at the same time if you first make a selection before pasting.

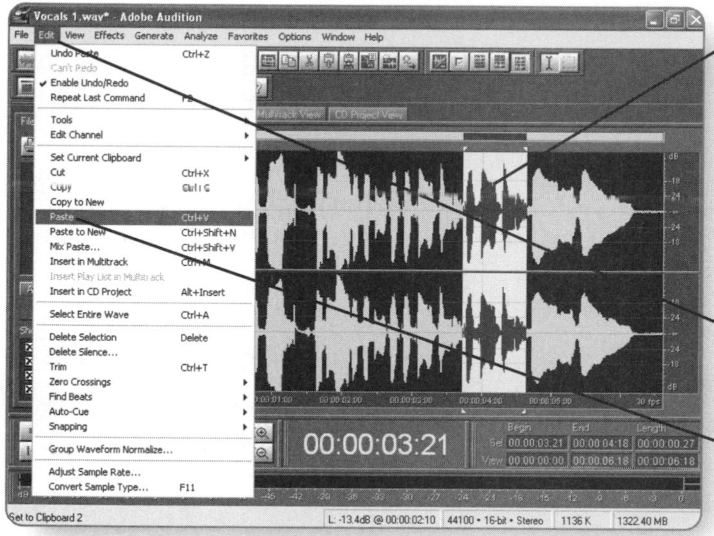

1. Select the **data** that you would like to remove, using one of the selection methods. The data will appear highlighted.

2. Click on **Edit**. The Edit menu will appear.

3. Click on **Paste**. The contents of the clipboard will replace the existing selection.

Overlapping

You can take the contents of the clipboard and overlap them with existing audio in your waveform. In essence you are mixing the contents of the clipboard with the current waveform together into one.

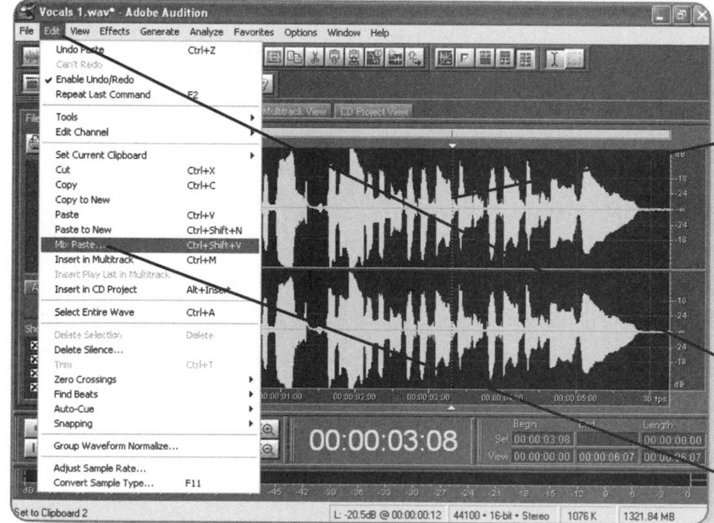

1. Click once where you would like to **insert** the data that you have on the clipboard. The playback cursor will appear where you have clicked.

2. Click on **Edit**. The Edit menu will appear.

3. Click on **Mix Paste**. The Mix Paste dialog box will open.

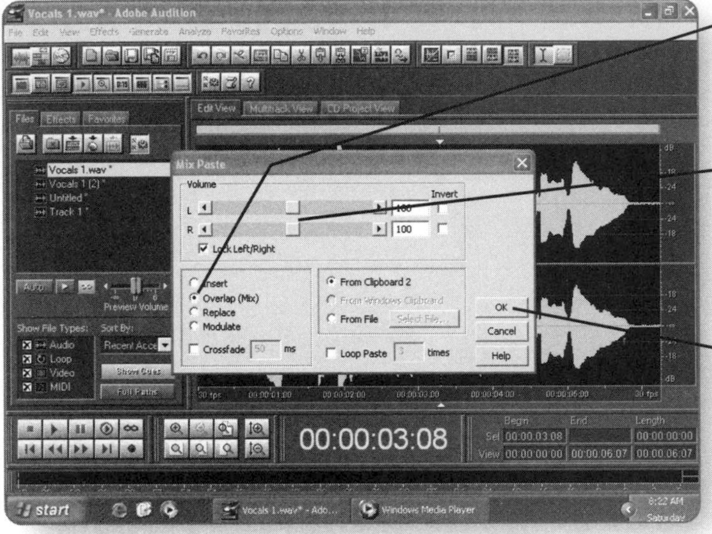

4. Click on the **circle** beside the Overlap (Mix) option. A dot will appear in the circle.

5. Click and drag the **volume controls** left or right to the desired levels. They will adjust as you drag.

6. Click on **OK**. The contents of the clipboard will overlap onto the existing waveform.

> **NOTE**
>
> When using the Overlap command, if the content of the clipboard is longer than the current waveform, the waveform will stretch to accommodate.

Replacing

When you use normal pasting, unless you have first made a selection, the existing data gets pushed farther into the timeline. If you want to replace the existing audio rather than push it further into the timeline, you can use the Replace command. In other words, let's say you had ten seconds of audio on the clipboard. By using the Replace command, you will replace ten seconds of audio in the current waveform with the audio that is on the clipboard.

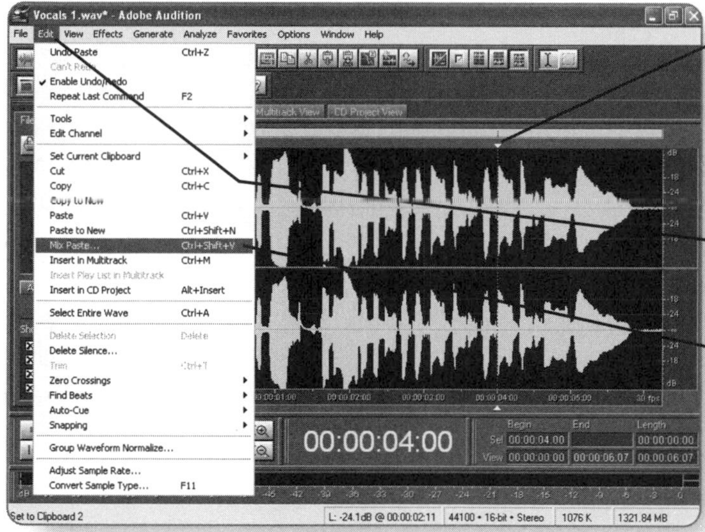

1. Click once where you would like to **insert** the data on the clipboard. The playback cursor will appear where you have clicked.

2. Click on **Edit**. The Edit menu will appear.

3. Click on **Mix Paste**. The Mix Paste dialog box will open.

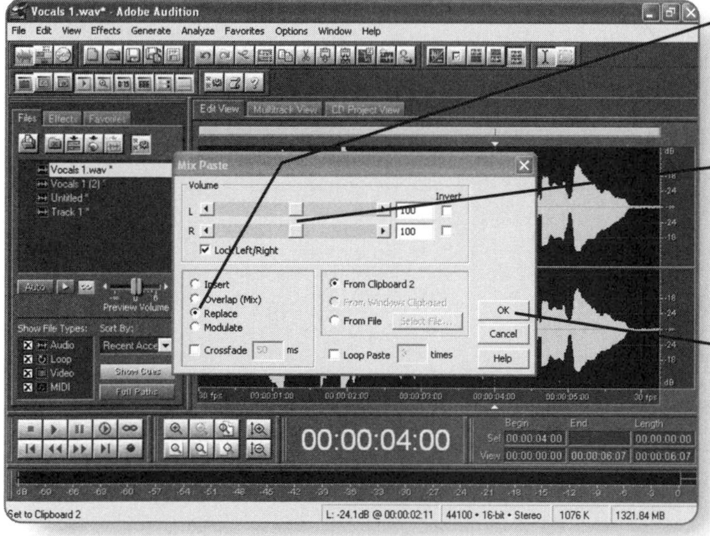

4. Click on the **circle** beside the Replace option. A dot will appear in the circle.

5. Click and drag the **volume controls** left or right to the desired levels. They will adjust as you drag.

6. Click on **OK**. The contents of the clipboard will replace the existing audio from the point of the playback cursor for the length of the clipboard contents.

Loop Pasting

If you wanted to insert the contents of the clipboard into your waveform and have it loop several times, you could do so without having to paste it over and over. This can be done in one step using the Loop Paste option in the Mix Paste dialog box.

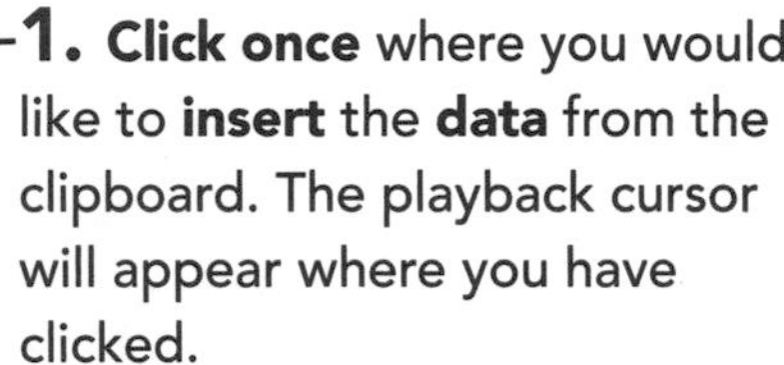

1. **Click once** where you would like to **insert** the **data** from the clipboard. The playback cursor will appear where you have clicked.
2. **Click** on **Edit**. The Edit menu will appear.
3. **Click** on **Mix Paste**. The Mix Paste dialog box will open.

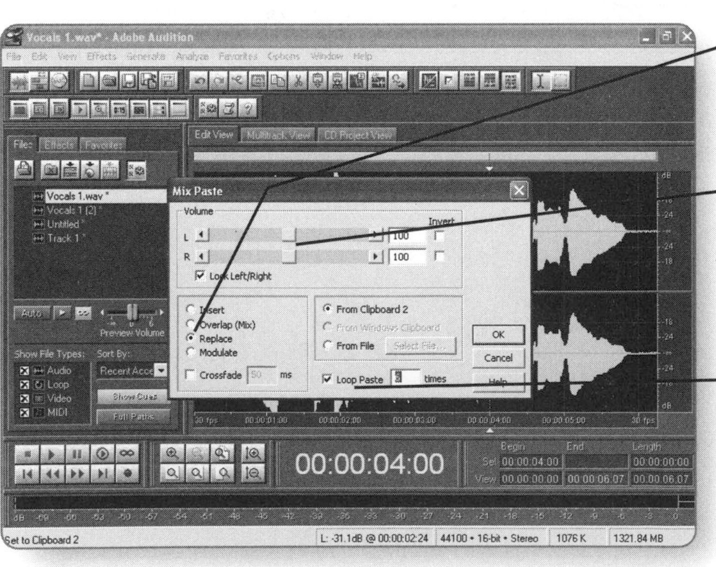

4. **Click** on the **circle** beside the desired Paste option. A dot will appear in the circle.
5. **Click and drag** the **volume controls** left or right to the desired levels. They will adjust as you drag.
6. **Click** on the **box** beside Loop Paste. A checkmark will appear in the box to indicate that it is selected.

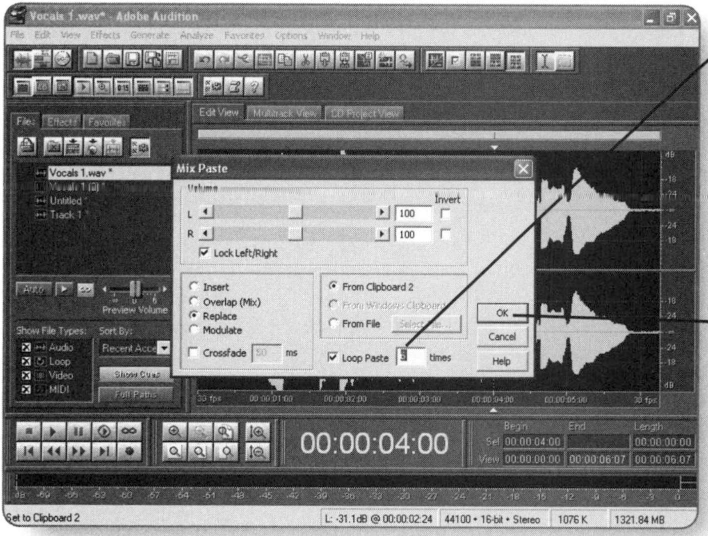

7. Double-click in the **number box**. It will be highlighted.

8. Type the **number** of times that you would like the contents of the clipboard to loop once pasted.

9. Click on **OK**. The contents of the clipboard will replace the existing audio from the point of the playback cursor and will be looped the specified number of times.

Creating Crossfades while Pasting

If you want a selection of audio to fade in and out for a specified period of time, you can apply a crossfade. Using the Mix Paste dialog box, you can create crossfades for the audio that you are pasting.

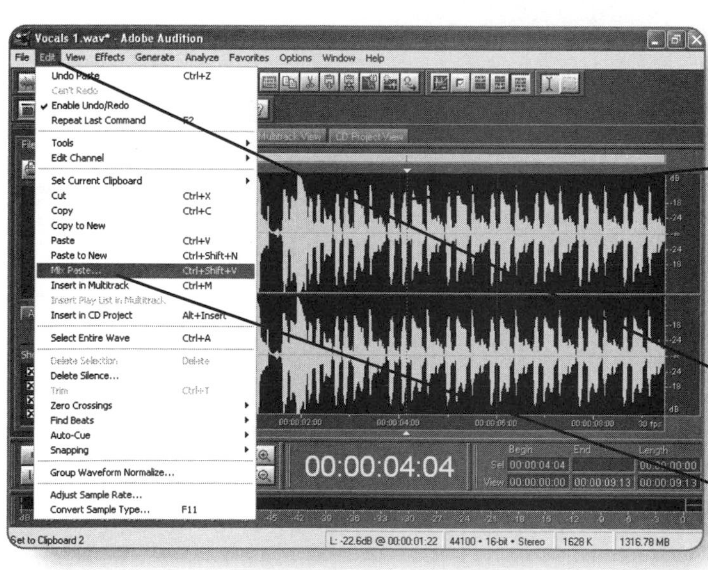

1. Click once where you would like to insert the data from the clipboard. The playback cursor will appear where you have clicked.

2. Click on **Edit**. The Edit menu will appear.

3. Click on **Mix Paste**. The Mix Paste dialog box will open.

4. **Click** on the **circle** beside the desired Paste option. A dot will appear in the circle.

5. **Click and drag** the **volume controls** left or right to the desired levels. They will adjust as you drag.

6. **Click** on the **box** beside Crossfade. A checkmark will appear in the box to indicate that it is selected.

7. **Double-click** in the **number box**. It will be highlighted.

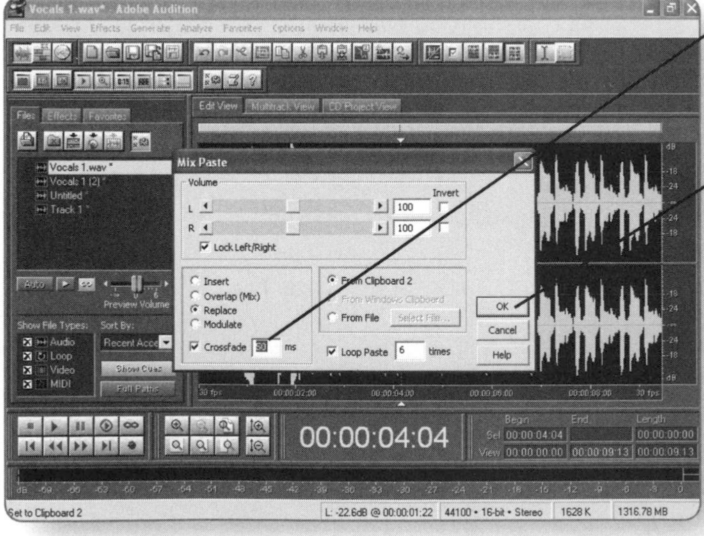

8. **Type** the **number** of milliseconds you want your selection to fade in and out.

9. **Click** on **OK**. The contents of the clipboard will be pasted and it will fade in and out based on the criteria that you have set.

Pasting to New

You can create a new waveform from the data on any clipboard by using the Paste to New command.

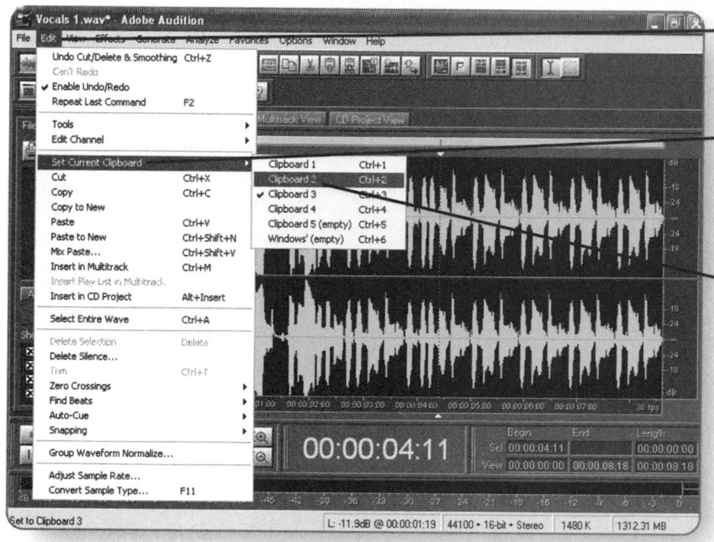

1. Click on **Edit**. The Edit menu will appear.

2. Click on **Set Current Clipboard**. A submenu will appear.

3. Click on the **clipboard** from which you would like to make a new waveform.

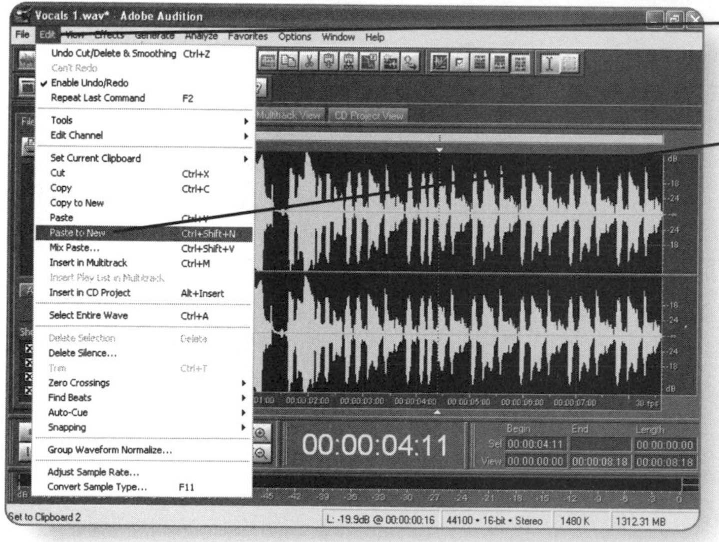

4. Click on **Edit**. The Edit menu will reappear.

5. Click on **Paste to New**. A new waveform file will be created from the contents of the clipboard you selected in Step 3.

Appending Files

You can merge two or more waveform files together by using the Append command. With a waveform open, the Append command allows you to select another waveform that will be added to the end of the existing one.

1. **Click** on **File**. The File menu will appear.

2. **Click** on **Open Append**. The Append a Waveform dialog box will open.

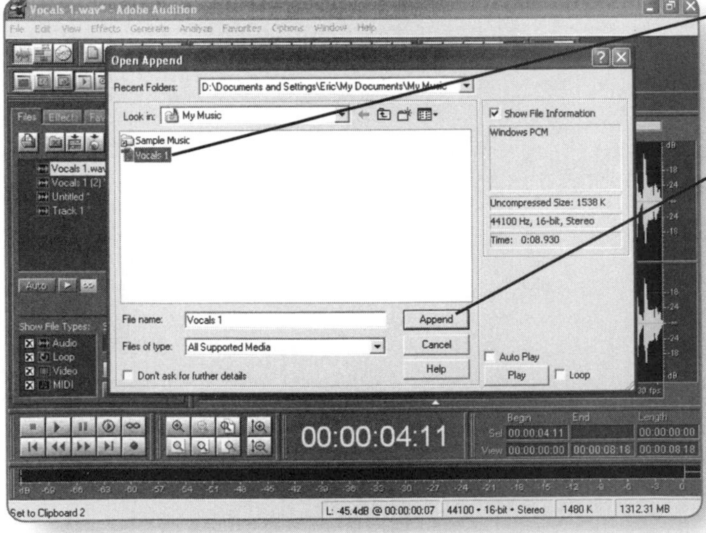

3. **Click** on the **file** that you would like to append. It will be highlighted.

4. **Click** on **Append**. The file will be appended to the end of the existing waveform.

5. **Repeat Steps 1-4** to add other waveforms to the existing one.

Normalizing

Because different audio files are typically recorded from a variety of sources, it's normal for them to have different loudness levels. This can pose a problem when editing, so Adobe Audition has a way for you to set consistent loudness levels for all of your waveforms.

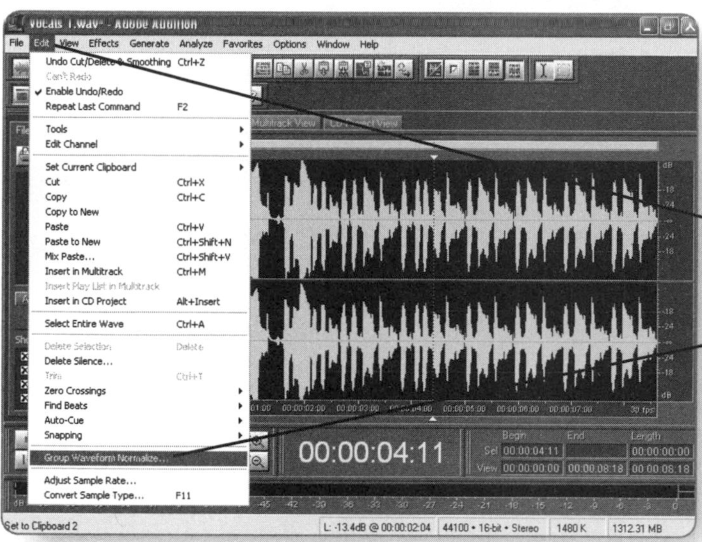

1. **Click** on **Edit**. The Edit menu will appear.

2. **Click** on **Group Waveform Normalize**. The Group Waveform Normalize dialog box will appear. All of the waveforms that are currently in your file will appear in a window.

3. **Click once** on the **top file**. It will be highlighted.

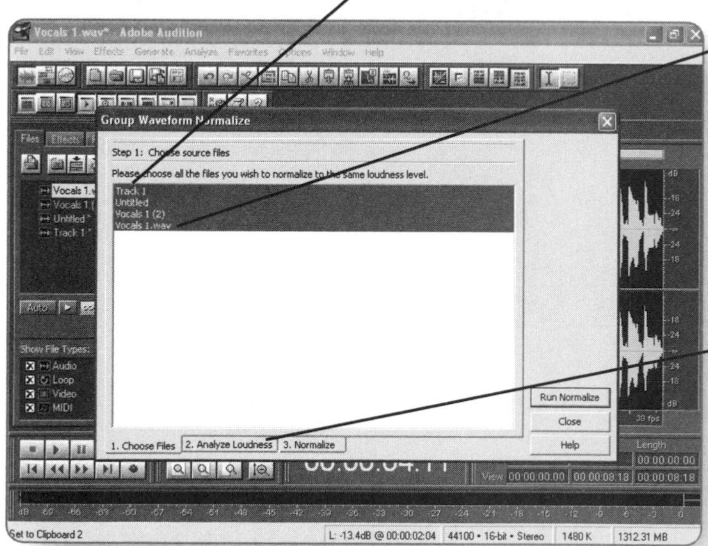

4. **Shift** + **click** on the **last file** in the window. All of the files in the window will be selected. Alternatively, if you don't want to select all of the files, you can **Ctrl + click** on only those **files** that you would like to normalize.

5. **Click** on the **2. Analyze Loudness tab** at the bottom of the dialog box. The screen will now change and you will be able to analyze the loudness of your files.

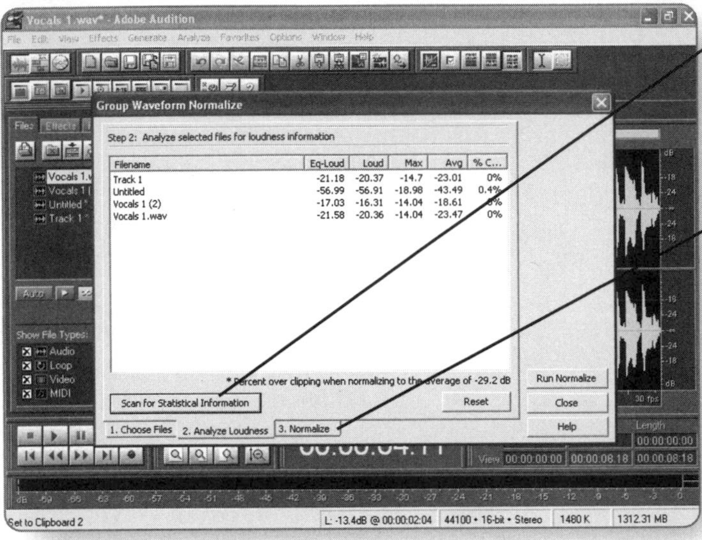

6. Click on the **Scan for Statistical Information button**. Statistics on each of your files will appear in the window.

7. Click on the **3. Normalize tab** at the bottom of the dialog box. You can now adjust the settings for the normalizing process.

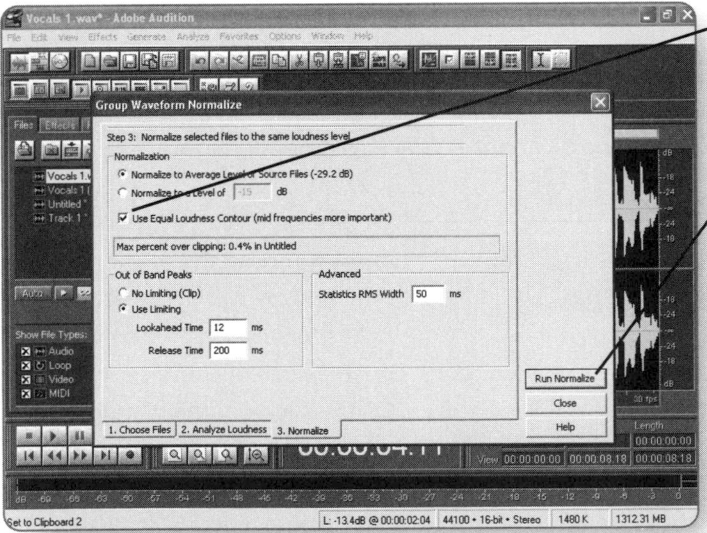

8. Click on the desired **settings**. They will adjust based on your selections.

9. Click on **Run Normalize**. The files will be normalized based on the settings you entered and the dialog box will close.

Deleting Silence

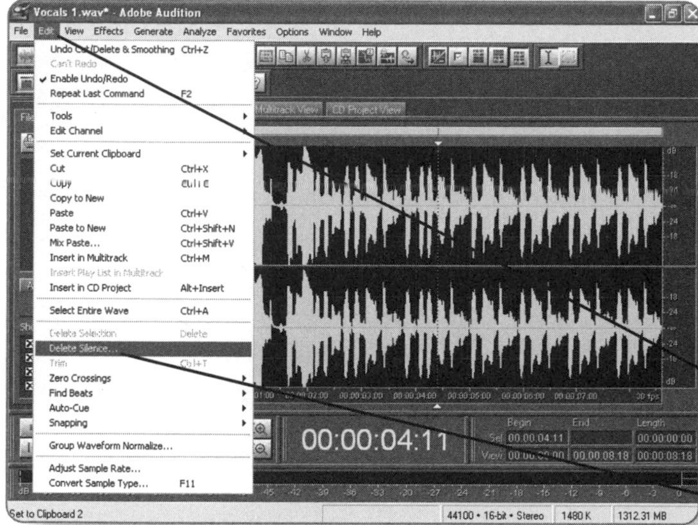

Ahhhh, sweet silence, why would you ever want to get rid of it? Well if you don't enjoy the silence, you can remove areas within your waveform that fall under a certain decibel level that you set.

1. **Click** on **Edit**. The Edit menu will appear.

2. **Click** on **Delete Silence**. The Delete Silence dialog box will appear.

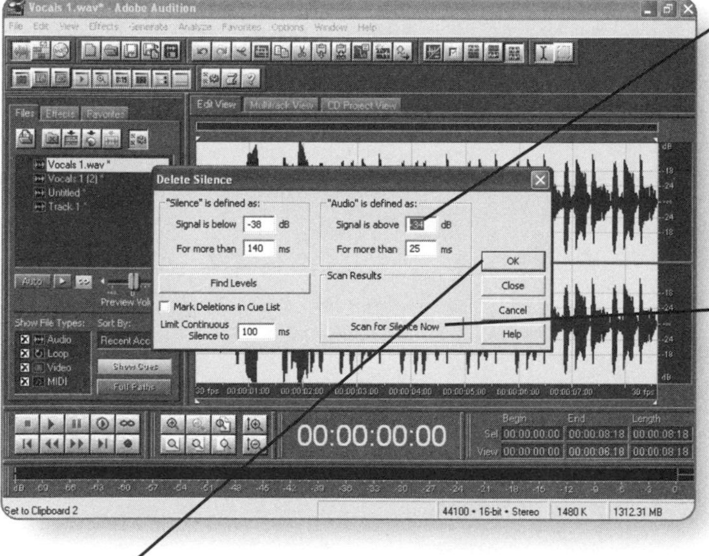

3. **Double-click** in any of the **value fields** that you would like to adjust. The box will be highlighted.

4. **Type** a **number**. The number will appear as you type.

5. **Click** on the **Scan for Silence Now button**. A description of the amount of silence in your waveform based on the criteria you have entered will appear in the dialog box.

6. **Click** on **OK**. The silences within your waveform will be removed.

Adjusting Sample Rate

Using the Adjust Sample Rate command will only change the sample rate for the playback on your soundcard and not the actual sample rate of the waveform file.

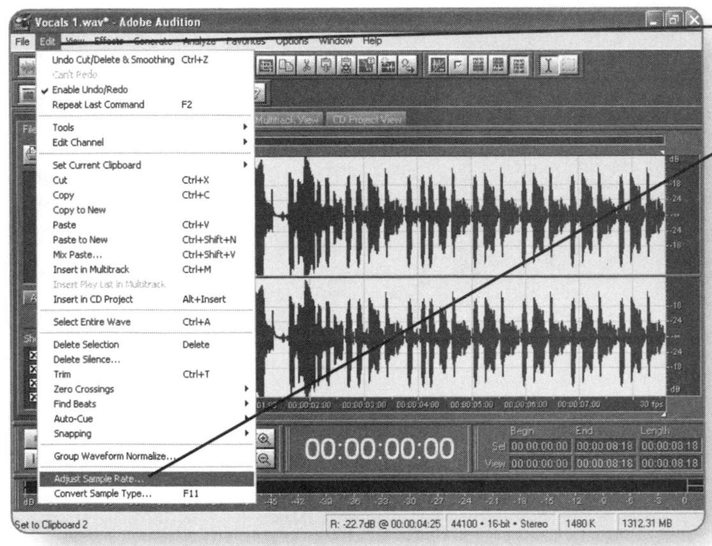

1. **Click** on **Edit**. The Edit menu will appear.

2. **Click** on **Adjust Sample Rate**. The Adjust Sample Rate dialog box will open.

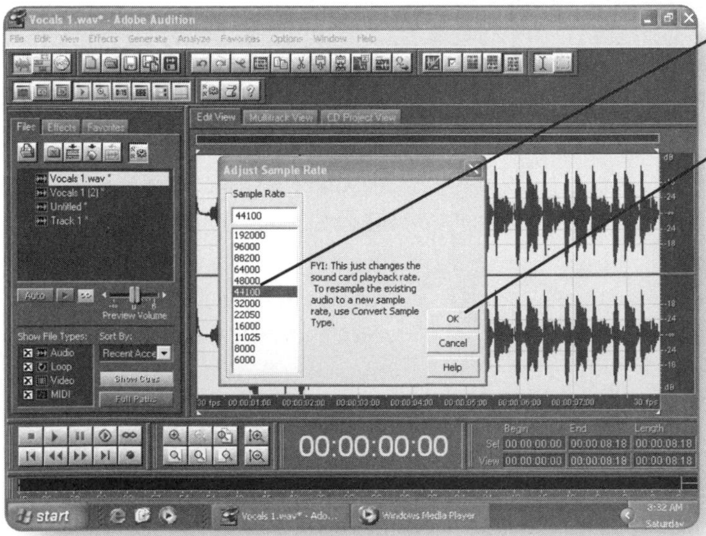

3. **Click** on the desired **sample rate**. It will appear highlighted.

4. **Click** on **OK**. The sample rate will be changed.

Converting Sample Types

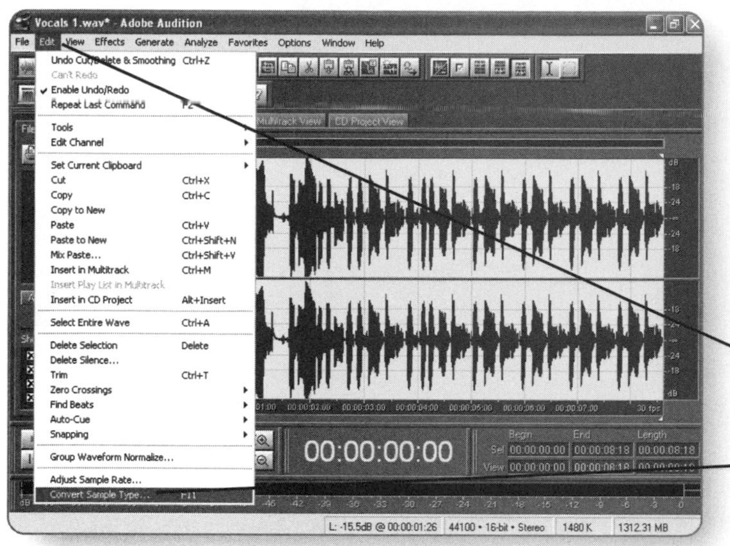

You can change the makeup of any waveform that you have open in the window by opening the Covert Sample Type dialog box. This box will allow you to change the sample rate, channel, distribution, and quality of the waveform.

1. **Click** on **Edit**. The Edit menu will appear.

2. **Click** on **Convert Sample Type**. The Convert Sample Type dialog box will open.

3. **Click** on the desired **sample rate**. It will be highlighted.

4. **Click and drag** the **Quality scroll box**. The quality level will change as you drag.

5. **Click** on the **circle** beside the desired Channel type. A dot will appear in the circle.

6. **Click** on the desired **resolution**. It will be highlighted once clicked.

7. **Click** on the **OK button**. The criteria that you have selected will be applied to the waveform.

6

Multitrack Editing

The projects that you create in Adobe Audition are called sessions. A session consists of different wave clips (music files) that are arranged in a particular sequence. The Multitrack view allows you to control how wave clips appear within the sequence. You are given a visual representation of your music files which can be quickly altered with a few clicks of the mouse.

In this chapter, you'll learn how to:

- Insert wave clips
- Move wave clips
- Name tracks
- Adjust track properties

Inserting Wave Clips

A typical session can be made up of potentially hundreds of different wave clips. These wave clips are inserted into different tracks to help manage both their timing and positioning within the session. Later in this chapter you'll learn to change track properties, but for now we'll cover the different ways you can get wave clips into tracks. Because inserting wave clips is such an essential task in Adobe Audition, you have several methods available to you.

Inserting Wave Clips from the Organizer Window

Files that you have previously imported are available in the Files area of the Organizer window. From the Organizer window, you simply have to click and drag the desired file onto a track. For more information on importing files to the Organizer window, see the section titled "Importing Recordings" in Chapter 4.

1. **Press F12** to toggle to Multitrack view, if you are not already there. Multitrack view will appear.

2. **Click** on the **Files tab** of the Organizer window, if it is not already selected. The Files tab will come to the front.

3. **Position** your **mouse pointer** over the file that you would like to insert into the session.

4. **Click and drag** the **file** to the desired track and location within that track. As you drag you will see a light shadow of the file name. The exact location of your mouse pointer is where the audio clip will start.

5. **Release** the **mouse button**. The file will be inserted into the track at the location where you released the mouse.

Inserting Wave Clips from the Session Display

Adobe Audition allows you to import an audio file directly from your computer's hard drive into the Session display.

1. **Right-click** at the approximate **location** where you would like to insert the wave clip. A menu will appear.

2. **Click** on **Insert**. A submenu will now appear.

3. **Click** on **Audio**. Alternatively, you can select MIDI, if you want to insert a MIDI file. A dialog box will now open from which you can select the file that you would like to import.

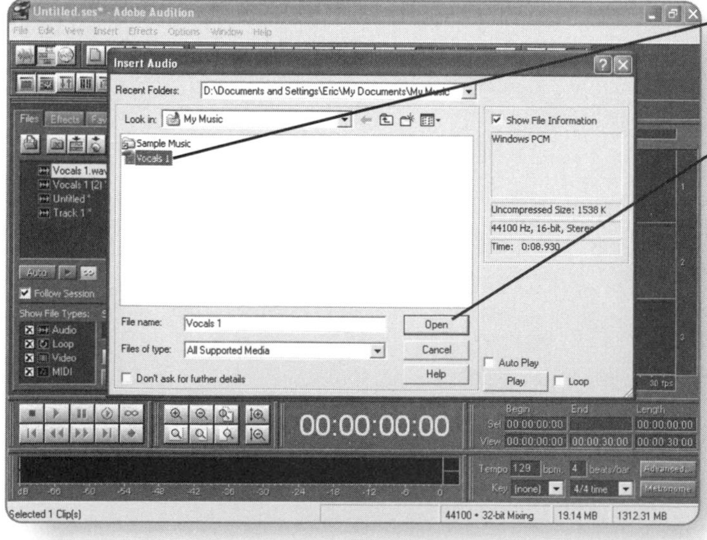

4. **Click** on the desired **file**. It will be highlighted.

5. **Click** on **Open**. The file will be inserted at the point where you right-clicked in Step 1.

Inserting Wave Clips from Windows Folders

Rather than opening several audio files to be stored in a session, some people prefer to store their audio files in a folder on their hard drive. Adobe Audition allows you to insert files from Windows folders by simply clicking and dragging.

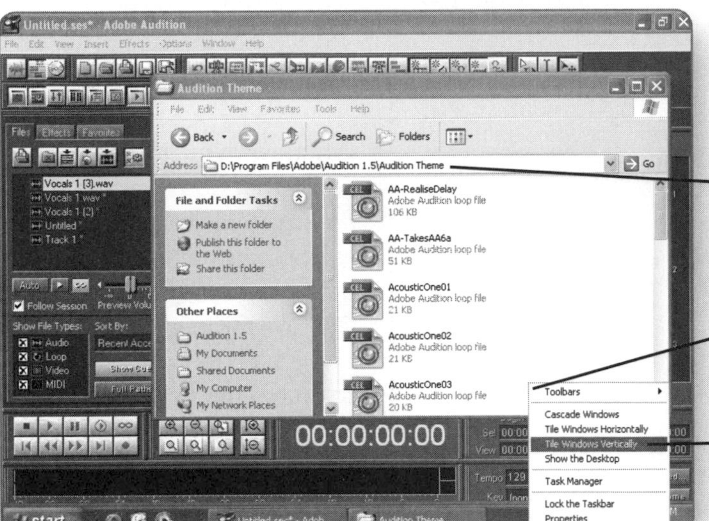

1. **Open** the **folder** that contains the audio files that you would like to import.

2. **Right-click** on the **Windows taskbar**. A menu will appear.

3. **Click** on **Tile Windows Vertically**. You will now be able to see the file window and Adobe Audition.

4. **Click and drag** the **file** from the file window to Adobe Audition. As you drag, the mouse pointer will have a little plus sign attached to it.

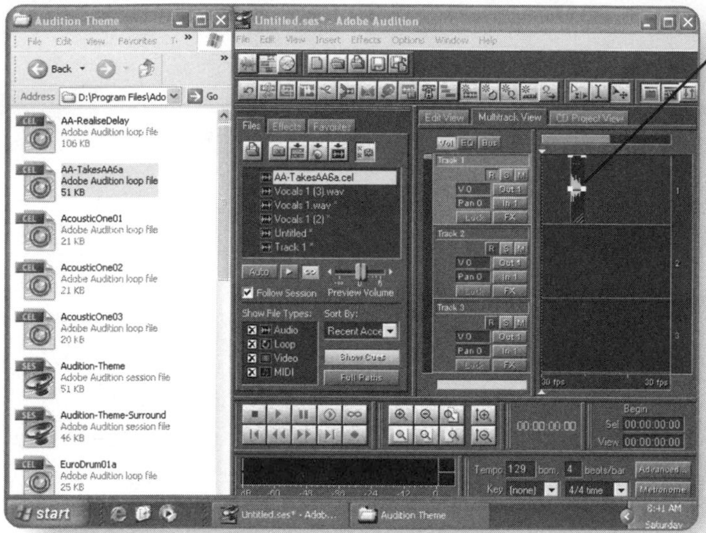

5. Release the **mouse button** when the mouse pointer is over the exact location where you would like to insert the audio. The wave clip will now be inserted into the track.

> **NOTE**
>
> Whenever you import audio that does not share the same audio properties as your current session, a dialog box will appear. Click on OK in that dialog box to convert the audio to match the existing properties of the session.

Moving a Wave Clip

When you import a wave file into a session, you can position the clip close to where you want it to appear within the session. There is a good likelihood that you may want to move that clip to either give it a precise location or simply move it to a different track. Moving a clip of audio in Adobe Audition is simply a matter of clicking and dragging.

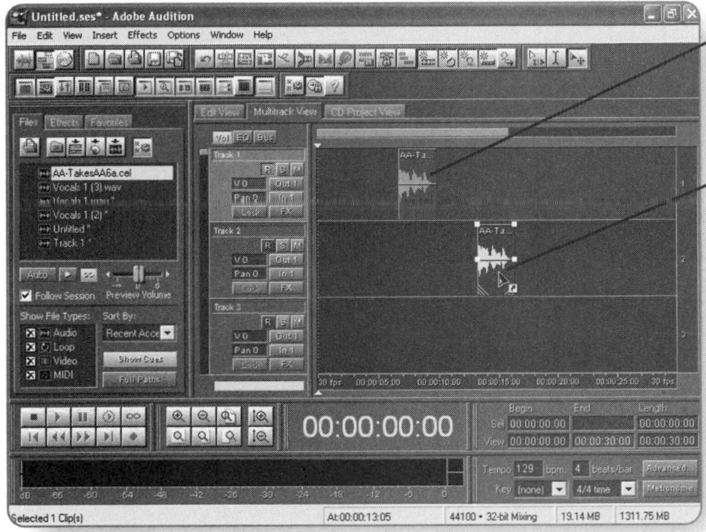

1. **Position** your **mouse pointer** over the wave clip that you would like to move.

2. **Right-click and drag** the **wave clip** to its new location. As you drag the wave clip will move.

3. **Release** the **mouse button**. A menu will appear.

4. **Click** on **Move Clip Here**. The clip will be moved.

Snapping

Think of the sound that is made when you put a positive and negative magnet together. They "snap" against each other when they get close. That's pretty much how snapping works in Adobe Audition. When the snapping feature is activated, the wave clips will snap to certain items as they are moved, allowing you to precisely position them. You can choose to have wave clips snap to each other, snap to positions on the ruler, or snap to other elements on the screen.

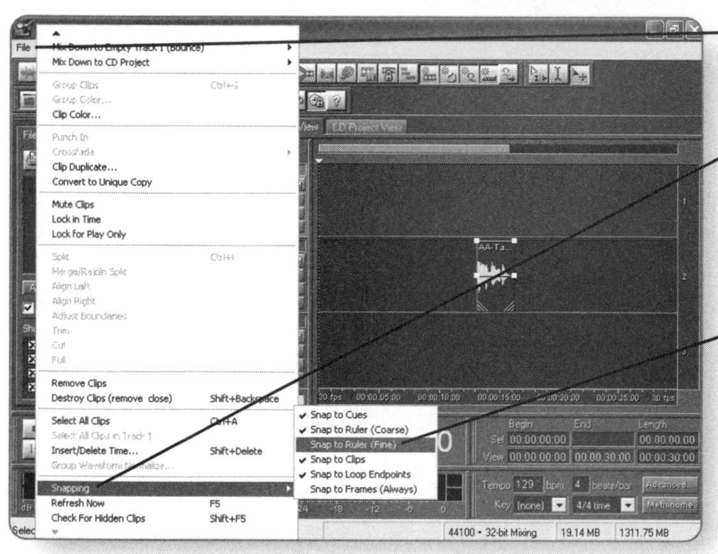

1. **Click** on **Edit**. The Edit menu will appear.

2. **Click** on **Snapping**. A submenu will appear, allowing you to choose a snapping method.

3. **Click** on the desired **Snapping method**. Those with a checkmark beside them are already selected. Now when you are moving a wave clip, it will snap together with whatever selection you made.

Copying

Unlike in Edit view, there are no commands to copy and paste selected wave clips. However, you can accomplish this by using the Ctrl key. If you hold down the Ctrl key while moving an audio clip, you'll actually leave the original in its place and a copy will be created where you release the mouse.

1. **Position** the **mouse pointer** over the wave clip that you would like to copy.

2. **Right-click and drag** the **wave clip** to the position where you would like to "paste" the copy. As you drag, a copy of the wave clip will appear and follow your cursor.

3. **Release** the **mouse button**. A menu will appear.

4. **Click** on **Copy Unique Here**. A copy of the original wave clip will appear at the point where you released the mouse button.

> **TIP**
>
> If you hold down the Shift key as you right-click and drag a clip, the clip will be copied.

Cloning

The future is now and cloning is alive and well and fully functioning in Adobe Audition. When you clone a wave clip you create an exact duplicate in a new location. The difference between copying and cloning is that unlike copying, which creates two distinct files, cloning simply references one file in more than one location. Anything that you do to a clone or the original file will also appear in all others. For example, after cloning, if you apply a special effect to the original, the same special effect will be applied to the clone; it's as if they are the same file.

1. **Position** the **mouse pointer** over the wave clip that you would like to clone.

2. **Right-click and drag** the **wave clip** to the position where you would like to create the clone. As you drag, a clone of the wave clip will appear and follow your cursor.

3. **Release** the **mouse button**. A menu will appear.

4. Click on **Copy Reference Here**. A clone of the original will be created.

5. Double-click on either the **original** or the **clone**. The waveform will open up in Edit view.

6. Click and drag across an area of the **waveform** to select it. The area will be highlighted.

7. Press the **Del key** to delete the highlighted section of the waveform.

8. Press F12 to toggle back to Multitrack view. Multitrack view will appear.

9. Observe the **clone** and the original wave clip. Although you edited only one of them, they both changed because they are clones.

Cutting

Cutting in Multitrack view is distinctly different from cutting in Edit view or cutting in any other Windows application, for that matter. When you cut a selection in Multitrack view, you are simply telling Adobe Audition to mute out that part of the wave clip as your session plays. Cutting is non-destructive, meaning that at any point you can reinstate any portion that you have cut.

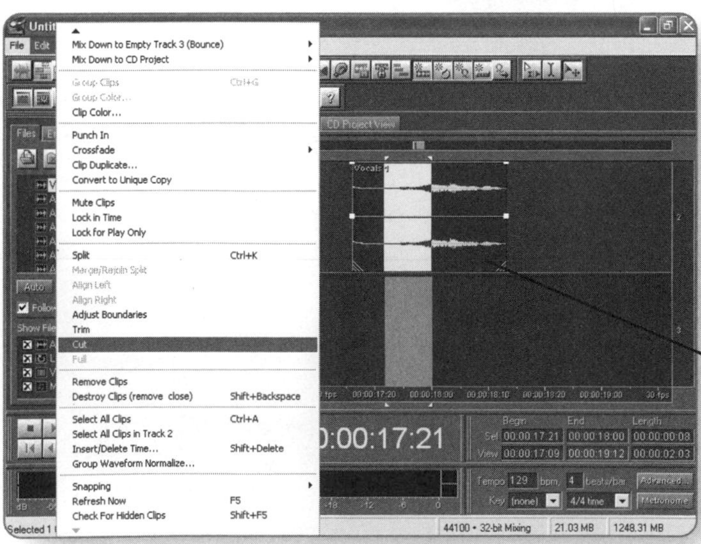

1. Click once on the **wave clip** that contains the audio that you would like to cut. The wave clip will be highlighted to indicate that it is selected.

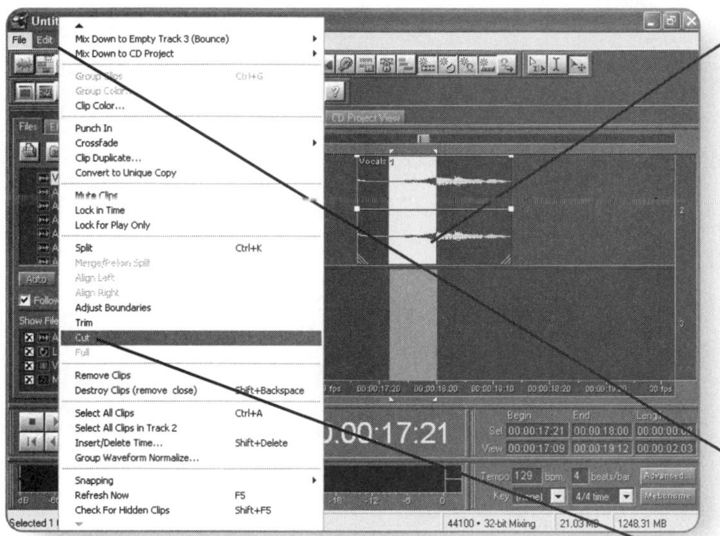

2. Click and drag across the portion of the **wave clip** that you would like to cut. The selection will be highlighted.

3. Click on **Edit**. The Edit menu will appear.

4. Click on **Cut**. The portion of the wave clip that was selected will be cut.

5. Click on the **Play button**. As the session plays you'll notice that there is no audio at the portion of the wave clip that you cut.

6. Click on the **Stop button**. The playback will stop.

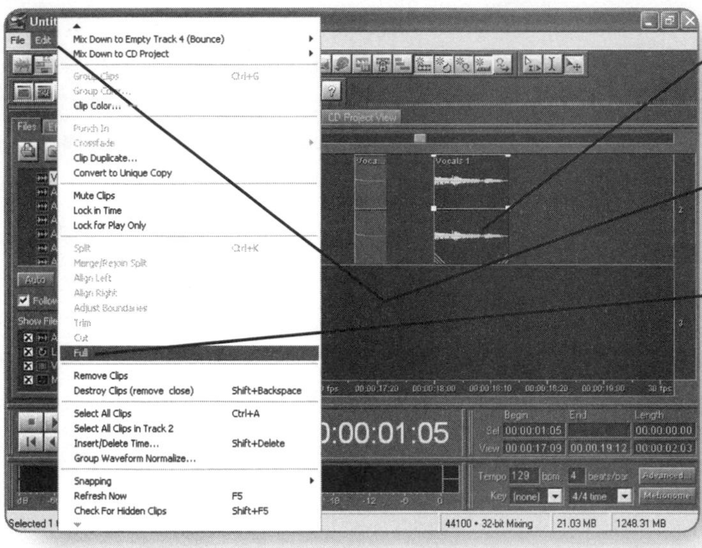

7. Click once on any **portion** of the wave clip that was cut. It will be highlighted.

8. Click on **Edit**. The Edit menu will appear.

9. Click on **Full**. The wave clip will be restored to its original, pre-cut state.

Splitting

Before the world of digital, audio editing was accomplished by physically cutting and pasting together pieces of audio tape. After a piece of tape was cut into slices, the individual slices could be moved and glued back anywhere in the sequence. Adobe Audition makes this much easier with a process called *splitting*. It will take a wave clip and split it into several distinct clips.

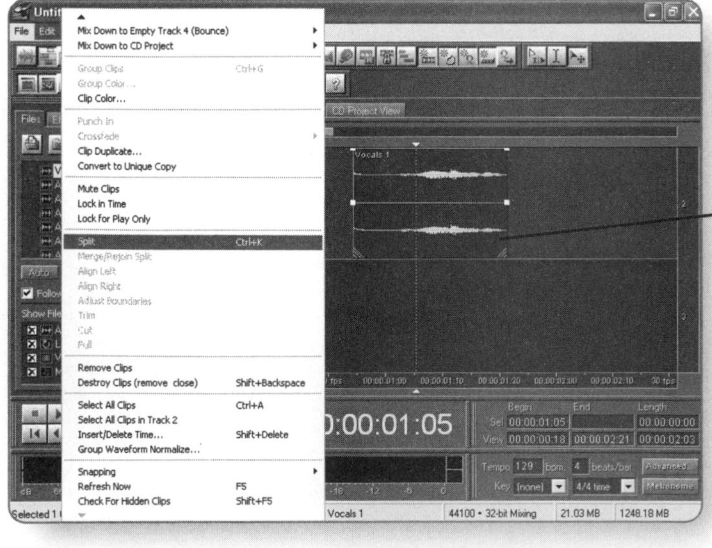

1. Click on the **clip** that you would like to split. It will be highlighted.

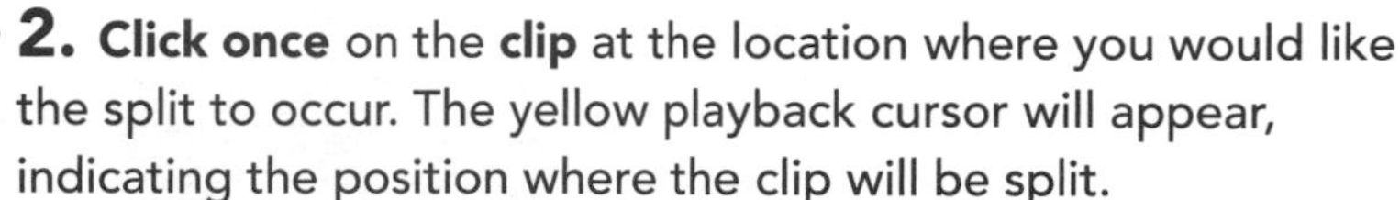

2. Click once on the **clip** at the location where you would like the split to occur. The yellow playback cursor will appear, indicating the position where the clip will be split.

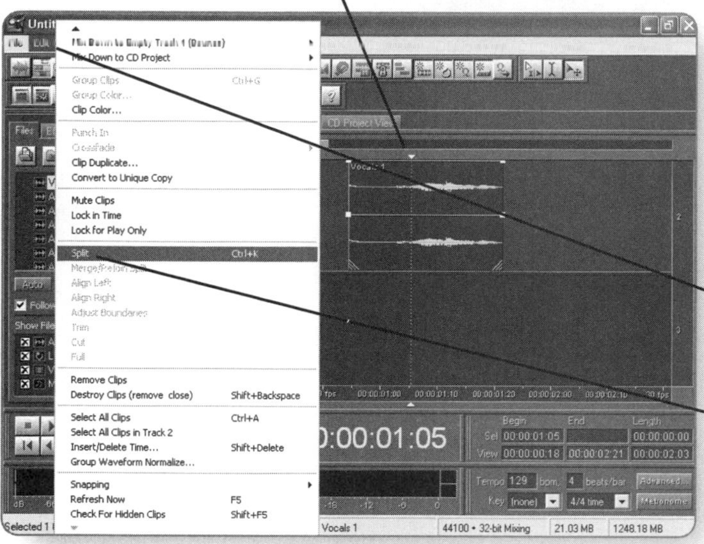

Alternatively, you can **click and drag across the clip** to make a selection. The beginning and end points of the selection are where the split will occur. If you skip this step, the clip will be split down the middle.

3. Click on **Edit**. The Edit menu will appear.

4. Click on **Split**. The wave clip will be split. It may not look like anything has happened, but as you'll see in Steps 5 and 6, the wave clip is indeed broken up.

5. Position your **mouse pointer** over any portion of the clip that you just split.

6. Right-click and drag the **split portion** to a new track. As you drag, the portion of the wave clip will follow your cursor.

7. Release the **mouse button**. A menu will appear.

8. Click on **Move Clip Here**. The split portion will move and remain selected.

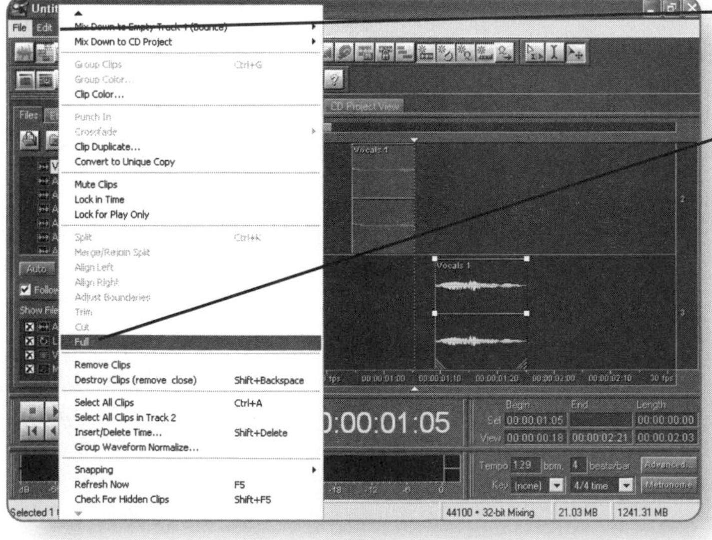

9. Click on **Edit**. The Edit menu will appear.

10. Click on **Full**. The split piece of audio will be returned to its original length and content, even though it has been moved.

Trimming

Trimming in Multitrack view works the same as it did in Edit view. The area of the wave clip that you select will remain in tact when you use the Trim command, whereas everything else will be removed.

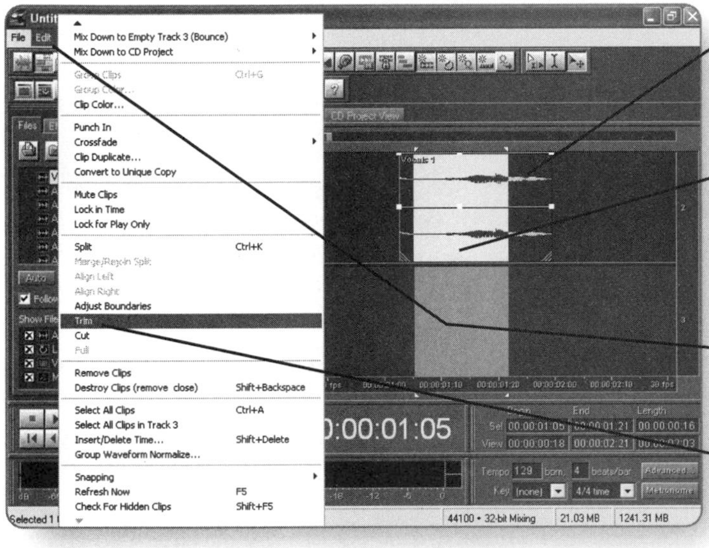

1. **Click once** on a **wave clip** to select it. It will become highlighted.
2. **Click and drag** across the **wave clip** to select the area that you would like to keep. The area will now be highlighted.
3. **Click** on **Edit**. The Edit menu will appear.
4. **Click** on **Trim**. Everything in the selected wave clip will be removed, except for the selected area.

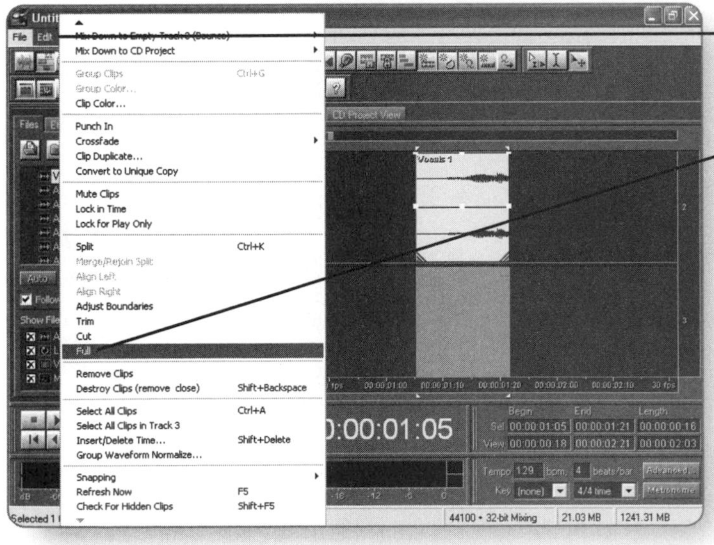

5. **Click** on **Edit**. The Edit menu will appear.
6. **Click** on **Full**. The wave clip will be returned to its pre-trimmed state.

> **TIP**
>
> You can always restore a wave clip that has been cut, split, trimmed, or had its boundaries adjusted by selecting it and then clicking Edit and then FULL from the menu bar.

Adjusting Boundaries

Using the Adjust Boundary command works almost exactly the same as trimming, with one exception. After you've executed the command, you can adjust the boundaries again to lengthen or shorten the area that has been trimmed.

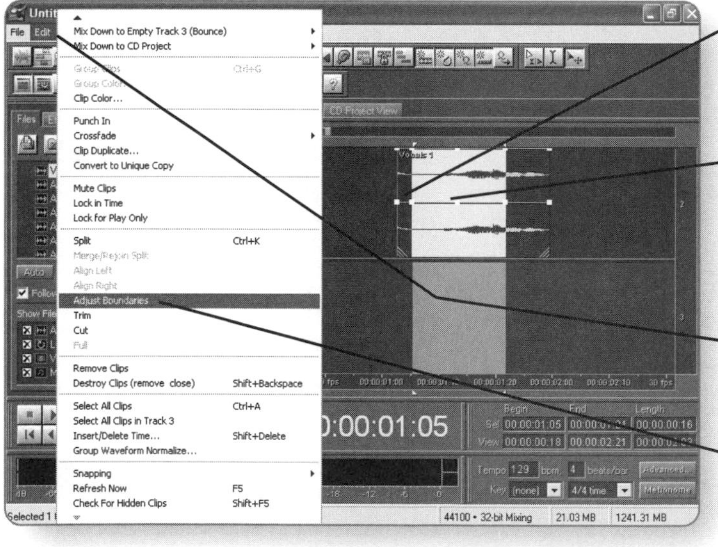

1. **Click once** on a **wave clip** to select it. It will become highlighted.

2. **Click and drag** across the **wave clip** to select the area that you would like to keep. The area will now be highlighted.

3. **Click** on **Edit**. The Edit menu will appear.

4. **Click** on **Adjust Boundaries**. Everything in the selected wave clip will be removed, except for the selected area.

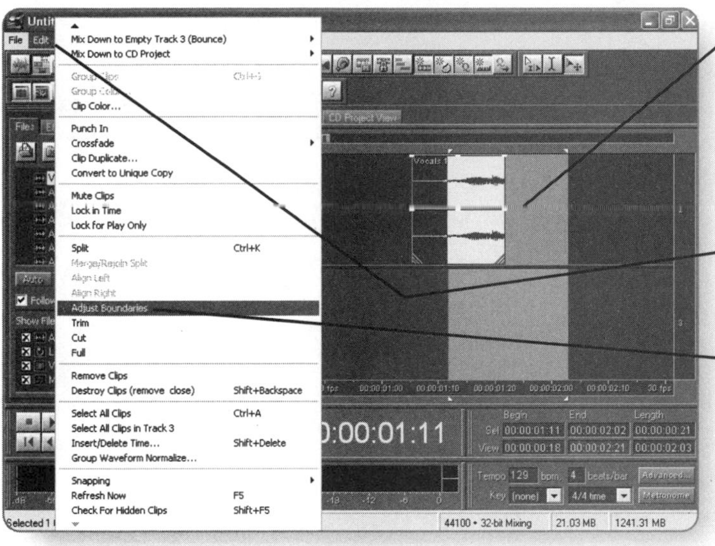

5. **Click and drag** across the remaining **wave clip**. Select an area beyond the boundaries of the waveform, to the left, right, or both.

6. **Click** on **Edit**. The Edit menu will appear.

7. **Click** on **Adjust Boundaries**. The area that was selected beyond the waveform will now be refilled with the original audio.

Removing a Wave Clip

If you no longer require a wave clip, you can quickly remove it from a track.

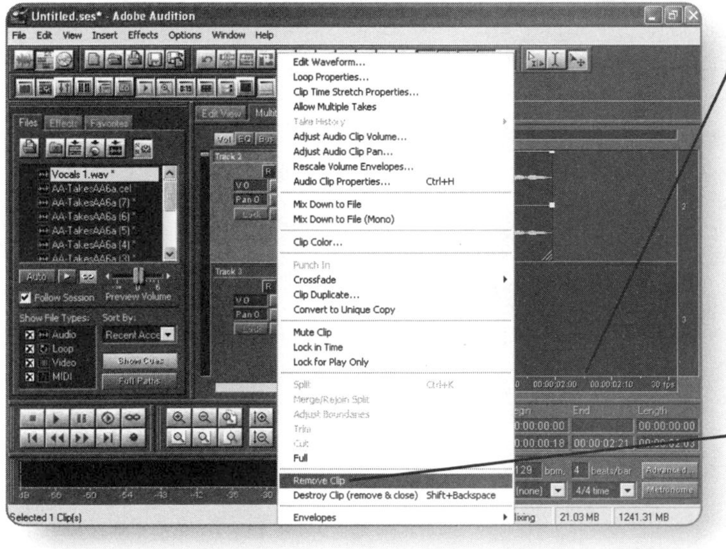

1. **Right-click** on the **wave clip** that you would like to remove. It will now be selected and a menu will appear.

2. **Click** on **Remove Clip**. The wave clip will be removed from the track.

Grouping

Grouping clips together allows you to get more done in less time. The beauty of grouping clips together is that all the clips within the group can be edited at one time.

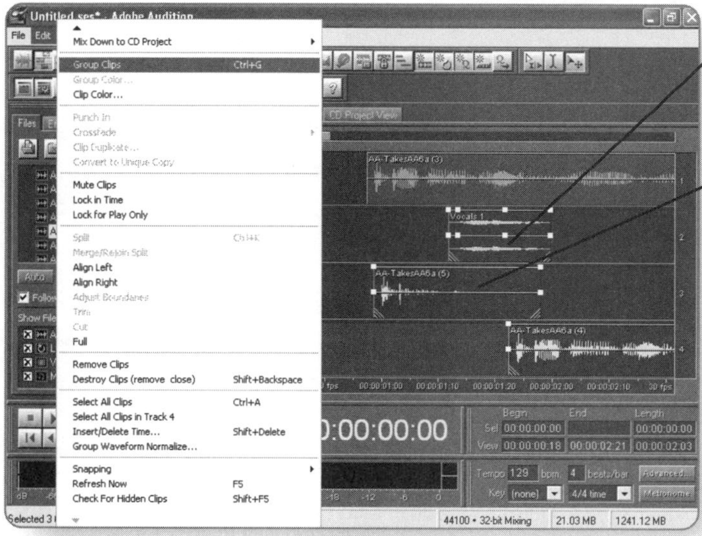

1. Click on a **clip** that you would like to have as part of a group. It will be selected.

2. Ctrl + **click** on **another clip**. It too will now be selected.

3. Repeat Step 2 until you have selected all of the wave clips that you would like to be part of the group.

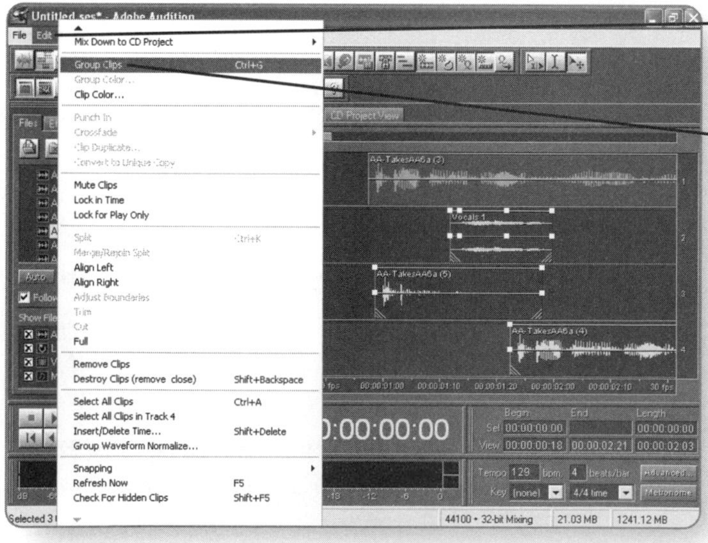

4. Click on **Edit**. The Edit menu will appear.

5. Click on **Group Clips**. The clips will appear purple to indicate that they are selected.

6. **Position** your **mouse pointer** over any of the clips within the group.

7. **Right-click and drag** the **clip** to a new location. As you drag, all of the clips within the group will move in harmony. In this example, we moved the clips to illustrate that they are grouped, but you can use any other editing command and all the clips within the group will be edited.

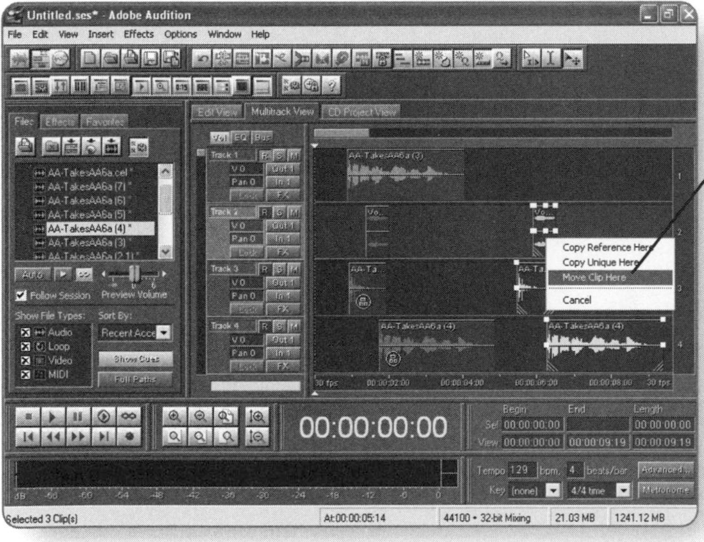

8. **Release** the **mouse button**. A menu will appear.

9. **Click** on **Move Clip Here.** All of the clips within the group will be moved.

> **TIP**
>
> The keyboard shortcut to select grouped clips is Ctrl + G.

Locking

You've painstakingly gone through the steps of creating the perfect wave clip. You cut, trimmed, moved, and copied the clip so that it's in the correct location and sounds perfect. It would be a shame to inadvertently move it or record over it when you've got it just right. As a measure of protection, Audition allows you to lock a wave clip so that it cannot be moved or recorded over.

Locking in Time

The Lock in Time feature will prevent a clip from being moved.

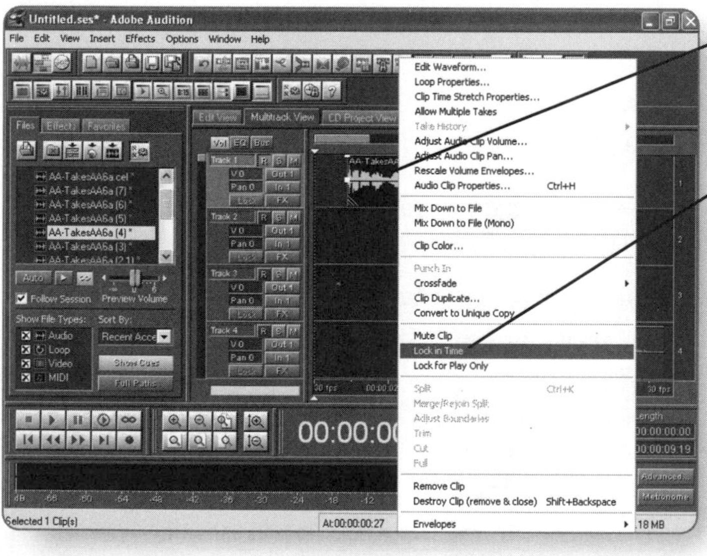

1. Right-click on the **wave clip** that you would like to lock. A menu will appear.

2. Click on **Lock in Time**. A picture of a lock will appear on the clip to indicate that it is locked.

3. Repeat Steps 1-2 to unlock the clip.

Locking for Play Only

When you record directly into a track, you take the chance of recording over existing audio. To prevent this from happening, you can lock the audio clips that you would like to protect.

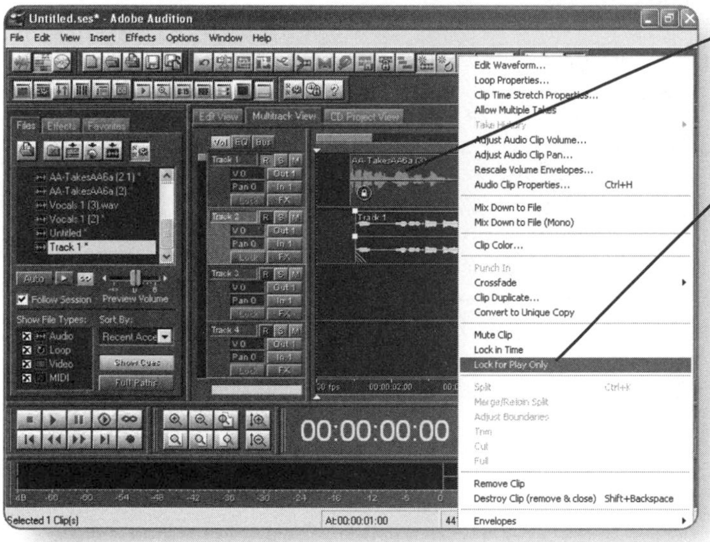

1. **Right-click** on the **wave clip** that you would like to lock. A menu will appear.

2. **Click** on **Lock for Play Only**. The clip will now be locked so that it cannot be recorded over.

3. **Repeat Steps 1-2** to unlock the clip.

Aligning

Instances will arise when you will want two clips of audio to begin playing at the exact same time. At other times, you may want two clips to end at the exact same moment. To accomplish this, you can use the Align function. There are two Align functions, Align Right, which will start the selected clips at the same time, and Align Left, which will end the selected clips at the same time.

1. **Click** on the **first clip** that you would like to align. It will be highlighted to indicate that it is selected.

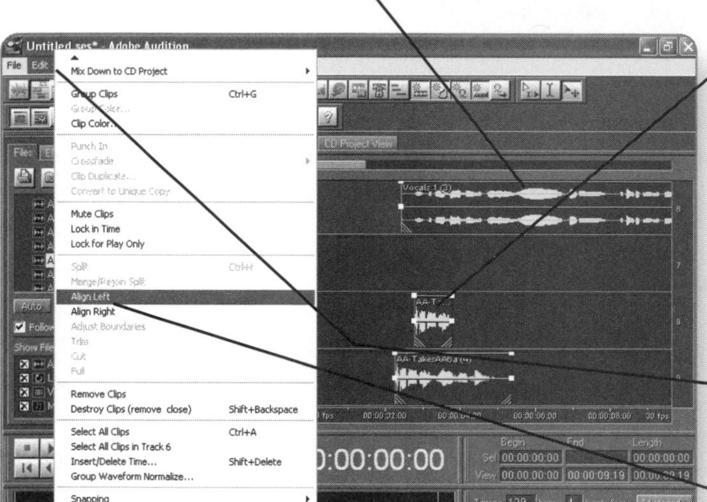

2. **Ctrl** + **click** on **another clip**. It too will now be selected.

3. **Repeat Step 2** until you have selected all the wave clips that you would like to align.

4. **Click** on **Edit**. The Edit menu will appear.

5. **Click** on **Align Left**. The clips will be aligned along the left edge of the clip you selected last.

6. **Observe** the **results**. If you want to align to the right edge, follow Steps 1–5, but select Align Right in Step 5.

> **NOTE**
>
> Your clips will be aligned based on the clip that you selected last.

Undoing

Just as in Edit view, you can correct any mistakes that you have made in the editing process by using the Undo command. Undo will take you back sequentially through the edits that you have made.

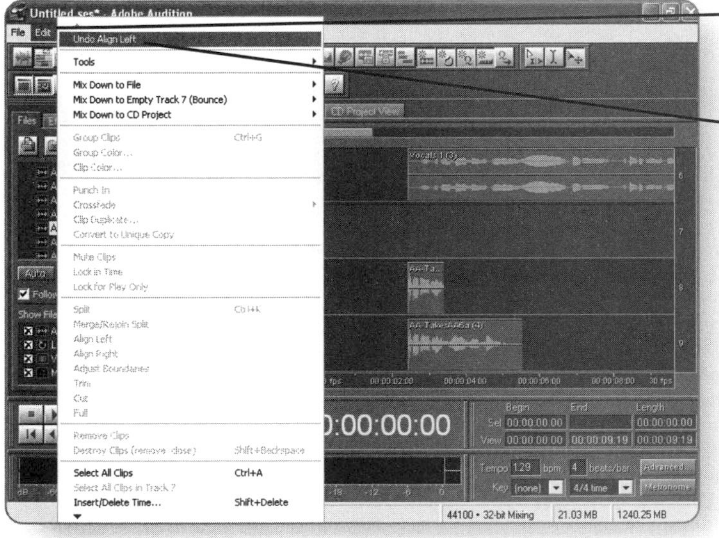

1. **Click** on **Edit**. The Edit menu will appear.

2. **Click** on **Undo *last action***. Rather than the words "last action," the actual name of the action will appear. For example, if the last thing that you did was aligned left (as in this screenshot), it would say Undo Align Left.

3. **Repeat Steps 1 and 2** until you've gone back to the point where you made your mistake.

> **TIP**
>
> The keyboard shortcut for undoing is Ctrl + Z.

Editing

You can bring any wave clip into Edit view to be edited simply by double-clicking on it.

1. **Double-click** on any **wave clip**. The clip will open in Edit view.

2. **Press F12** to toggle back to Multitrack view, once you have completed editing the clip. Multitrack view will appear.

7

Multitrack Editing, Part Deux

Did Chapter 6 give you a taste of Multitrack editing, but leave you wanting more? Well, look no further because here in Chapter 7 we will dive even deeper into Multitrack editing. Adobe Audition gives you many tools to manage the tracks that you have created and further edit waveforms within those tracks.

In this chapter, you'll learn how to:

- Create crossfades
- Match song tempos
- Find beats
- Manage tracks

Adjusting Wave Clip Volume

The volume envelope is a visual representation of the volume level in a wave clip, in the form of a green line. Once the volume envelope is activated, you can manipulate it by simply clicking and dragging at any point across the green line. If you want the volume level to remain constant throughout the wave clip, the green volume line must remain straight; otherwise, the volume level will change throughout.

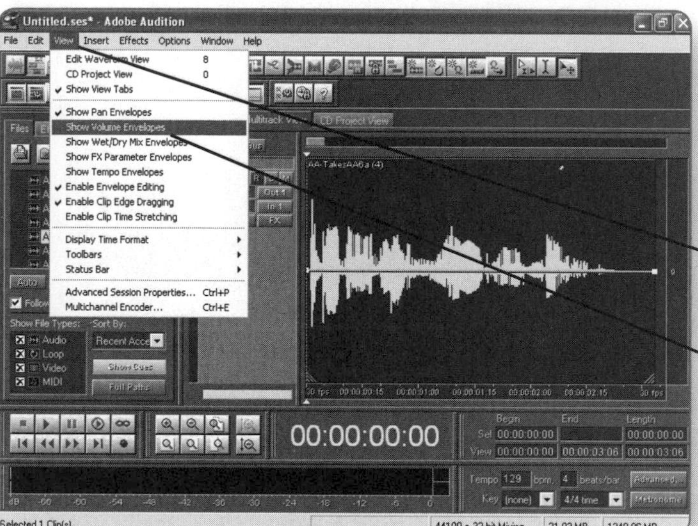

1. **Click** on **View**. The View menu will appear.

2. **Click** on **Show Volume Envelopes**. If no previous volume changes have been made to the wave clip, a green line will appear across the very top of the wave clip.

3. **Position** the **mouse pointer** over the white node at the beginning of the green line. This green line indicates the volume level of the wave clip.

4. **Click and drag downward** to adjust the volume at that point. The line will move as you drag.

5. **Release** the **mouse button**. The volume will now be adjusted and will go from low volume to full volume as it travels across the waveform.

6. **Position** the **mouse pointer** over the white node at end of the green line.

7. **Click and drag downward** until the line is straight.

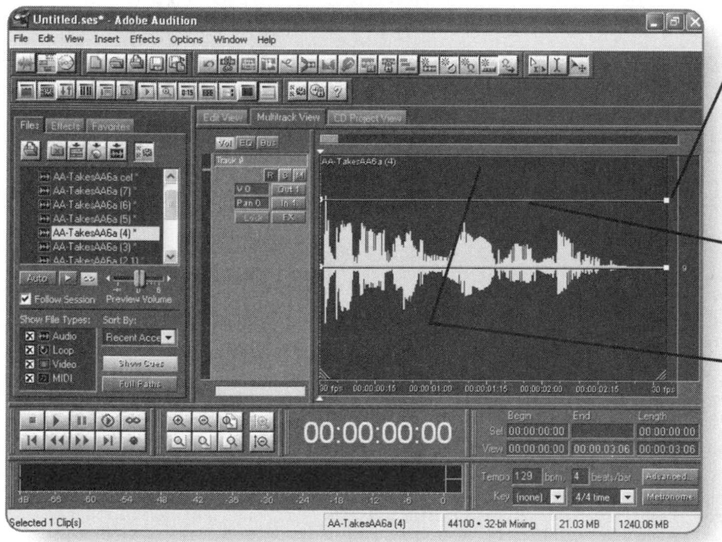

8. **Release** the **mouse button** when the line is perfectly straight. You will now have a constant volume level across the wave clip.

9. **Position** the **mouse pointer** over any point on the green line.

10. **Click and drag up or down**. As you drag, a white node will be created at the point where you clicked. This will allow you to adjust the volume at any point in the wave clip.

11. Release the **mouse button**. The volume level will now change as the wave clip is played.

12. Repeat Steps 9-11 until the desired volume changes are achieved.

> **TIP**
>
> Another way to quickly create a volume adjustment is to use a preset fade from the Amplitude effect dialog box. Instructions on applying this effect can be found in the "Applying Amplitude Presets" section of Chapter 9.

Adjusting Pan Levels of Wave Clips

Adjusting pan levels using the pan envelope works in much the same way as the volume envelope. Pan levels indicate how strong the volume of a wave clip will be to either the left or the right side. The pan envelope provides you with a visual representation of the pan in the form of a blue line. You can click and drag this blue line to adjust the pan settings. When the blue line appears through the middle of the wave clip, then volume levels are equal on both the left and the right. Dragging the blue line upward will increase the volume on the left side, whereas dragging it downward will increase the volume on the right.

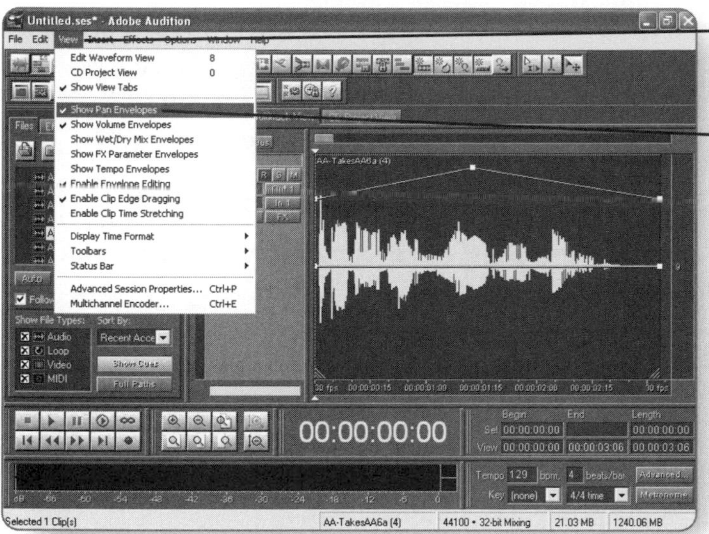

1. Click on **View**. The View menu will appear.

2. Click on **Show Pan Envelopes**, if it is not already checked. If no previous pan changes have been made to the wave clip, a blue line will appear across the middle of the wave clip.

3. Position the **mouse pointer** over the white node at the beginning of the blue line. This blue line indicates the pan level of the wave clip.

4. Click and drag downward to adjust the pan at that point. The line will move as you drag.

5. Release the **mouse button**. The pan will now be adjusted and go from the right to the left as the wave clip is played.

6. Position the **mouse pointer** over the white node at end of the blue line.

7. Click and drag downward until the line is straight. The pan level will now be constant throughout.

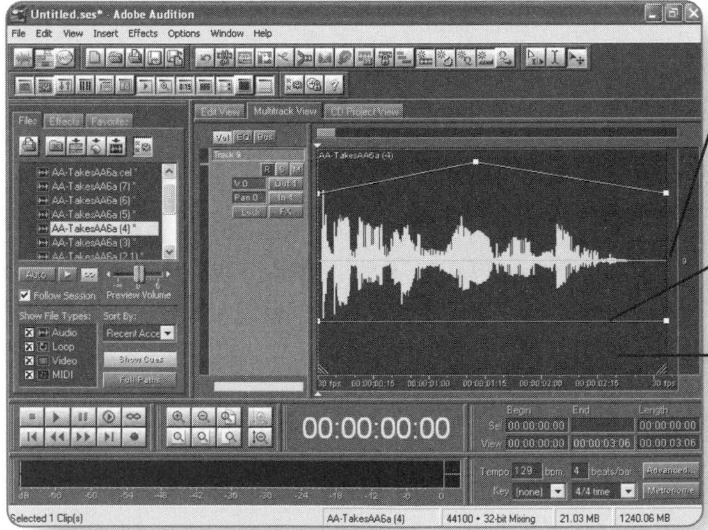

8. Release the **mouse button** when the line is perfectly straight. You will now have a constant pan level across the wave clip.

9. Position the **mouse pointer** over any point on the blue line.

10. Click and drag up or down. As you drag, a white node will have been created at the point where you clicked. This will allow you to adjust the pan level at any point in the wave clip.

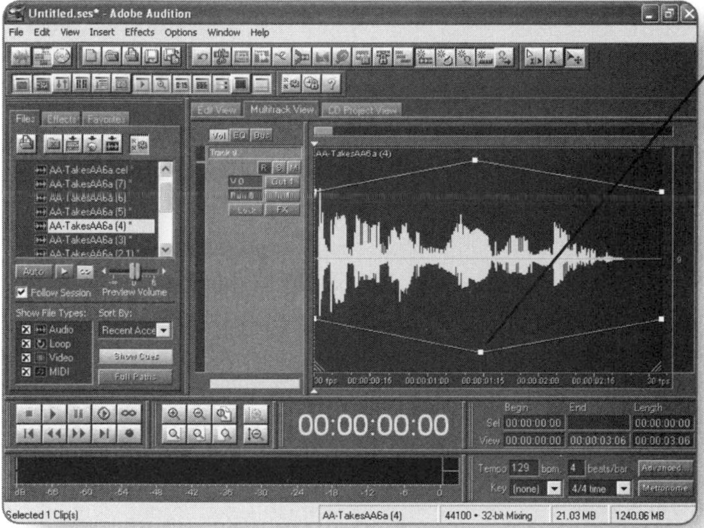

11. Release the **mouse button.** The pan level will now change as the wave clip is played.

12. Repeat Steps 8-10 until the desired pan changes are achieved.

> **TIP**
>
> Another way to adjust pan levels is to use a preset pan from the Amplitude effect dialog box. Instructions on applying this effect can be found in the "Applying Amplitude Presets" section of Chapter 9.

Creating Crossfades

Crossfades allow you to create a smooth transition between two or more pieces of audio. In essence, what a crossfade does is adjust the volume of a track so that it fades in or out. Within Adobe Audition, you can quickly create crossfades by selecting a region where you want the crossfade to occur and then determining what type of crossfade to use.

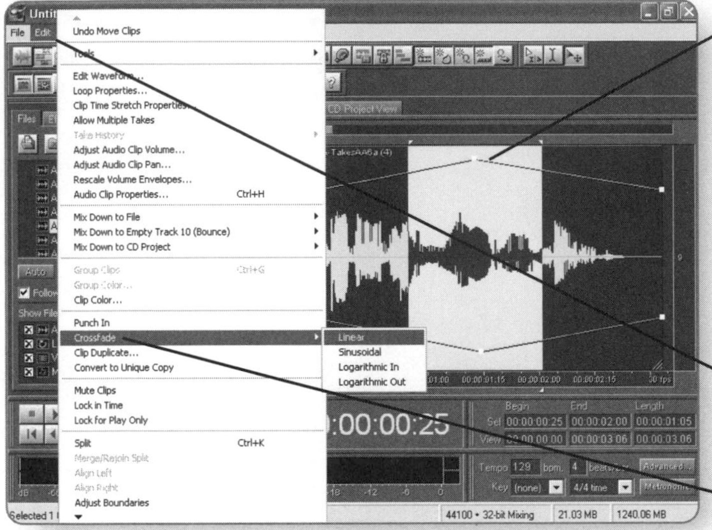

1. **Create** a **selection** across the area of the wave clip in which you would like to have the audio fade in or out. If your selection goes across the beginning of the wave clip, the crossfade will fade in. Creating a selection around the end will make the audio fade out.

2. **Click** on **Edit**. The Edit menu will appear.

3. **Click** on **Crossfade**. A submenu of different crossfades will appear.

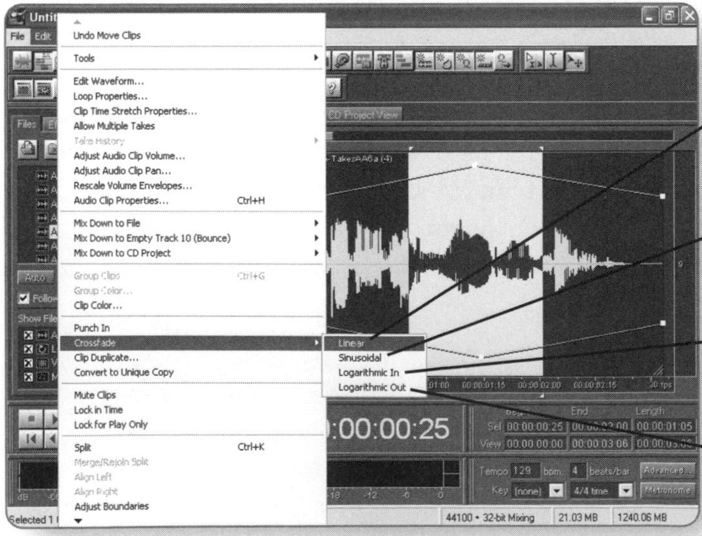

4. **Click** on the desired **crossfade**. Your choices include:

- **Linear**. This option will create an even fade in or out across the selection.
- **Sinusoidal**. This option will create a curved fade in or fade out across the selection.
- **Logarithmic In**. This option will fade in the amplitude at a constant rate.
- **Logarithmic Out**. This option will fade out the amplitude at a constant rate.

Adjusting Crossfades

Because a crossfade is simply a change to the volume envelope, you can adjust your crossfades just as you would volume envelopes.

1. **Position** your **mouse pointer** over any white node of the crossfade. You don't actually have to be over a node, you can be over any point of the crossfade and a new node will be created as you drag.

2. **Click and drag** to adjust the **volume envelope**. It will move as you drag.

3. **Release** the **mouse button**. The crossfade will be adjusted accordingly.

Working with Tracks

With the ability to create over 128 tracks in any given session, being able to manage those tracks becomes an essential part of audio editing. Adobe Audition provides you with several tools to work with individual tracks.

Naming Tracks

You are in for a world full of hurt if you don't get into the habit of naming your tracks. Once you have inserted audio into any more than two different tracks, you'll be hard pressed to remember what was on those tracks if you don't name them. Unless you want to spend half of your audio editing time just auditioning tracks to remember what was on them, I implore you to start naming your tracks.

1. **Click once** on the **track name**. The track name will be highlighted.

2. **Type** a **name** for the track. It's a good idea to give the track a descriptive name. The name will appear as you type.

3. **Repeat Steps 1-2** for any other track that you would like to name.

Moving Tracks

To make editing easier, you can relocate tracks to any place within the session. This is particularly handy if there are two or three tracks that you are working on in particular. Rather than having to jump back and forth to those tracks, you can simply move them so that they are on top of one another.

1. **Position** your **mouse pointer** in any gray area underneath the track name of the track that you would like to move.

2. **Right-click and drag** the **track** to its new location. As you drag, a white line will appear, indicating the current location of the track.

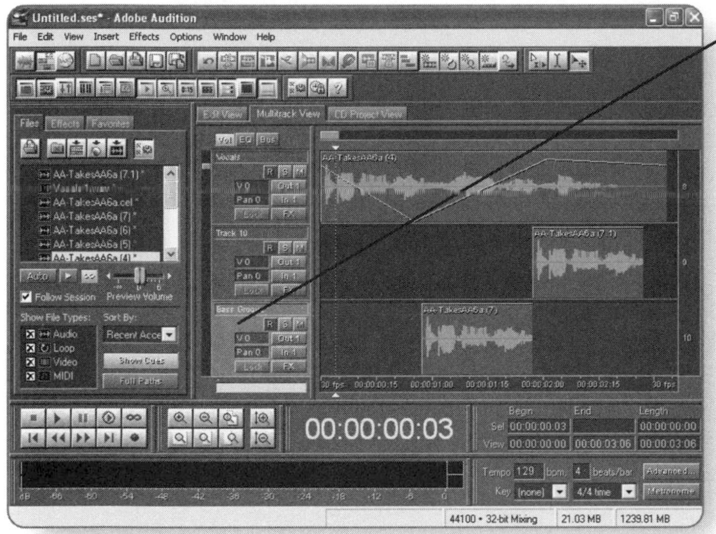

3. Release the **mouse button**. The track will be moved to the location where you released the mouse button. In this example, we moved the Bass Groove track down by two tracks.

Adjusting Track Volume

Adobe Audition allows you to adjust the volume of an entire track. When you adjust the volume of a track, all the waveforms within that track will go up or down by the adjustment you have made.

1. Click on the **Volume tab** in the Tracks Controls window, if it is not already selected. The Volume tab will come to the front.

2. Right-click on the **VO button**. A volume slider will appear.

3. Click and drag the **slider** to the desired volume level for the track. Alternatively, you can simply type a number for the volume at the top of the slider window.

4. Click on the **X** in the top-right corner of the volume window to close it. The volume settings for that track will now be set.

Adjusting Panning for a Track

If you've been to a movie in the last 10 years you know all about audio panning. Modern movie theaters have full surround speakers so you can distinctly tell which side of the theater a sound is coming from. Panning controls the volume levels of audio from left to right. Adobe Audition allows you to adjust the panning controls for an entire track so you can choose whether it is higher or lower to the left or right.

1. **Click** on the **Volume tab** in the Tracks Controls window, if it is not already selected. The Volume tab will come to the front.

2. **Right-click** on the **Pan button** for the track that you would like to edit. A pan slider will appear.

3. **Click and drag** the **slider** to the desired pan level for the track. As you drag to the left or right, the number in the window will change.

4. **Click** on the **X** in the top-right corner of the pan window to close it. The pan settings for that track will now be set.

Track Muting

If you do not want to hear a specific track during playback you can mute it. Adobe Audition allows you to mute multiple tracks.

1. Click on the **M button** in any track that you would like to mute. The button will appear depressed and bright green to indicate it is selected.

2. Repeat Step 1 for any other track that you would like to mute.

3. Click on the **Play button**. You will hear all tracks except for the ones that you have muted.

4. Click on the **M button** on any track that you have muted to turn off muting.

Soloing Tracks

A quick way to preview how one track sounds is to solo it. When you solo a track, you mute all others so that only the soloed track can be heard on playback.

1. Click on the **S button** on any track that you would like to solo. The S button will appear bright yellow to indicate that it is selected.

2. **Click** on the **Play button**. Only the track that you have soloed will be heard.

3. **Repeat Step 1** to turn soloing off. The S button will no longer appear bright yellow, which indicates that soloing is turned off.

Track Equalizers

You can open a Track Equalizer window for any track to adjust its high, med, and low frequencies and amplitude. Within this window you can also adjust the band settings for the track.

1. **Click** on the **EQ tab** of the Tracks Controls window. The window will change to show you EQ settings for each track.

2. **Right-click** on any of the **H, M, or L settings** for the track that you would like to adjust. The Track Equalizer window will now open.

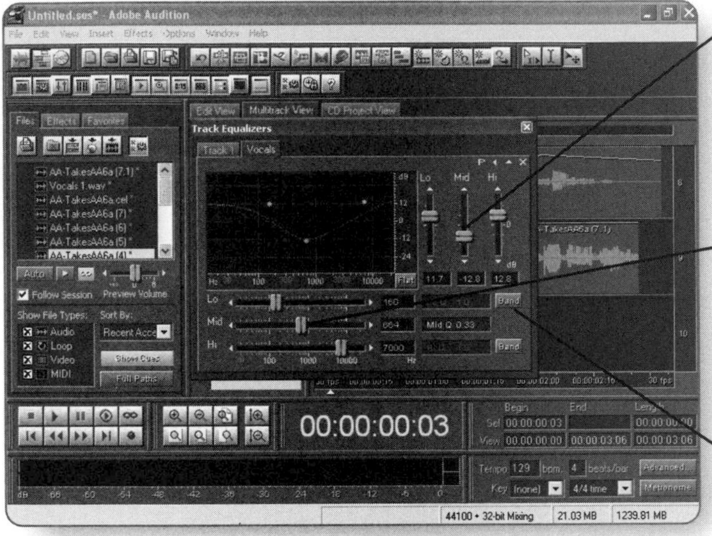

3. **Click and drag** on any of the **sliders** to adjust the high, medium, and low frequencies. As you drag the settings will adjust.

4. **Click and drag** on any of the **sliders** to adjust the high, medium, and low amplitudes. As you drag, the settings will adjust.

5. **Click** on the **Band buttons** to activate or deactivate the Hi Q or Low Q settings.

6. **Click** on the **X** in the top-right corner to close the window and apply the settings. The window will close.

Busses

Imagine if you would, five separate roads that all happen to converge at the same point through a tunnel. If you wanted to collect a toll from everyone who traveled on those roads, you wouldn't set up five different toll booths at the beginning of each road; rather, you would set up one toll booth at the tunnel because all the roads meet at that point. That's similar to the way busses work in Adobe Audition. Rather than having to apply effects and change certain properties for individual tracks, you can set up a bus, which will apply effects to all tracks that pass through it. Then, when tracks pass through the bus, the changes that you specified to take place will affect each track. Not only do busses save time, but they also reduce the processing power required by your computer.

To create a bus you simply have to select the first track that you want to add to the bus, open a dialog box, and then name it. Once the bus is created, you can add additional tracks to it. Once you have a bus created and have added tracks to it, any effects you apply to that bus or properties you change will affect all the tracks that pass through it. Effects will be discussed in detail in a later chapter, but here you'll learn the steps to apply any effect to a bus.

1. **Click** on the **Bus tab** of the Tracks Controls window. The window will change to show you Bus settings for each track.

2. **Click** on the **Out button** in the first track that you would like to add to the bus. The Playback Devices dialog box will open.

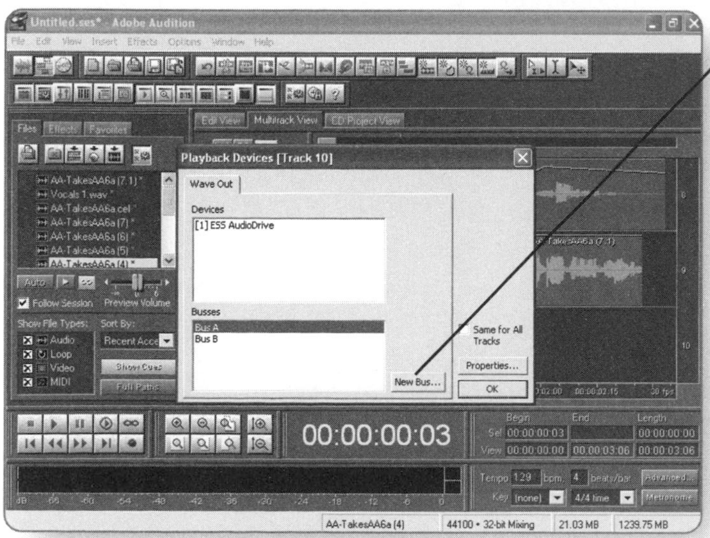

3. **Click** on the **New Bus button**. Another dialog box will appear where you can name and apply effects to your bus.

4. **Click** on the **+** to expand any effects to add to the bus. A list of effects that fall under that category will appear.

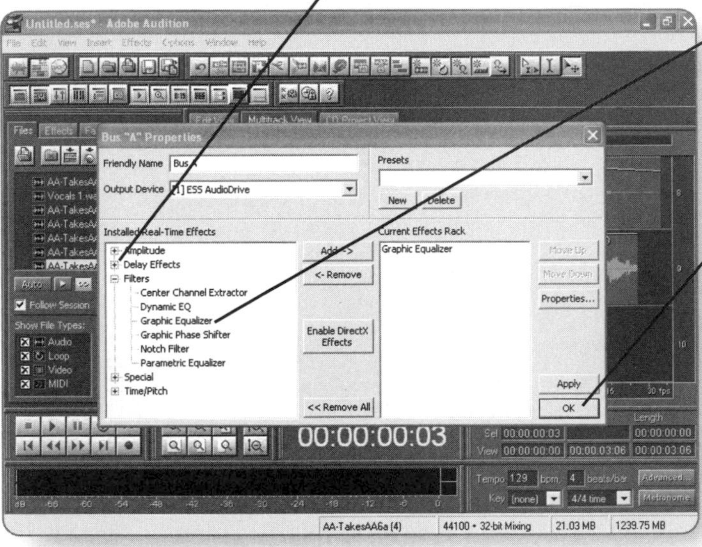

5. **Double-click** any **effects** you would like to apply to the bus. They will be added to the effects rack.

6. **Click** on the **OK button** after you've added any effects to this bus. You will be returned to the Playback Devices dialog box.

7. **Repeat Steps 3–6** to add any other busses.

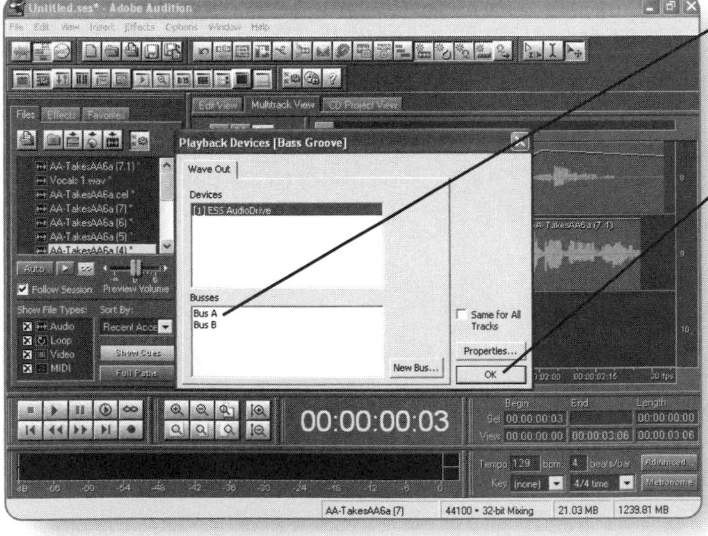

8. **Click** on the **name** of a bus that was just created. It will be highlighted.

9. **Click** on **OK**. That track will now be added to the selected bus and the dialog box will close.

10. **Repeat Steps 2–9** to add a bus to any other tracks.

Adjusting Playback and Recording Devices for Tracks

The bus area of the Tracks Control window also allows you to change which devices are used when recording or playing back tracks.

1. **Click** on the **Out or Bus button** for any track. The Playback Devices dialog box will open.

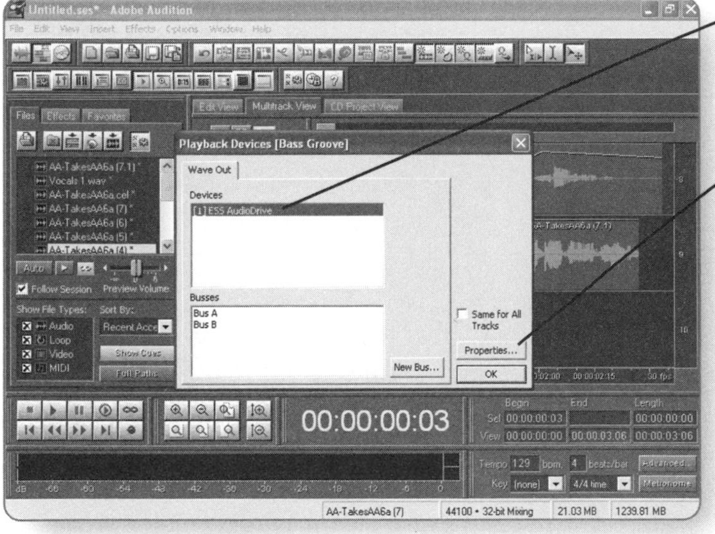

2. **Click** on any of the **devices** in the window. The device will be highlighted.

3. **Click** on the **Properties button**. The Device Ordering Preferences dialog box will open.

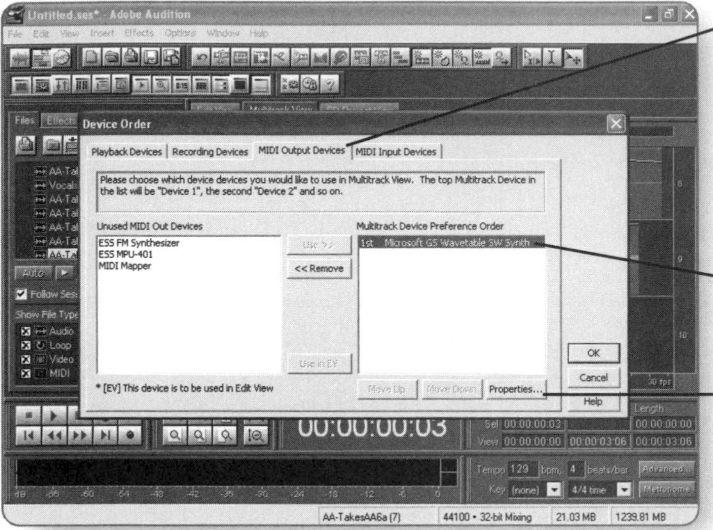

4. **Click** on the **tab** of the type of device you would like to adjust. Your options include playback devices, recording devices, MIDI output devices, and MIDI input devices.

5. **Click** on the desired **device**. It will be highlighted.

6. **Click** on the **Properties button**. The Device Properties dialog box will open so that you can view and adjust any properties for that device.

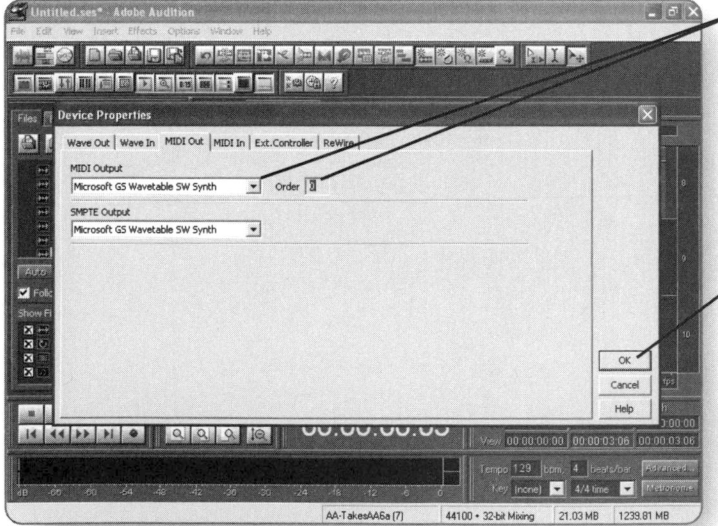

7. **Make** the desired **changes** to the settings for that device. By clicking on the various tabs at the top of the dialog box, you can view the different properties of that device.

8. **Click** on **OK**. The changes that you have made to the settings for that device will be stored and you will be returned to the Device Ordering Preferences dialog box.

9. **Repeat Steps 4-8** for any other device.

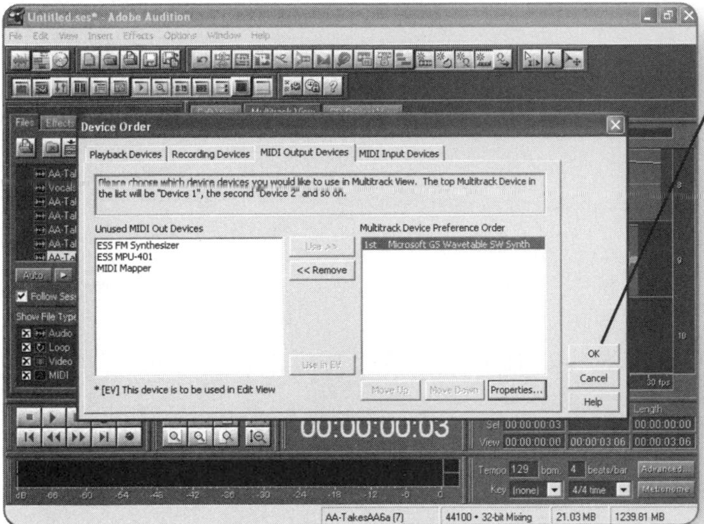

10. **Click** on **OK**. The dialog box will close and you will return to the Playback Devices dialog box.

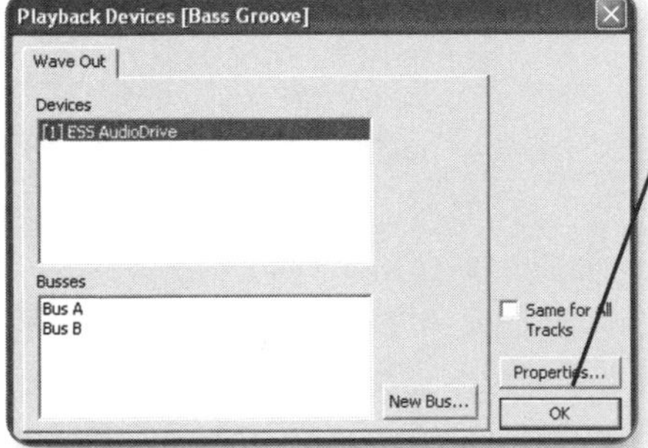

11. **Click** on **OK**. The Playback Devices dialog box will close and your settings will take effect.

8

Looping

It used to be that a composer would sit down with a piano or other instrument and painstakingly scribe music to create his masterpiece. Modern-day music is a little different. If you find a few three-second clips of audio and play them over and over, you'll have a hit on your hands in no time. Well, the truth is, it may not be that simple, but looping audio is a fundamental part of audio editing.

In this chapter, you'll learn how to:

- Use the Loop Duplicate command
- Create loops with loop properties
- Create loops from wave files
- Edit loops

Creating Loops with Loop Duplicate

The fastest way to loop an existing wave clip is to use the Loop Duplicate command. Loop Duplicate is basically a fancy copy and paste, where you can specify how many times you'd like your waveform to repeat. Loop Duplicate also allows you to create time breaks between loops.

Creating Gap Free Loops

The typical way for a loop to be created is to have the audio repeat continuously, starting again as soon as it reaches its endpoint.

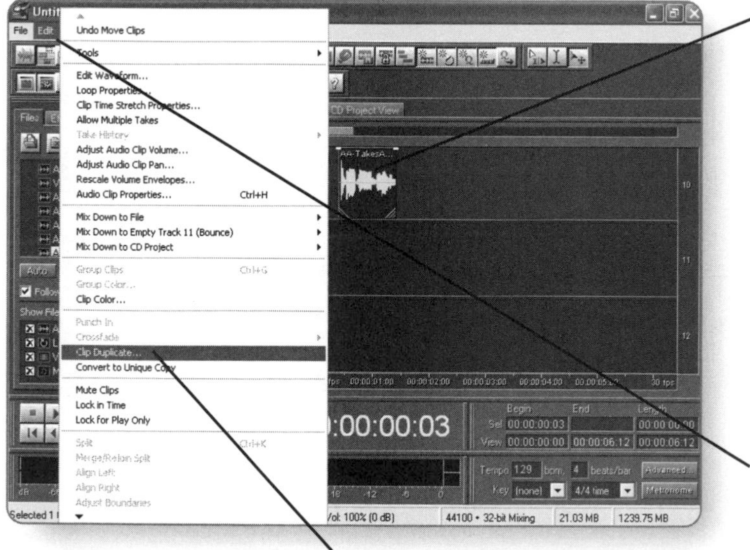

1. **Click once** on the **wave clip** in Multitrack view that you would like to duplicate. It will be highlighted to indicate that it is selected.

2. **Click** on **Edit**. The Edit menu will appear.

3. **Click** on **Clip Duplicate**. The Clip Duplicate dialog box will open, allowing you to set how many times you would like to loop the file.

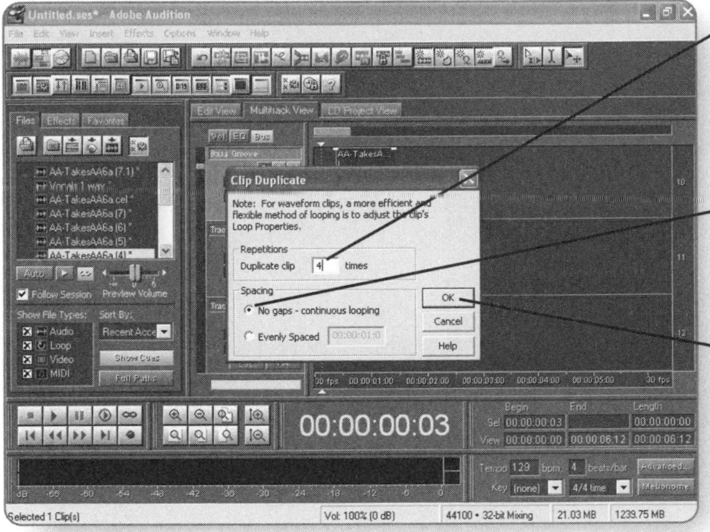

4. Type the **number** of times you would like the audio file to loop. The number will appear in the box.

5. Click on the **No gaps-continuous looping circle**, if it is not already selected.

6. Click on **OK**. The loop will be created based on the criteria you set.

7. Observe the **results**. A number of instances of the audio will appear based on the number you set in the Clip Duplicate dialog box.

NOTE

By using the Loop Duplicate function, you are actually creating clones of your selected audio. This means that any change you make to the original piece of audio or any changes that you make to a duplicate, will be reflected in all others.

Creating Loops with Gaps

Rather than having a piece of audio repeat as soon as it reaches its end point, you can create a loop that repeats at specific intervals.

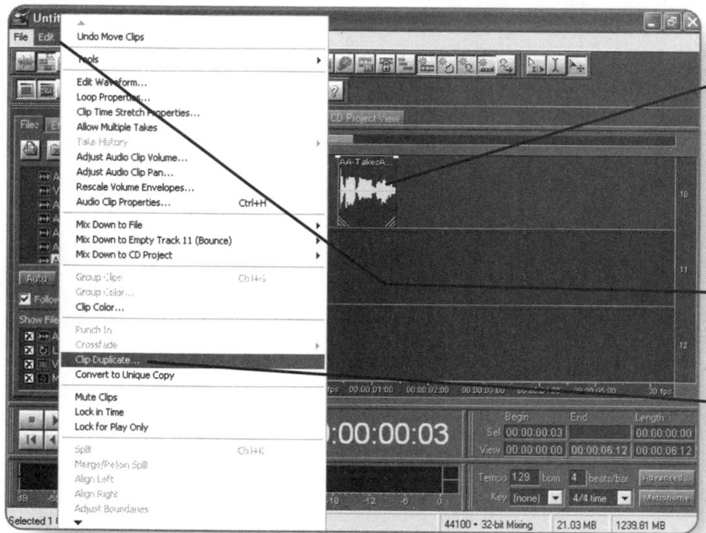

1. **Click once** on the **wave clip** in Multitrack view that you would like to duplicate. It will be highlighted to indicate that it is selected.

2. **Click** on **Edit**. The Edit menu will appear.

3. **Click** on **Clip Duplicate**. The Clip Duplicate dialog box will open, allowing you to set how many times you would like to loop the file.

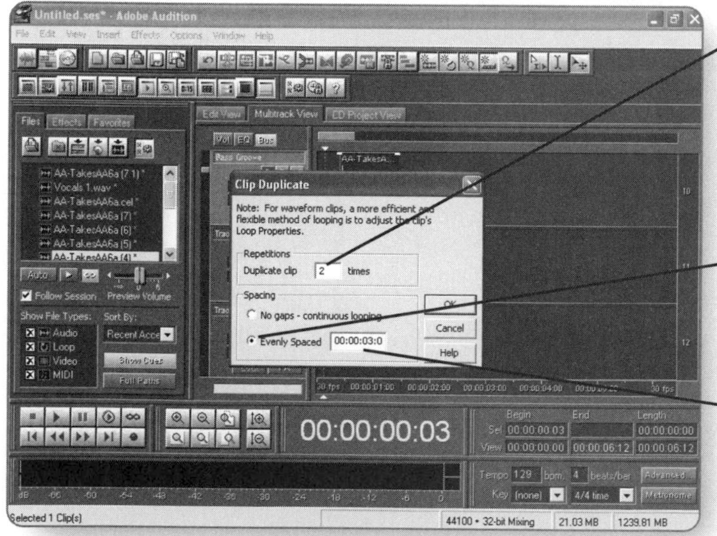

4. **Type** the **number** of times that you would like the audio file to loop. You can enter any number into this box. The number will appear.

5. **Click** on the **circle** beside Evenly Spaced. A dot will appear in the circle.

6. **Type** a **number** for the space interval. This will be the amount of time that will occur between each loop.

7. **Click** on **OK**. The loop will be created based on the criteria you set.

8. Observe the **results.** A number of instances of the audio will appear based on the number you set in the Clip Duplicate dialog box.

Looping with Loop Properties

A more proficient and accommodating way of creating loops is to use Loop Properties. Loop Properties allows you to create a loop but also adjust its pitch and tempo.

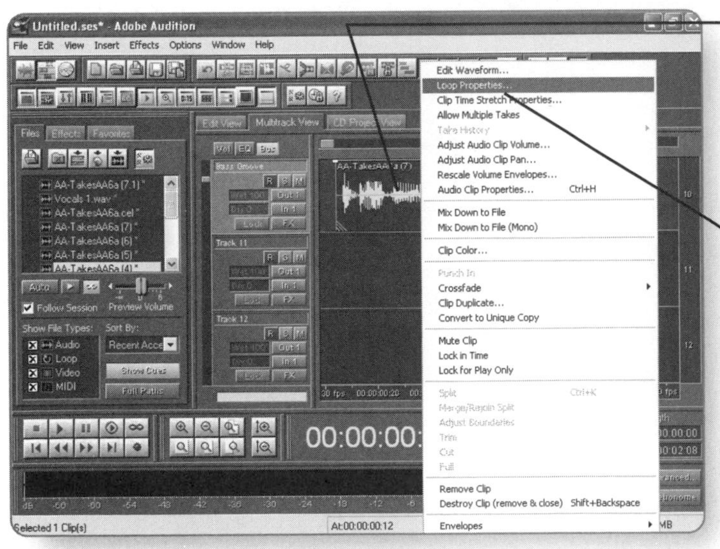

1. Right-click on the **wave clip** in Multitrack view that you would like to loop. It will be highlighted to indicate that it is selected. A submenu will appear.

2. Click on **Loop Properties.** The Wave Clip Looping dialog box will appear.

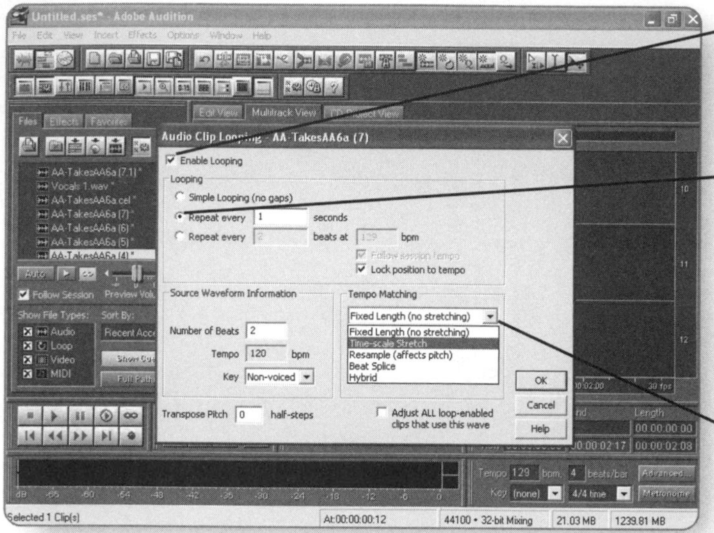

3. Click on the **Enable Looping check box**, if it is not already selected.

4. Click on the **circle** beside the desired loop method. If you select one of the Repeat Every methods, then you must also enter the number of seconds or beats between each loop.

5. Click on the **down arrow** under the Tempo Matching section. A list of different tempo matching options will appear.

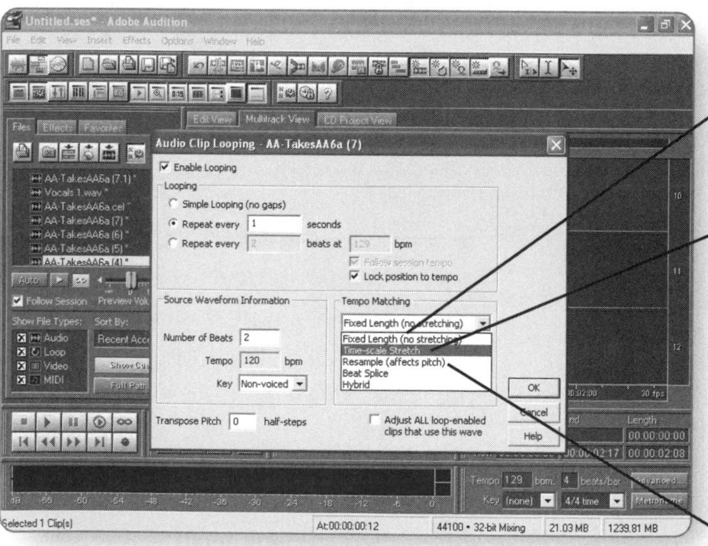

6. Click on the desired **tempo matching option**. It will be selected.

- **Fixed Length**. The tempo of the waveform will remain unchanged.
- **Time-Scale Stretch**. The tempo of the waveform will be stretched to match that of the current session. When you select this option, you will be given the opportunity to select several different subsettings.
- **Resample**. The tempo of the waveform will be resampled to match the tempo of the session. This method will affect pitch, and you'll be able to adjust the quality settings.

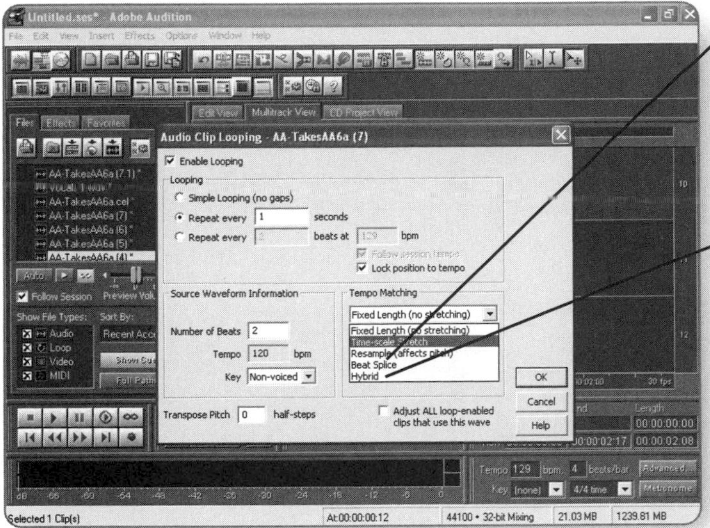

- **Beat Splice**. This method examines the beats detected within the file and matches the tempo accordingly.
- **Hybrid**. If you lower the BPM, the hybrid method will stretch the audio file, and if you raise the BPM, the hybrid method will use splicing.

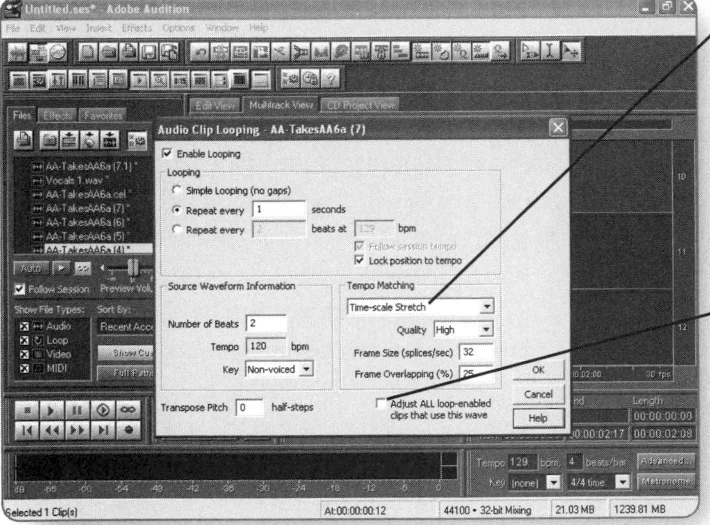

7. **Click** on the desired **setting** for the tempo matching option that you have selected. Depending on the method you have selected, you may or may not have to enter additional data.
8. **Click** on the **Adjust All Loop Enabled Clips that Use this Wave check box**, if you want all other instances of this wave to share these properties. A checkmark will appear in the check box.

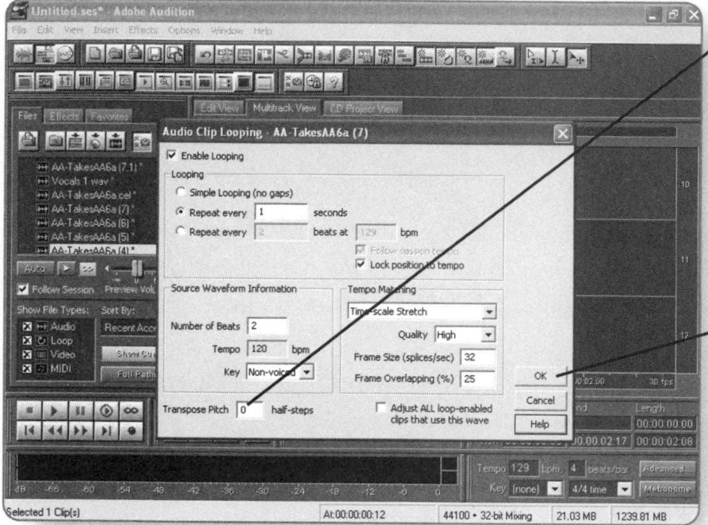

9. **Type** a **number** in the Transpose Pitch field if you want to change the pitch of the loop. If you enter a positive number the pitch will raise, whereas negative numbers will lower the pitch.

10. **Click** on **OK**. The loop will be created based on the criteria you set.

Creating Loops from a Wave File

Although Adobe Audition comes with dozens of different audio files that can easily be looped into fantastic sounding pieces, there will be many occasions where you'll want to create loops from existing audio. You can create a loop from audio that you've ripped from CD, from original recordings that you have made, or from downloaded files. Getting a loop to sound right is both an art and a science, so Adobe Audition gives you several tools to help you with this endeavor. The first step is to select and adjust the audio for the loop. After that you can create a separate wave file and then adjust the loop settings. Finally, you can insert and click and drag to create loops in Multitrack view.

Finding Beats

Typically, loops are a phrase of music that contains two bars with eight beats. This isn't a steadfast rule, but it's a good guide to follow. Ultimately it's your ear that will let you know if a loop sounds right. Ideally you want your loop to start and end on a certain beat. Adobe Audition has a tool that will allow you to find the next beat outside of your selection, so that you can create the perfect loop.

1. **Press F12** to toggle to Edit view if you are not already there. Edit view will appear.

2. **Double-click** on the **waveform** from which you'd like to create a loop. It will open in the wave display.

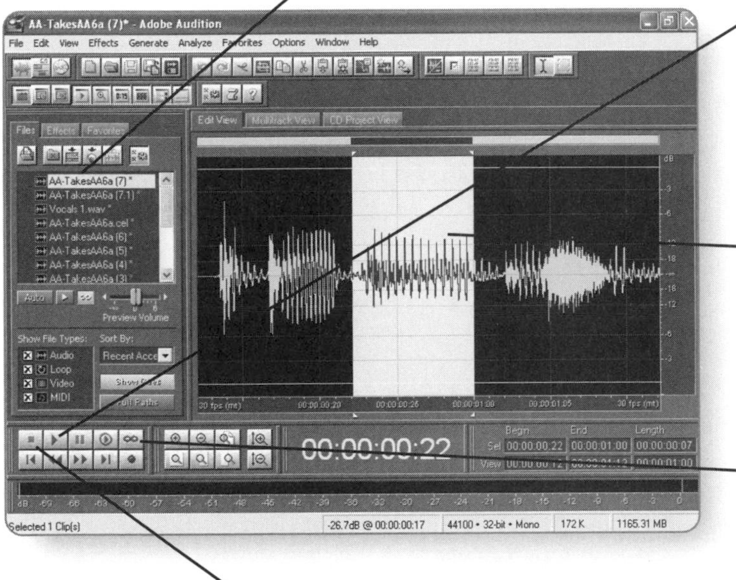

3. **Click** on the **Play button**. The waveform will begin to play. Listen closely for the area from which you would like to create a loop.

4. **Click and drag** across the approximate **area** of the waveform that contains the audio that you would like to loop. The area will be highlighted.

5. **Click** on the **Play Looped button**. The selection you have made will play over and over as if it was looped, so you can preview how your loop will sound.

6. **Click** on the **Stop button**. The playback will stop.

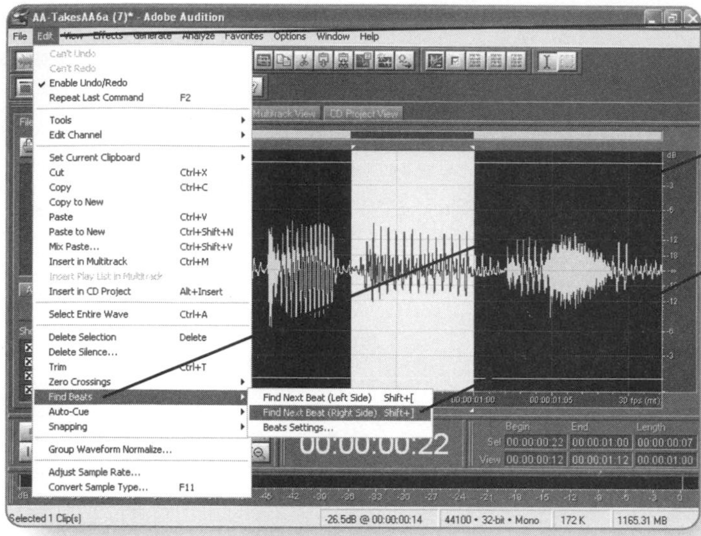

7. Click on **Edit**. The Edit menu will appear.

8. Click on **Find Beats**. A submenu will appear.

9. Click on **Find Next Beat (Left Side) or Find Next Beat (Right Side)**. The selection will expand to the next beat on the side that you have selected.

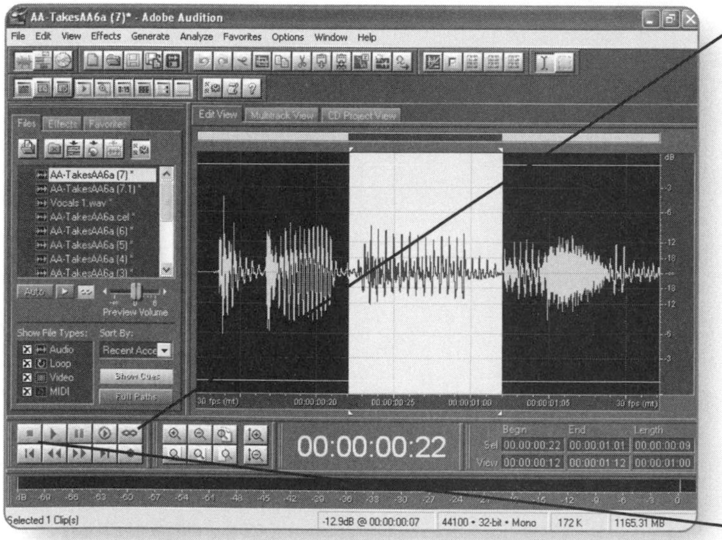

10. Click on the **Play Looped button**. The selection you have made will play over and over as if it was looped, so you can preview how your loop will sound.

11. Click on the **Stop button**. The playback will stop.

12. Repeat Steps 7-11 to further adjust the selection until it is just right.

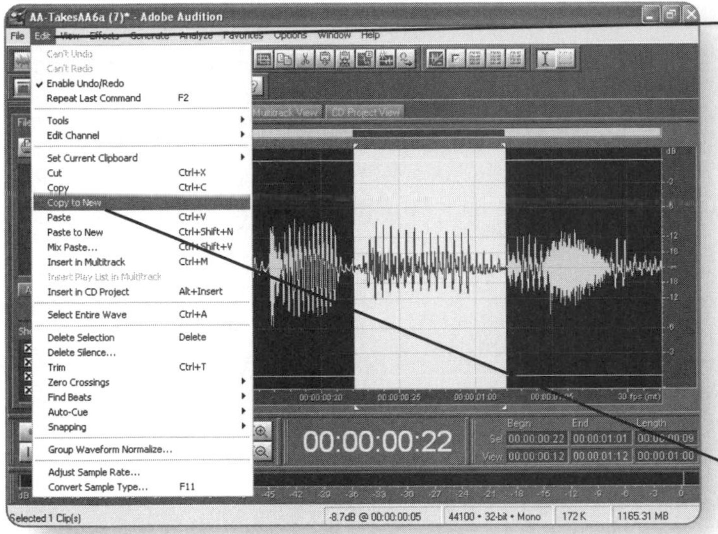

13. Click on **Edit**. The Edit menu will appear. Follow this and the next step only when you are completely satisfied with your loop selection. If your selection still needs minor tweaking, see the following two sections. Otherwise, after you have completed Step 14, go to the Creating the Loop section later in this chapter.

14. Click on **Copy to New**. The selection will be opened as a new file in Edit view.

Adjusting Your Selection

If you need to slightly tweak your selection so that the loop has a seamless transition, you can simply click and drag the selection while holding the Shift key.

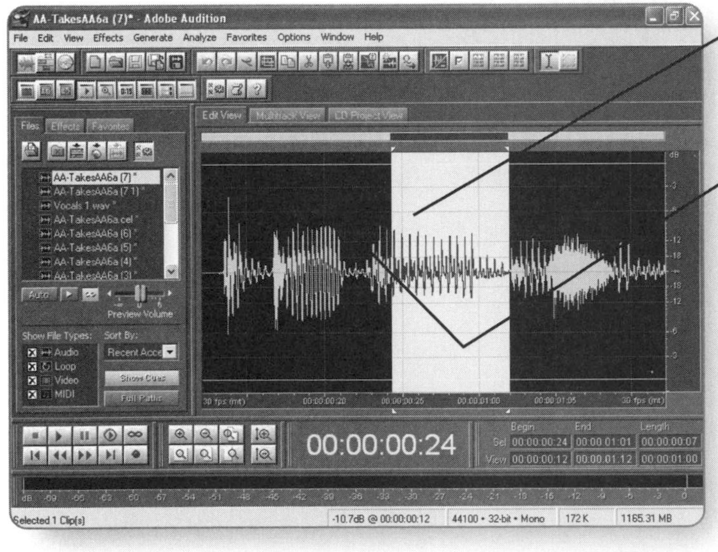

1. Position the **mouse pointer** over the left or right edge of the selection.

2. Click and drag any of the **selection markers** to adjust the selection.

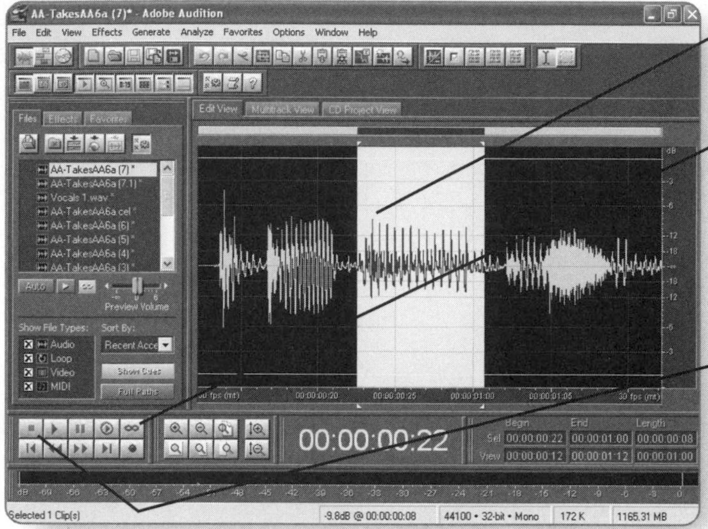

3. Release the **mouse button**. The selection will be readjusted.

4. Click on the **Play Looped button**. The selection you made will play over and over as if it was looped, so you can preview how your loop will sound.

5. Click on the **Stop button**. Playback will stop.

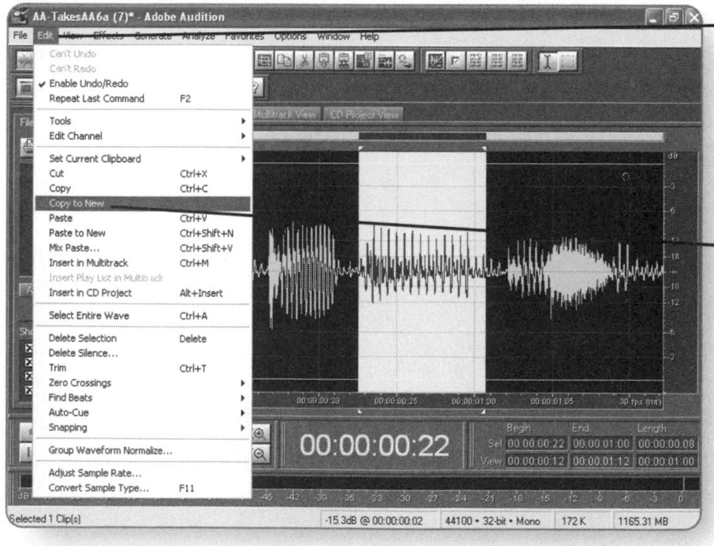

6. Click on **Edit**. The Edit menu will appear. Follow this and the next step only when you are completely satisfied with your loop selection.

7. Click on **Copy to New**. The selection will be opened as a new file in Edit view.

Zero Crossings

A zero crossing is a point in your audio where the amplitude is equal to zero. When creating loops, it may be helpful to find the points of zero crossing for the start and end point.

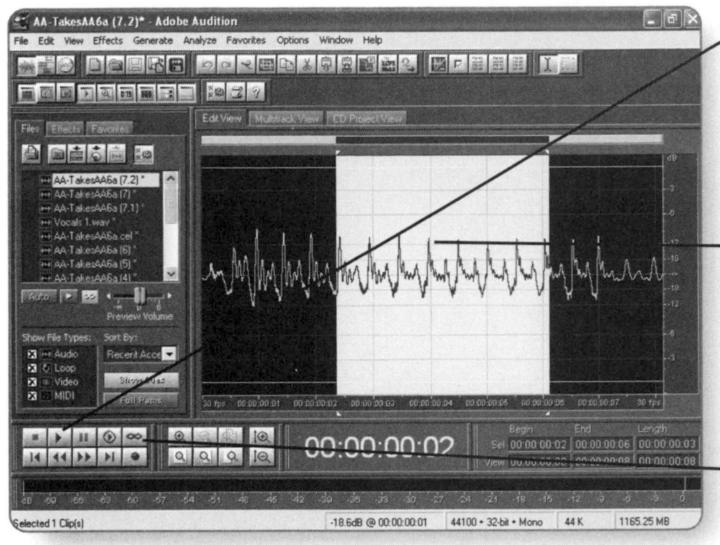

1. **Click** on the **Play button**. The waveform will begin to play. Listen closely for the area from which you would like to create a loop.

2. **Click and drag** across the approximate **area of the waveform** that contains the audio that you would like to loop. The area will be highlighted.

3. **Click** on the **Play Looped button**. The selection you made will play over and over as if it was looped, so you can preview how your loop will sound.

4. **Click** on the **Stop button**. Playback will stop.

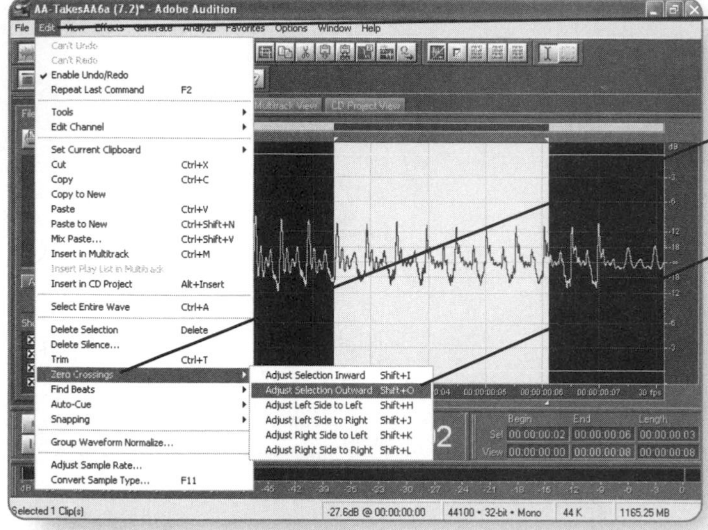

5. Click on **Edit**. The Edit menu will appear.

6. Click on **Zero Crossings**. A submenu will appear.

7. Click on the desired **zero crossing method**. The selection will expand based on the zoom crossing method you selected.

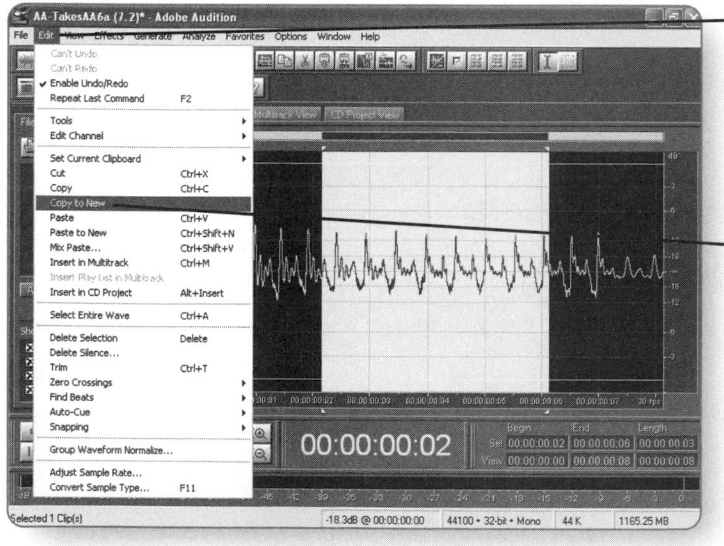

8. Click on **Edit**. The Edit menu will appear. Follow this and the next step only when you are completely satisfied with your loop selection.

9. Click on **Copy to New**. The selection will be opened as a new file in Edit view.

Creating the Loops with Your Mouse

Once you have a wave file created from which you want to create a loop, you can follow any of the steps outlined earlier in this chapter to create the loop, or you can create a loop by simply clicking and dragging.

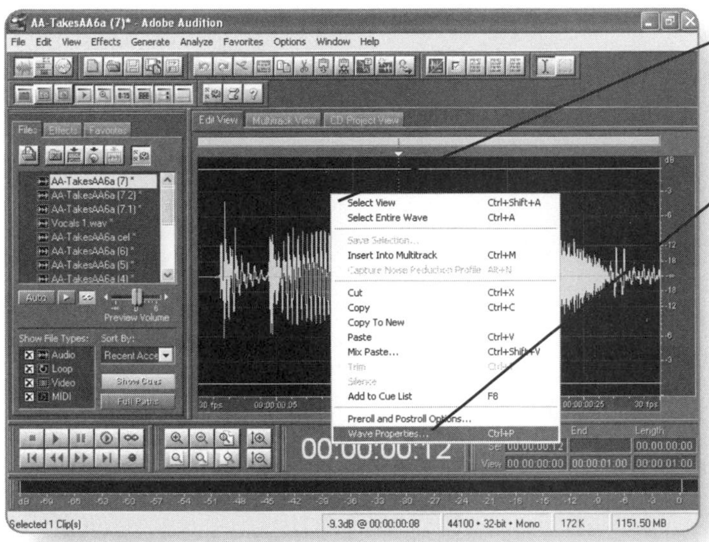

1. **Right-click** on the **wave file** that you created in Edit view. A menu will appear.

2. **Click** on **Wave Properties**. A dialog box will appear allowing you to adjust the wave properties.

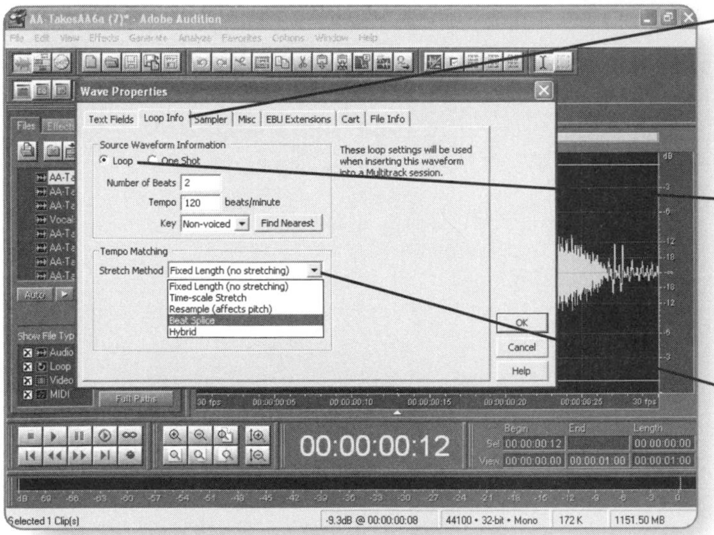

3. **Click** on the **Loop Info tab**. The dialog box will change to give you information on the looping properties.

4. **Click** on the **circle** beside Loop, if it is not already selected. This will make your wave file loopable.

5. **Click** on the **down arrow** beside Stretch Method. A list of different stretch methods will appear.

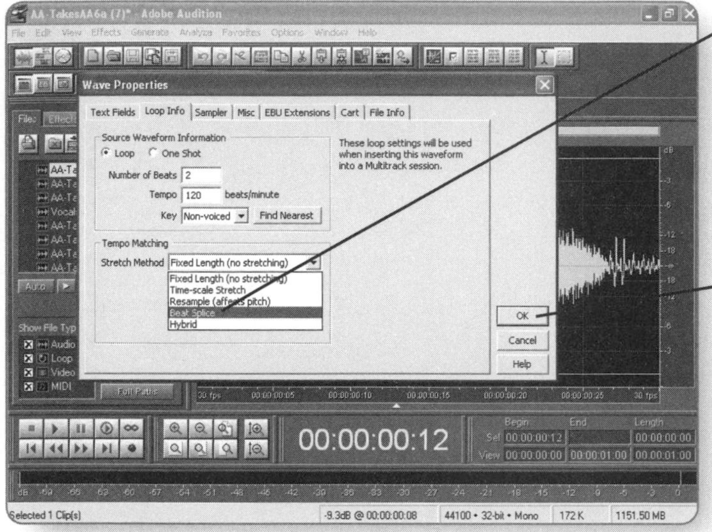

6. Click on the desired **stretch method**. For more information on the different stretch methods, see the "Looping with Loop Properties" section earlier in this chapter.

7. Click on **OK**. The wave file will now be loopable.

8. Press F12 to toggle to Multitrack view. Multitrack view will appear.

9. Position the **mouse pointer** over the name of the file you were working on in Edit view.

10. Click and drag the **wave file** from the Organizer window to the desired track.

11. **Release** the **mouse button**. It will be inserted into the track. The wave clip will have three diagonal lines in the bottom-right corner to indicate that it is loopable.

12. **Position** the **mouse pointer** over the diagonal lines in the bottom-right or left corner of the wave clip.

13. **Click and drag** to the **right or left**. As you drag, the file will loop repeatedly. You can always adjust this by clicking and dragging to the right to extend the loop, or to the left to reduce the loop.

14. **Release** the **mouse button**. The wave clip will now be looped. The number of times the file is looped is determined by how far you dragged in Step 13.

Editing Loops

After you've created a loop, you can modify its properties by accessing the Wave Properties dialog box.

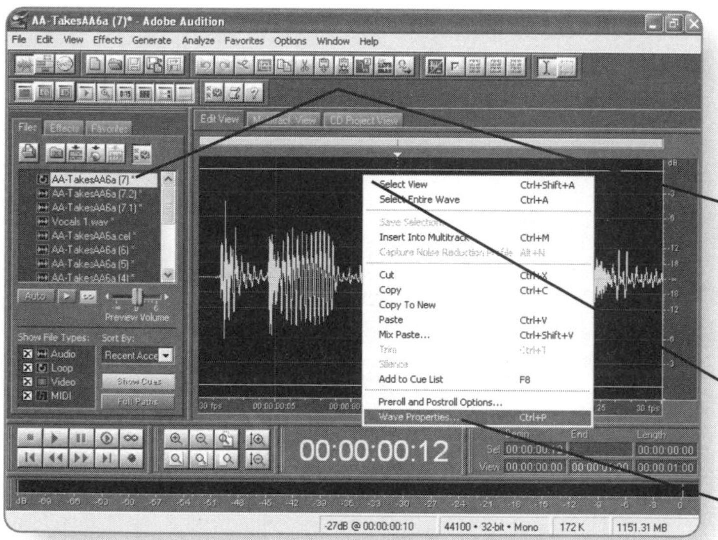

1. **Press F12** to toggle to Wave Edit view, if you are not already there. Wave Edit view will appear.

2. **Double-click** on the **wave loop file** that you would like to edit. It will open in the wave display.

3. **Right-click** anywhere on the **wave**. A menu will appear.

4. **Click** on **Wave Properties**. The Wave Properties dialog box will open.

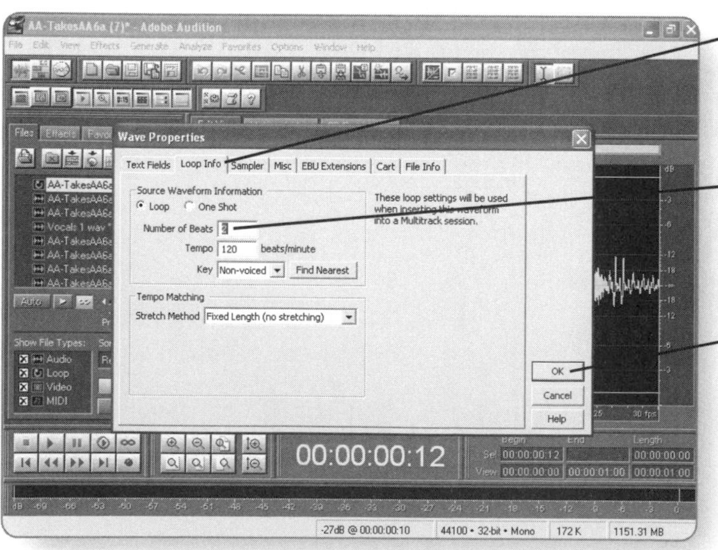

5. **Click** on the **Loop Info tab**. You will now be provided with loop options.

6. **Make** any **changes** to the loop. You can change any of the available settings.

7. **Click** on **OK**. The changes that you made will be saved.

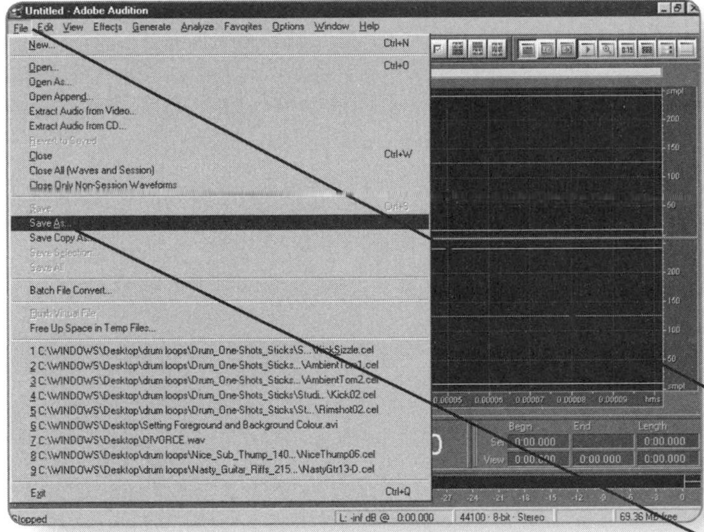

Saving to Loop Format

After you have created your loop, you can save it in loop format, so that when it is placed in tracks of other sessions, it can simply be clicked and dragged to create loops.

1. **Click** on **File** with the wave open in Edit view. The File menu will appear.

2. **Click** on **Save As**. A dialog box will appear.

3. **Type** a **name** for your loop. It's a good idea to give it a name that reflects its contents.

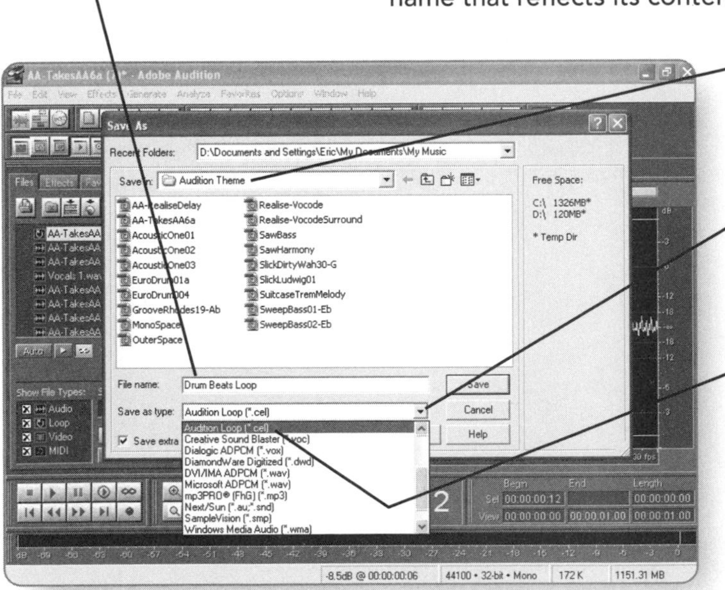

4. **Click** on a **location** to save your loop. The file will be stored in this location.

5. **Click** on the **Save as type down arrow**. A list of different file types will appear.

6. **Click** on **Audition Loop (*.cel)**, if it is not already selected. It will be highlighted.

7. **Click** on **Save**. The loop will be saved.

9

Repair and Adjustment Effects

Adobe Audition has a full line of special effects that you can add to your audio. Some are effects designed to create wild, out of the ordinary sounds, whereas others are meant to fix problems. In this chapter, the concentration will be on those effects that can tweak your audio when the quality is not quite right or does not fit in with your sequence. Audio can be recorded or downloaded from many sources, some of which do not provide the greatest results. Audition's line of repair effects will help you clean up those files.

In this chapter, you'll learn how to:

- Use the Spectral view
- Repair common audio problems
- Adjust the time and pitch of audio
- Change the amplitude of audio

Using the Spectral View

Up to this point, audio in the Edit view has appeared in waveform. When you are viewing a waveform, you can see the amplitude of the audio but not its frequency. Spectral view, by contrast, allows you to view both the frequency and the amplitude in the form of a color. Spectral view shows the results of applying effects and filter better than Wave view.

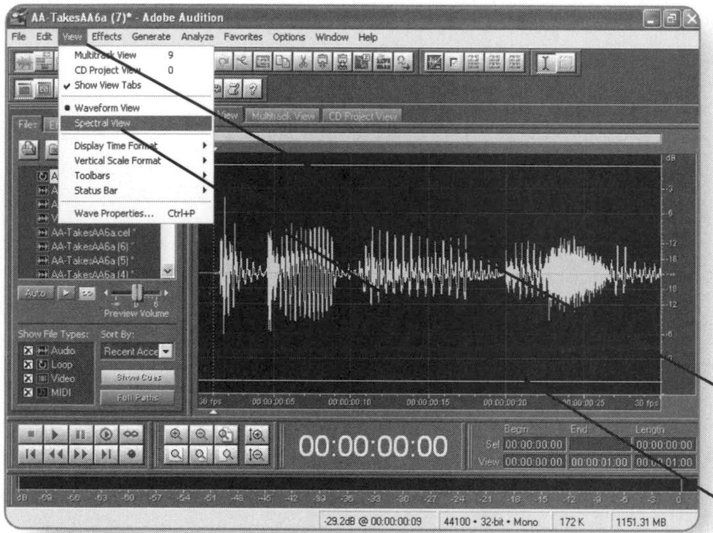

1. **Press F12** to toggle to Edit view if you are not already there. Edit view will appear.

2. **Click** on **View**. The Spectral menu will appear.

3. **Click** on **Spectral View**. The wave display will change to Spectral view.

> **NOTE**
>
> While in Spectral view, the Amplitude ruler will become a Frequency ruler which measures frequencies in Hertz.

4. **Click** on **View**. The View menu will appear.

5. **Click** on **Waveform View**. You will switch back to Waveform view.

Audio Repair Effects

Depending on the original source of your audio, it may have one or more problems associated with it. Some recording sources produce clicks and pops, especially when recording from turntables and old records. Other audio problems include hissing, noise, and clipping. Adobe Audition has several tools to help clean up these common problems.

> **NOTE**
>
> For all of the audio repair effects, you must have your wave open in the Edit view. You can press F12 on your keyboard to toggle to Edit view, if you are not already there.

Removing Clicks and Pops

Recording from vinyl records typically produces some type of audio problem. Old records (nowadays every record is old) tend to produce scratches, pops, and clicks. You can digitally remaster almost any old recording using the Click and Pop Eliminator.

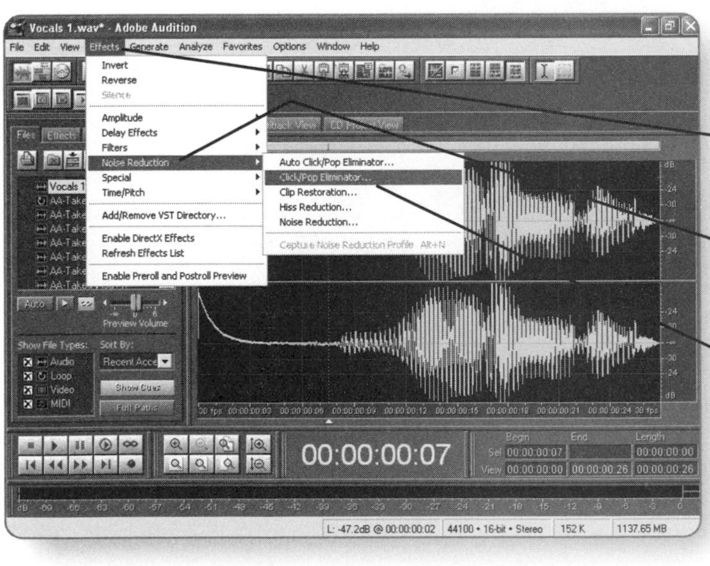

1. **Click** on **Effects**. The Effects menu will appear.
2. **Click** on **Noise Reduction**. A submenu will appear.
3. **Click** on **Click/Pop Eliminator**. The Click/Pop Eliminator dialog box will open.

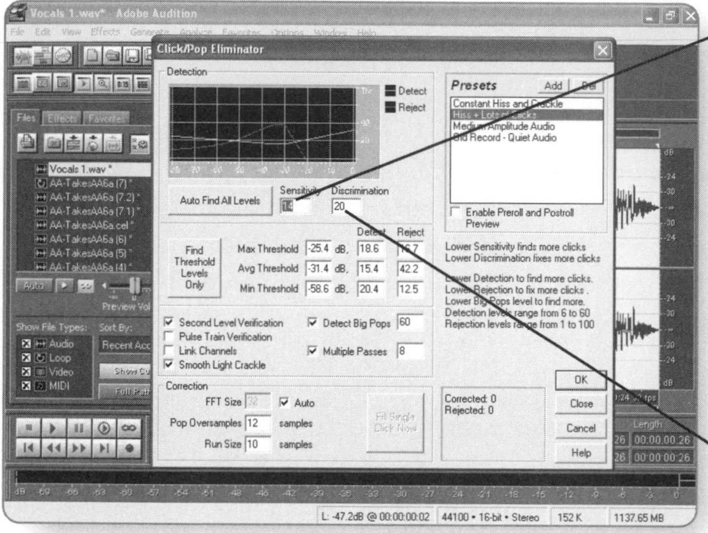

4. Double-click in the **Sensitivity field box**. The box will be highlighted.

5. Type a **sensitivity number**. Lower sensitivity numbers will find the more subtle clicks. Higher sensitivity numbers will find the louder, more obvious clicks. The range must be between 4 and 50.

6. Double-click in the **Discrimination field box**. The box will be highlighted.

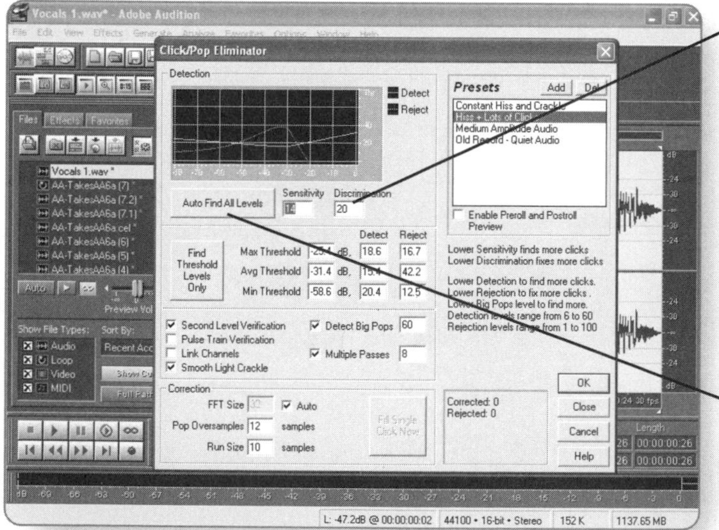

7. Type a **number** for the discrimination. The higher the number you set here, the fewer clicks will be found, but audio will remain intact.

8. Click on the **Auto Find All Levels button**. The audio will be scanned for all clicks based on your sensitivity and discrimination settings.

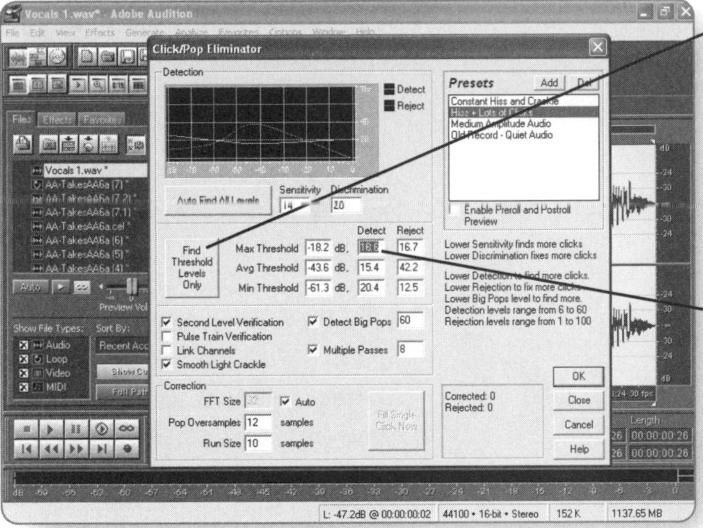

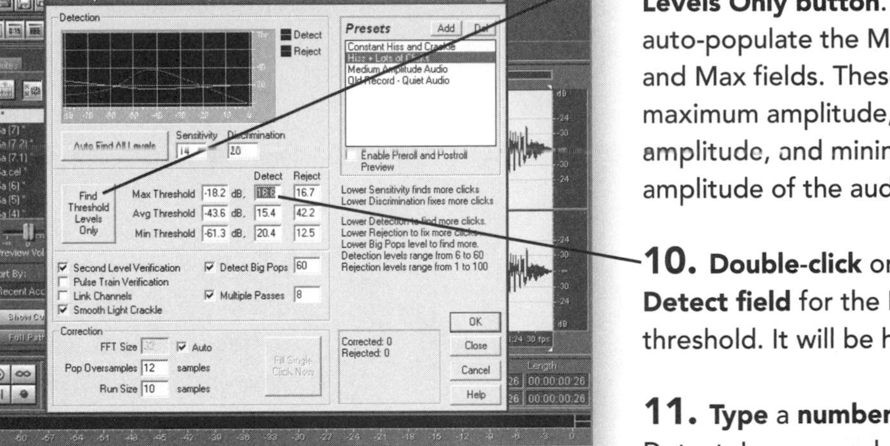

9. Click on the **Find Threshold Levels Only button**. This will auto-populate the Min, Avg, and Max fields. These are the maximum amplitude, average amplitude, and minimum amplitude of the audio.

10. Double-click on the **Detect field** for the Max threshold. It will be highlighted.

11. Type a **number** for the Detect. Lower numbers will find more clicks. Higher numbers will find less clicks.

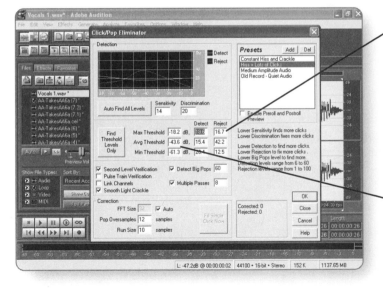

12. Double-click on the **Reject field** for the Max threshold. It will be highlighted.

13. Type a **number** for the Reject. Lower numbers will repair more clicks, whereas higher numbers will repair fewer clicks.

14. Repeat Steps 11-13 for the Avg and Min fields for Detect and Reject.

> **NOTE**
>
> The Detect field allows you to enter values from 6-60, whereas the Reject field allows you to enter values from 1-100.

15. **Click** the **check box** beside Detect Big Pops, if it is not already checked. This will enable you to detect and remove large clicks that may not be detected using the regular method.

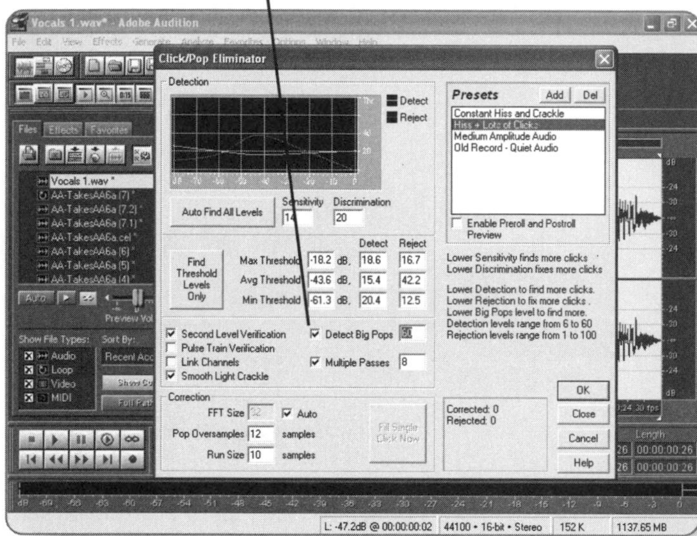

16. **Double-click** in the **Detect Big Pops field**. The number will be highlighted.

17. **Type** a **number** from 30 to 200. This is the value that Audition will look for when removing large clicks. This number represents the threshold for pops, so the larger the number the more pops will be found.

CAUTION

Only use Detect Big Pops when you are sure there are large pops in your audio. Some audio contains similar characteristics to a big pop and you want to avoid inadvertently removing it.

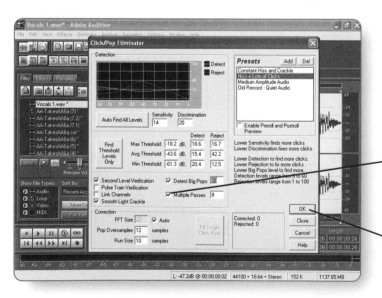

18. **Click** the **check boxes** to enable or disable any other settings.

19. **Click** on **OK**. Your audio will be repaired based on the settings you have entered.

Auto Click/Pop Eliminator

Now that you've learned the hard way to remove clicks and pops, here's the easy way. The Auto Click/Pop Eliminator allows you to adjust only Noise Threshold and Complexity and will then scan your document and automatically remove clicks and pops.

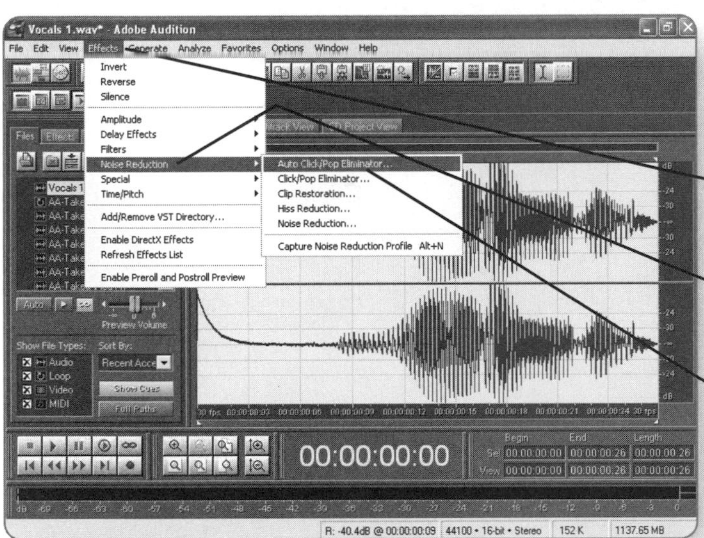

1. **Click** on **Effects.** The Effects menu will appear.
2. **Click** on **Noise Reduction**. A submenu will appear.
3. **Click** on **Auto Click/Pop Eliminator**. The Auto Click/Pop Eliminator dialog box will open.

4. **Click** on the desired **preset**. It will be highlighted.

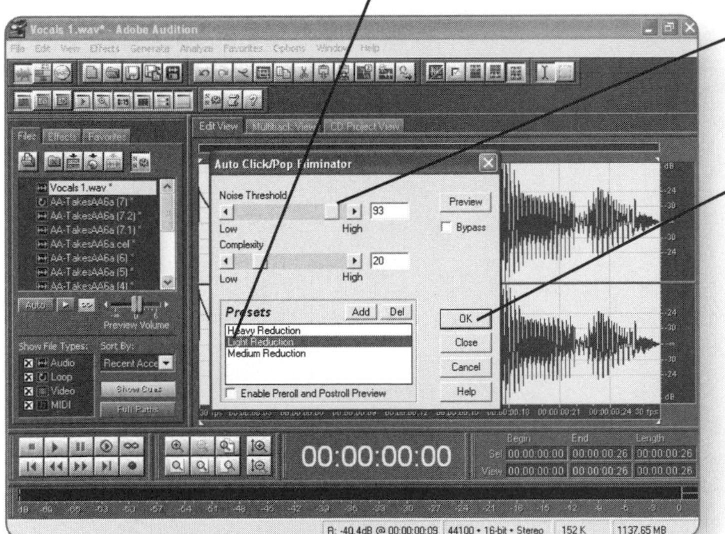

5. **Click and drag** to adjust the **Noise Threshold and/or the Complexity settings**.
6. **Click** on **OK**. Your audio will be scanned and clicks and pops will be removed based on your settings.

Removing Clipping

Clipping is the result of too much amplification being applied to a waveform or improperly adjusted equipment. The result of clipping is that you have areas of your waveform cut out at the top and bottom. The Clip Restoration feature in Adobe Audition will fill in these areas.

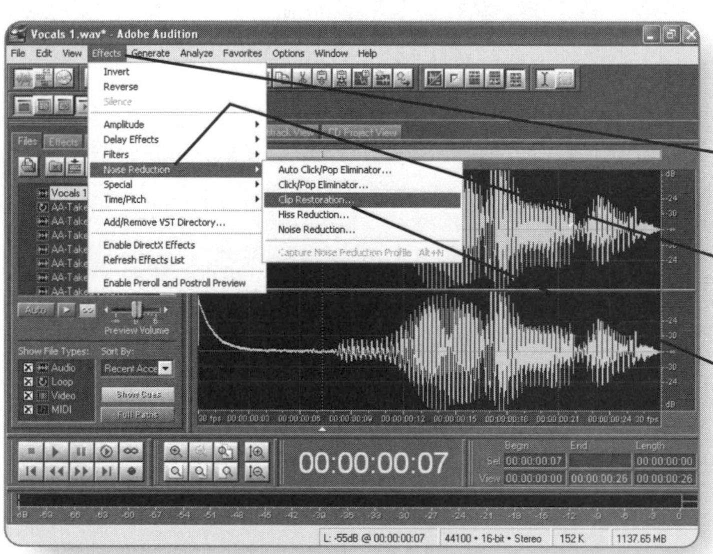

1. **Click** on **Effects**. The Effects menu will appear.

2. **Click** on **Noise Reduction**. A submenu will appear.

3. **Click** on **Clip Restoration**. The Click Restoration dialog box will open.

4. **Click** on the **Gather Statistics Now button**. Statistics on your audio will appear in the window.

5. **Double-click** on the **Input Attenuation field**. The number will be highlighted.

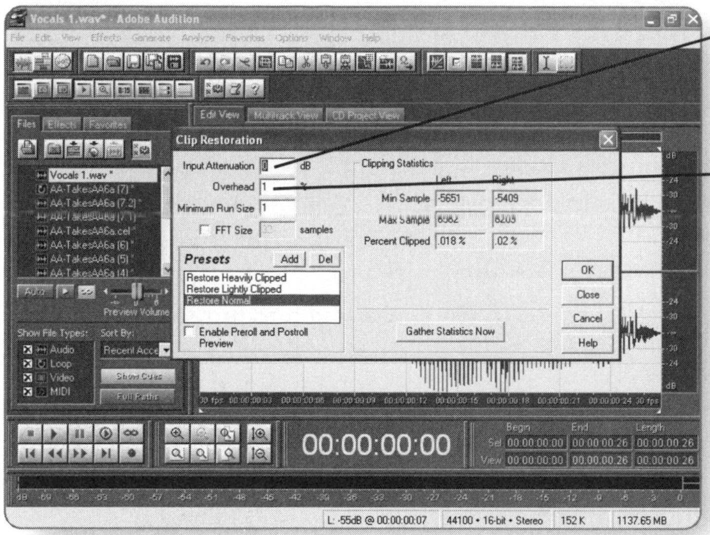

6. **Type** a **number** for the Input Attenuation. This specifies the amount to amplify the signal.

7. **Press** the **Tab key**. You will advance to the Overhead field and the number will be highlighted.

8. **Type** a **number** for the Overhead. This number represents the percentage variance for detecting clipped areas.

> **TIP**
>
> Typically you should set the Overhead number at 1% to catch most of the problems.

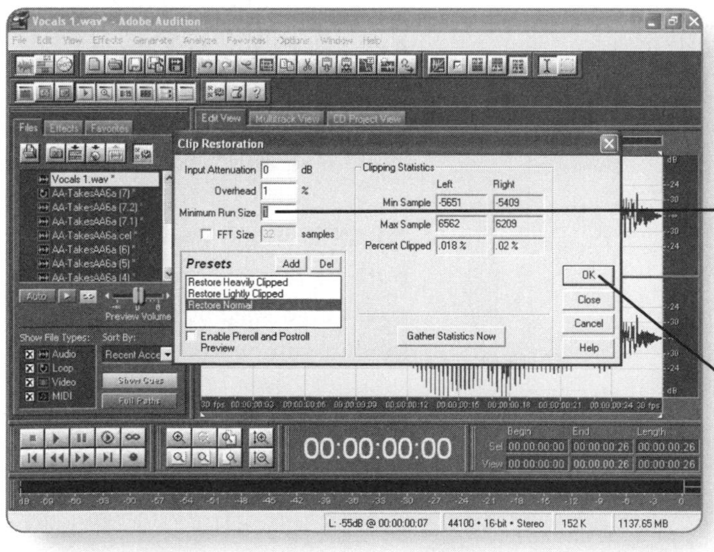

9. **Press** the **Tab key**. You will advance to the Minimum Run Size field and the number will be highlighted.

10. **Type** a **number** for the Minimum Run Size. This number represents the shortest run of clipped audio to repair.

11. **Click** on the **OK button**. Your audio will be repaired based on the settings you have entered.

Removing Hiss

Typically from audio tape recordings, hiss is the snake-like sound that appears in the background of some recordings. Because hiss is usually at a constant level, Audition can eliminate it by removing all audio in all frequencies that are below a certain threshold. The Hiss Reduction dialog box allows you to preview the changes as you are making them.

1. **Click** on **Effects**. The Effects menu will appear.

2. **Click** on **Noise Reduction**. A submenu will appear.

3. **Click** on **Hiss Reduction**. The Hiss Reduction dialog box will open.

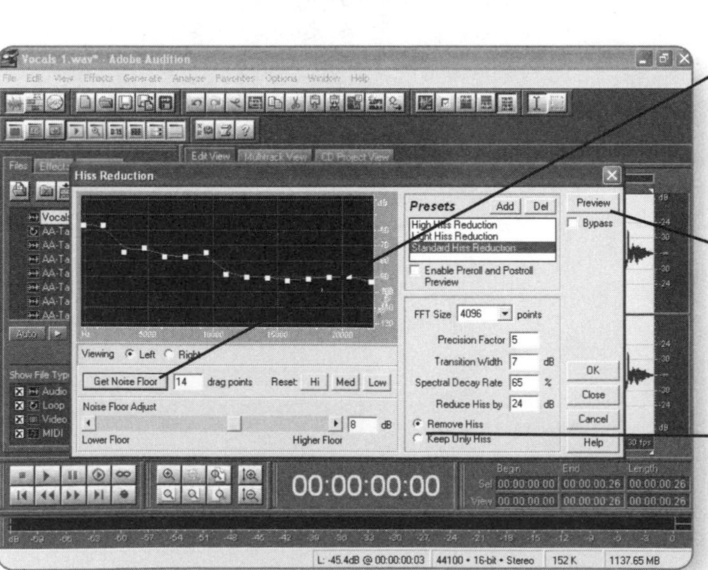

4. **Click** on the **Get Noise Floor button**. The will search your audio for an area containing only hiss.

5. **Click** on the **Preview button**. This will preview what your audio will sound like with the hiss removed.

6. **Click** on the **circle** beside Keep only Hiss. This will allow you to hear the hiss that will be removed.

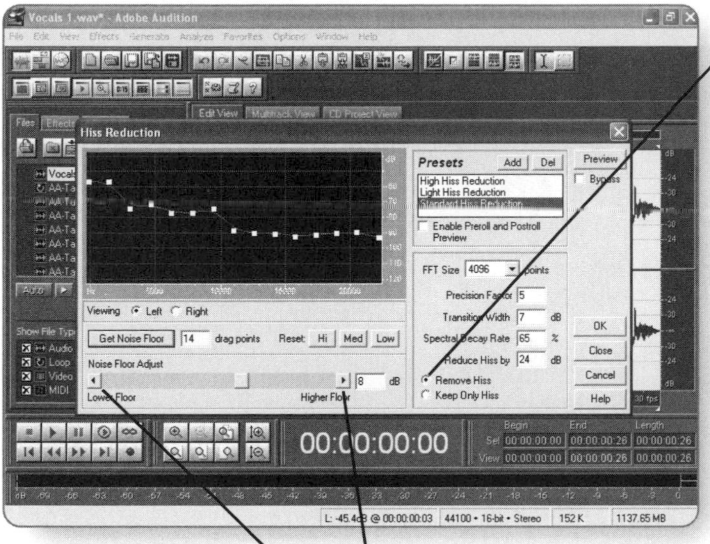

7. **Click** on the **circle** beside Remove Hiss to return to normal mode.

8. **Click** on the **arrows** to adjust the Noise Floor. As the audio is being previewed, you can **click** these **buttons** to listen to the difference it makes.

9. **Click** on **OK** once you have successfully removed the hiss to your satisfaction.

Removing Noise

It is almost impossible to record noise-free audio. There is so much noise around us that it does not even register with us. Noise can come from just about anything, including subtle things like computer monitors, lights, vents, heaters, fans, and many other sources. Typically we only notice the noise when we play back our audio. Unless you have a state-of-the-art sound studio, there's a good likelihood that your audio has some form of noise in the background. That being said, Audition gives you a nice, easy-to-use tool for removing noise. With this tool you select an area of audio that contains the noise, then Audition processes it and removes that noise throughout the file.

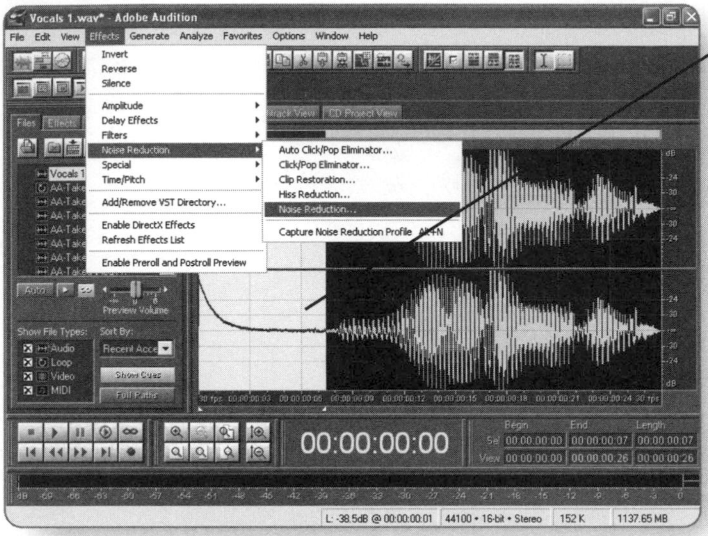

1. **Click and drag** across a **portion** of your audio file that contains only the noise that you want to remove. Typically you can find this at the very beginning or end of the audio.

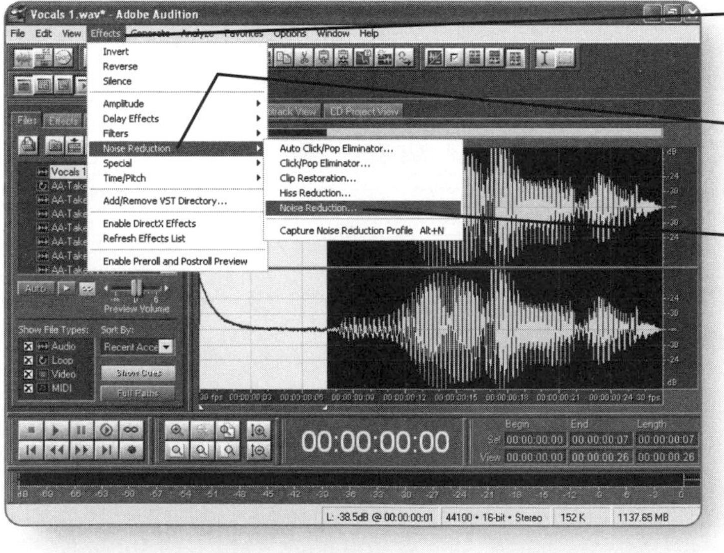

2. **Click** on **Effects**. The Effects menu will appear.

3. **Click** on **Noise Reduction**. A submenu will appear.

4. **Click** on **Noise Reduction**. The Noise Reduction dialog box will open.

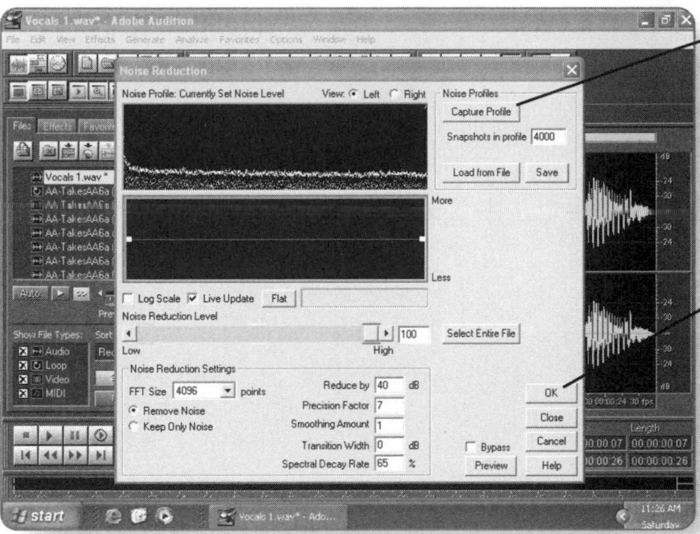

5. Click on the **Capture Profile button**. A profile will be created based on the selection that you made and a visual representation of the noise will appear in the window.

6. Click on the **OK button**. The noise will be removed from your audio.

Amplitude Effects

Adobe Audition comes with audio effects to satisfy almost every appetite. Among them are the Amplitude effects that deal with how loud or soft the volume of your audio is at certain points. To apply any of the Amplitude effects, you should be in Edit view.

Amplification

Adobe Audition provides you with different ways to change the volume level of a wave. One method is to use the Amplify effect. Within the Amplify dialog box you can select from different amplification presets or you can manually adjust the volume level.

1. **Press F12** to toggle to Edit view if you are not already there. Edit view will appear.

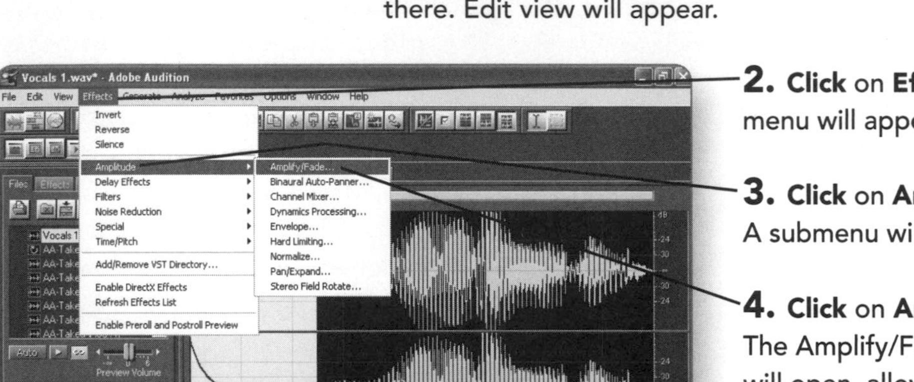

2. **Click** on **Effects**. The Effects menu will appear.

3. **Click** on **Amplitude**. A submenu will appear.

4. **Click** on **Amplify/Fade**. The Amplify/Fade dialog box will open, allowing you to adjust the amplitude of the wave.

Applying Amplitude Presets

Audition comes with several preset amplitude effects that you can select from. These presets provide a convenient way to apply common amplitude effects such as fades and pans.

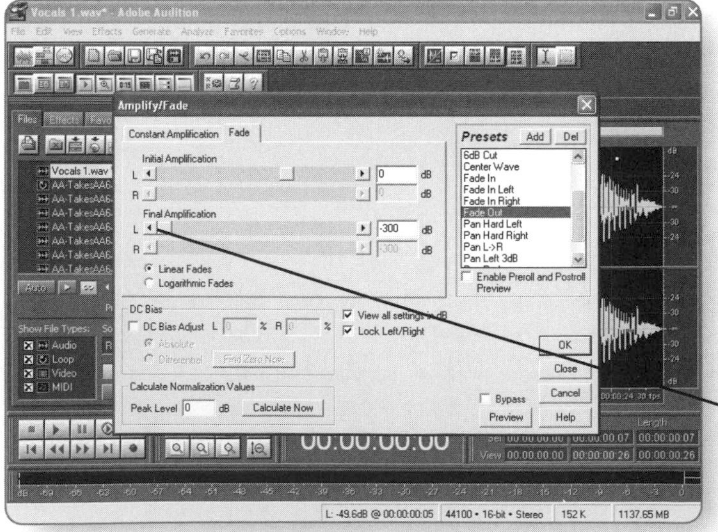

1. **Click** on the **scroll buttons** to view the different presets.

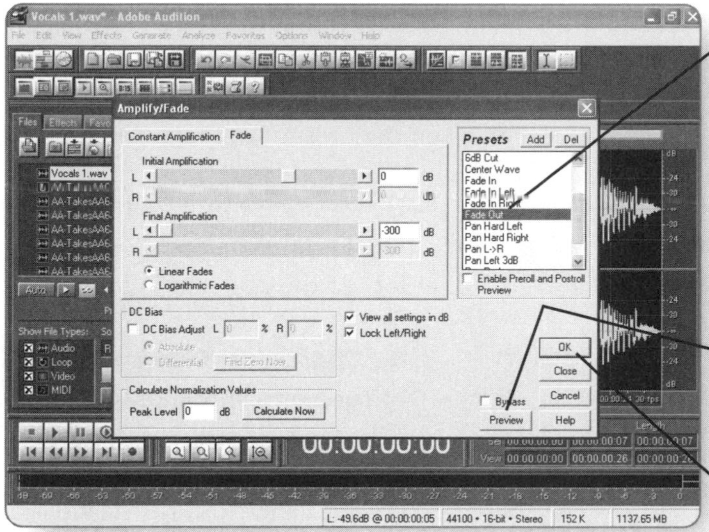

2. Click on the desired **preset**. It will appear highlighted.

3. Click on the **Preview button** to hear how the effect sounds applied to your audio. If you are satisfied with the audio, skip to Step 5.

4. Make the desired **adjustments** to the settings until you are satisfied with the sound.

5. Click on **OK**. The dialog box will close and the effect will be applied to your audio.

Manually Adjusting Amplitude

Using the Amplitude dialog box you can manually adjust the constant volume level of your audio or create fades.

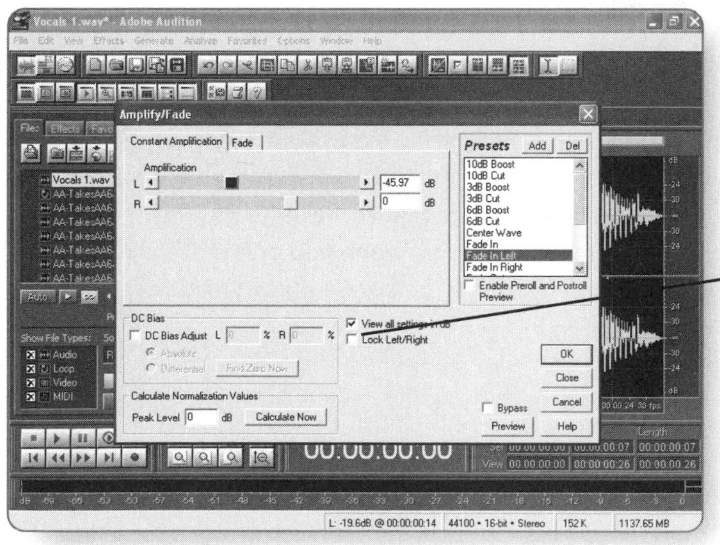

Adjusting Constant Amplification

Using this adjustment will change the constant level of volume for the entire wave.

1. Uncheck the **Lock Left/Right check box** if you want to set different levels for the left and right channel.

2. Click and drag the **left amplification scroll box** to change the volume level for that channel. Alternatively, you can enter a number in the dB box. Positive numbers will make the audio louder, whereas negative numbers will make the audio softer.

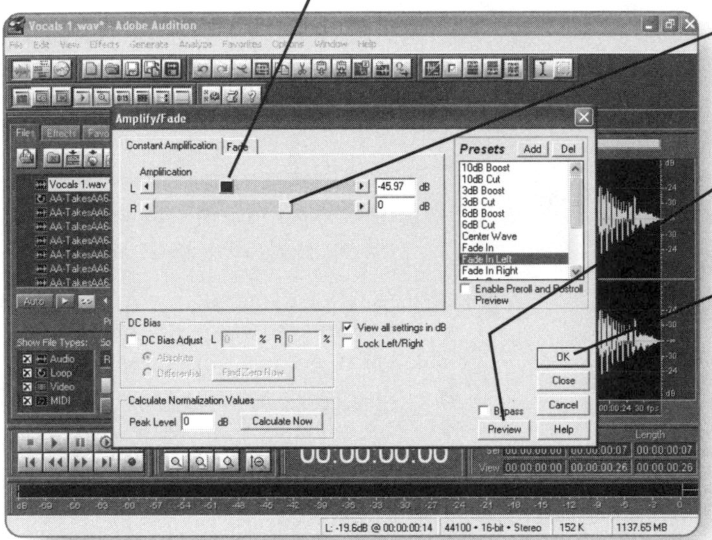

3. Repeat Step 2 for the right amplification if you have not locked the channels in Step 1.

4. Click on the **Preview button** to audition the sound.

5. Click on **OK** to accept the changes and close the dialog box.

Creating Fades

Creating a fade is similar to adjusting constant amplification in that you simply click and drag the scroll boxes to adjust the amplification. The difference is that you actually adjust the volume for two settings, one that represents the initial amplification and the other that represents the final amplification. In other words, when you create a fade, you change the amplification level over a period of time.

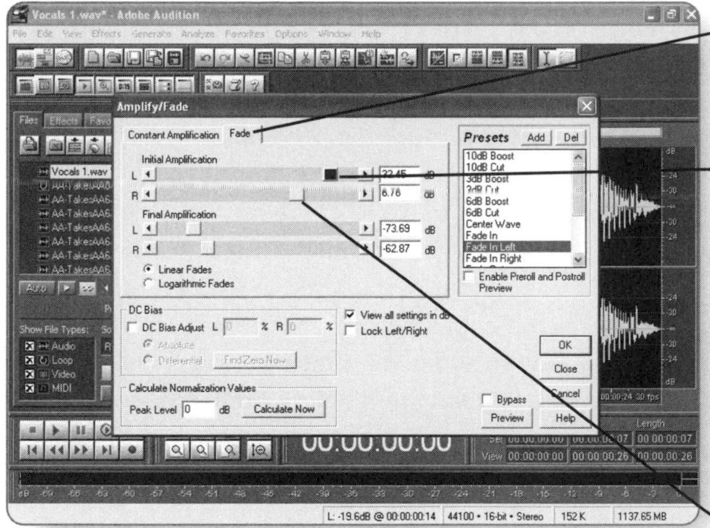

1. Click on the **Fade tab**. This will allow you to create a fade over time.

2. Click and drag the **Initial Amplification left scroll box** to change the volume level for that channel. Alternatively, you can enter a number in the dB box. Positive numbers will make the audio louder, whereas negative numbers will make the audio softer.

3. Repeat Step 2 for the right amplification or enter a number into the dB box.

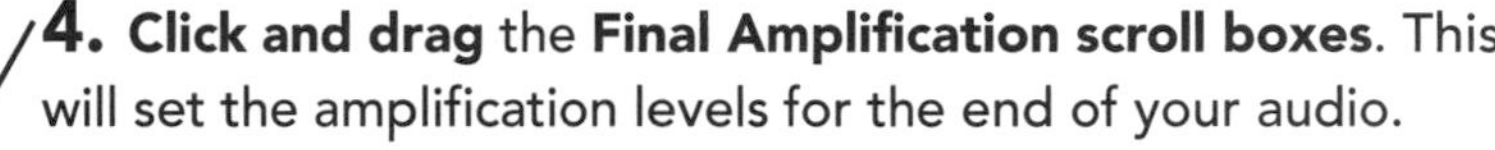

4. Click and drag the **Final Amplification scroll boxes**. This will set the amplification levels for the end of your audio.

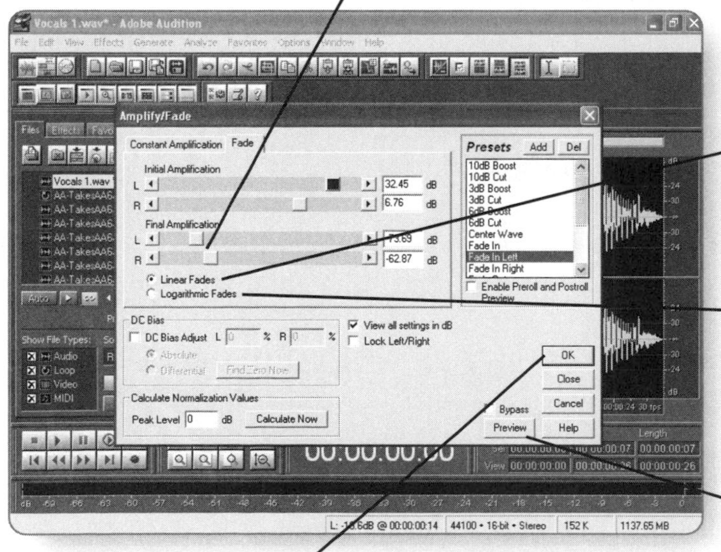

5. Click on the **circle** beside the desired fade type. Your choices include:

- **Linear Fades**. This will fade the audio evenly from the initial state to the final amplification.
- **Logarithmic Fades**. The fade will occur stronger on one of the ends of the audio, depending on whether you are fading in or out.

6. Click on the **Preview button** to audition the sound.

7. Click on **OK** to accept the changes and close the dialog box.

Blowing Your Mind with the Binaural Auto-Panner

The original developers of Audition, a company called Syntrillium Software, certainly could be described as "a little out there" when it comes to some of the features they included in the program. One of those features, called the Brainwave Synchronizer has reappeared in Adobe Audition as the Binaural Auto-Panner. If you're in to creating hypnotic suggestions, relaxation audio, meditation music, or subconscious mantras, then the Binaural Auto-Panner is for you. The creators claim that it can produce stereo files that will put the listener into any desired state of awareness.

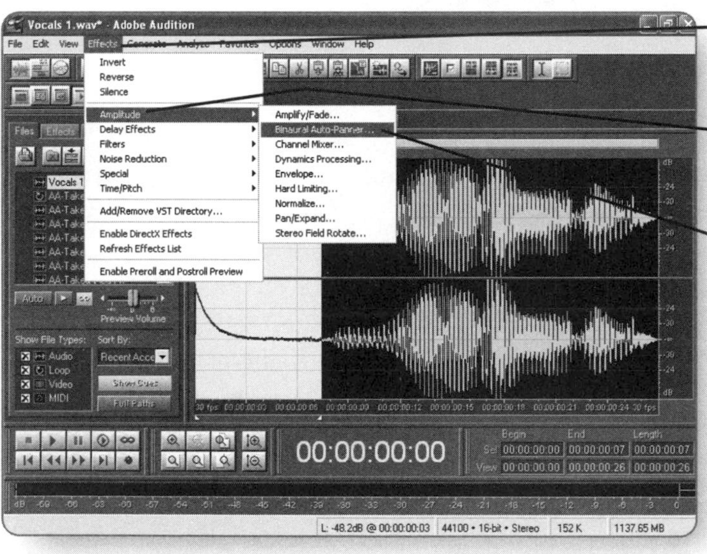

1. **Click** on **Effects**. The Effects menu will appear.

2. **Click** on **Amplitude**. A submenu will appear.

3. **Click** on **Binaurial Auto-Panner**. The Binaurial Auto-Panner dialog box will open.

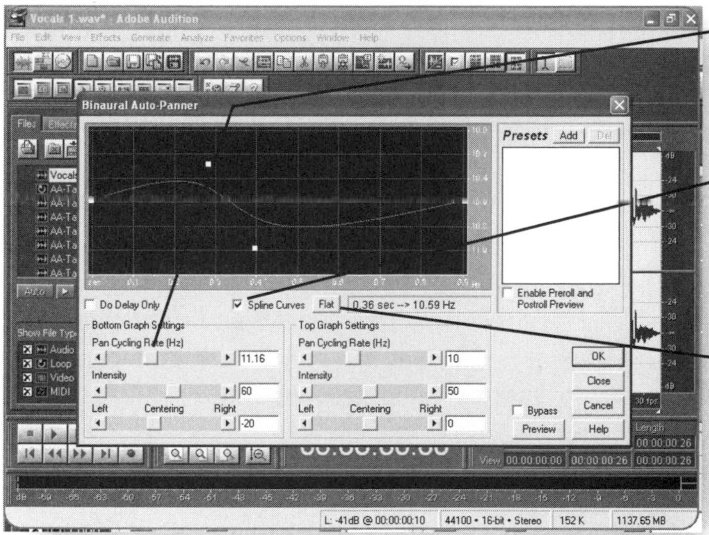

4. **Click and drag** any of the **scroll boxes** to change the settings.

5. **Click** on the **Spline Curves check box** if you want to create a curved line rather than a straight line.

6. **Click** on the **Flat button** if you want to reset the graph.

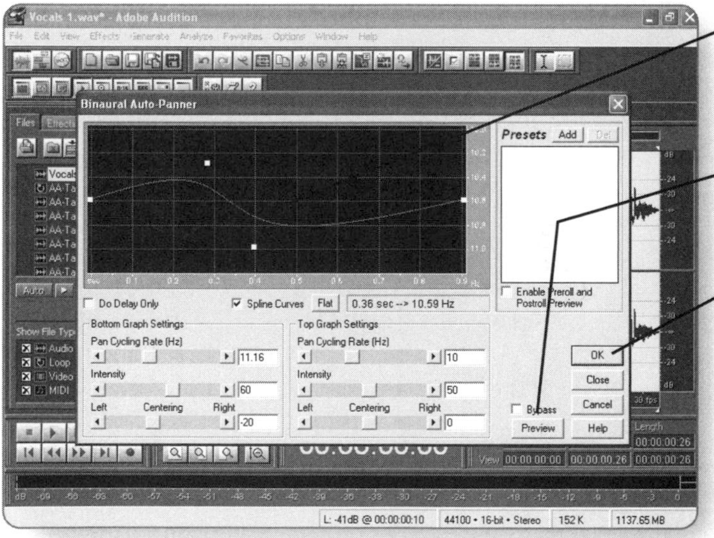

7. **Click and drag** anywhere on the **line** to adjust the curve. As you drag a handle will appear.

8. **Click** on the **Preview button** to audition the sound.

9. **Click** on **OK** to accept the changes and close the dialog box.

Channel Mixer

This effect combines the two different sides of a stereo waveform to create some interesting audio. The way in which the two sides are mixed depends on the preset that you select or the settings that you adjust. Because the Channel Mixer mixes together the audio from the left and right channels, it can only be used on stereo waveforms.

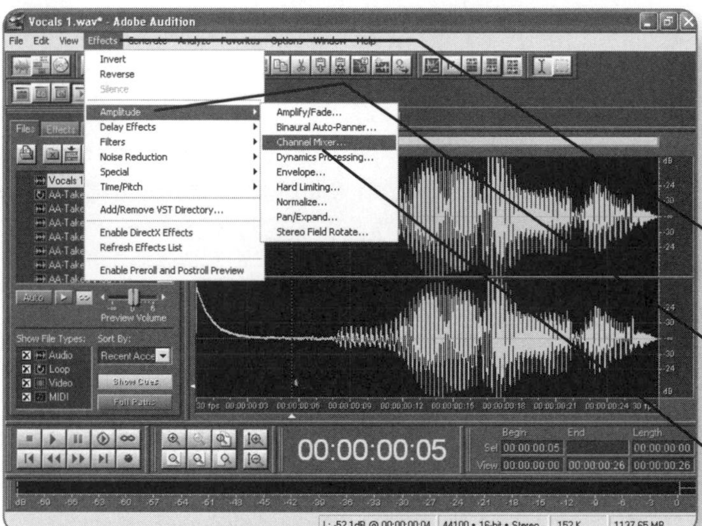

1. **Click** on **Effects**. The Effects menu will appear.
2. **Click** on **Amplitude**. A submenu will appear.
3. **Click** on **Channel Mixer**. The Channel Mixer dialog box will open.

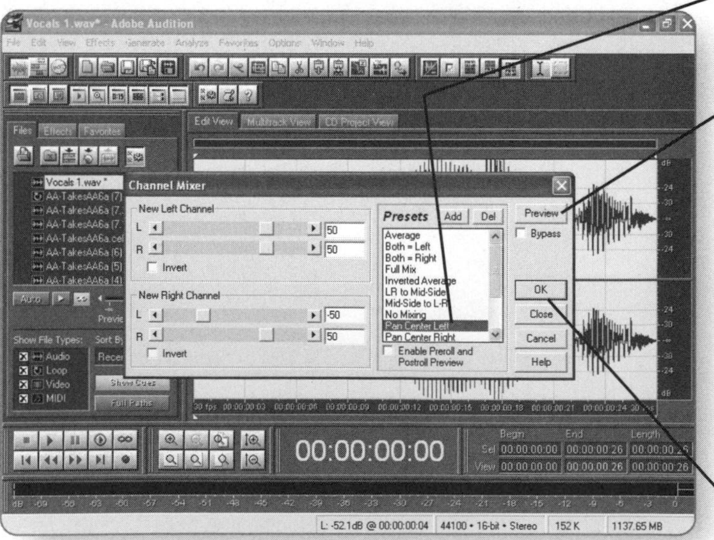

4. **Click** on the desired **preset**. It will be highlighted.
5. **Click** on the **Preview button**. You will preview how the effect sounds when applied to your waveform.
6. **Click and drag** the **slider box** to adjust the channels.
7. **Repeat Steps 5 and 6** until the desired results are achieved.
8. **Click** on **OK**. The dialog box will close and the effect will be applied to your waveform.

> **TIP**
>
> The Channel Mixer is a great tool for karaoke enthusiasts, because it allows you to remove vocals from most audio. Within the Channel Mixer dialog box there is a Voice Cut preset that will invert the channels, which causes the information in the center of the channel (typically where vocals reside) to be removed.

Dynamics Processing

It's almost impossible to create a recording, especially when recording vocals, that isn't too high or too low in volume at certain points. The Dynamics Processor will allow you to create a consistent level of volume based on the input levels. Within the Dynamics Processor dialog box there are several tabs that will allow you to adjust the different settings. You can either manually adjust settings or choose from a variety of presets.

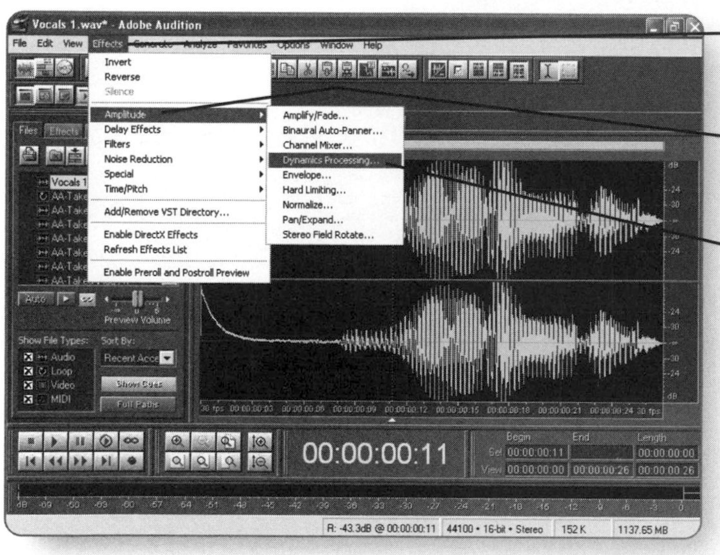

1. **Click** on **Effects**. The Effects menu will appear.

2. **Click** on **Amplitude**. A submenu of effects will appear.

3. **Click** on **Dynamics Processing**. The Dynamics Processing dialog box will open.

The Graphic Tab

The first window that appears in the Dynamic Processing dialog box is the Graphic window. The graph that is provided gives you a visual representation of input vs. output. The x axis shows you the input level and the y axis illustrates how the signal will be output. You can manipulate the graph simply by clicking and dragging on it.

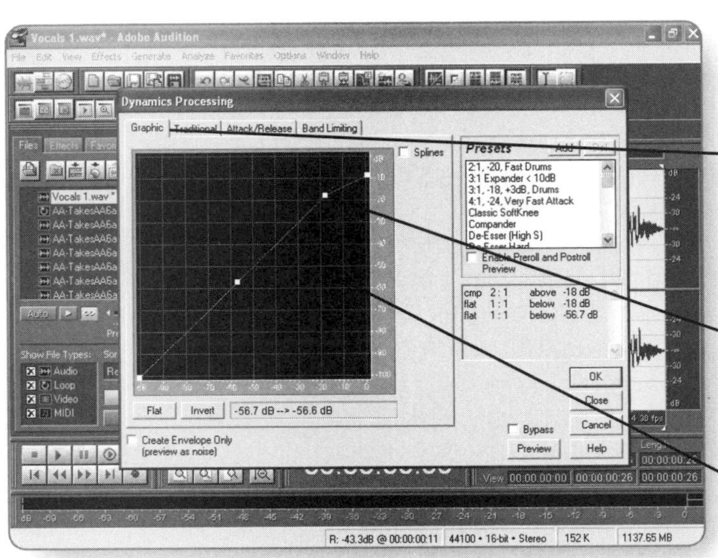

1. **Click** on the **Graphic tab**, if it is not already selected. The Graphic tab will come to the front.

2. **Position** your **mouse pointer** at the point on the graph that you would like to adjust.

3. **Click and drag** to the desired **location**. As soon as you click a white handle will appear.

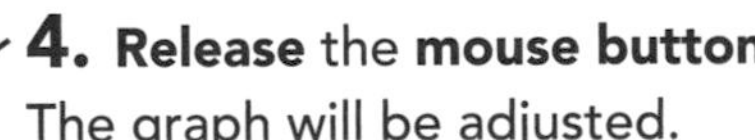

4. **Release** the **mouse button**. The graph will be adjusted.

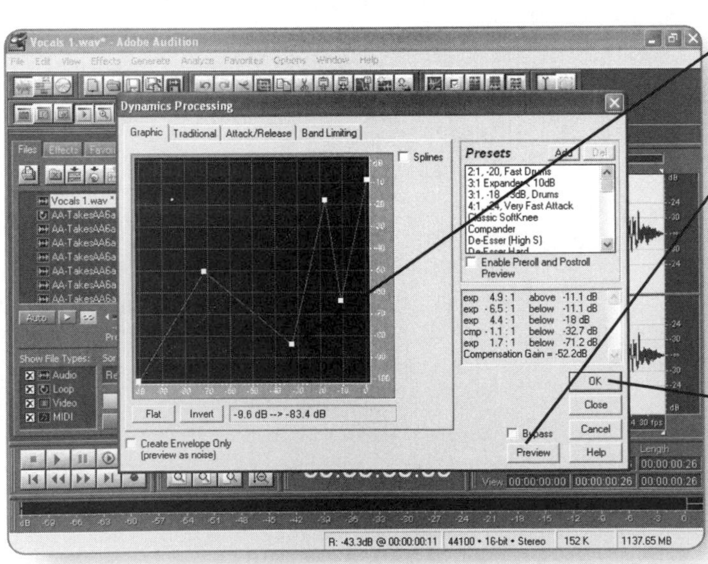

5. **Click** on the **Preview button** to audition your audio based on the changes you have made.

6. **Repeat Steps 2-5** until you are satisfied with the audio.

7. **Click** on the **OK button** to accept the changes and close the dialog box. Alternatively, you can continue to the following sections for further adjustments.

> **TIP**
>
> You can return the graph to its default state by clicking on the Flat button.

Using the Traditional Tab

The Traditional tab of the Dynamics Processing dialog box allows you to alter audio by using the Compress, Flat, or Expand commands. Within the dialog box, you choose which setting you would like, then enter the ratio for that setting and the decibel threshold. You can enter up to six different commands.

1. Click on the **Traditional tab**. You can now enter data into the dialog box.

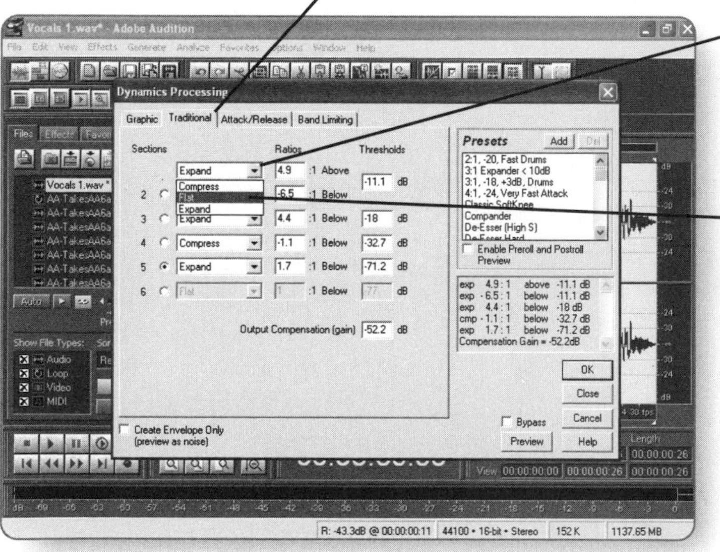

2. Click on the **down arrow** in the first line. You will now be able to choose between Compress, Flat, and Expand.

3. Click on the desired **command**. It will be selected.

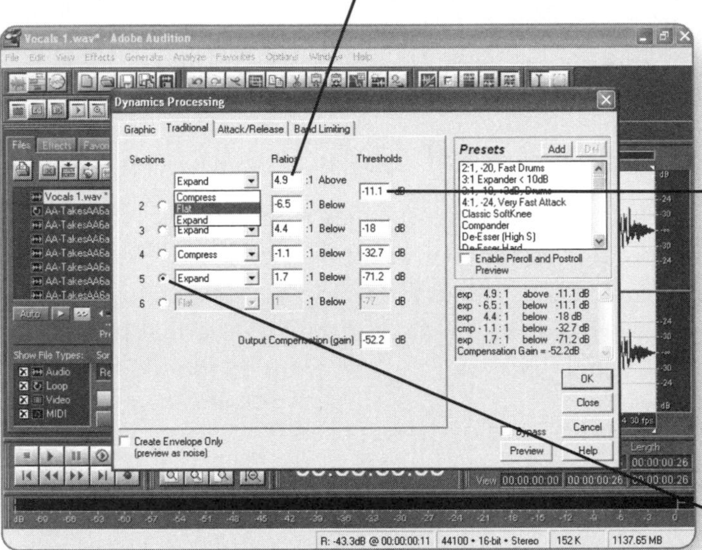

4. Double-click in the **Ratios field** of the first line. The number in the field will be highlighted.

5. Type a **number**. This will be the ratio of the setting to be applied.

6. Double-click in the **dB field**. The number will be highlighted.

7. Type a **number**. This will be the number of decibels the audio will be expanded, compressed, or flatted based on the ratio you have entered.

8. Repeat Steps 2-7 for any of the other lines to add additional settings.

NOTE

No line can have a setting higher than its preceding line. For example, if you had an expand setting of -20dB in line two, line three would have to have settings less than –20dB.

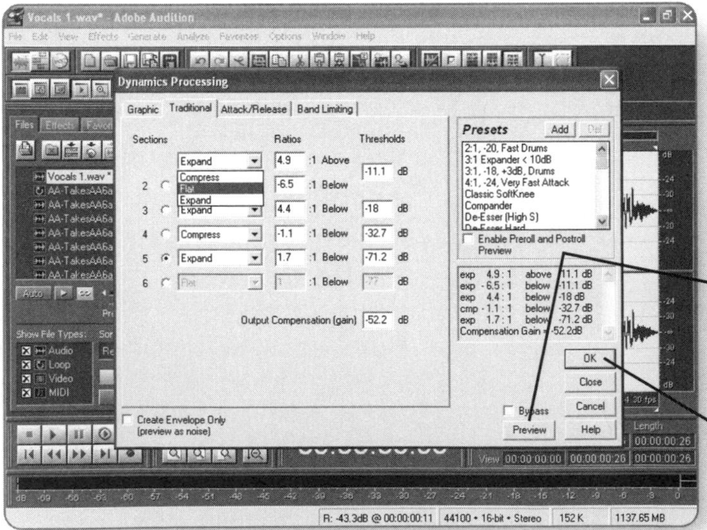

9. Click on the **Preview button** to listen to how the effect sounds on your audio.

10. Click on **OK** to accept the changes and close the dialog box. Alternatively, you can continue to the following sections for further adjustments.

The Attack/Release Tab

The Attack Release section of the window is broken up into two parts, the Gain Processor and the Level Detector. The Gain Processor amplifies the signal, whereas the Level Detector determines the input amplitude.

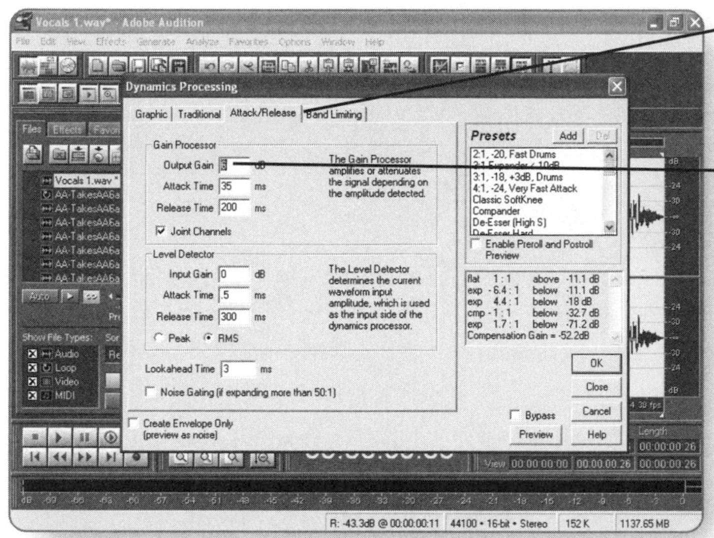

1. Click on the **Attack/Release tab**. The Attack/Release tab will come to the front.

2. Double-click in the **Output Gain box**. The number will be highlighted, allowing you to enter a new number.

3. Type a **value** for the Output Gain. This is the amount of gain that will be added to the output signal.

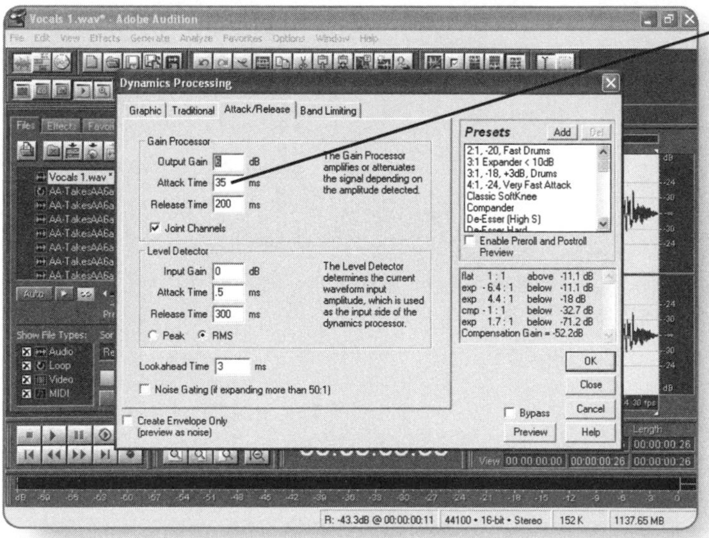

4. Double-click in the **Attack Time box**. The number will be highlighted, allowing you to enter a new number.

5. Type a **value** for the Attack Time. This is the time that it will take for the output signal to reach its volume level.

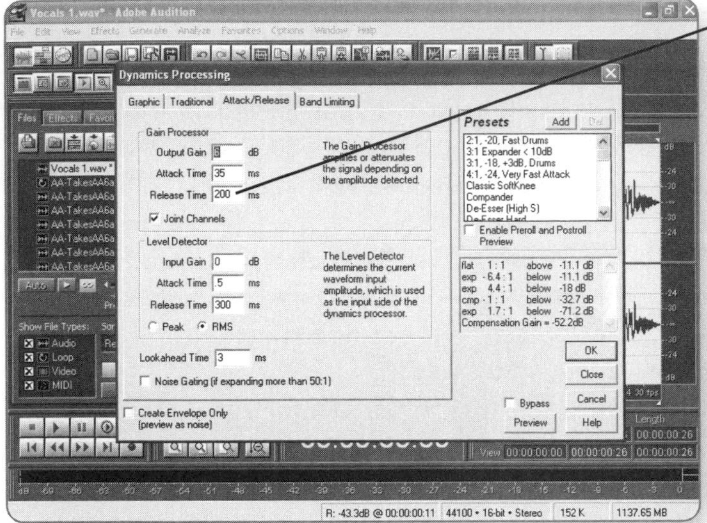

6. Double-click in the **Release Time box.** The number will be highlighted, allowing you to enter a new number.

7. Type a **value** for the Release Time. This is the time it will take the end of a previous output level to reach the specified volume level.

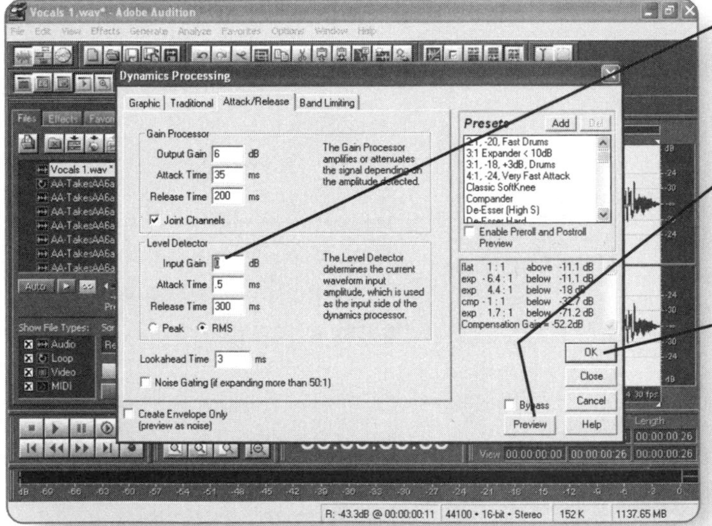

8. Type values for the Level Detector as you did for the Gain Processor.

9. Click on the **Preview button** to listen to how the effect sounds on your audio.

10. Click on **OK** to accept the changes and close the dialog box. Alternatively, you can continue to the following sections for further adjustments.

Band Limiting Tab

This final tab of the Dynamics Processing dialog box allows you to set a range within which dynamics processing will occur. You simply set a high and low limit for the frequency, and the effects will be restricted to within that border.

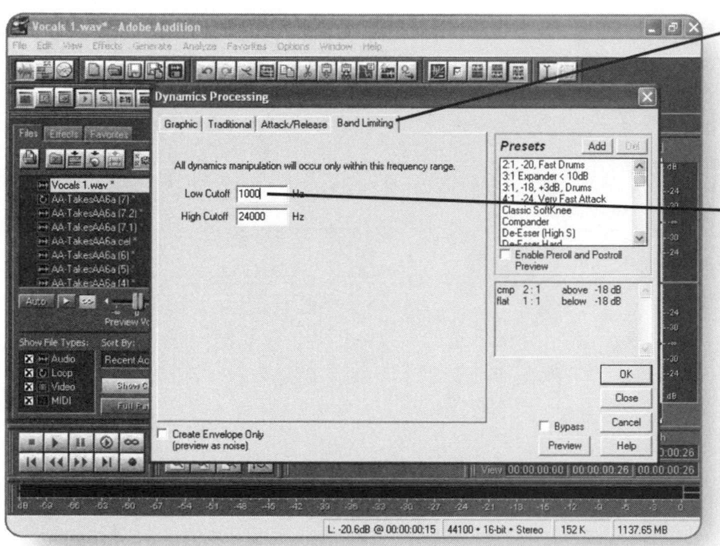

1. **Click** on the **Band Limiting tab**. The dialog box will change so that you can enter a low and high frequency cutoff.

2. **Double-click** in the **Low Cutoff box**. The number will be highlighted, allowing you to enter a new number.

3. **Type** a **value** for the Low Cutoff. Any frequency below this will not be affected by dynamics processing.

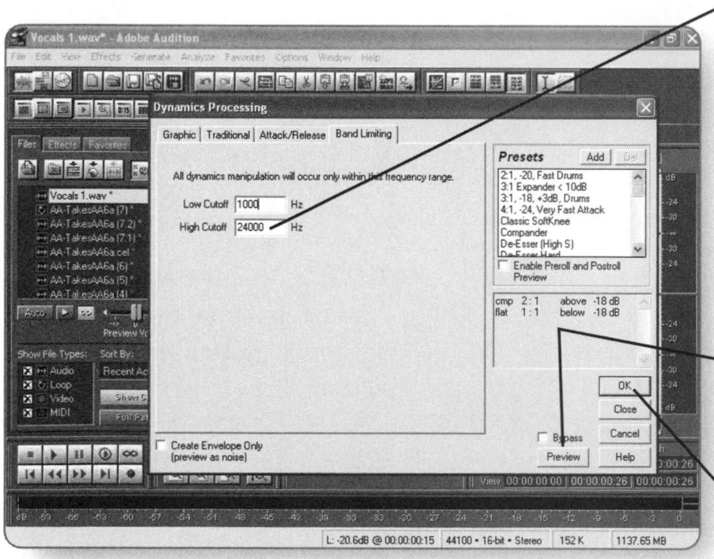

4. **Double-click** in the **High Cutoff box**. The number will be highlighted, allowing you to enter a new number.

5. **Type** a **value** for the High Cutoff. Any frequency higher than this will not be affected by dynamics processing.

6. **Click** on the **Preview button** to listen to how the effect sounds on your audio.

7. **Click** on **OK** to accept the changes and close the dialog box.

Envelope

In Chapter 7, editing envelopes within Multitrack view was covered. The Envelope effect in the Edit view provides you with even more control when manipulating the volume levels of a waveform. Just as in Multitrack view, an envelope provides you with a visual representation of the volume that can be adjusted at different points in your waveform.

1. Click and drag across the **selection** that you want to adjust. Alternatively, you can skip this step if you want to apply the envelope to the entire waveform.

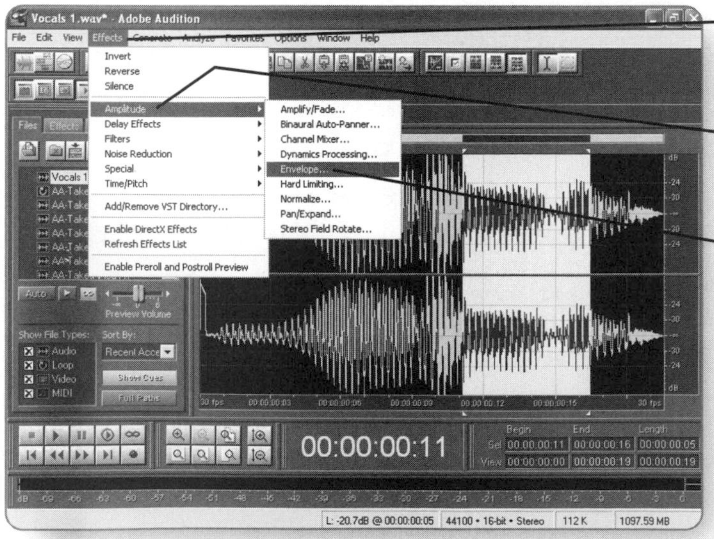

2. Click on **Effects**. The Effects menu will appear.

3. Click on **Amplitude**. A submenu will appear.

4. Click on **Envelope**. The Create Envelope dialog box will appear with a graph of your volume.

5. Click on a **preset envelope**. It will be highlighted. Alternatively, you can skip to Step 7 if you want to manually adjust the envelope.

6. Click on the **Preview button** to preview how the envelope will sound.

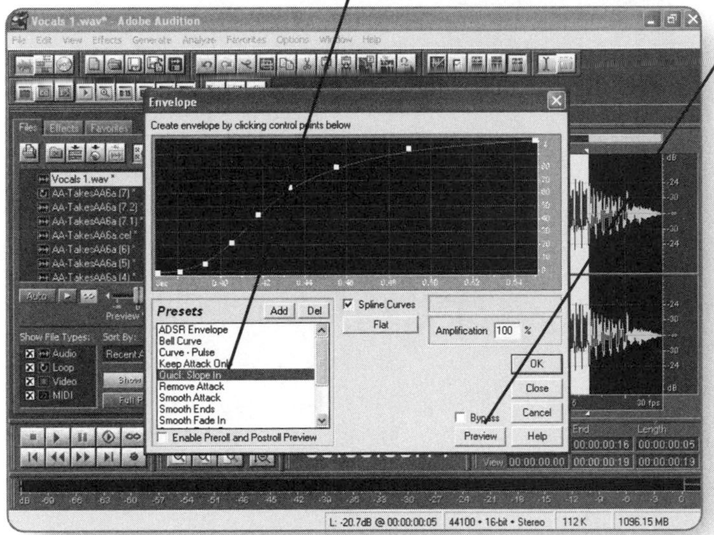

7. Position the **mouse pointer** over the envelope line at the point where you would like to adjust the volume level.

8. Click and drag up or down to adjust the envelope. Dragging upwards will increase the volume, whereas dragging downwards will decrease the volume.

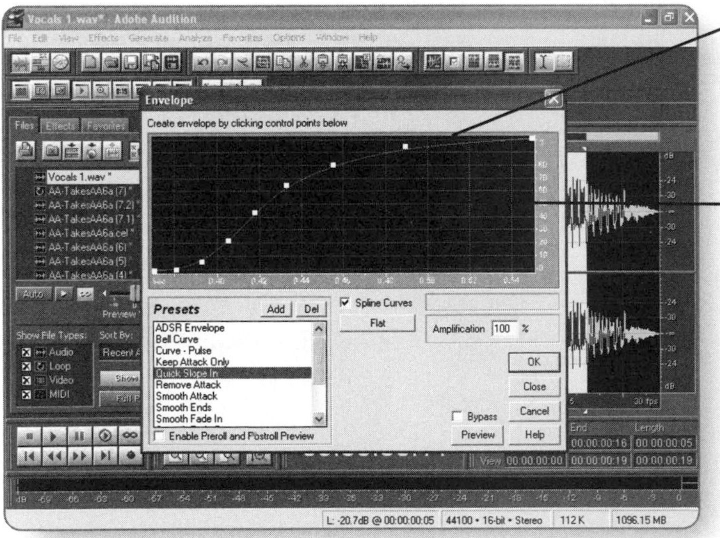

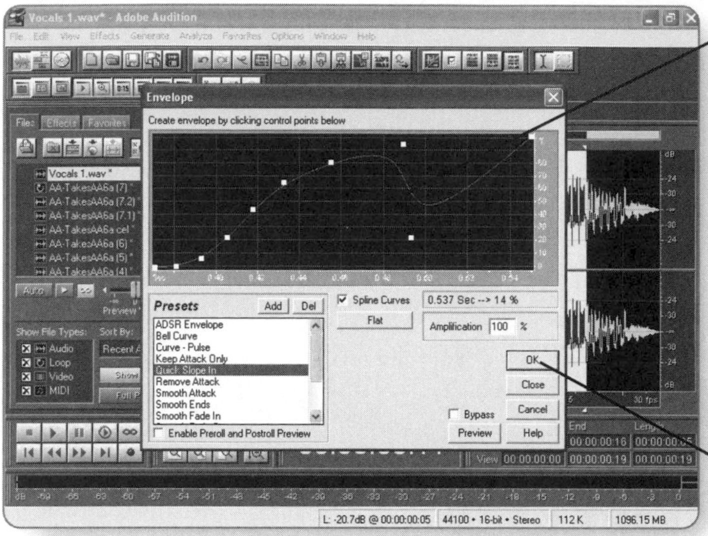

9. Release the **mouse button**. The envelope line will be adjusted.

10. Click on the **Preview button** to preview how the envelope will sound.

11. Repeat Steps 7–10 until you are satisfied with the audio volume levels.

12. Click on the **OK button**. The envelope will be applied to the audio and the dialog box will close.

Hard Limiting

Hard Limiting is one of those effects that if used properly can be of great help, but if used on the wrong file, it can have disastrous effects. Hard Limiting is meant for those waveforms that have occasional jumps in level. Hard Limiting will reduce levels at the jump points and amplify the rest of the waveform.

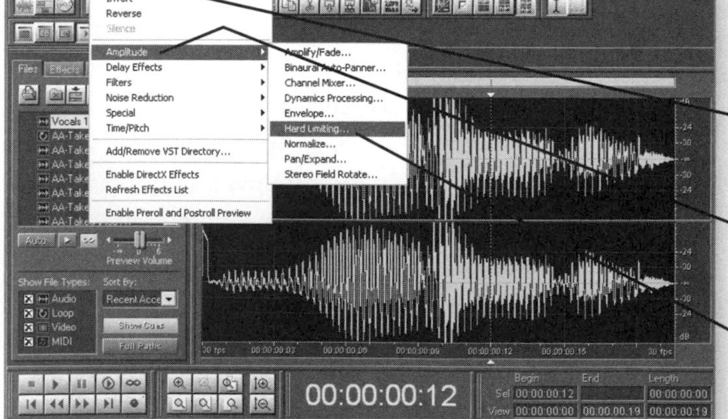

1. Click on **Effects**. The Effects menu will appear.

2. Click on **Amplitude**. A submenu will appear.

3. Click on **Hard Limiting**. The Hard Limiting dialog box will appear with a graph of your volume.

4. Click on the **Gather Statistics Now button**. This will show the percentage of the waveform that would be clipped without applying this effect.

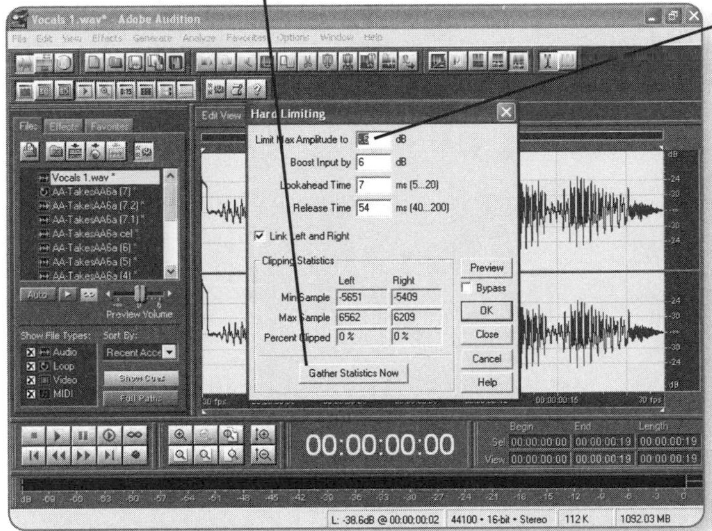

5. Double-click on the **Limit Max Amplitude to field box**. The box will be highlighted.

6. Type a **number**. This number represents the maximum sample amplitude that will be allowed.

> **TIP**
>
> If you are working with 16-bit audio, you should not set the Limit Maximum Amplitude level to more than –0.1dB.

7. Repeat Steps 5 and 6 for the other fields. These fields include: Boost Input By, Look Ahead Time, and Release Time.

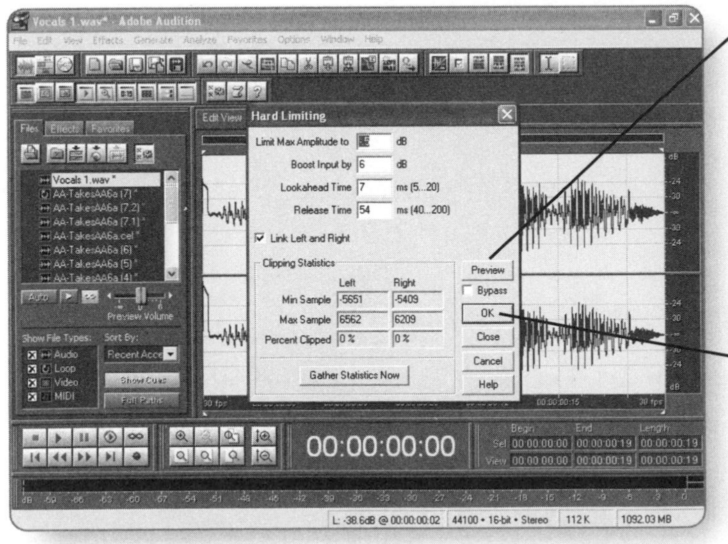

8. Click on the **Preview button**. You will be able to listen to the effect as it is applied to your audio.

9. Readjust any of the **settings** that you made until the effect is just right.

10. Click on **OK**. The dialog box will close and the effect will be applied.

Normalize

The Normalize effect will increase the dB level of a selection or an entire waveform, up to a maximum of 0dB. This is the maximum level that can be set before clipping will occur. Take, for example, a waveform that has a high point of –20dB and a low point of –30dB. Running Normalize at 100% would raise the high point to 0dB (the max point before clipping) and it would raise the lowest point to –10dB, because the amount of amplification has to be even throughout.

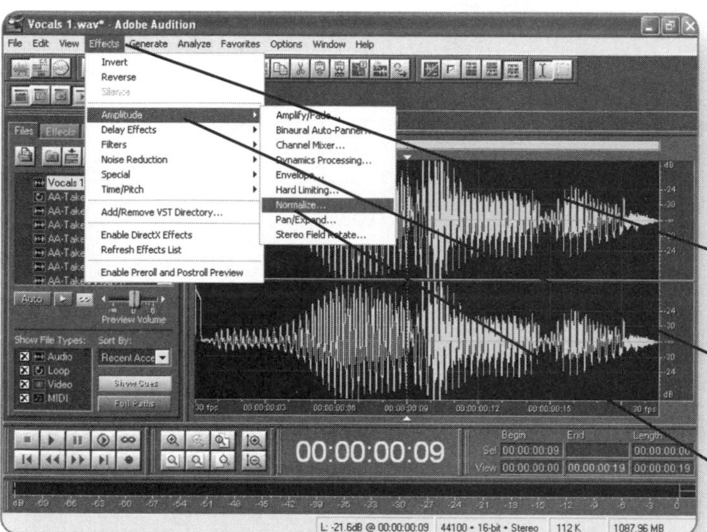

1. Click on **Effects**. The Effects menu will appear.

2. Click on **Amplitude**. A submenu will appear.

3. Click on **Normalize**. The Normalize dialog box will open.

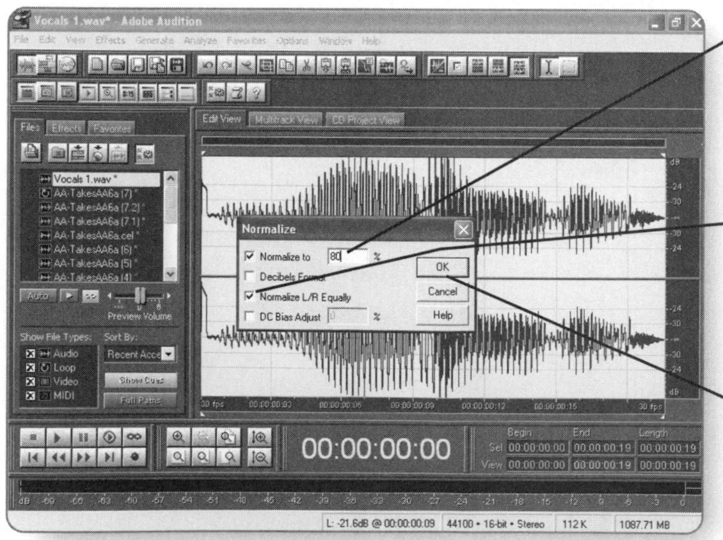

4. Type in a **number**. This number represents the maximum percentage to Normalize.

5. Click on the **check boxes** beside any of the other options you would like to enable or disable.

6. Click on **OK**. The settings will take effect and the dialog box will close.

Pan/Expand

As its name would suggest, the Pan/Expand effect allows you to either pan the audio from one channel to another or expand (or narrow) the stereo separation of the channels. You can select from preset settings or you can manually adjust the graphs to adjust the settings.

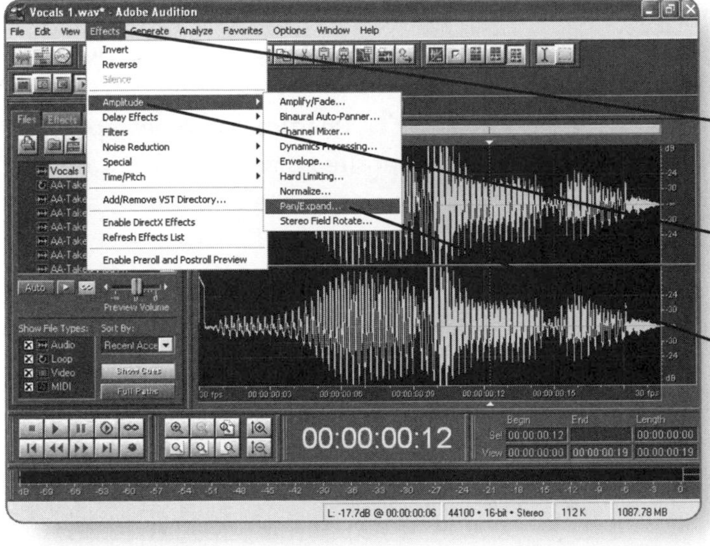

1. **Click** on **Effects**. The Effects menu will appear.

2. **Click** on **Amplitude**. A submenu of effects will appear.

3. **Click** on **Pan/Expand**. The Pan/Expand dialog box will open.

4. **Click** on a **preset**. The two graphs in the dialog box will change to show the effect on pan and expand.

5. **Click** on the **Preview button**. You can audition the effect on your audio.

6. **Click** on **OK** if you are satisfied with your audio. The settings will take effect and the dialog box will close. Otherwise, you can manually adjust the settings by following the directions in the next section.

Manually Adjusting Pan

The top window in the Pan/Expand dialog box is a graph that represents how the audio will flow from the left and right channels through the duration of the song. Anything above center will be stronger on the left channel and anything below will be stronger on the right.

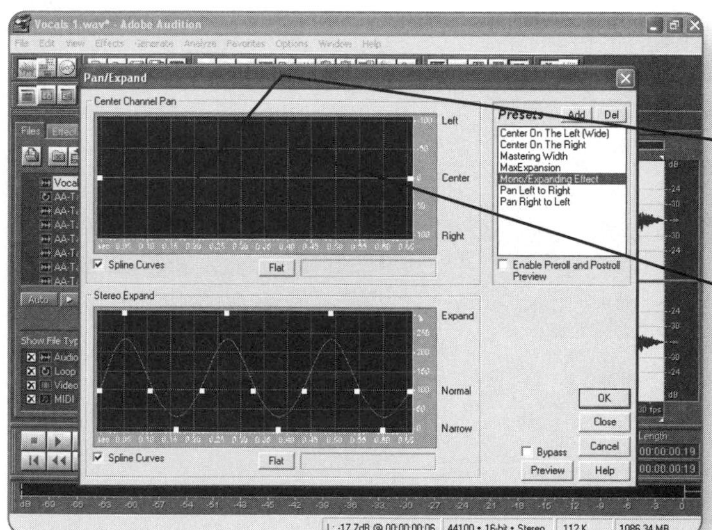

1. **Position** the **mouse pointer** at the point on the line where you want to adjust the pan line.
2. **Click and drag** the **line** to the desired location. A handle will be created as soon as you begin dragging.

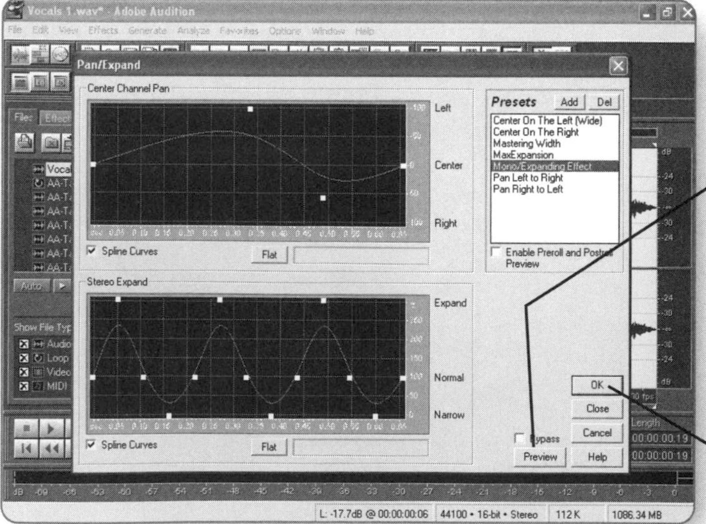

3. **Release** the **mouse button**. The line will be adjusted to this point.
4. **Click** on the **Preview button** to listen to the effect that adjusting the pan had on your audio.
5. **Repeat Steps 1-4** until you are satisfied with the audio.
6. **Click** on the **OK button** to accept the changes and close the dialog box.

Manually Adjusting Expand

Every stereo track has two channels, left and right. The difference between the two channels is called the surround channel, and the sum of the two is called the center channel. Using the Stereo Expand graph, you can increase or decrease the differences between the channels, which helps create a wider stereo image.

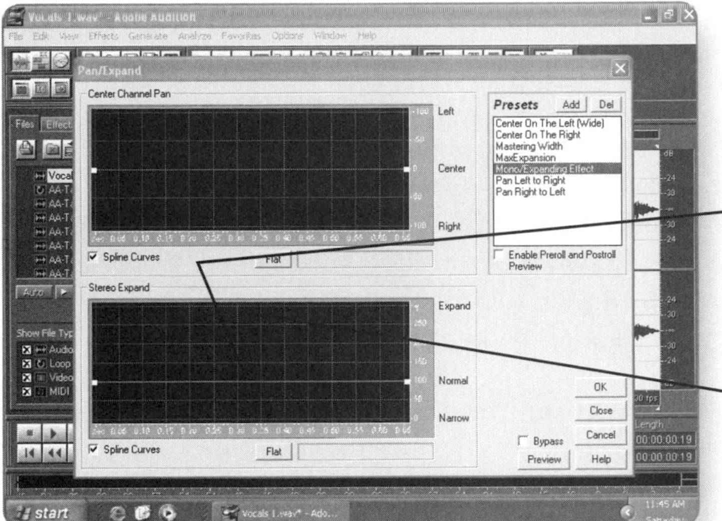

1. **Position** the **mouse pointer** at the point on the line where you want to adjust the expand line.

2. **Click and drag** the **line** to the desired location. A handle will be created as soon as you begin dragging.

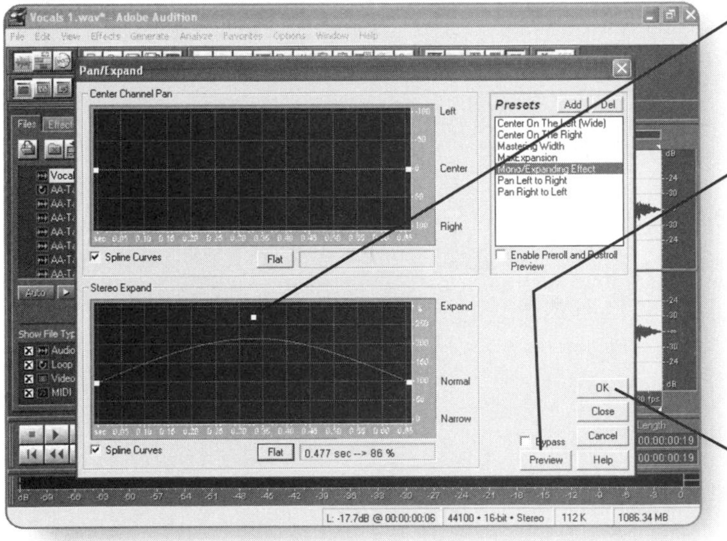

3. **Release** the **mouse button**. The line will be adjusted to this point.

4. **Click** on the **Preview button** to listen to the effect that adjusting the expand had on your audio.

5. **Repeat Steps 1-4** until you are satisfied with the audio.

6. **Click** on the **OK button** to accept the changes and close the dialog box.

> **TIP**
>
> You can reset the graphs in the Pan/Expand dialog box to their default state by clicking the Flat option.

Stereo Field Rotate

Imagine two people having a conversation while riding a Ferris wheel. If you were listening to the audio of the conversation, their voices would seem to be moving. The Stereo Field Rotate effect allows you to create the illusion of movement in your audio by providing you with a graph that plots time against degrees, which you can manipulate.

1. **Click** on **Effects**. The Effects menu will appear.

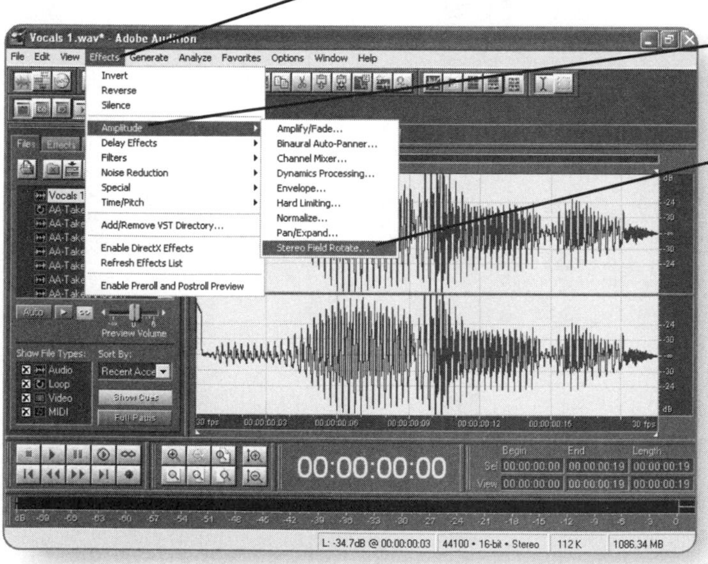

2. **Click** on **Amplitude**. A submenu of effects will appear.

3. **Click** on **Stereo Field Rotate**. The Stereo Field Rotate dialog box will open.

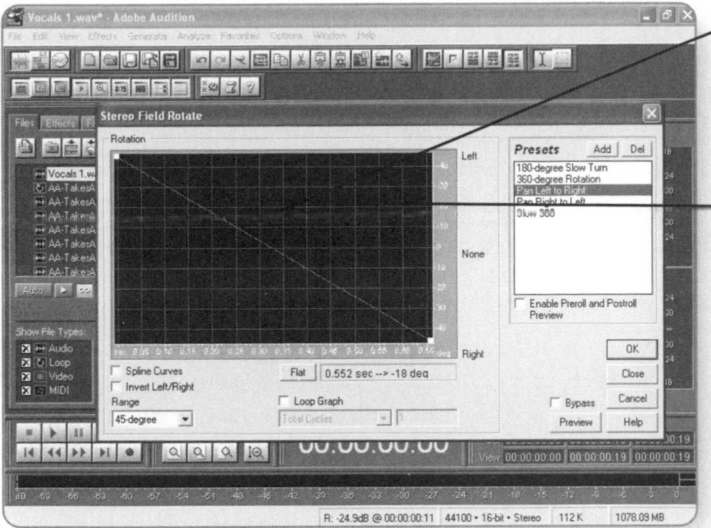

4. Position your **mouse pointer** over the point on the line that you would like to adjust.

5. Click and drag to the desired **location**. As soon as you click, a white handle will appear on the line.

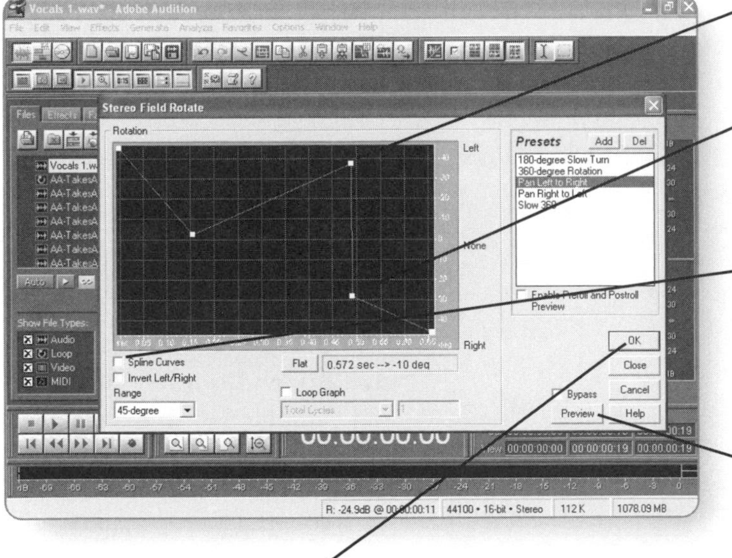

6. Release the **mouse button**. The graph will be reshaped.

7. Repeat Steps 4-6 with any other areas of the graph that you would like to adjust.

8. Click in the **Spline Curves check box** if you would prefer curves rather than straight lines for your graph adjustments.

9. Click on the **Preview button** to hear how the changes to your audio sound.

10. Click on **OK** to accept the changes and close the dialog box.

Time/Pitch Effects

You don't need a flux capacitor or the ability to fly around at supersonic speeds to be able to manipulate time in Adobe Audition. Within the software, there are three powerful tools for changing how a piece of audio sounds over time. These effects allow you to adjust the pitch, tempo, and panning of your waveforms.

Doppler Shifter

When I was younger we lived near a railway track, and every day the train would pass by. The sound would start off as a low murmur in the distance, getting stronger and stronger as it got closer to our house. Then it would roar by and then slowly fade away into the distance. Using the Doppler Shifter, you can create the illusion of movement in sound, such as a train passing by, an airplane taking off, or a racecar speeding around a track. The Doppler Shifter will alter both the pitch and the panning of audio over a period of time.

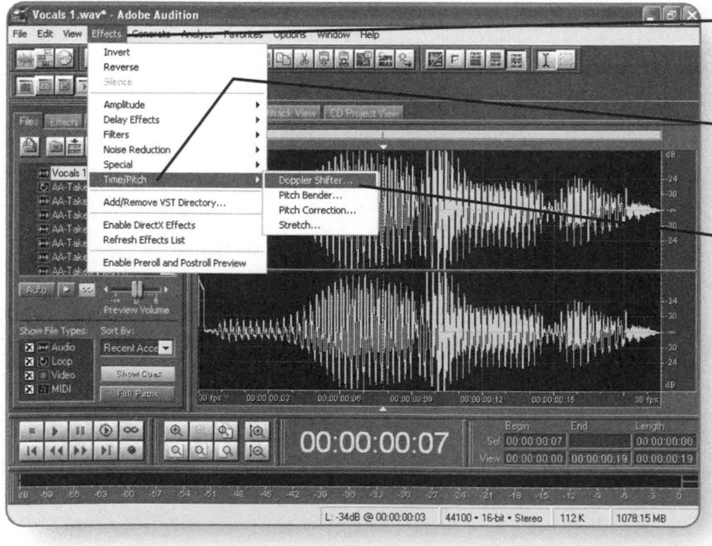

1. **Click** on **Effects**. The Effects menu will appear.

2. **Click** on **Time/Pitch**. A submenu of effects will appear.

3. **Click** on **Doppler Shifter**. The Doppler Shifter dialog box will open and you will be presented with a visual representation of the pitch of your audio.

4. **Click** on a **preset** that most closely matches the effect you are trying to accomplish. The preset will be highlighted and a graphical representation of that effect will appear in the dialog box.

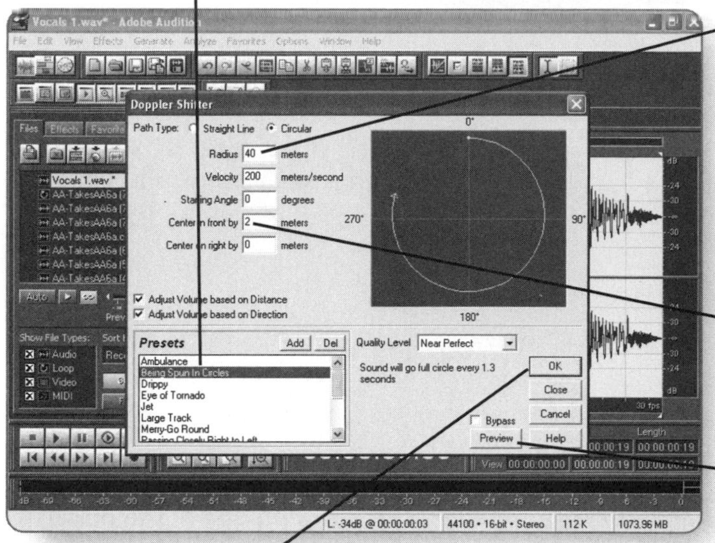

5. **Double-click** in any **field box**. The box will become highlighted.

6. **Type** a **new number** for the setting that you have selected. It will appear as you type.

7. **Repeat Steps 5 and 6** for any of the other settings that you would like to adjust.

8. **Click** on the **Preview button** to listen to how the effect sounds on your audio.

9. **Click** on **OK** to accept the changes and close the dialog box.

Pitch Bender

The Pitch Bender dialog box will plot the pitch of your audio onto a graph. You can then alter the pitch by changing the graph manually or selecting one of the presets. If you ever wanted to take your voice and make it sound like one of those creepy kidnappers, this effect is for you. It can take any soprano and turn them into Barry White at the click of a mouse button.

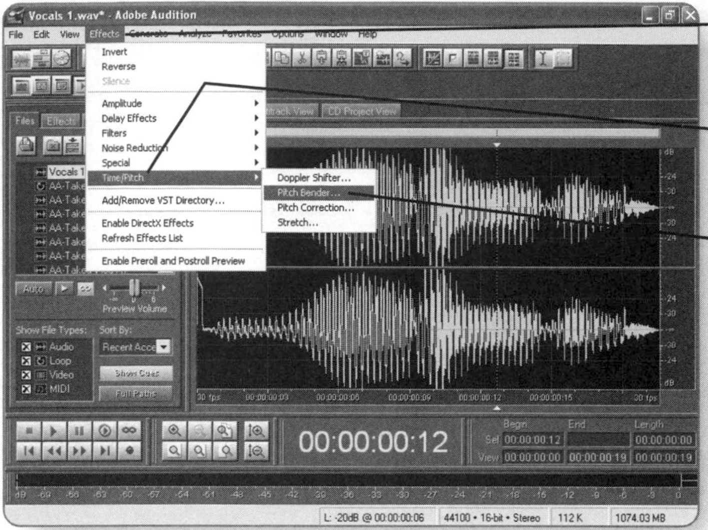

1. **Click** on **Effects**. The Effects menu will appear.

2. **Click** on **Time/Pitch**. A submenu of effects will appear.

3. **Click** on **Pitch Bender**. The Pitch Bender dialog box will open and you will be presented with a visual representation of the pitch of your audio.

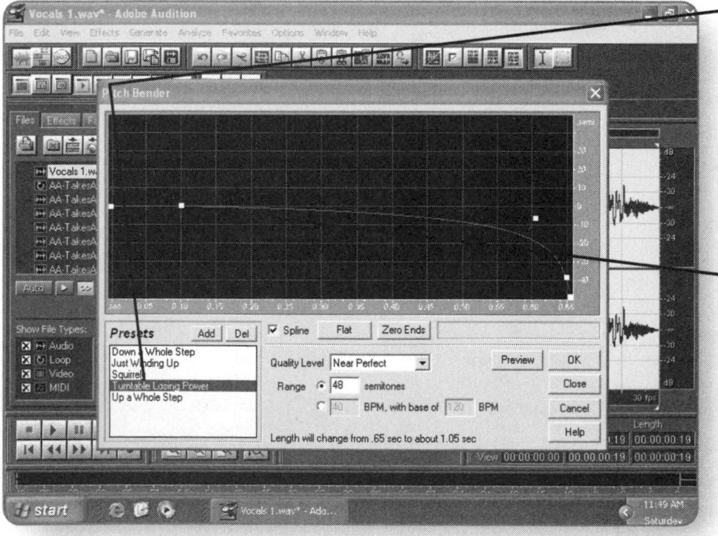

4. **Click** on **one** of the **presets**. It will be highlighted. Alternatively, you can create a manual adjustment of the pitch by continuing with Step 5. Otherwise, skip to Step 9.

5. **Position** your **mouse pointer** over the point on the line that you would like to adjust.

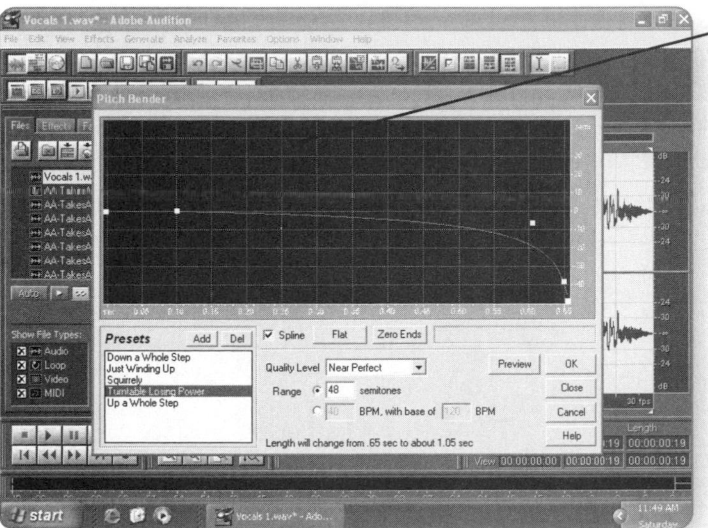

6. Click and drag to the desired **location**. As soon as you click, a white handle will appear on the line.

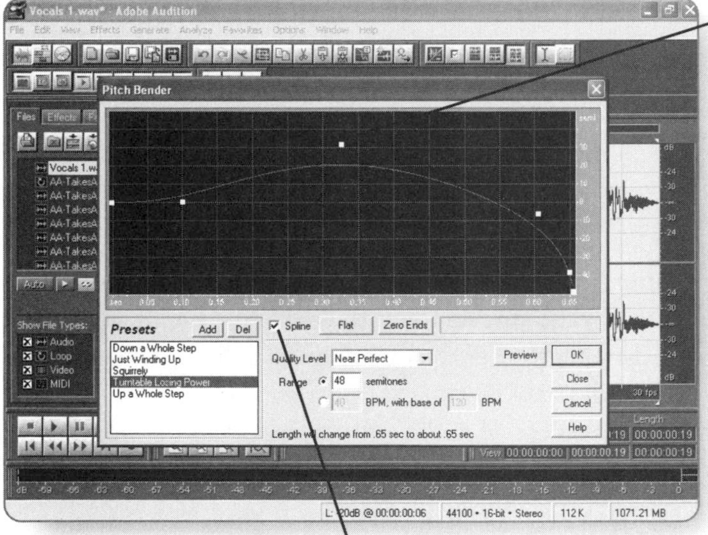

7. Release the **mouse button**. The graph will be repositioned based on where you released the mouse button.

> **TIP**
>
> If you want to create a constant pitch change throughout the selected audio, drag only the first and last white handle so that the graph of the pitch is a straight horizontal line.

8. Click on the **Spline check box** to enable or disable spline curves. When it's enabled, your graph will appear as curves between two points; otherwise, it will be straight lines.

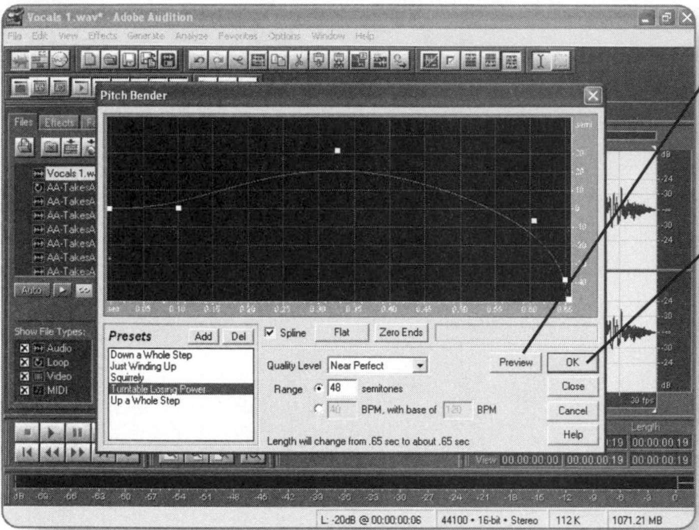

9. Click on the **Preview button** to listen to how your audio will sound with the effect applied to it.

10. Click on **OK** to apply the changes and close the dialog box.

> **TIP**
>
> Rather than using crossfades to fade a piece of audio in or out, try using the Turntable Losing Power preset or similar graph configuration as a way to bring audio in or out.

Changing Tempos Using Stretch

Most audio editing is about taking different pieces of audio, looping them, and mixing them to create the ultimate session. One problem that arises when you bring in audio files from different sources is that their tempos may not match. Putting together two pieces of audio with mismatched tempos sounds awkward at best. Within Adobe Audition you can change the tempo of the entire session, but this still won't help you if you have wave blocks with different tempos. The Stretch function will allow you to change the tempo of a block of audio to match others. Not only can you adjust tempos with the Stretch effect, you can also adjust the pitch of the selection. Whether pitch or tempo gets affected is determined by the choice you make in Step 5 below.

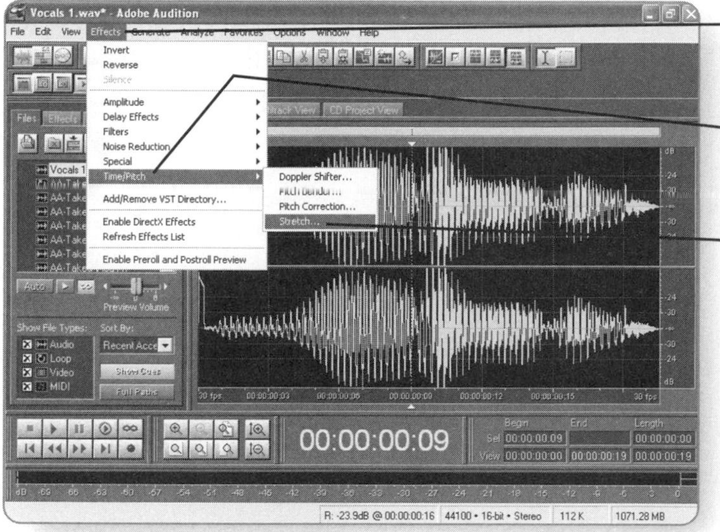

1. **Click** on **Effects**. The Effects menu will appear.

2. **Click** on **Time/Pitch**. A submenu of effects will appear.

3. **Click** on **Stretch**. The Stretch dialog box will open. You can now alter the tempo and pitch of your audio.

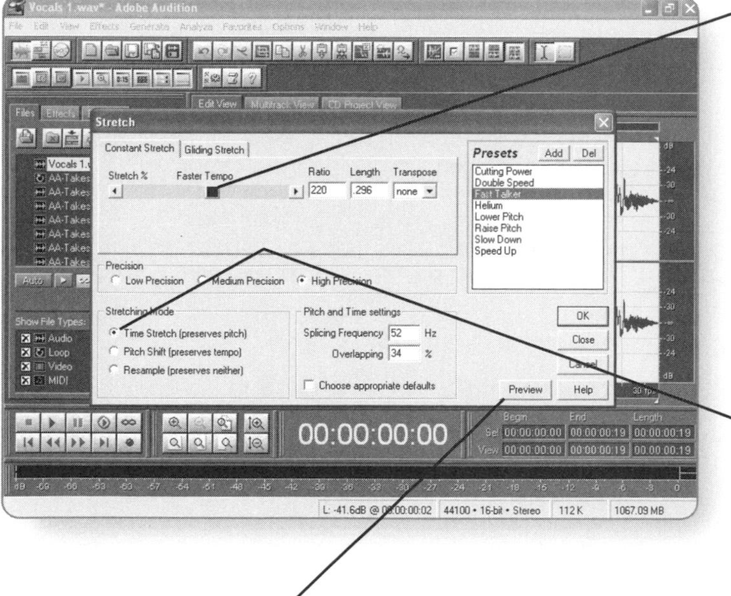

4. **Click and drag** the **Faster Tempo scroll box** to the right or the left. As you drag, the number in the Ratio box will change. When at 100% the audio will not be affected at all. Anything above 100% will increase the tempo or pitch, and anything below 100% will decrease the tempo or pitch.

5. **Click** on the **circle** beside the desired Stretching Mode. One mode preserves the pitch, one preserves the temp, and the third preserves neither.

6. **Click** on the **Preview button** to listen to how your audio sounds with the effect applied to it.

7. Click on **OK** to apply the changes and close the dialog box.

10

Special Effects

Adobe Audition comes with a laundry list of different effects that you can apply to your audio files. Some of these effects have very practical uses, whereas others are simply there to create weird, cool, funky, and creative sounds. The process of applying special effects in Audition is quite simple. Each effect has a dialog box associated with it, from which you can adjust the various settings.

In this chapter, you'll learn how to:

- Apply special effects
- Create and save presets
- Use alternate methods for applying effects

Delay Effects

Typically, delay effects work by playing the original audio, then creating a copy of that audio that is changed in some respect, and then playing it along with or after the original audio. Using the delay effects, you can create different types of echoes and reverbs that result in some interesting sounding effects.

> **NOTE**
>
> If you don't create a selection before you apply an effect, the effect will be applied to your entire wave file.

Chorus

If you want to create the illusion of many people singing or playing an instrument, but don't have a lot of friends who can carry a tune, don't worry, Audition has the answer. The Chorus effect allows you to specify as many people as you want to be singing or playing a piece of audio. There are several different settings that you can adjust to change the way your virtual choir sounds.

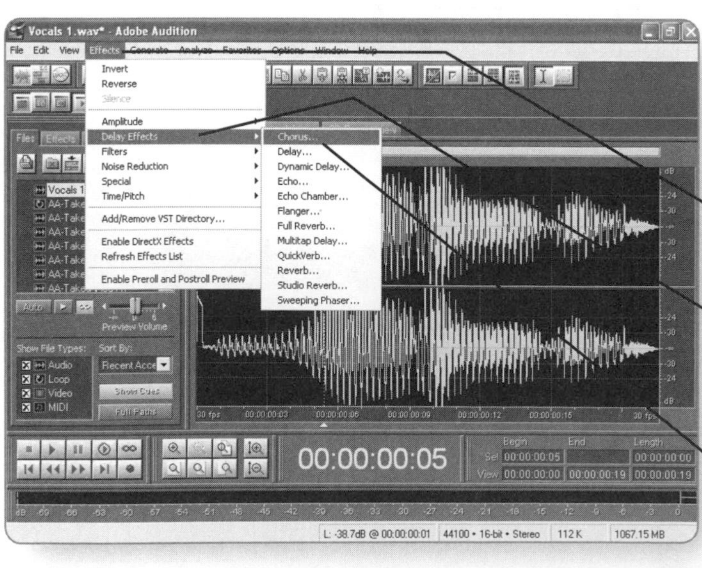

1. **Click** on **Effects**. The Effects menu will appear.

2. **Click** on **Delay Effects**. A submenu of different delay effects will appear.

3. **Click** on **Chorus**. The Chorus dialog box will open, allowing you to adjust the settings for that effect.

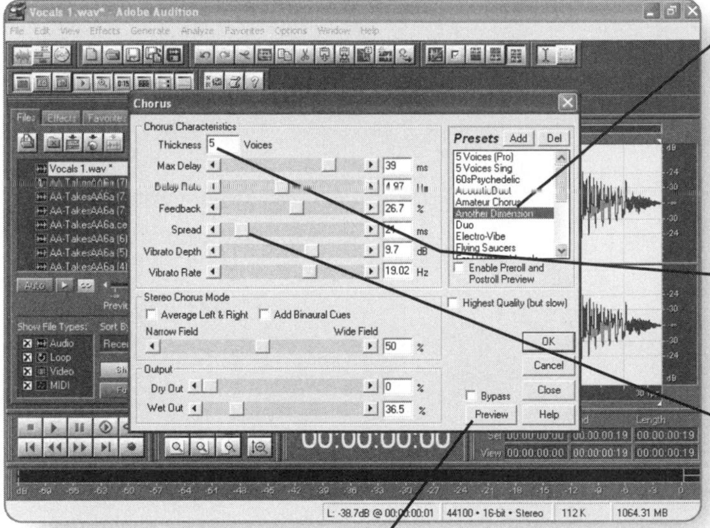

4. Click on a **preset** that most closely matches the effect you'd like to achieve for your audio. Alternatively, you can skip to Step 5 and manually adjust the settings.

5. Type the **number** of voices you want to sing your piece of audio.

6. Click and drag any of the **slider boxes** to adjust the settings.

7. Click on the **Preview button**. You will hear how your audio sounds with the effect applied. If you are satisfied, you can proceed to Step 8; otherwise, repeat Steps 5 and 6.

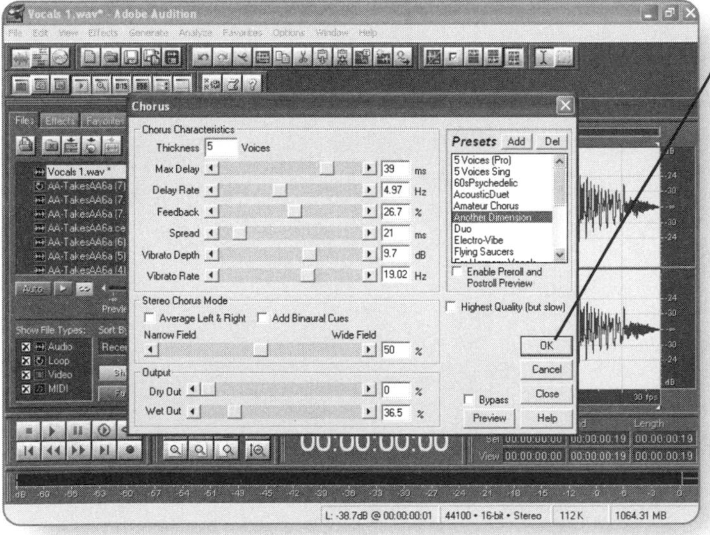

8. Click on **the OK button**. The changes you made will be accepted and the dialog box will close.

Delay

The Delay effect will repeat your audio, delayed by a specific amount of time that you specify. With the Delay effect, you not only adjust the delay time but you also adjust the mixing of the original signal and the delayed signal.

1. **Click** on **Effects**. The Effects menu will appear.

2. **Click** on **Delay Effects**. A submenu of different delay effects will appear.

3. **Click** on **Delay**. The Delay dialog box will open, allowing you to adjust the settings for that effect.

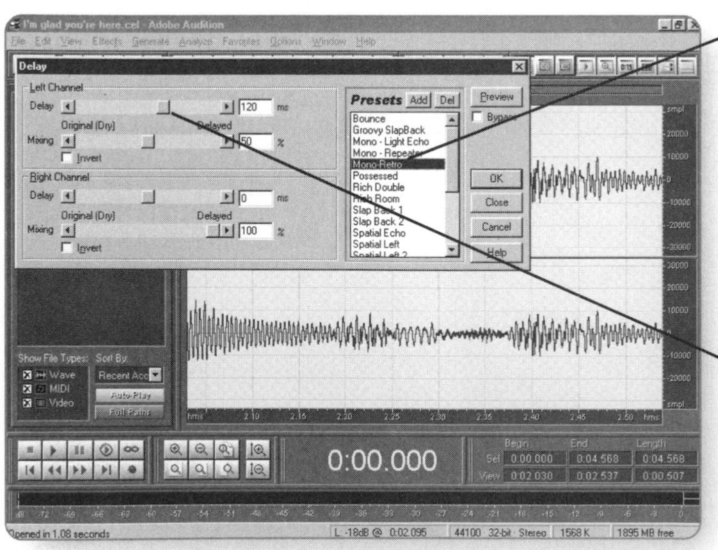

4. **Click** on a **preset** that most closely matches the effect you'd like to achieve for your audio. Alternatively, you can skip to Step 5 and manually adjust the settings.

5. **Click and drag** the **Left Channel Delay scroll box** to the left or right. This will allow you to set the delay amount in milliseconds.

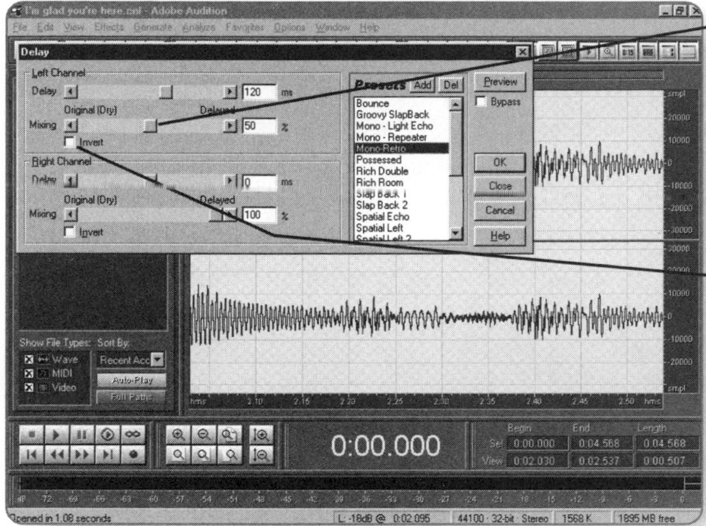

6. Click and drag the **Left Channel Mixing scroll box** to the left or right. This will allow you to set the percentage that the delayed signal will mix with the original signal.

7. Click on the **Invert check box** if you want to change the positive values of the selected waveform to negative values.

8. Repeat Steps 5-7 for the Right Channel.

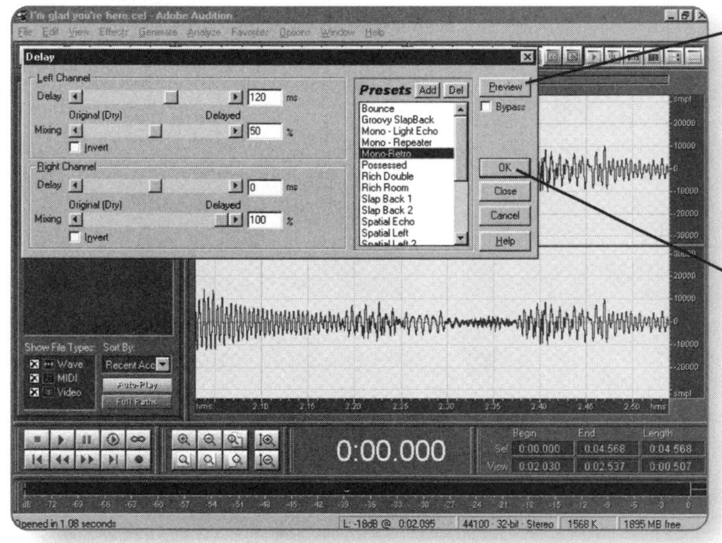

9. Click on the **Preview button**. You will hear how your audio sounds with the effect applied. If you are satisfied, you can proceed to Step 10; otherwise, repeat Steps 4-8.

10. Click on the **OK button**. The changes you made will be accepted and the dialog box will close.

Dynamic Delay

Using the Delay effect, you set a delay that is constant throughout your selection or the entire waveform. With the Dynamic Delay effect, you can specify different delays for different sections of your waveform.

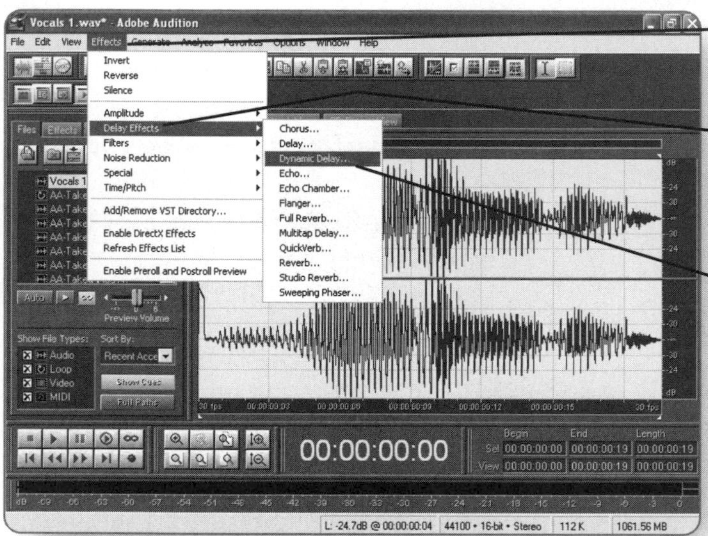

1. **Click** on **Effects**. The Effects menu will appear.
2. **Click** on **Delay Effects**. A submenu of different delay effects will appear.
3. **Click** on **Dynamic Delay**. The Dynamic Delay dialog box will open, allowing you to adjust the settings for that effect.

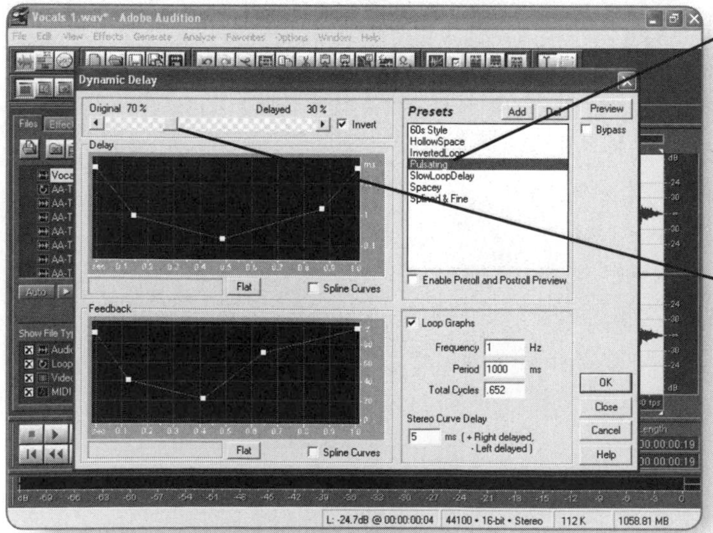

4. **Click** on a **preset** that most closely matches the effect you'd like to achieve for your audio. Alternatively, you can skip to Step 5 and manually adjust the settings.
5. **Click and drag** the **Mixing scroll box** left or right. This will allow you to set the percentage that the delayed signal will mix with the original signal.

6. **Position** your **mouse pointer** over the line in the Delay graph. This graph is a visual representation of the delay in your audio. The x axis represents the point in time and the y axis represents the length of the delay in milliseconds.

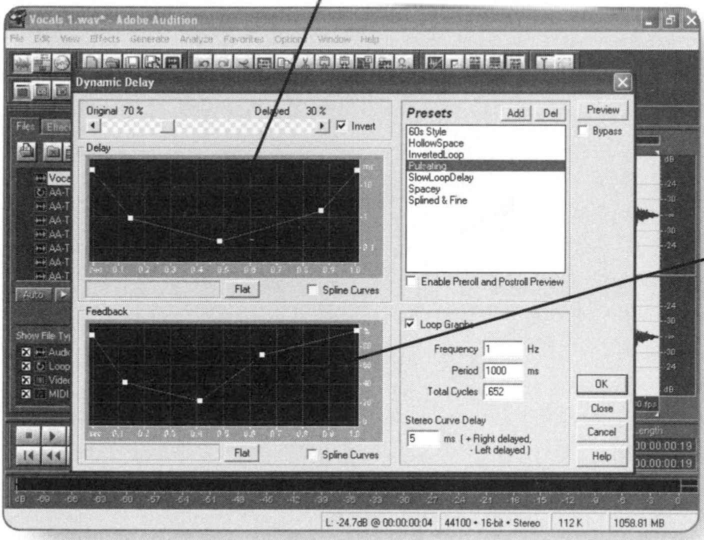

7. **Click and drag** the **point on the graph** to a new location to adjust the setting. A handle will appear on the graph as soon as you click.

8. **Position** your **mouse pointer** over the line in the Feedback graph. This graph represents the amount of feedback for the delay.

9. **Click and drag** the **point on the graph** to a new location to adjust the setting. A handle will appear on the graph as soon as you click.

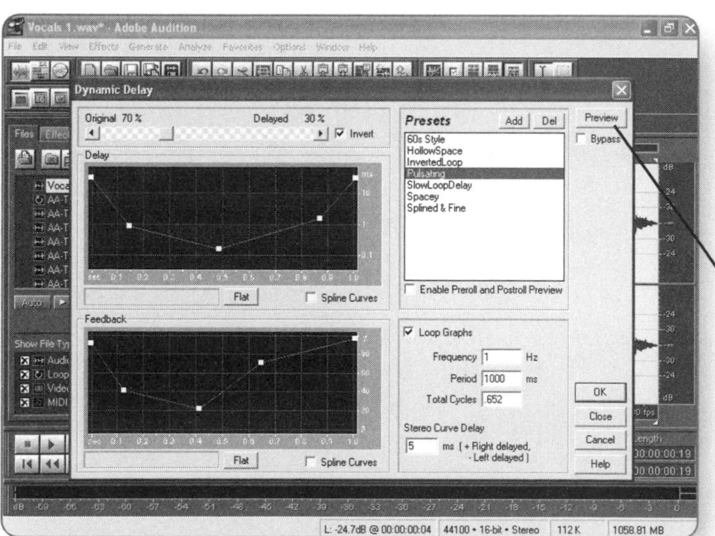

> **TIP**
>
> You can click on the Flat button at any time to reset either of the graphs.

10. **Click** on the **Preview button**. You will hear how your audio sounds with the effect applied. If you are satisfied, you can proceed to Step 11; otherwise, repeat Steps 5-9.

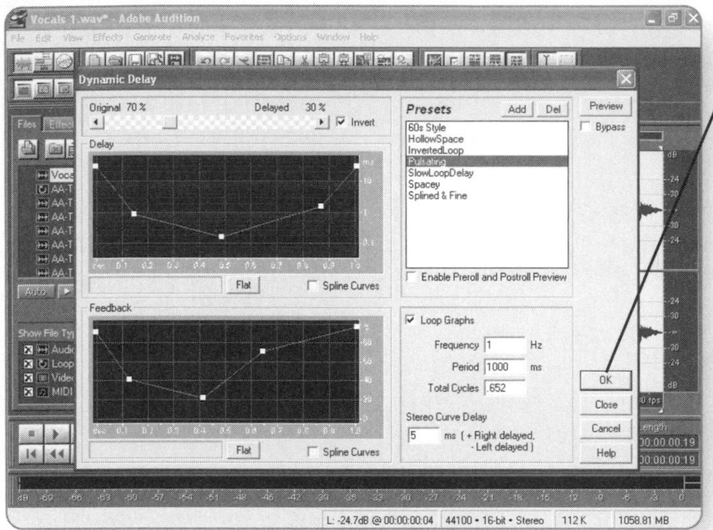

11. Click on the **OK button**. The changes you made will be accepted and the dialog box will close.

Echo

Unlike the Delay effect that creates one constant echo, the Echo effect allows you to create multiple echoes that can fade away, away, away, away, away.

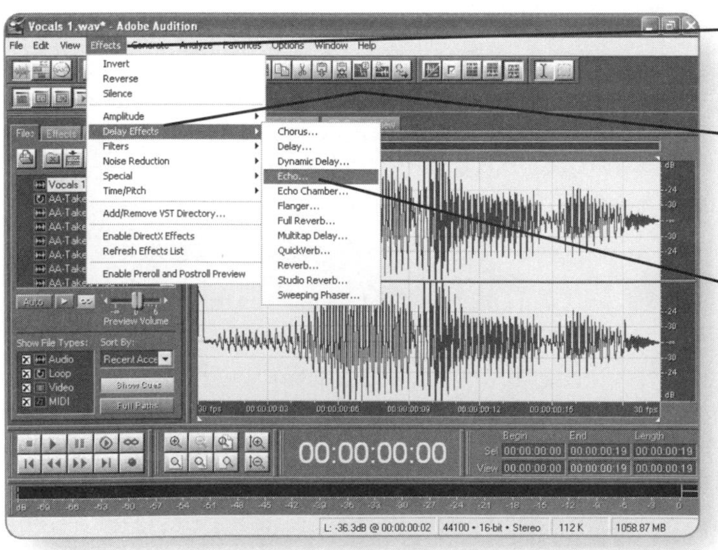

1. Click on **Effects**. The Effects menu will appear.

2. Click on **Delay Effects**. A submenu of different delay effects will appear.

3. Click on **Echo**. The Echo dialog box will open, allowing you to adjust the settings for that effect.

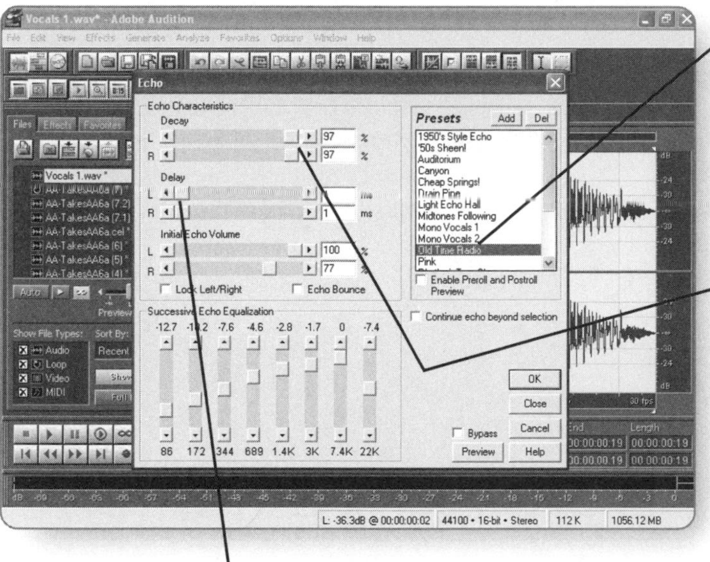

4. Click on a **preset** that most closely matches the effect you'd like to achieve for your audio. Alternatively, you can skip to Step 5 and manually adjust the settings.

5. Click and drag the **Decay scroll box** left or right. Decay determines how quickly the echo will fade away. For example, if you set a level of 50%, the first echo will be half the force of the original sound, the next echo will be half of that, and so on until it can't be heard.

6. Click and drag the **Delay scroll box** left or right. This will determine the length of time between each echo.

7. Click and drag the **Initial Echo Volume scroll box** left or right. This will determine how much of the original signal will be mixed with the echo.

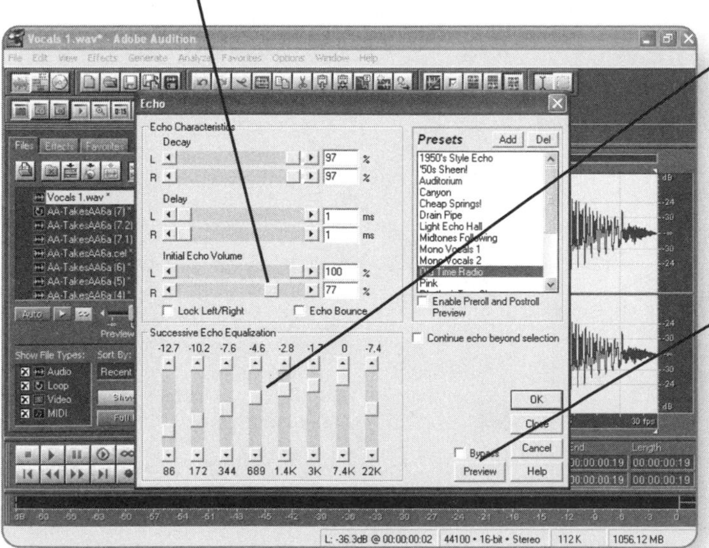

8. Click and drag any of the **Successive Echo Equalization scroll boxes** up or down to adjust their settings. This will allow you to specify the order of decay for each frequency.

9. Click on the **Preview button**. You will hear how your audio sounds with the effect applied. If you are satisfied, you can proceed to Step 10; otherwise, repeat Steps 5-8.

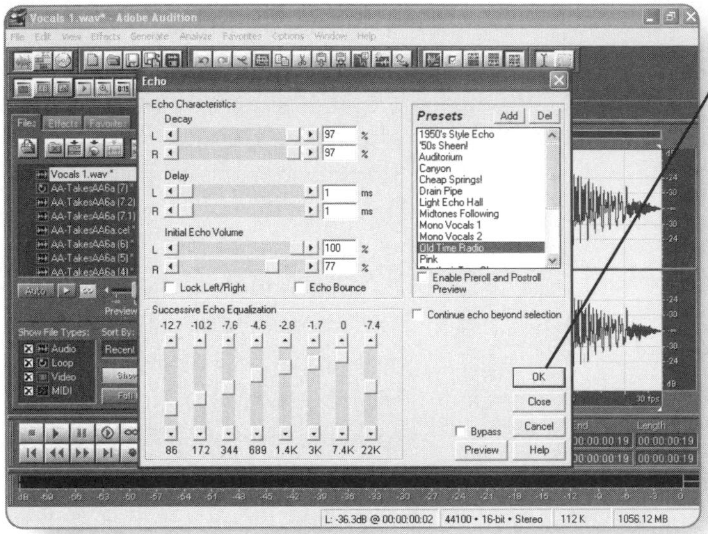

10. Click on the **OK button**. The changes you made will be accepted and the dialog box will close.

Echo Chamber

Imagine being able to perform in a room of any size, dimension, and material. That's what the Echo Chamber effect allows you to do. The effect allows you to create a virtual room in which you can play your audio. And, you can change the characteristics of the room to change the ambiance.

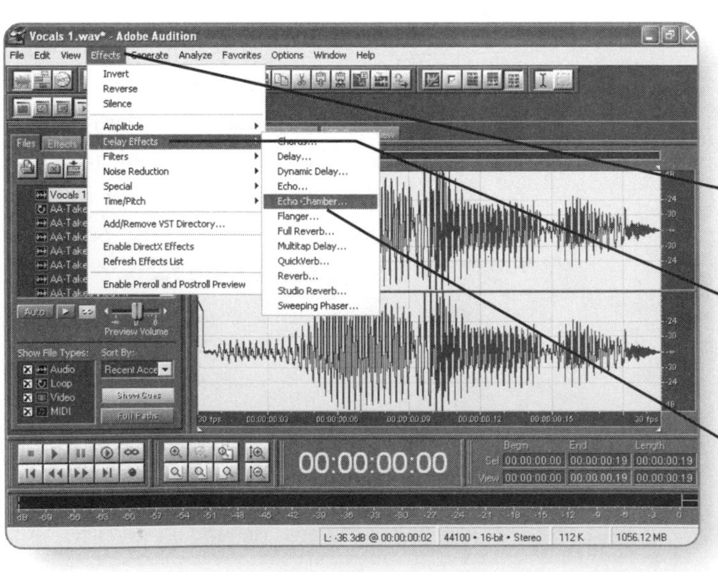

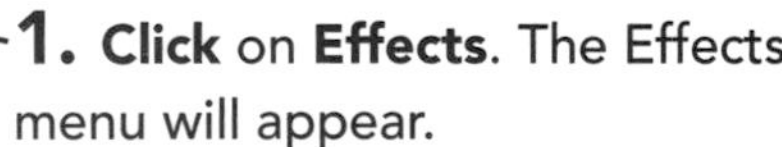

1. Click on **Effects**. The Effects menu will appear.

2. Click on **Delay Effects**. A submenu of different delay effects will appear.

3. Click on **Echo Chamber**. The Echo Chamber dialog box will open, allowing you to adjust the settings for that effect.

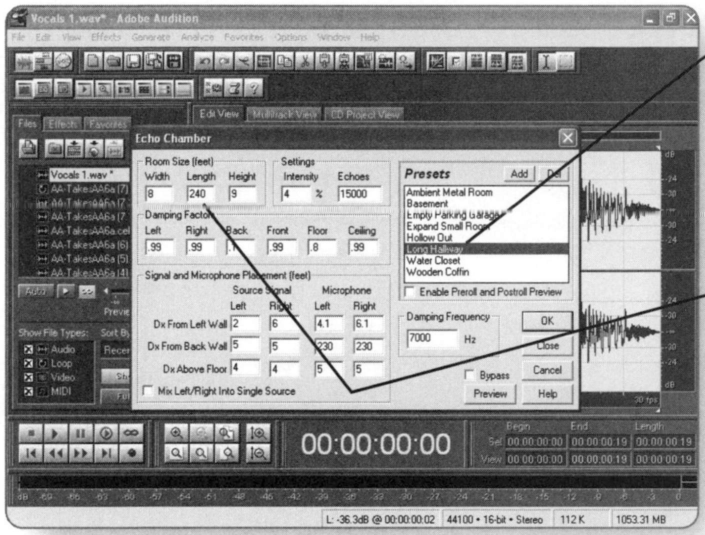

4. Click on a **preset** that most closely matches the room type you would like to create for your echo. Alternatively, you can skip to Step 5 and manually adjust the settings.

5. Enter Room Size values. You can do this by **double-clicking** in any field and **typing** in the numbers. These numbers will represent the dimensions of the room in feet.

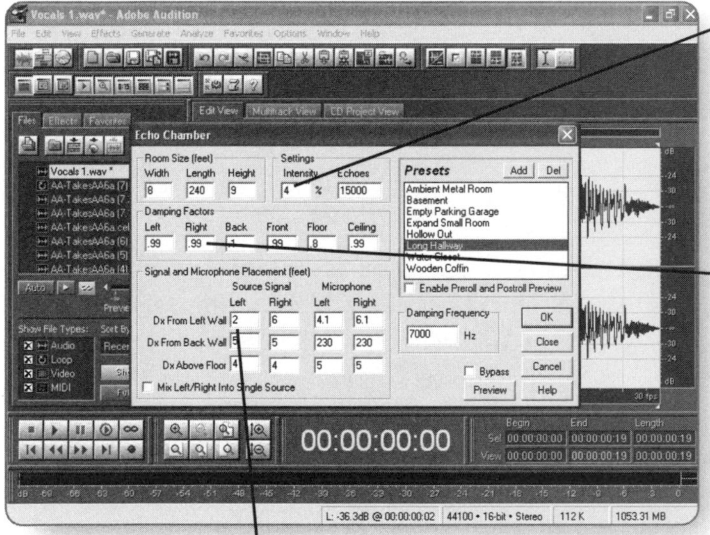

6. Enter Settings values. Intensity represents the percentage of amplitude of the original signal and Echoes represents the number of echoes that you would like to produce.

7. Enter Damping Factors values. These values will reflect things in the room that may deflect, absorb, or enhance the echo.

8. Enter Signal Source and Microphone Placement values. These values will indicate where in the room your audio is coming from and where the microphones are placed.

9. **Enter** a **Damping Frequency value**. This is the amount that the frequency will be decreased over time.

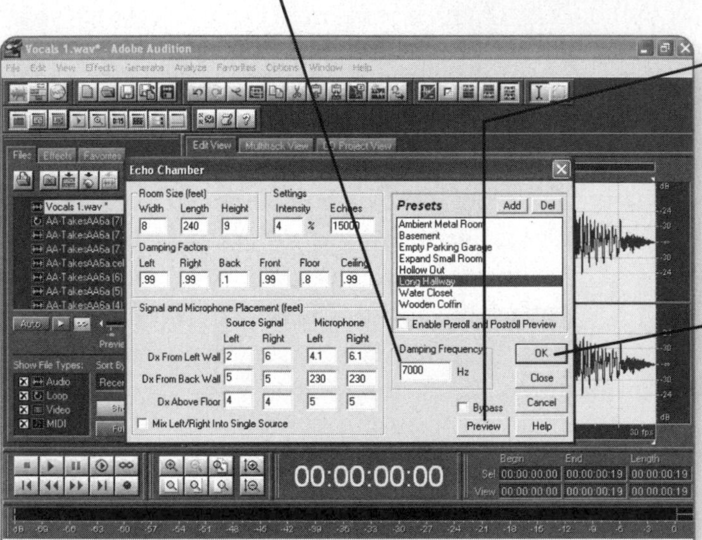

10. **Click** on the **Preview button**. You will hear how your audio sounds with the effect applied. If you are satisfied, you can proceed to Step 11; otherwise, repeat Steps 5-9.

11. **Click** on the **OK button**. The changes you made will be accepted and the dialog box will close.

Flanger

Flanging is the result of mixing an audio signal with a delayed duplicate of itself. This effect came about in the '60s, when audio would be recorded to tape machines. If you touched the rim of a tape reel (known as a flange), it would change the pitch and timing of the audio and create some unique-sounding effects. The Flanger effect in Audition provides several different adjustable settings.

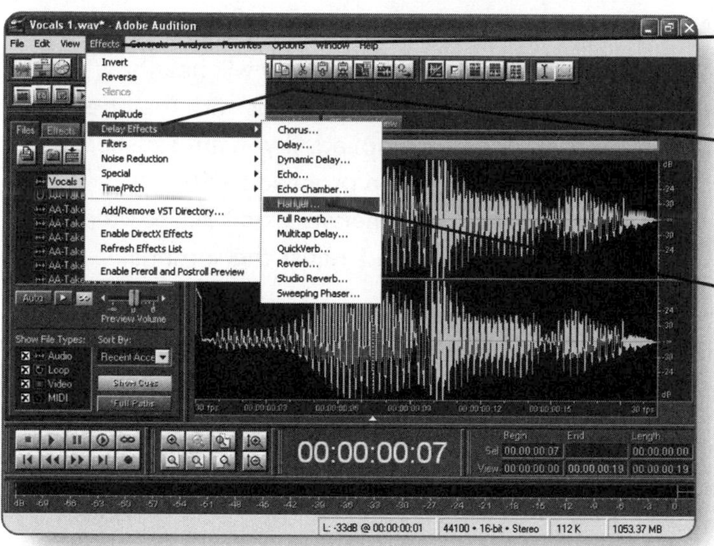

1. Click on **Effects**. The Effects menu will appear.

2. Click on **Delay Effects**. A submenu of different delay effects will appear.

3. Click on **Flanger**. The Flanger dialog box will open, allowing you to adjust the settings for that effect.

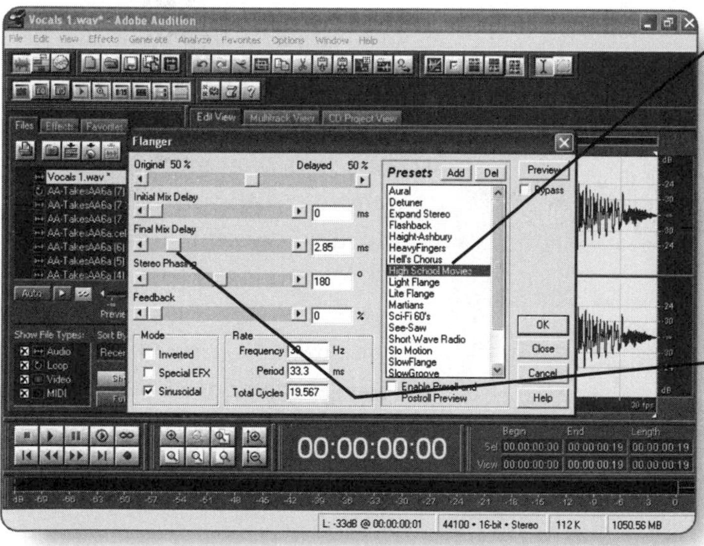

4. Click on a **preset** that most closely matches the type of effect that you would like to create. The Flanger effect has a long list of presets that you can choose from. Alternatively, you can skip to Step 5 and manually adjust the settings.

5. Click and drag any of the **scroll box settings** to adjust the levels. As you drag the scroll boxes, the values for each of the settings will change.

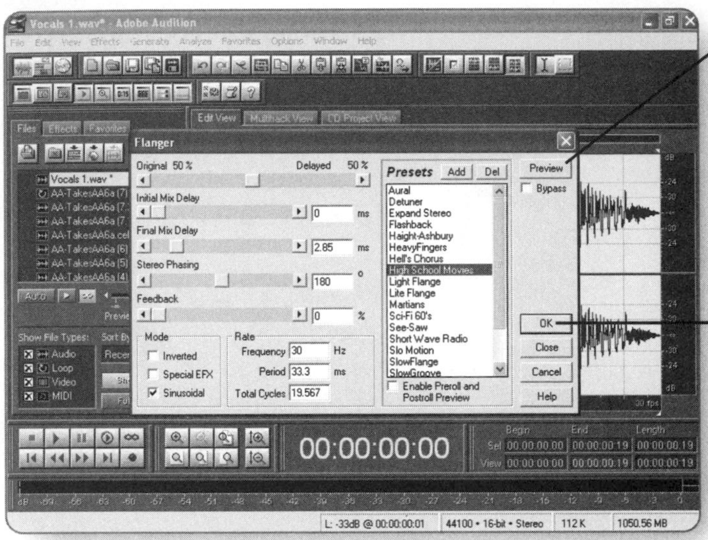

6. Click on the **Preview button**. You will hear how your audio sounds with the effect applied. If you are satisfied, you can proceed to Step 7; otherwise, go back to Step 5 and adjust the settings.

7. Click on the **OK button**. The changes you made will be accepted and the dialog box will close.

Full Reverb

In a nutshell, reverb is the environment that surrounds a piece of audio. The reason you sound so good singing in the shower rather than in an auditorium has a lot to do with the echo that is created with reverb. If you want to create a natural-sounding reverb for your audio, Full Reverb is the tool for you. The Full Reverb dialog box has a multitude of presets and settings to choose from.

1. Click on **Effects**. The Effects menu will appear.

2. Click on **Delay Effects**. A submenu of different delay effects will appear.

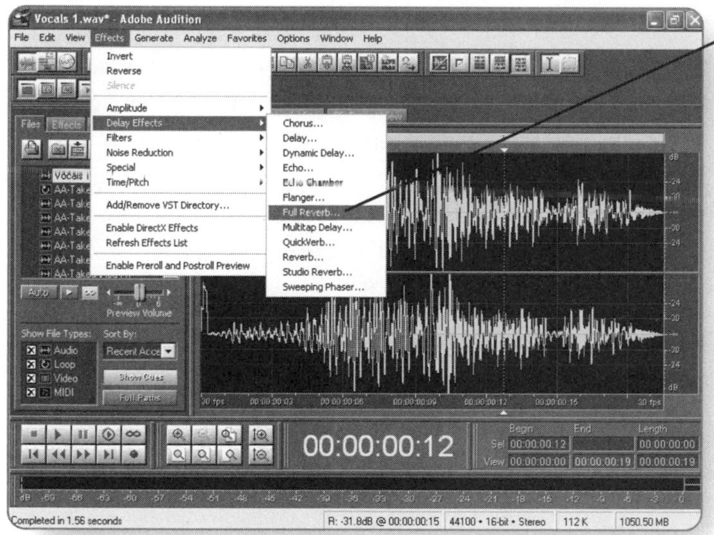

3. Click on **Full Reverb**. The Full Reverb dialog box will open, allowing you to adjust the settings for that effect.

4. Click on a **preset** that most closely matches the type of effect that you would like to create. Alternatively, you can skip to Step 5 and manually adjust the settings.

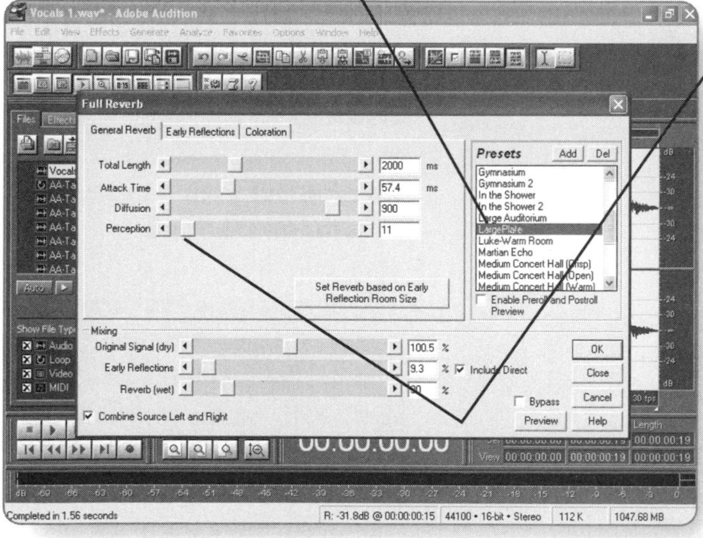

5. Click and drag any of the **scroll box settings**. These settings include:

- **Total Length**. This is the total length of time that it takes for your signal to decay to 60dB.
- **Attack Time**. This is how long it will take in milliseconds for the signal to reach its most powerful amplitude.
- **Diffusion**. This determines the quality of the echo, from very distinct to blended together.
- **Perception**. The greater the value for perception, the more external objects will affect the echo.

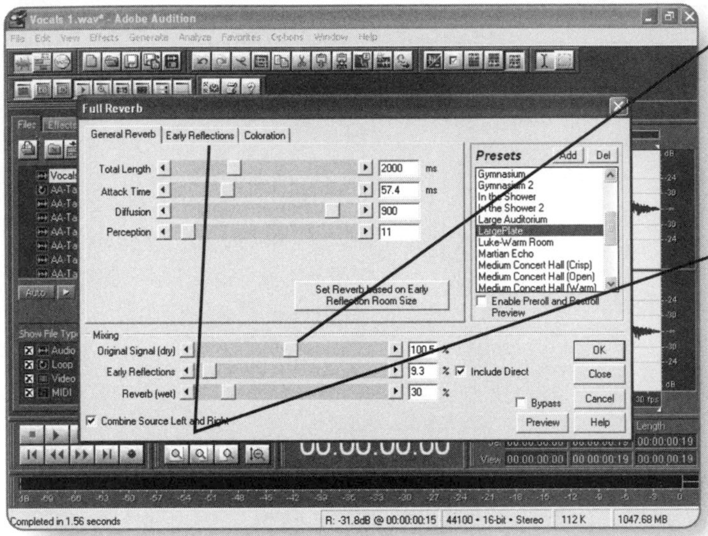

6. Click and drag the **sliders** to adjust the Mixing settings. This will allow you to control how the delay signal is mixed with the original signal.

7. Click on the **Early Reflections tab**. The Early Reflections tab will come to the front.

8. Click and drag the **sliders** to adjust the settings. These settings will allow you to adjust the dimensions and size of the virtual room that will create the reverb.

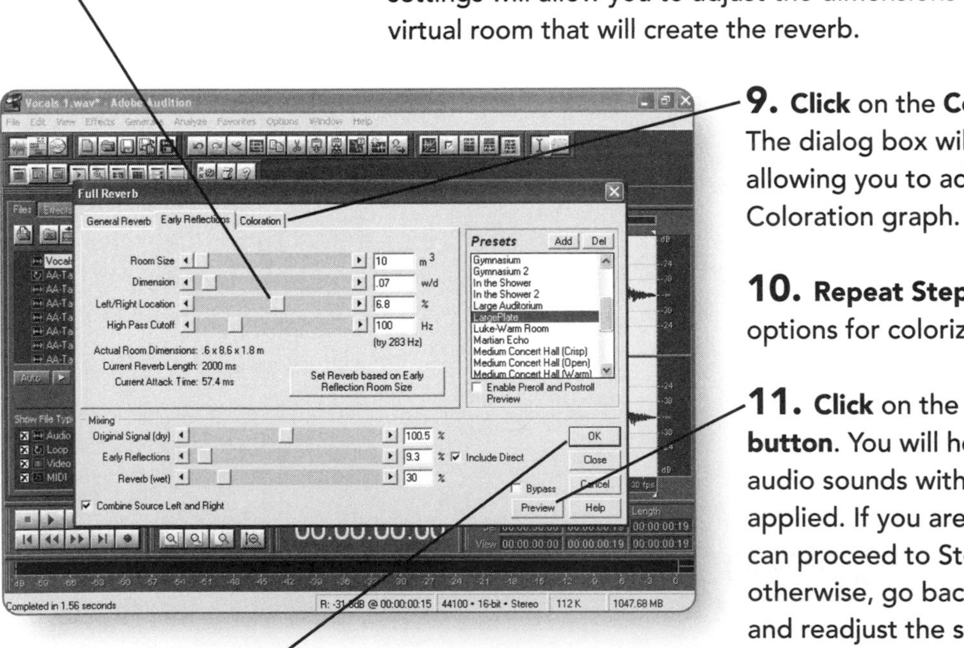

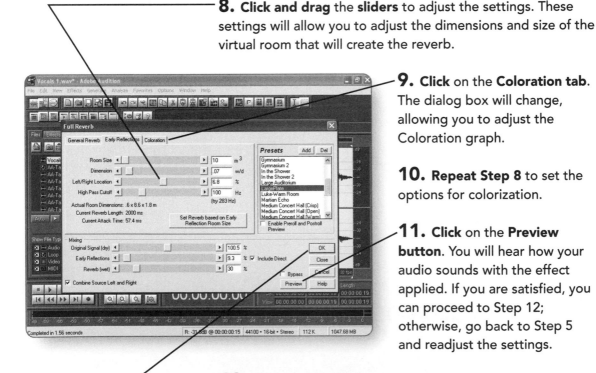

9. Click on the **Coloration tab**. The dialog box will change, allowing you to adjust the Coloration graph.

10. Repeat Step 8 to set the options for colorization.

11. Click on the **Preview button**. You will hear how your audio sounds with the effect applied. If you are satisfied, you can proceed to Step 12; otherwise, go back to Step 5 and readjust the settings.

12. Click on the **OK button**. The changes you made will be accepted and the dialog box will close.

Multitap

With the Multitap effect, you can create multiple echo effects that build on one another.

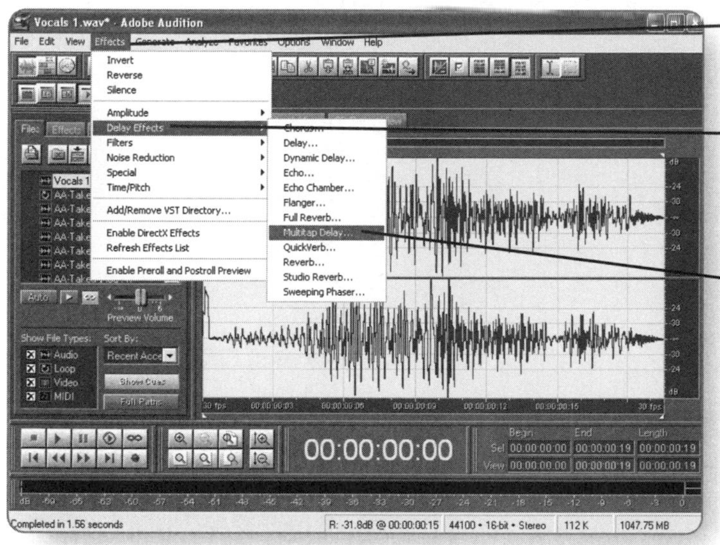

1. Click on **Effects**. The Effects menu will appear.

2. Click on **Delay Effects**. A submenu of different delay effects will appear.

3. Click on **Multitap Delay**. The Multitap Delay dialog box will open, allowing you to adjust the settings for that effect.

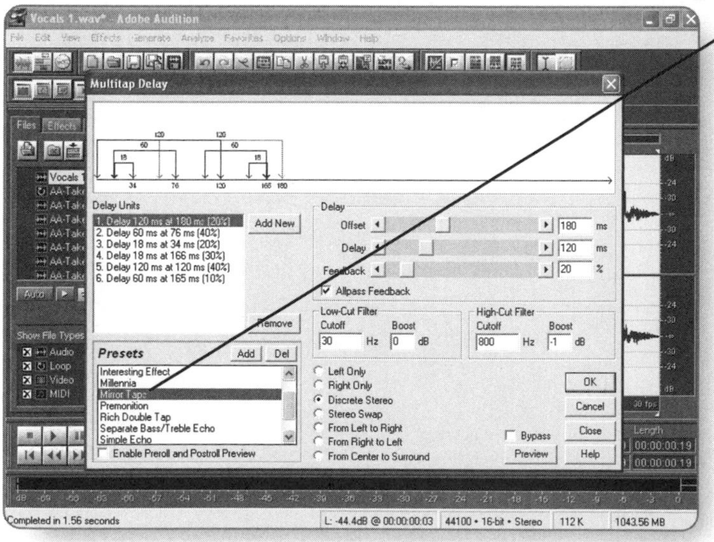

4. Click on a **preset** that most closely matches the type of effect that you would like to create. Alternatively, you can skip to Step 5 and manually adjust the settings.

5. **Click** on the **first echo** in the Delay units list. It will be highlighted.

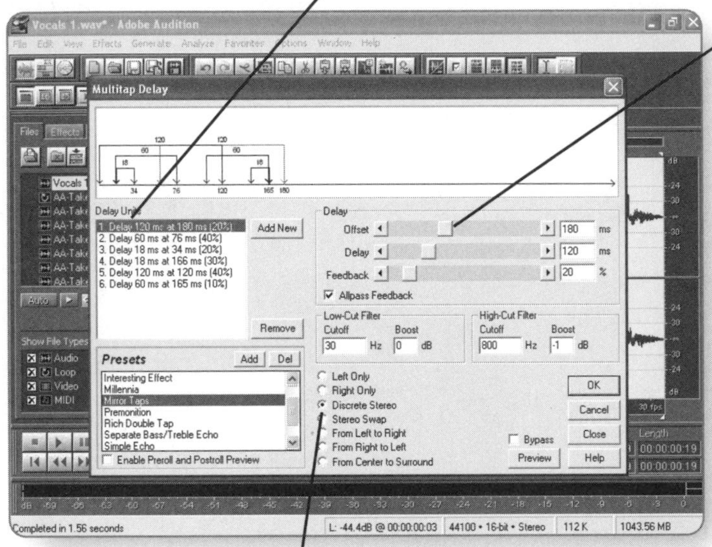

6. **Click and drag** the **scroll boxes** to adjust the settings. Your options include:

- **Offset**. The Offset indicates where in the delay the audio will begin to be mixed to cause an echo.
- **Delay**. The Delay is the time in milliseconds between echoes.
- **Feedback**. Feedback is the amount of original signal that is to be mixed with the echo.

7. **Click** on the **circle** beside the desired channel option. A dot will appear in the circle.

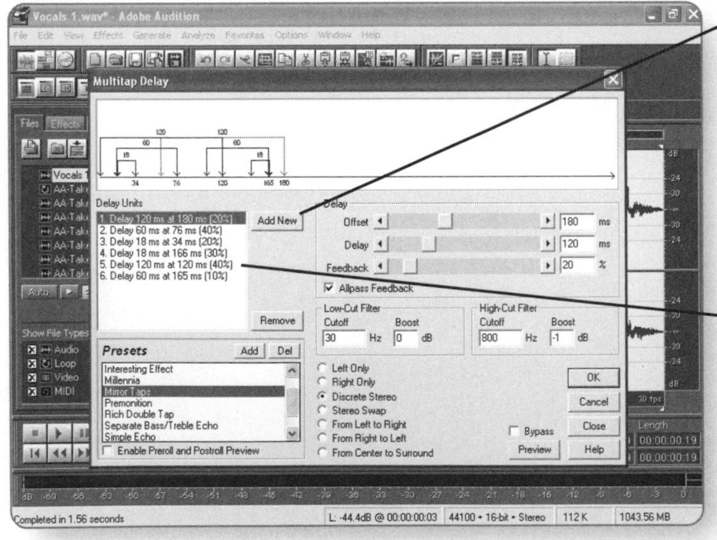

8. **Click** on the **Add New button** to enter settings for another echo.

9. **Repeat Steps 5-8** for this echo. Each echo can have its own settings.

10. **Repeat Steps 8-9** until you have added the desired number of echoes. You can add up to a maximum of ten echoes.

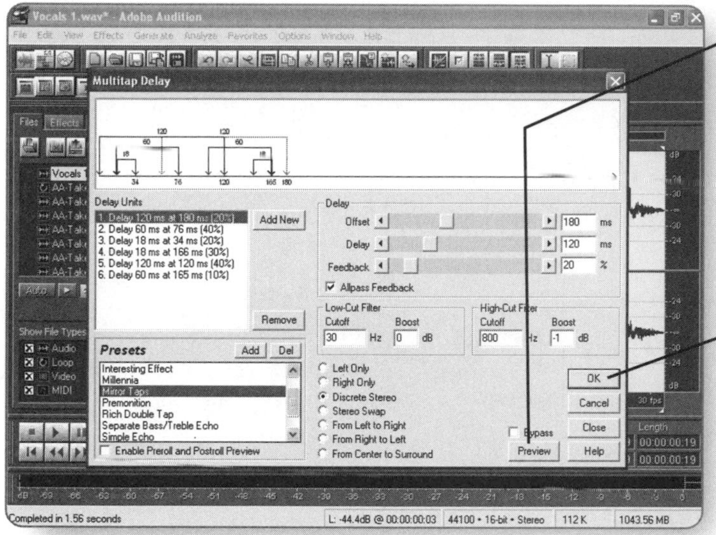

11. Click on the **Preview button**. You will hear how your audio sounds with the echoes applied. If you are satisfied, you can proceed to Step 12; otherwise, go back to Step 5 and readjust the settings.

12. Click on the **OK button**. The changes you made will save and the dialog box will close.

QuickVerb

QuickVerb is a fast way to create reverb on your audio, because it doesn't tax system resources like other reverb methods. Even though it doesn't use as many system resources, the QuickVerb effect still provides you with a variety of options and settings.

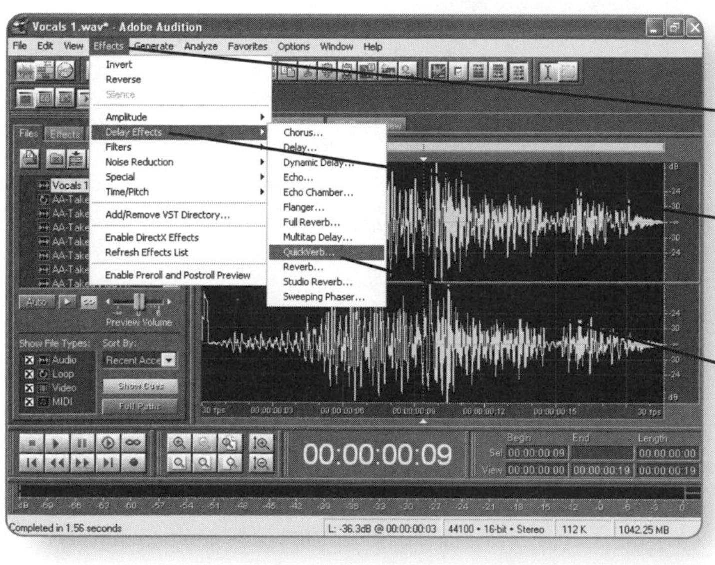

1. Click on **Effects**. The Effects menu will appear.

2. Click on **Delay Effects**. A submenu of different delay effects will appear.

3. Click on **QuickVerb**. The QuickVerb dialog box will open, allowing you to adjust the settings for that effect.

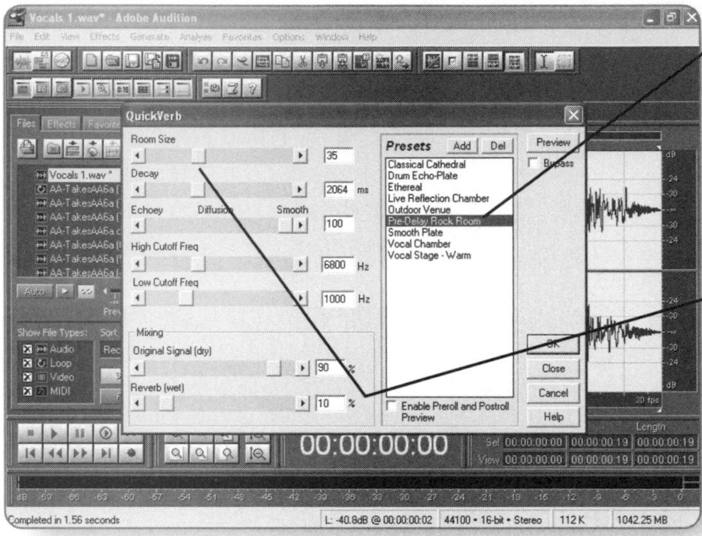

4. **Click** on a **preset** that most closely matches the type of effect that you would like to create. Alternatively, you can skip to Step 5 and manually adjust the settings.

5. **Click and drag** any of the **scroll box settings** to adjust their levels. As you drag the scroll boxes, the values for each of the settings will change.

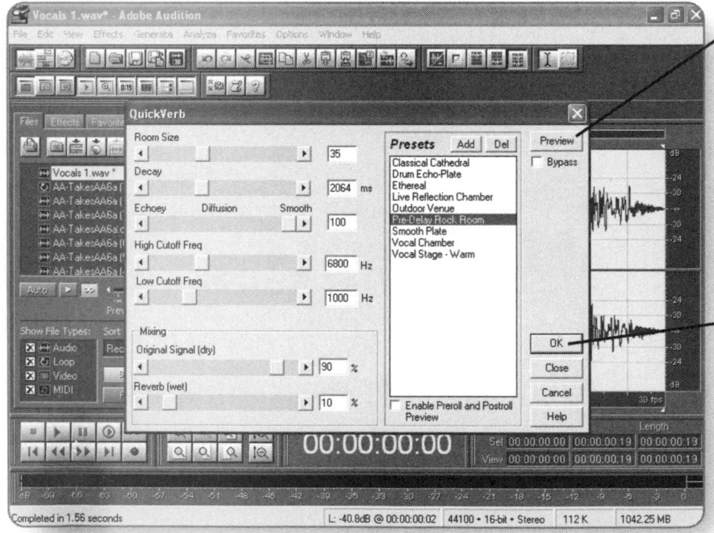

6. **Click** on the **Preview button**. You will hear how your audio sounds with the effect applied. If you are satisfied, you can proceed to Step 7; otherwise, go back to Step 5 and readjust the settings.

7. **Click** on the **OK button**. The changes you made will be accepted and the dialog box will close.

Reverb

The Reverb effect is the middleground between QuickVerb and the other reverb effects. It doesn't use as many system resources as Full Reverb, but it is still a convolution-based effect, so it takes longer to process than QuickVerb. You can choose from several presets or adjust the settings manually.

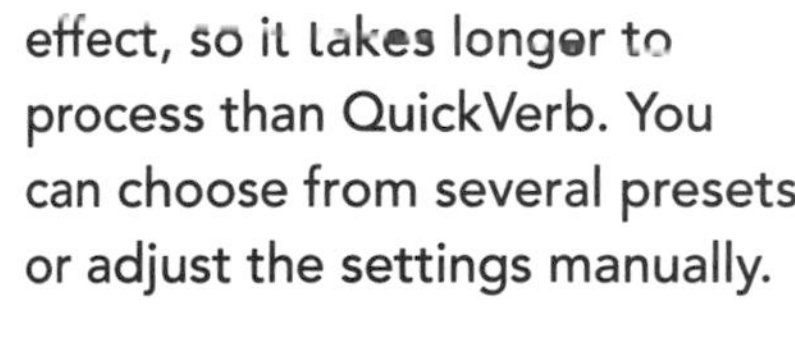

1. **Click** on **Effects**. The Effects menu will appear.

2. **Click** on **Delay Effects**. A submenu of different delay effects will appear.

3. **Click** on **Reverb**. The Reverb dialog box will open, allowing you to adjust the settings for that effect.

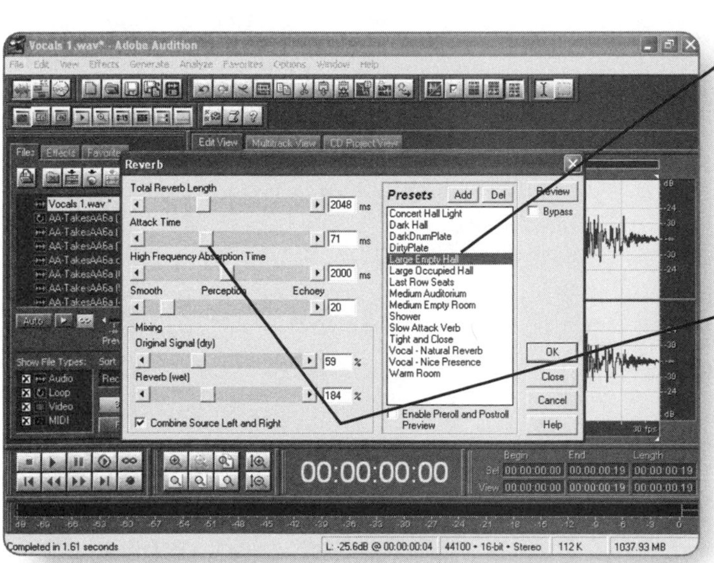

4. **Click** on a **preset** that most closely matches the type of effect that you would like to create. Alternatively, you can skip to Step 5 and manually adjust the settings.

5. **Click and drag** any of the **scroll box settings** to adjust their levels. As you drag the scroll boxes, the values for each of the settings will change.

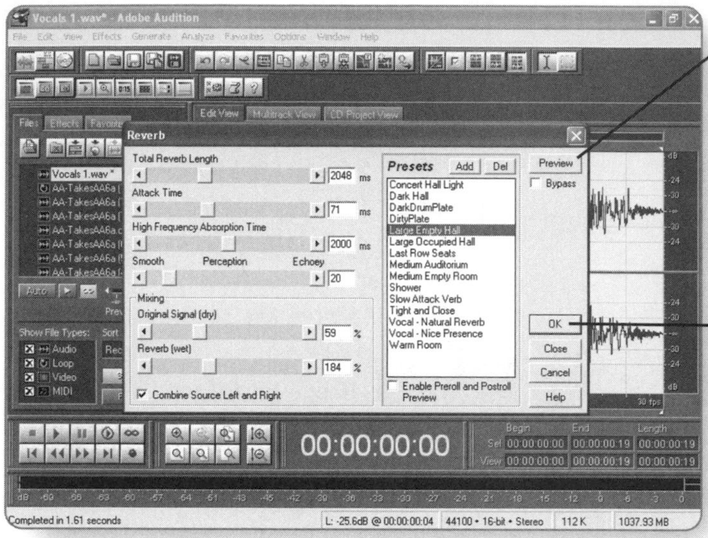

6. Click on the **Preview button**. You will hear how your audio sounds with the effect applied. If you are satisfied, you can proceed to Step 7; otherwise, go back to Step 5 and readjust the settings.

7. Click on the **OK button**. The changes you made will be accepted and the dialog box will close.

Studio Reverb

This sounds like a tool meant only for the pros in the studio, but it can also be used by regular Joes like you and me. The beauty of the Studio Reverb effect is that it takes up limited computer resources when applied and it can be applied in both Edit and Multitrack views. It provides you with a means of creating high-quality reverb that can be used in real time.

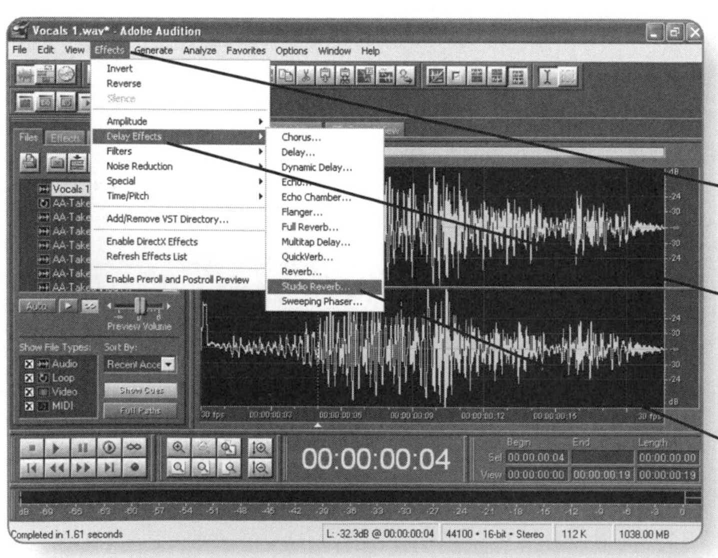

1. Click on **Effects**. The Effects menu will appear.

2. Click on **Delay Effects**. A submenu of different delay effects will appear.

3. Click on **Studio Reverb**. The Studio Reverb dialog box will open, allowing you to adjust the settings for that effect.

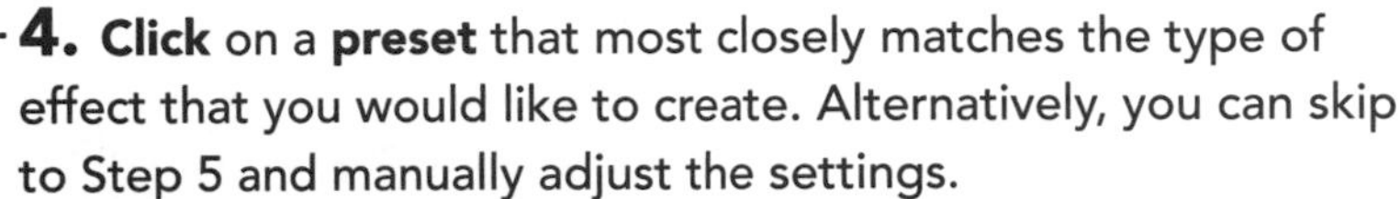

4. **Click** on a **preset** that most closely matches the type of effect that you would like to create. Alternatively, you can skip to Step 5 and manually adjust the settings.

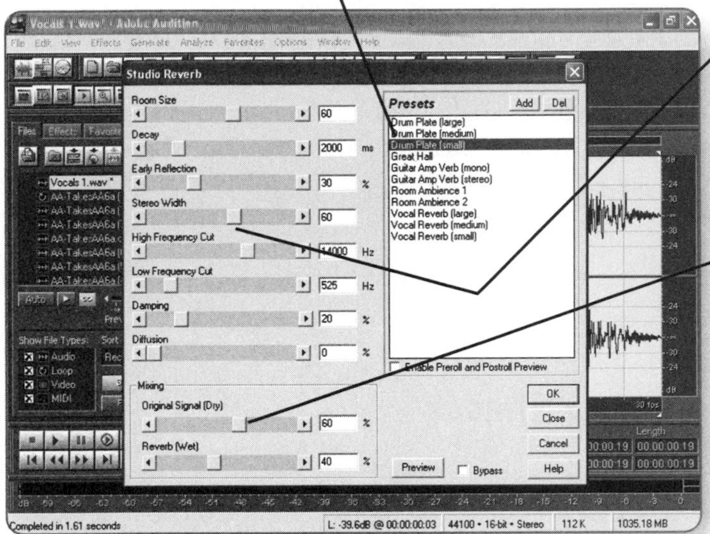

5. **Click and drag** any of the **scroll box settings** to adjust their levels. As you drag the scroll boxes, the values for each of the settings will change.

6. **Click and drag** on the **Mixing settings**. This will control how much of the original signal will be mixed with the adjusted settings.

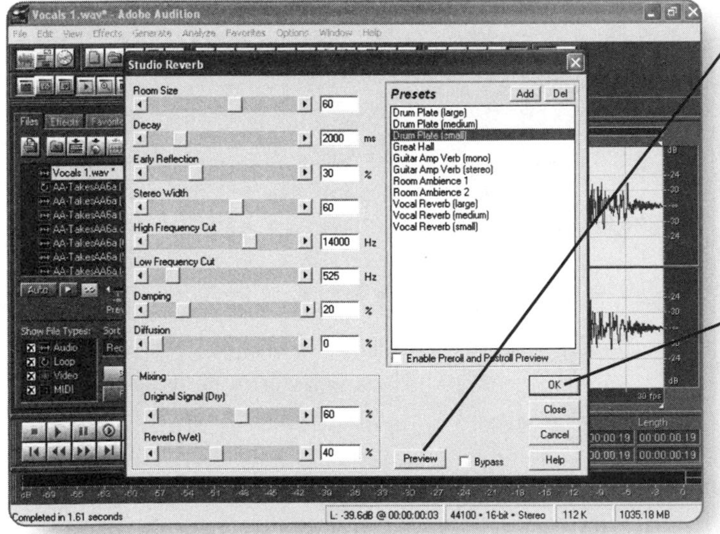

7. **Click** on the **Preview button**. You will hear how your audio sounds with the effect applied. If you are satisfied, you can proceed to Step 8; otherwise, go back to Step 5 and readjust the settings.

8. **Click** on the **OK button**. The changes you made will be accepted and the dialog box will close.

TIP

If you are applying an effect to a selection of audio, rather than an entire audio file, you may find the Preroll and Postroll previews useful. By clicking on the Preroll or Postroll preview, you can listen to the transition between the original audio and the selection. Preroll and Postroll previews are not available for every effect in Audition. You can edit the setting for Preroll and Postroll by selecting Preroll and Postroll Options from the Options menu.

Sweeping Phaser

If you're a fan of music from the '60s, then you'll recognize the sound that the Sweeping Phaser creates on your audio. It's very similar to the Flanger effect, but instead of just using a delay, frequencies are phase-shifted over time. The result is a type of psychedelic, mind-bending retro sound.

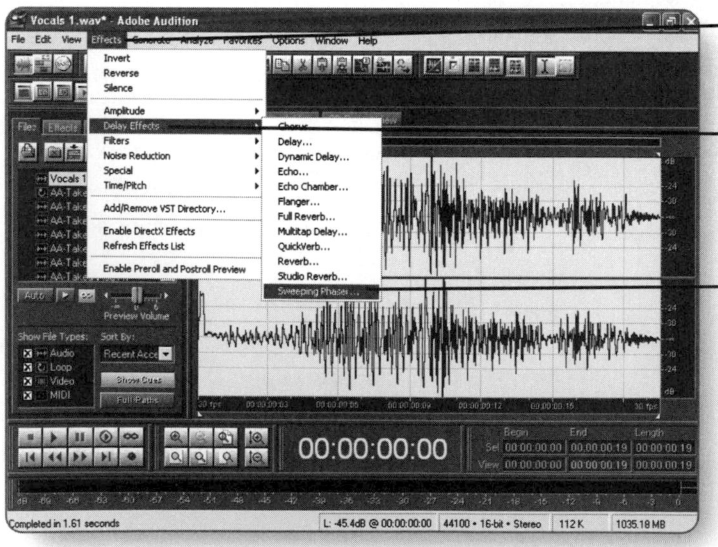

1. **Click** on **Effects**. The Effects menu will appear.
2. **Click** on **Delay Effects**. A submenu of different delay effects will appear.
3. **Click** on **Sweeping Phaser**. The Sweeping Phaser dialog box will open, allowing you to adjust the settings for that effect.

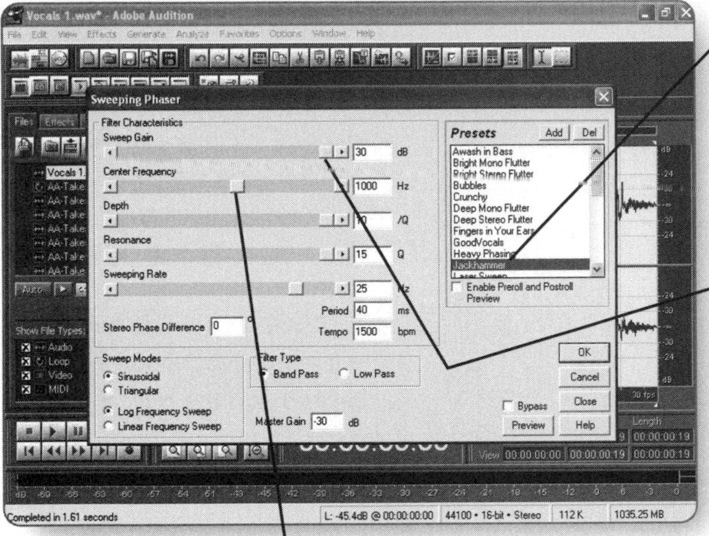

4. Click on a **preset** that most closely matches the type of effect that you would like to create. Alternatively, you can skip to Step 5 and manually adjust the settings.

5. Click and drag the **Sweep Gain scroll box** to the left or right. This will adjust the level of gain.

6. Click and drag the **Center Frequency scroll box** to the left or right. Since the phase sweeps around the center frequency, this will adjust where the phasing takes place.

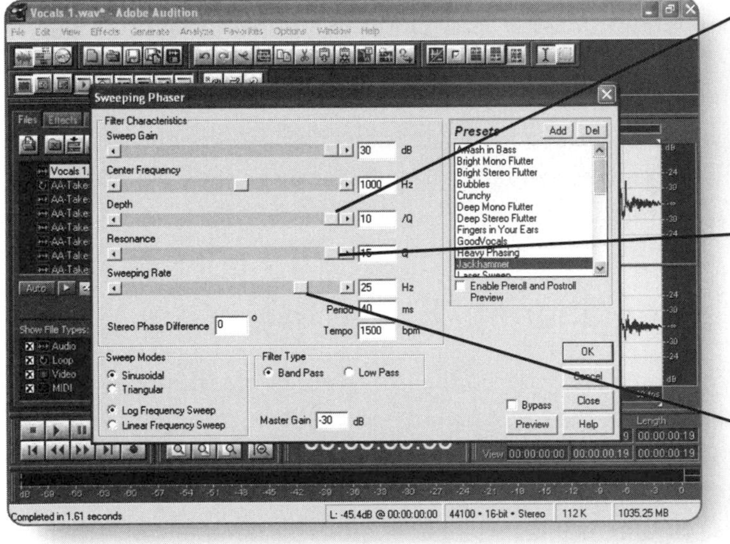

7. Click and drag the **Depth scroll box** to the left or right. This will determine how close or how far the sweep will extend from the center frequency.

8. Click and drag the **Resonance scroll box** to the left or right. This will set the amount of phase shift for the signal.

9. Click and drag the **Sweeping Rate scroll box** to the left or right. This will determine the speed of the sweep.

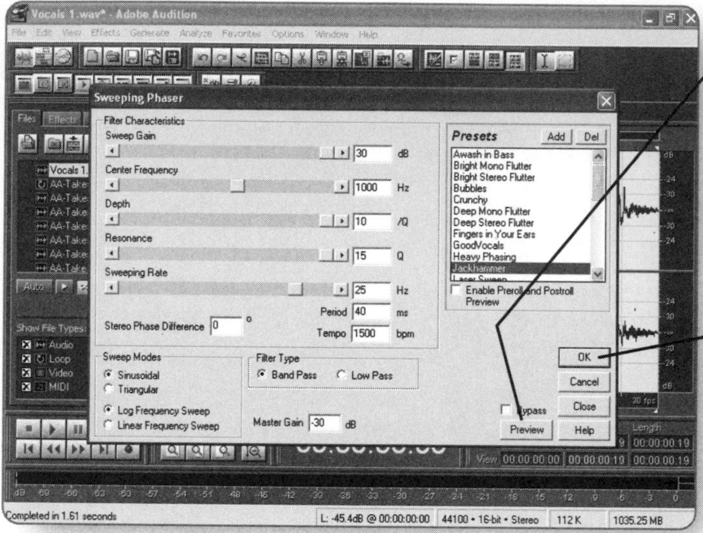

10. **Click** on the **Preview button**. You will hear how your audio sounds with the effect applied. If you are satisfied, you can proceed to Step 11; otherwise, go back to Step 5 and readjust the settings.

11. **Click** on the **OK button**. The changes you made will be accepted and the dialog box will close.

Filter Effects

Think of how a water filter works in a purifier. Water passes through one end and a chemical is applied to it. Then the filtered water comes out the other end. That's pretty much how audio filters work in Audition. Your audio enters the filter and has certain elements filtered out to provide an interesting sound effect.

Center Channel Extractor

When you have a stereo file, there are some sounds that occur only in the left channel, some only in the right, and others that are common to both. Those that are common to both are called the center channel. Typically, things like vocals, bass, and certain drums reside in this center channel. The Center Channel Extractor allows you to manipulate audio that falls in the center channel.

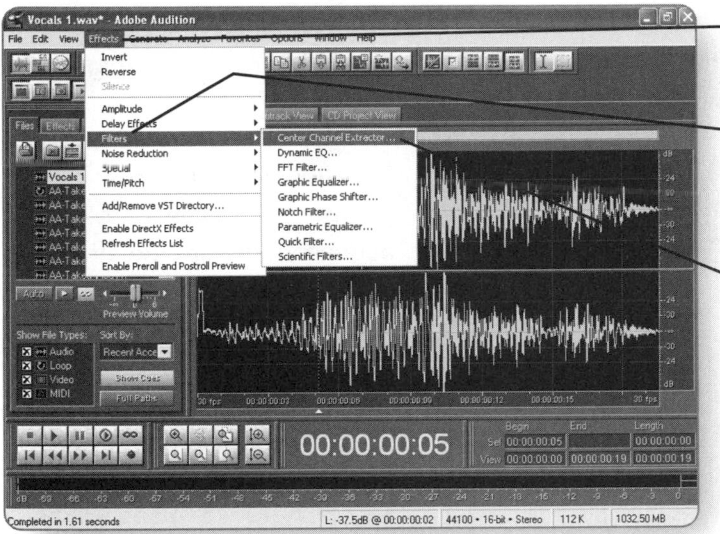

1. **Click** on **Effects**. The Effects menu will appear.

2. **Click** on **Filters**. A submenu of different filter effects will appear.

3. **Click** on **Center Channel Extractor**. The Center Channel Extractor dialog box will open, allowing you to adjust the settings for that effect.

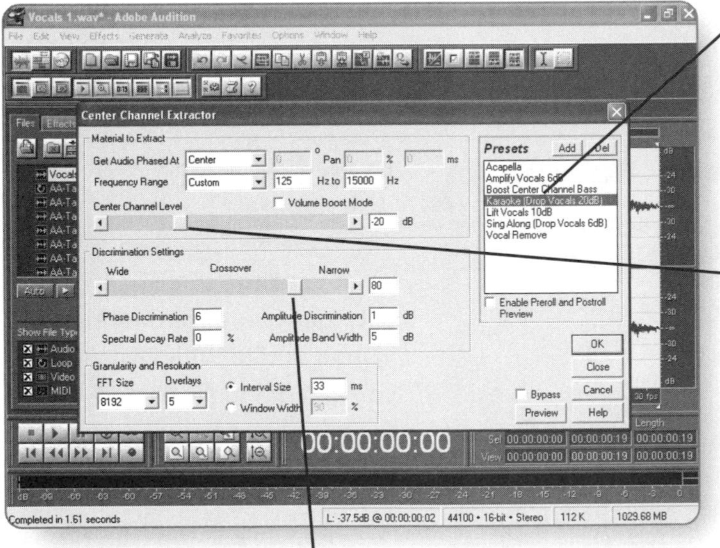

4. **Click** on a **preset** that most closely matches the type of effect that you would like to create. Alternatively, you can skip to Step 5 and manually adjust the settings.

5. **Click and drag** the **Center Channel Level scroll box**. Negative values will remove center channel frequencies, whereas positive values will extract stereo channels.

6. **Click and drag** the **Crossover scroll box**. This will control the level of audio bleed. Dragging to the right will allow less bleed, whereas dragging to the right will allow more.

7. **Adjust** any of the other **settings** in the dialog box, by either typing them directly into field boxes or selecting them from drop-down menus.

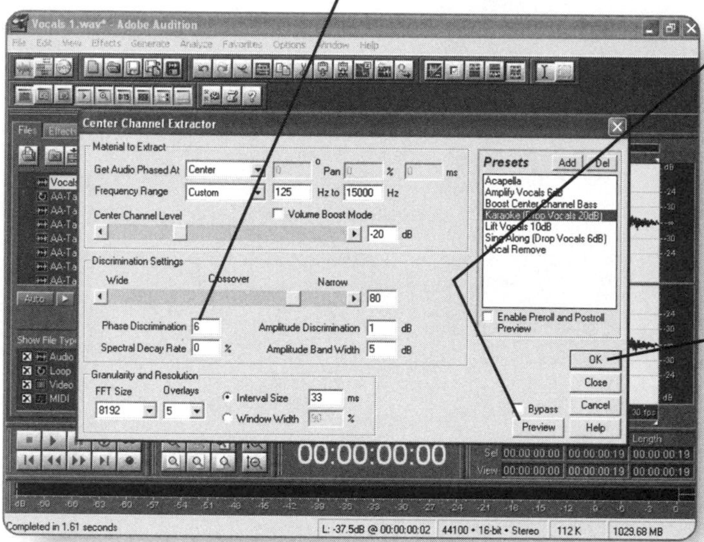

8. **Click** on the **Preview button**. You will hear how your audio sounds with the effect applied. If you are satisfied, you can proceed to Step 9; otherwise, go back to Step 5 and readjust the settings.

9. **Click** on the **OK button**. The changes you made will be accepted and the dialog box will close.

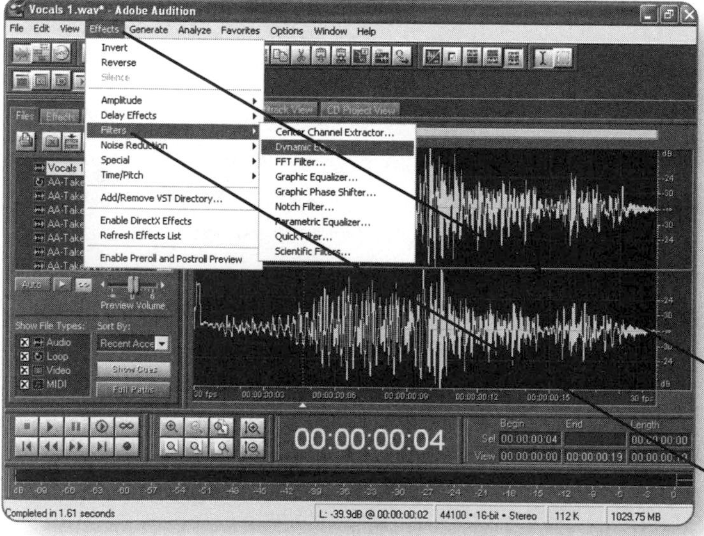

Dynamic EQ

The Dynamic EQ effect allows you to change the EQ levels automatically at different points in your audio. With Dynamic EQ, you can gradually change the EQ level of a frequency over time.

1. **Click** on **Effects**. The Effects menu will appear.

2. **Click** on **Filter Effects**. A submenu of different filter effects will appear.

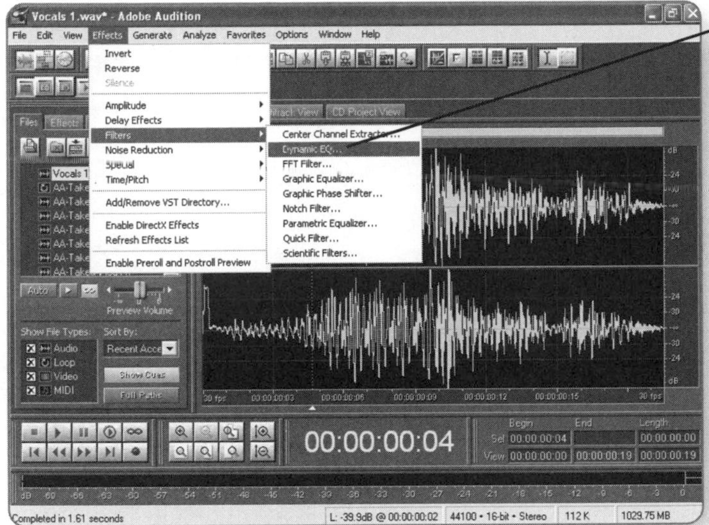

3. Click on **Dynamic EQ**. The Dynamic EQ dialog box will open, allowing you to adjust the settings for that effect.

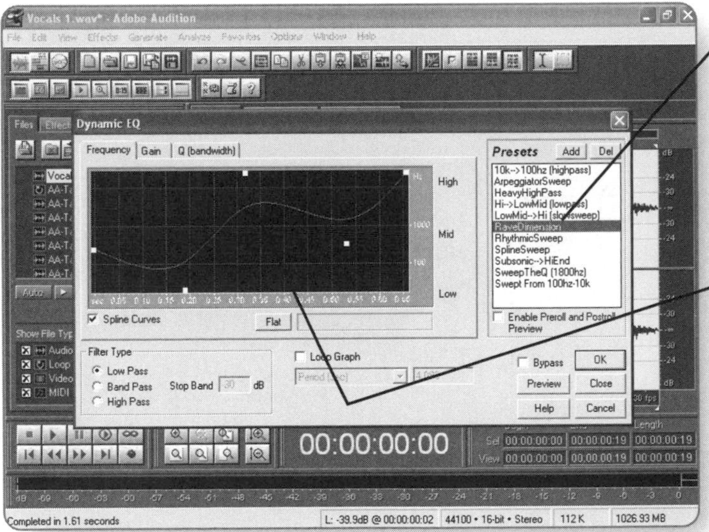

4. Click on a **preset** that most closely matches the type of effect that you would like to create. Alternatively, you can skip to Step 5 and manually adjust the settings.

5. Position your **mouse pointer** over the point on the Frequency graph that you would like to adjust. The Frequency graph will display the frequency over the length of your selection.

6. Click and drag the **point** on the graph to a new location. As soon as you click, a handle will appear.

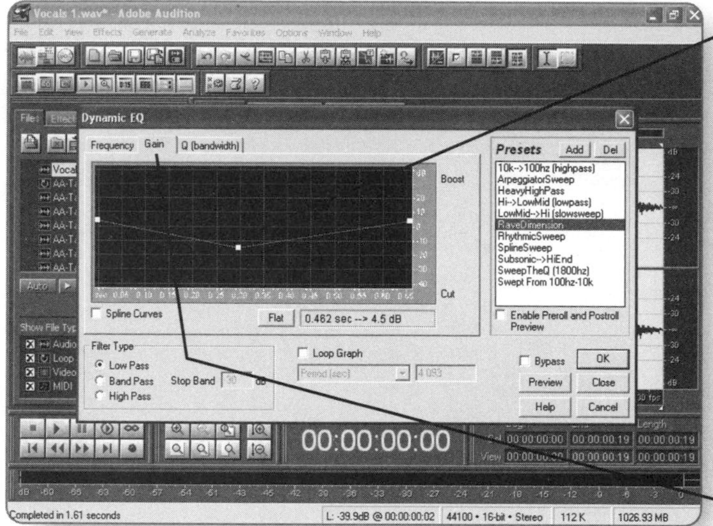

7. Release the **mouse button**. The graph will be adjusted.

8. Click on the **Gain tab**. The Gain graph will appear.

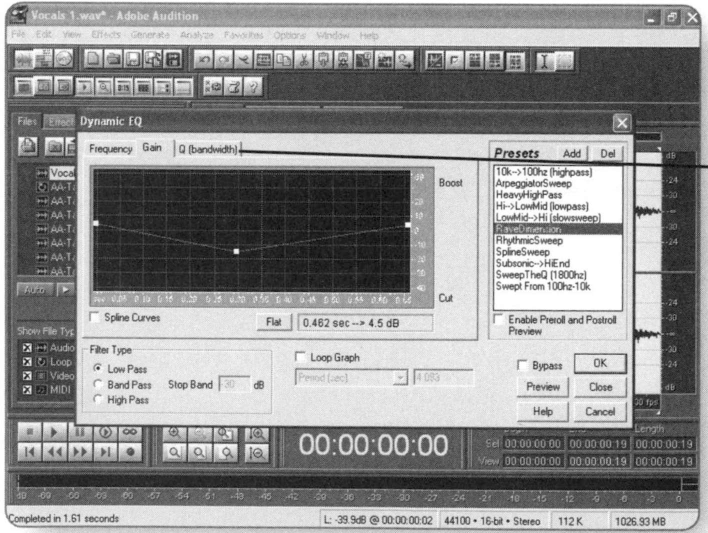

9. Repeat Steps 5-8 to adjust the settings for the gain of your audio.

10. Click on the **Q (bandwidth) tab**. The dialog box will display a graph where you can adjust the Q level.

11. Repeat Steps 5-8 to adjust the settings for the Q level of your audio. The settings will change.

12. Click on the **circle** beside the desired filter option. Your options include:

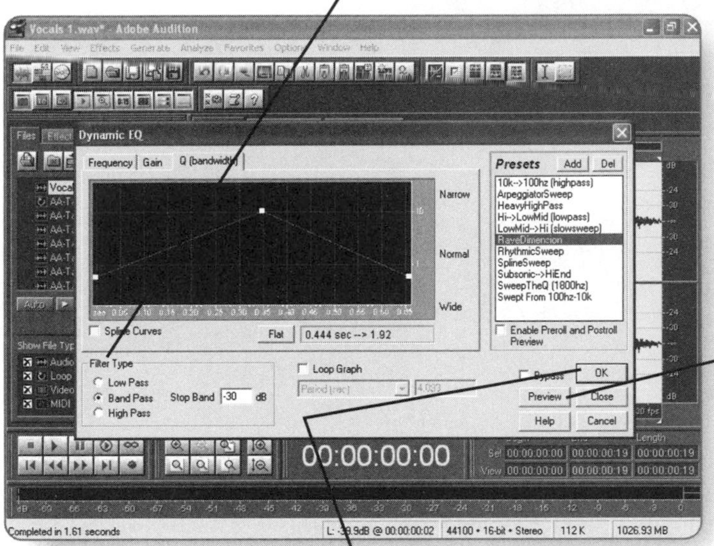

- **Band Pass**. This option will protect a certain band of frequencies and remove all others.
- **High Pass**. This option will remove low frequencies.
- **Low Pass**. This option will remove high frequencies.

13. Click on the **Preview button**. You will hear how your audio sounds with the effect applied. If you are satisfied, you can proceed to Step 14; otherwise, go back to Step 5 and readjust the settings.

14. Click on the **OK button**. The changes you made will be accepted and the dialog box will close.

FFT Filter

If you took advanced math or engineering at the university level, then you should be very familiar with Fast Fourier Transform (FFT). In math terms, an FFT is an efficient algorithm used to compute the Discrete Fourier Transform (DFT) and its inverse. If you're shaking your head at this point, don't worry, that's normal. All you need to know is that in Audition, it allows you to manipulate the frequency by clicking and dragging on a graph in the dialog box.

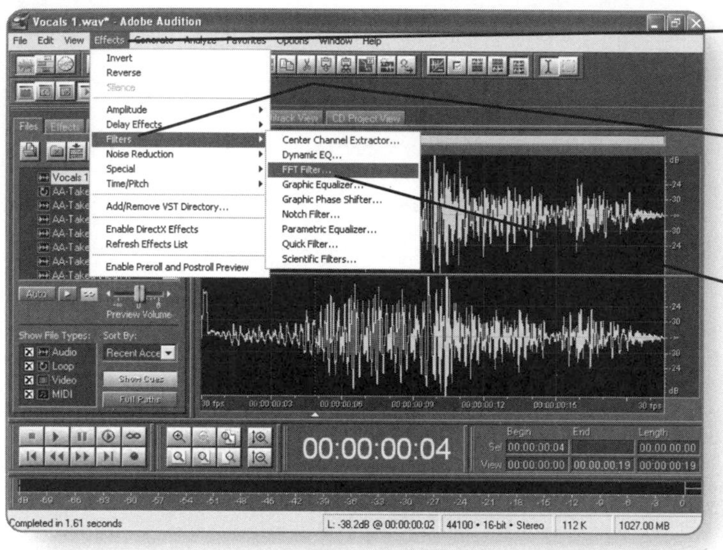

1. **Click** on **Effects**. The Effects menu will appear.

2. **Click** on **Filters**. A submenu of different filter effects will appear.

3. **Click** on **FFT Filter**. The FFT Filter dialog box will open, allowing you to adjust the settings for that effect.

4. **Click** on a **preset** that most closely matches the type of effect that you would like to create. Alternatively, you can skip to Step 5 and manually adjust the settings.

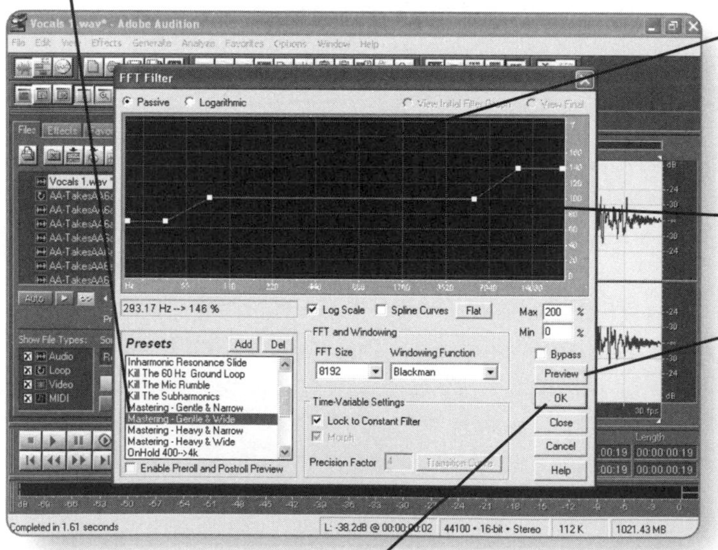

5. **Click** on **any point** of the background of the graph. The line in the graph will automatically jump to that point.

6. **Repeat Step 5** for any other points in the graph.

7. **Click** on the **Preview button**. You will hear how your audio sounds with the effect applied. If you are satisfied, you can proceed to Step 8; otherwise, go back to Step 5 and readjust the settings.

8. **Click** on the **OK button**. The changes you made will be accepted and the dialog box will close.

Graphic Equalizer

The Graphic Equalizer effect allows you to increase and decrease frequency levels at different points in the audio. With the Graphics Equalizer, you can adjust settings for frequency bands, gain, accuracy level, and range. If you move a band above the center line, you will increase the frequency, whereas moving it below will reduce the frequency.

1. **Click** on **Effects**. The Effects menu will appear.

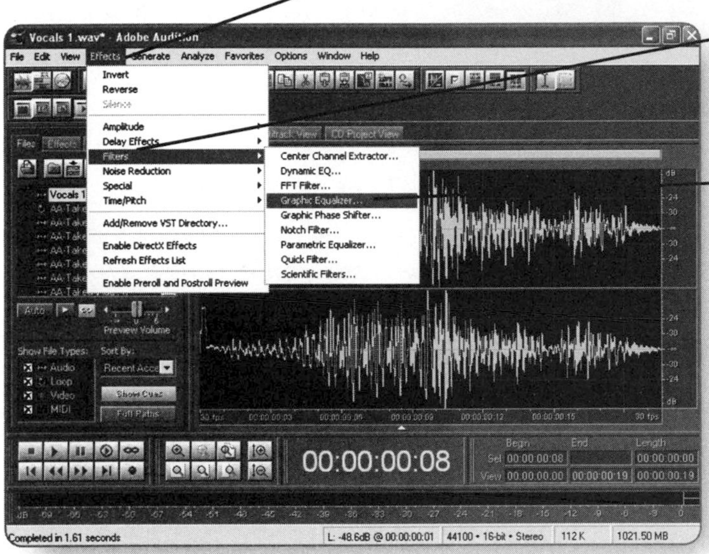

2. **Click** on **Filters**. A submenu of different filter effects will appear.

3. **Click** on **Graphic Equalizer**. The Graphic Equalizer dialog box will open, allowing you to adjust the settings for that effect.

4. Click on a **preset** that most closely matches the type of effect that you would like to create. Alternatively, you can skip to Step 5 and manually adjust the settings.

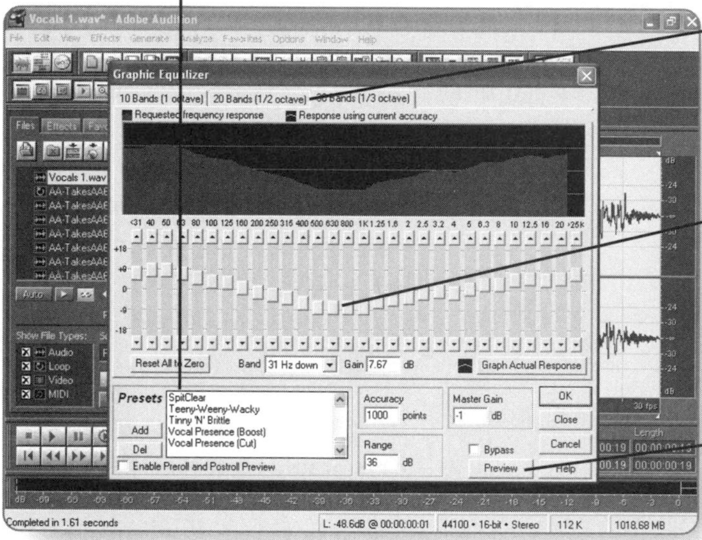

5. Click on the desired **tab**. Depending on which tab you select, you will have 10, 20, or 30 bands to adjust.

6. Click and drag up or down to adjust any of the band settings. As you drag, the graph of the EQ curve will adjust accordingly.

7. Click on the **Preview button**. You will hear how your audio sounds with the effect applied. If you are satisfied, you can proceed to Step 8; otherwise go back to Step 5 and readjust the settings.

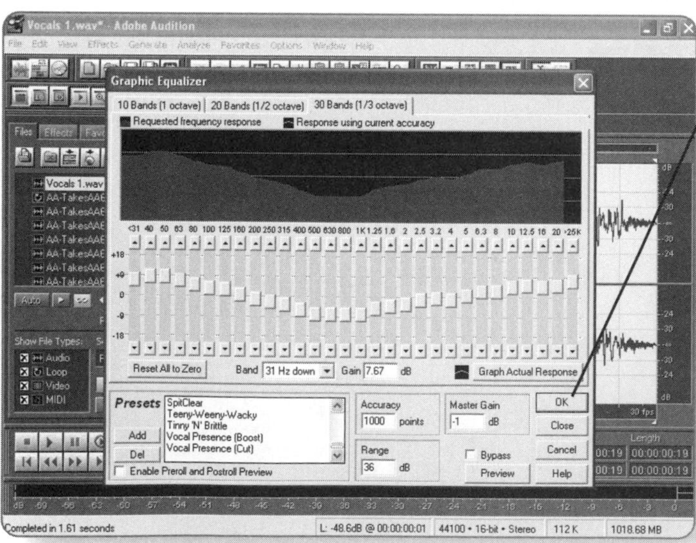

8. Click on the **OK button**. Your changes will be saved and the dialog box will close.

Graphic Phase Shifter

The Graphic Phase Shifter gives you a 360-degree range in which to adjust your frequencies. Typically, it is used to correct any phase problems that your audio may have.

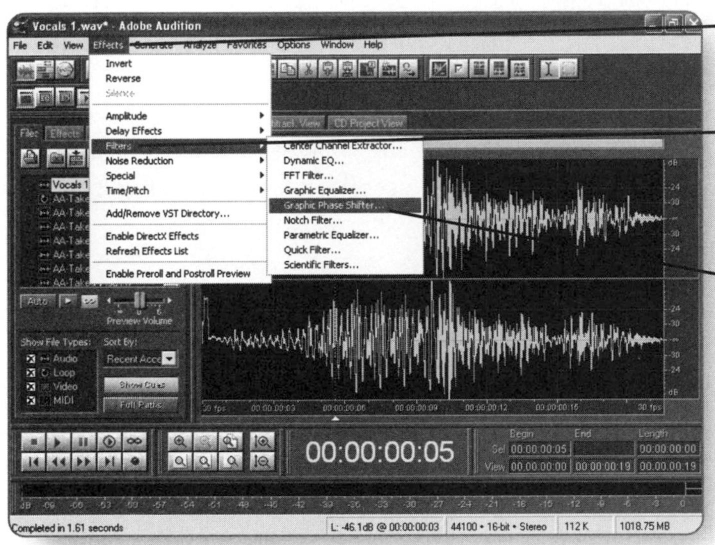

1. **Click** on **Effects**. The Effects menu will appear.

2. **Click** on **Filters**. A submenu of different filter effects will appear.

3. **Click** on **Graphic Phase Shifter**. The Graphic Phase Shifter dialog box will open, allowing you to adjust the settings for that effect.

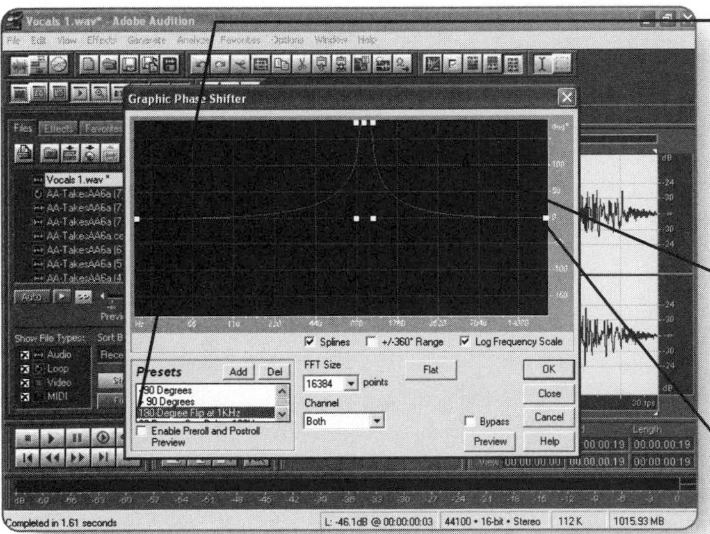

4. **Click** on a **preset** that most closely matches the type of effect that you would like to create. Alternatively, you can skip to Step 5 and manually adjust the settings.

5. **Click** on any **point** of the background of the graph. The line in the graph will automatically jump to that point.

6. **Repeat Step 5** for any other points in the graph.

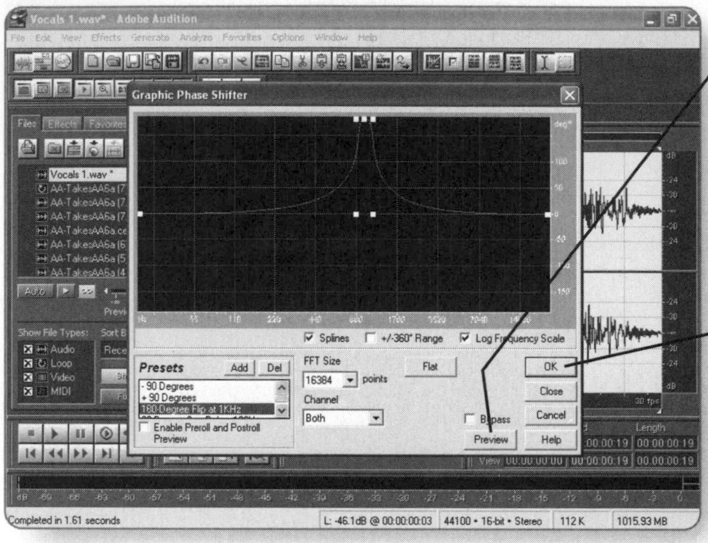

7. Click on the **Preview button**. You will hear how your audio sounds with the effect applied. If you are satisfied, you can proceed to Step 8; otherwise, go back to Step 5 and readjust the settings.

8. Click on the **OK button**. The changes you made will be accepted and the dialog box will close.

Notch Filter

The Notch Filter is a precision tool that allows you to manipulate individual frequencies without affecting neighboring frequencies. Using this tool, you can remove up to six different frequencies. Typically, this is used to remove noise from certain frequencies. As with most effects in Audition, there are several different presets that you can select, or you can manually adjust the settings.

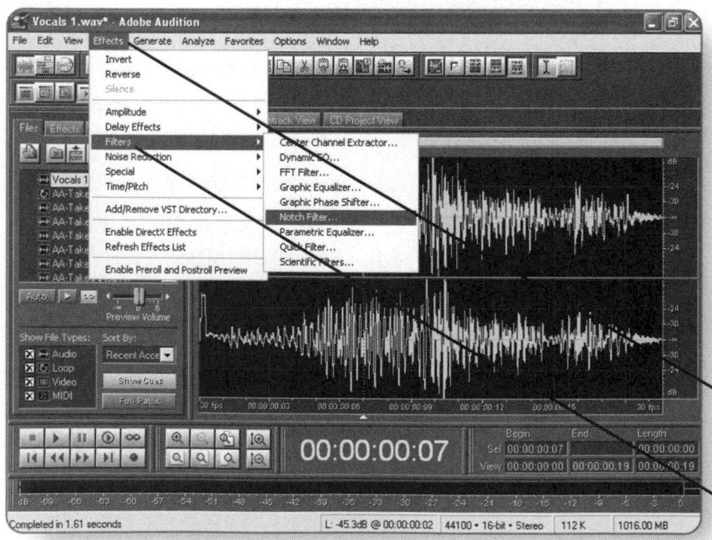

1. Click on **Effects**. The Effects menu will appear.

2. Click on **Filters**. A submenu of different filter effects will appear.

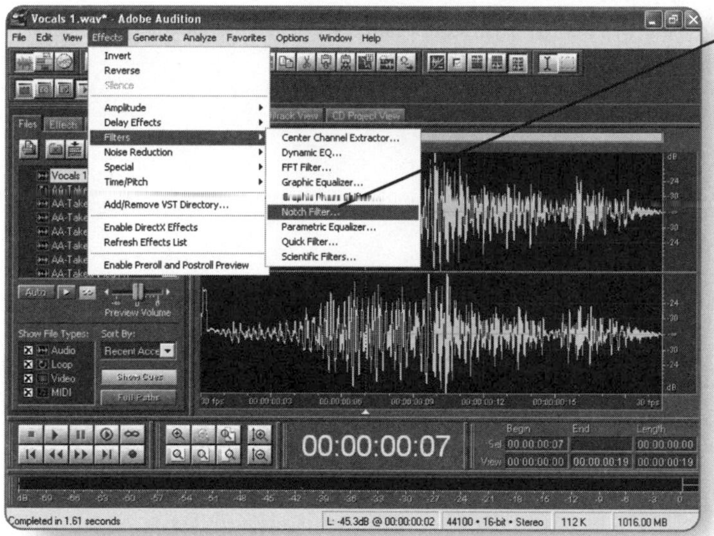

3. Click on **Notch Filter**. The Notch Filter dialog box will open, allowing you to adjust the settings for that effect.

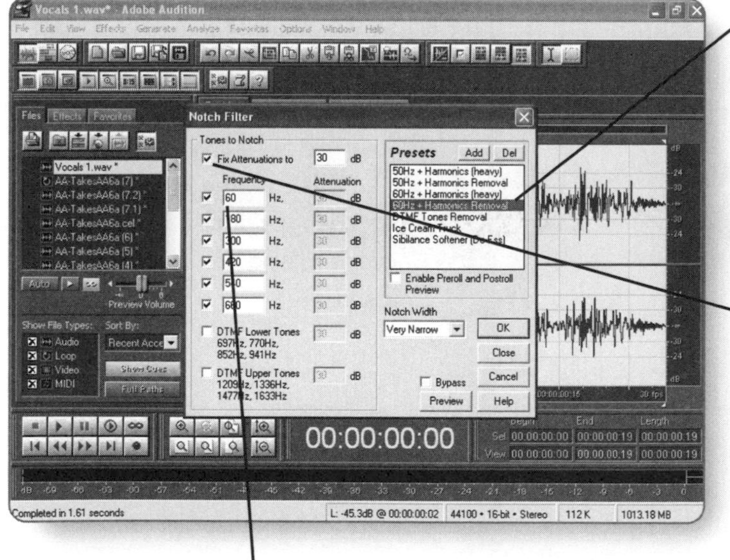

4. Click on a **preset** that most closely matches the type of effect that you would like to create. Alternatively, you can skip to Step 5 and manually adjust the settings.

5. Click in the **Fix Attenuations to check box** if you want to attenuate all of the specified channels to the same level. If you select this, then you will have to specify a number for the attenuation.

6. Type in a **value** for the **frequency** that you would like to attenuate. You will then have to specify a value for the attenuation.

7. Type a **value** for the **attenuation**. It will appear in the box.

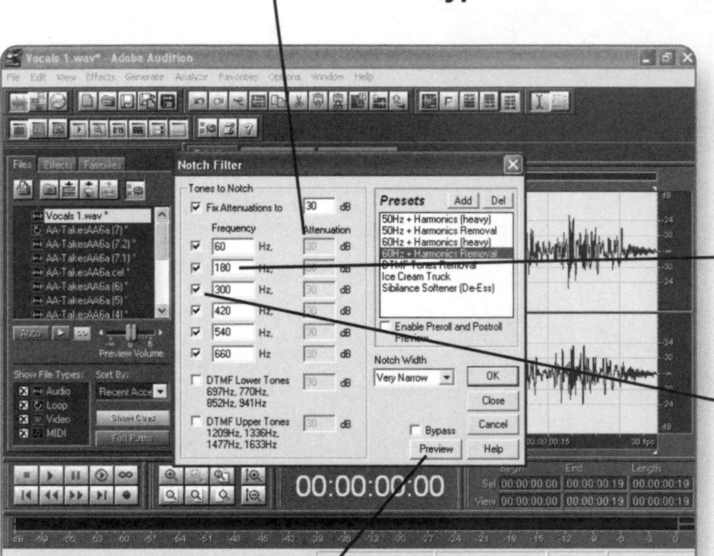

8. Repeat Steps 6 and 7 for any other frequencies that you would like to attenuate.

9. Click on the **check box** beside the frequency to activate the attenuation, if it is not already checked.

10. Click on the **Preview button**. You will hear how your audio sounds with the effect applied. If you are satisfied, you can proceed to Step 11; otherwise, go back to Step 5 and readjust the settings.

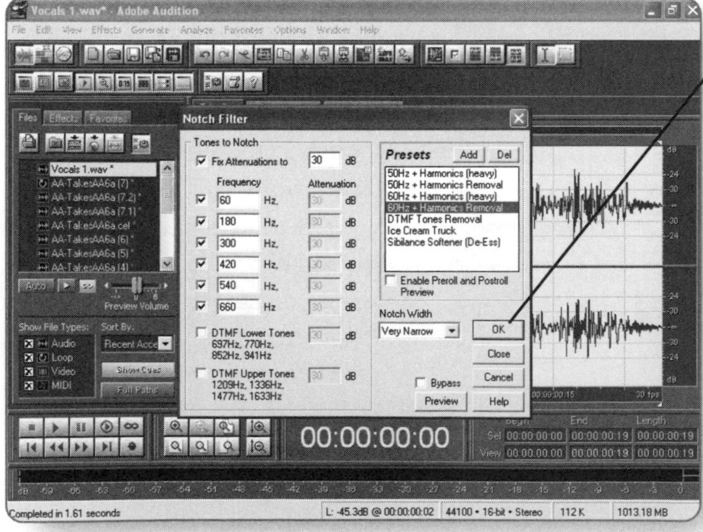

11. Click on the **OK button**. The changes you made will be accepted and the dialog box will close.

Parametric Equalizer

The Parametric Equalizer is another precision effect that allows you to adjust frequency, Q, and gain settings. With it you can also adjust a group of frequencies all at once.

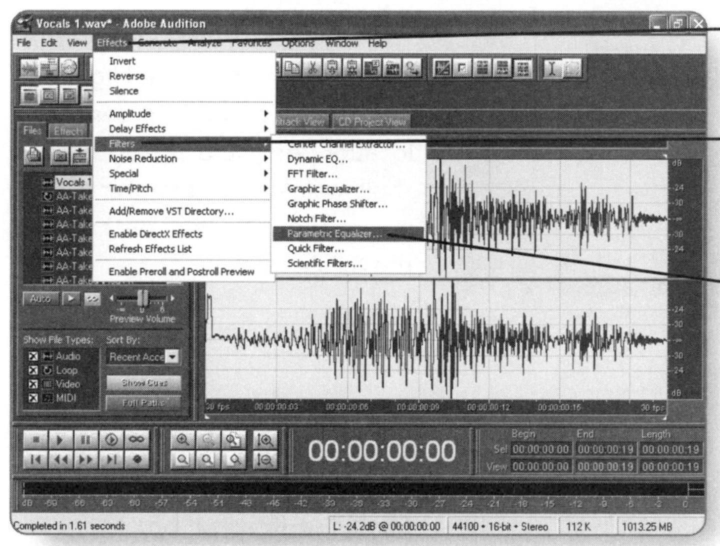

1. **Click** on **Effects**. The Effects menu will appear.
2. **Click** on **Filters**. A submenu of different filter effects will appear.
3. **Click** on **Parametric Equalizer**. The Parametric Equalizer dialog box will open, allowing you to adjust the settings for that effect.

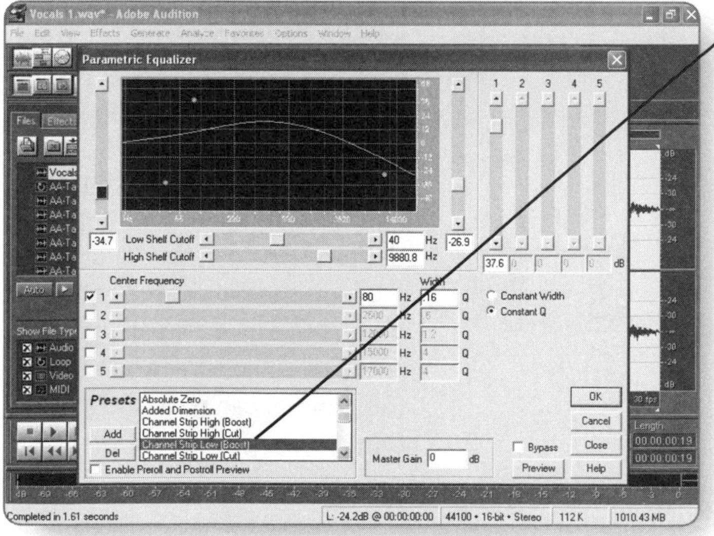

4. **Click** on a **preset** that most closely matches the type of effect that you would like to create. Alternatively, you can skip to Step 5 and manually adjust the settings.

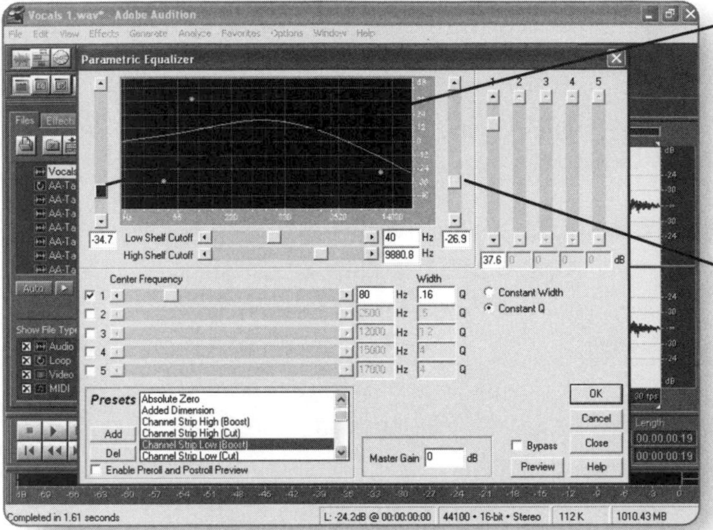

5. **Click and drag** the **Low Shelf scroll box** to the desired location. As you drag, the low shelf indicator on the graph will move. The low shelf determines the bass level.

6. **Click and drag** the **High Shelf scroll box** to the desired location. As you drag, the high shelf indicator on the graph will move. The high shelf determines the treble level.

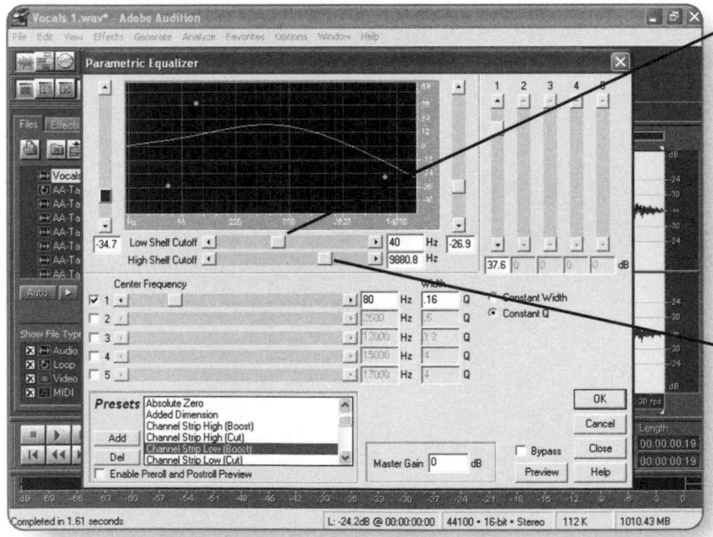

7. **Click and drag** the **Low Shelf Cutoff scroll box** to the desired location. As you drag, the low shelf indicator on the graph will move. The low shelf cutoff sets the level where low frequencies can pass and high frequencies get removed.

8. **Click and drag** the **High Shelf Cutoff scroll box** to the desired location. As you drag, the high shelf indicator on the graph will move. The high shelf cutoff sets the level where high frequencies can pass and low frequencies get removed.

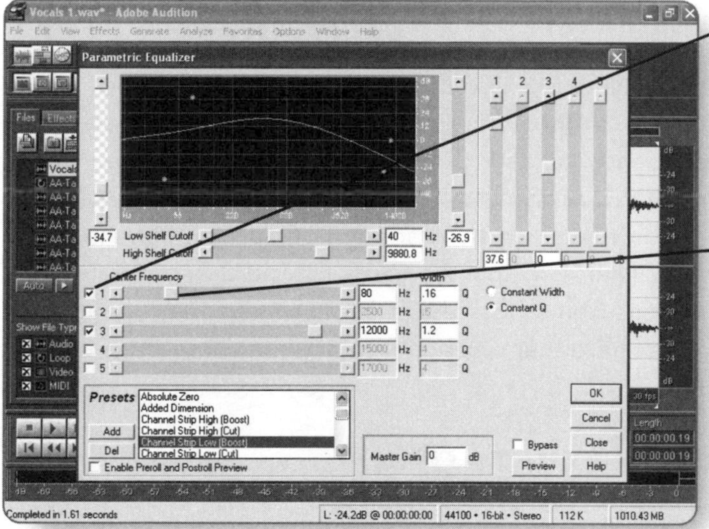

9. **Click** on the **check box** beside the number 1 in the Center Frequency area of the dialog box. That frequency will now be adjustable.

10. **Click and drag** the **Frequency scroll box** to the desired location. As you drag, the values for Hz and Q will adjust and the equalization curve will adjust.

11. **Repeat Steps 7 and 8** for any other frequencies that you would like to adjust.

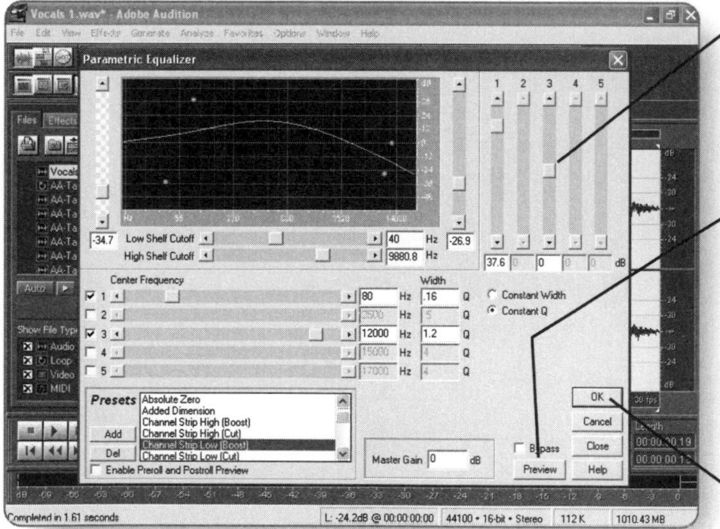

12. **Click and drag** the **sliders** to adjust the amount of boost or cut. As you drag, the dB value will change.

13. **Click** on the **Preview button**. You will hear how your audio sounds with the effect applied. If you are satisfied, you can proceed to Step 14; otherwise, go back to Step 5 and readjust the settings.

14. **Click** on the **OK button**. The changes you made will be accepted and the dialog box will close.

Quick Filter

The Quick Filter is a little different than typical graphic equalizers. The frequencies that you adjust do not operate independently. Adjusting one will affect the others. The Quick Filter dialog box also allows you to adjust the master volume so that the adjustments you set do not place an unwanted effect on volume. Within the Quick Filter dialog box you have two options: You can set the levels to be constant throughout or you can have them change from their initial settings to final settings.

1. **Click** on **Effects**. The Effects menu will appear.

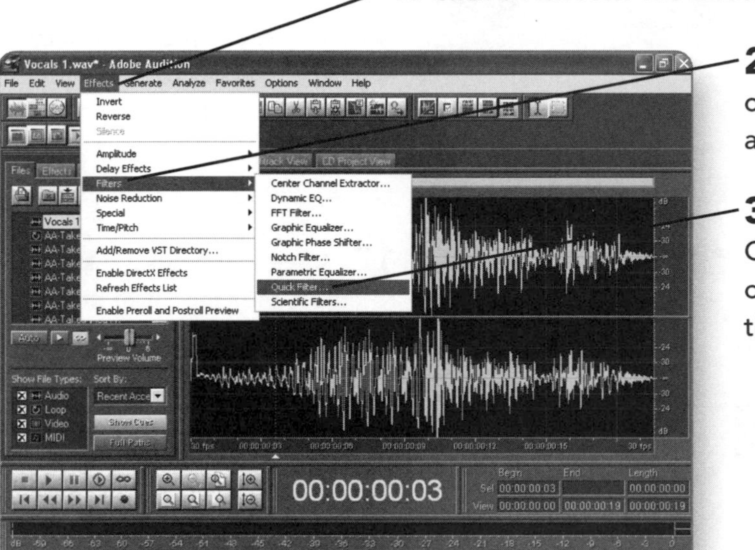

2. **Click** on **Filters**. A submenu of different filter effects will appear.

3. **Click** on **Quick Filter**. The Quick Filter dialog box will open, allowing you to adjust the settings for that effect.

Setting Constant Levels

If you want to keep the levels consistent throughout your audio selection, you can set constant levels. In other words, your levels will stay the same at every point in your audio.

1. **Click** on a **preset** that most closely matches the type of effect that you would like to create. Alternatively, you can skip to Step 2 and manually adjust the settings.

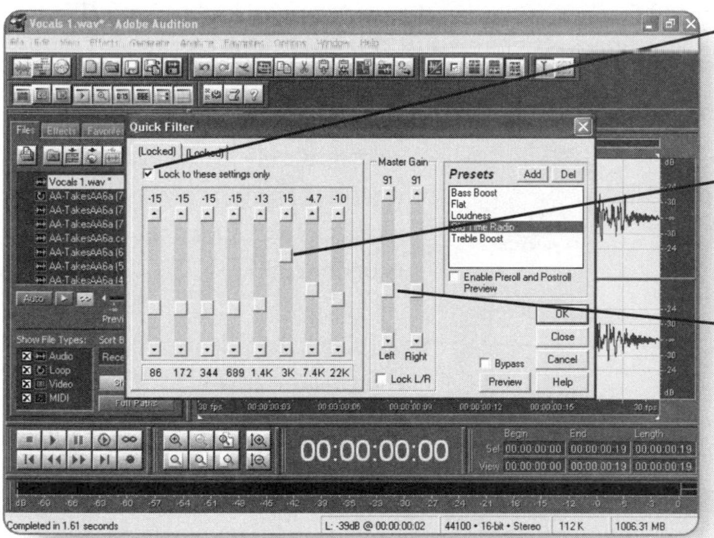

2. **Click** on the **Lock to these settings only check box**, if it is not already checked.

3. **Click and drag** the **sliders** to the desired levels. As you drag, the settings will adjust.

4. **Click and drag** the **Master Gain settings**. If you are working with mono audio you will only be able to adjust the left slider; otherwise, you can adjust both the left and the right.

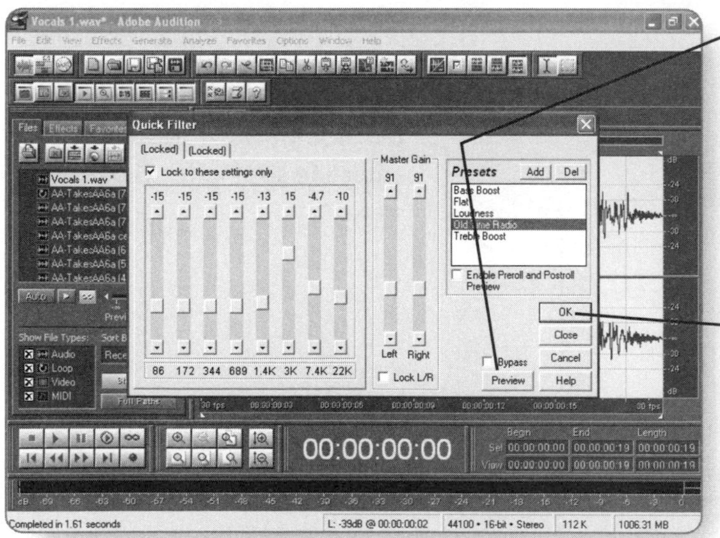

5. **Click** on the **Preview button**. You will hear how your audio sounds with the effect applied. If you are satisfied, you can proceed to Step 6; otherwise, go back to Step 3 and readjust the settings.

6. **Click** on the **OK button**. The changes you made will be accepted and the dialog box will close.

Setting Changing Levels

The Quick Filter allows you to set initial settings and then have them gradually move to a set of final settings while the audio plays. To accomplish this, you simply have to set the initial and final settings and Audition will do the rest.

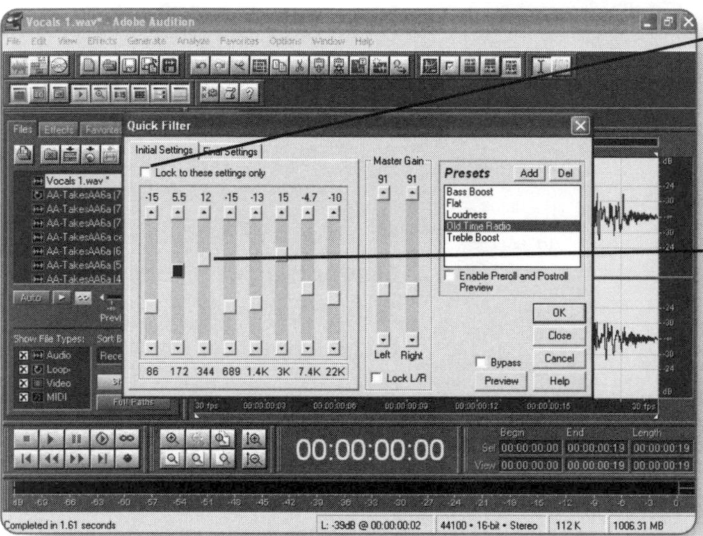

1. **Click** on the **Lock to these settings only check box** to deselect this option. In other words, make sure that this box is unchecked.

2. **Click and drag** the **sliders** to the desired levels for the initial state. As you drag, the settings will adjust.

3. **Click** on the **Final Settings tab**. You will now be able to enter the setting for the final state.

4. Click and drag the **sliders** to the desired levels for the final state. As you drag, the settings will adjust.

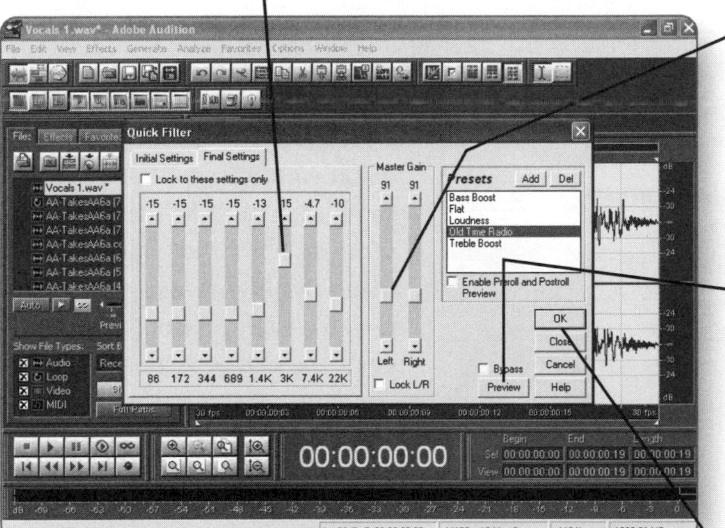

5. Click and drag the **Master Gain settings**. If you are working with mono audio, you will only be able to adjust the left slider; otherwise, you can adjust both the left and the right.

6. Click on the **Preview button**. You will hear how your audio sounds with the effect applied. If you are satisfied, you can proceed to Step 7; otherwise, go back to Steps 4 and 5 and readjust the settings.

7. Click on the **OK button**. The changes you made will be accepted and the dialog box will close.

Special Effects

Although all effects should consider themselves honored to be a part of Adobe Audition, three in particular have been deemed as "special." These three effects don't really seem to fit in any other category so they've been exiled to the ranks of special effects. The three effects that fall under this category are indeed unique because they allow you to make your music talk, add distortion to your audio, and allow you to compose your own tunes that can be played back with any audio file.

Making Music Talk with Convolution

It takes years of practice and some considerable talent to make it seem like the instrument you are playing is actually talking. Well, you can save the money you would spend on expensive music lessons because the Convolution effect allows you to achieve similar results in seconds. The Convolution effect works by multiplying the samples in one waveform by the samples in another waveform. Using this effect, you must first load a waveform (for instance a vocal track) that will become the impulse that other waveforms are multiplied by (such as a guitar track).

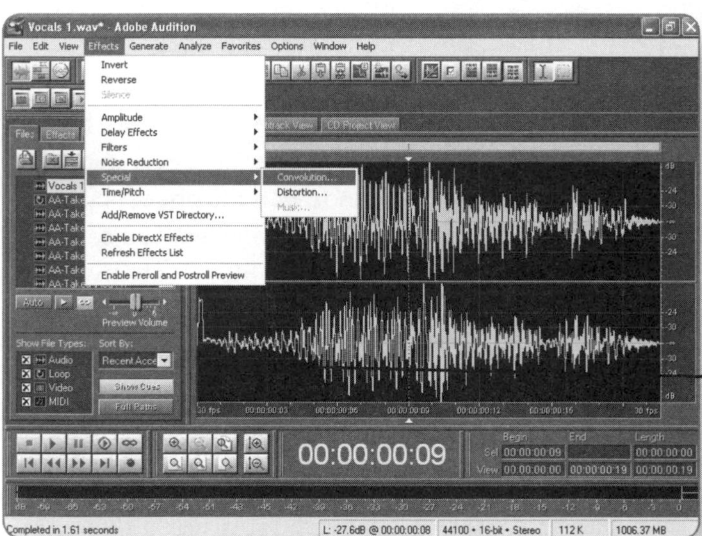

1. **Open** the **waveform** that you would like to use as the template for others to be multiplied by. If you want to make your music talk, choose a piece of audio with spoken word, such as a vocal track. The waveform or a selection within the waveform must be at least 5 seconds long.

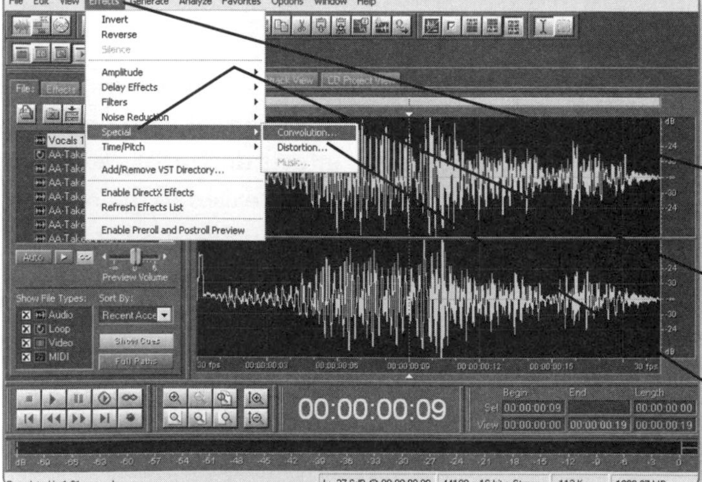

2. **Click** on **Effects**. The Effects menu will appear.

3. **Click** on **Special**. A submenu of special effects will appear.

4. **Click** on **Convolution**. The Digital Convolution dialog box will open.

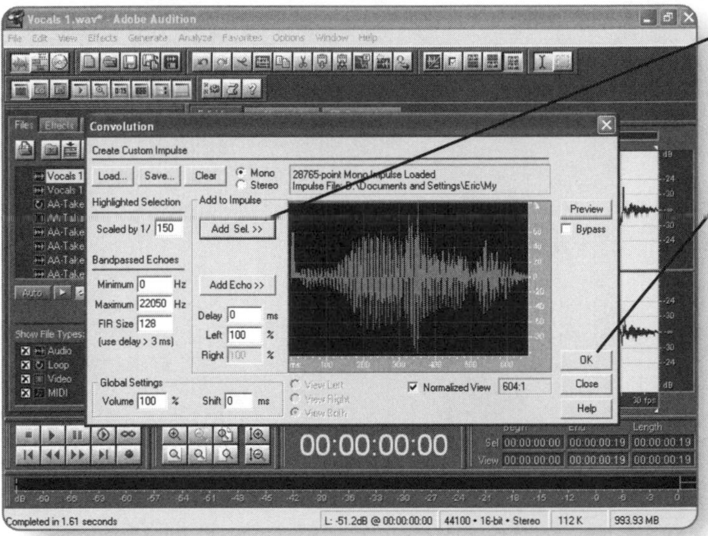

5. Click on the **Add Sel button**. Your entire waveform or the current selection will be added.

6. Click on the **Save button**. A dialog box will appear from which you can save your waveform as an impulse that will be applied to future waveforms.

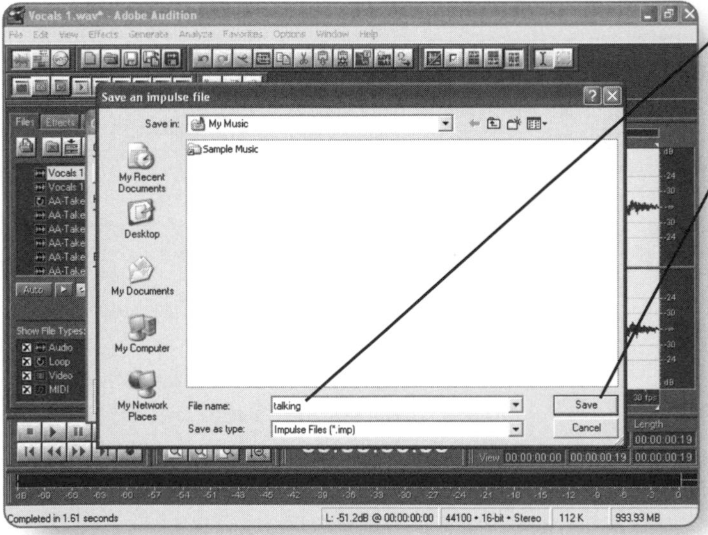

7. Type a **descriptive** name for your impulse.

8. Click on the **Save button**. The dialog box will close and you will return to the Digital Convolution dialog box.

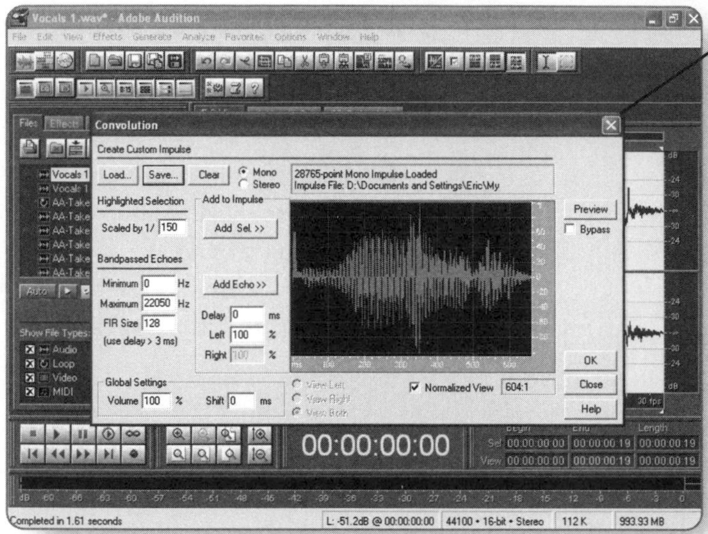

9. Click on the **X** in the top-right corner of the dialog box. This will close the effect without applying any changes to your audio. At this point, we only had the dialog box open to save our impulse.

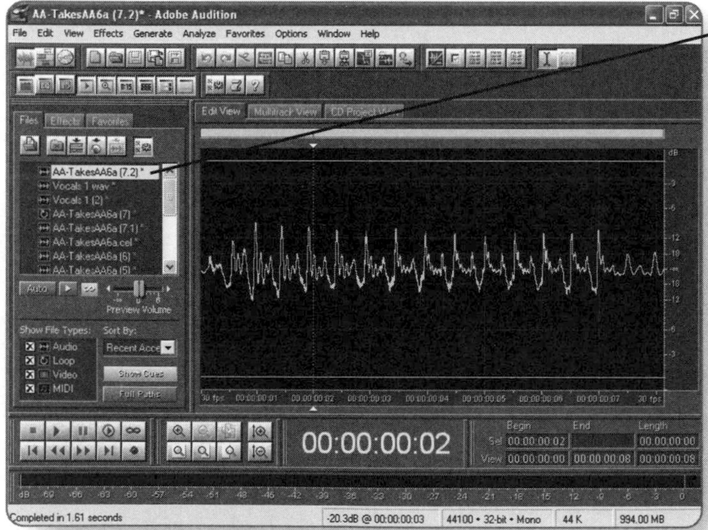

10. Double-click to **open the waveform** that you would like to multiply (the guitar track, for example). It will open in the window.

> **TIP**
>
> Guitar riffs are particularly good tracks to apply Convolution effects with spoken audio because the guitar really sounds like it is talking.

11. Repeat Steps 2-4 to open up the Digital Convolution dialog box.

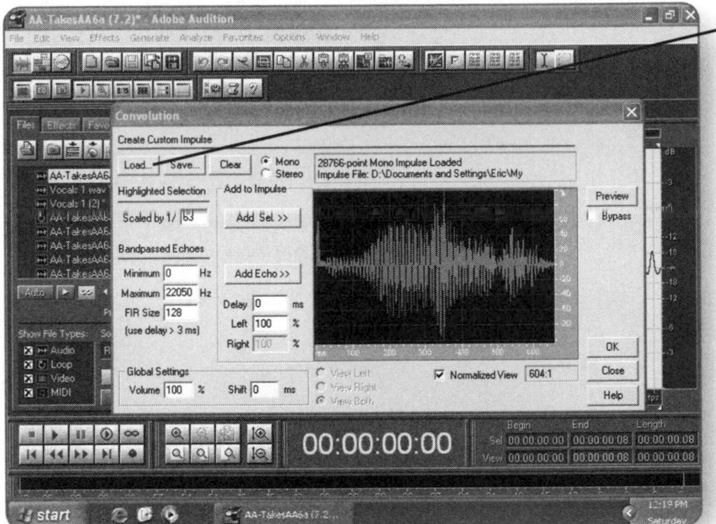

12. Click on the **Load button** to load the impulse that you created earlier so that it can be applied to this audio. A dialog box will open from which you can choose the file.

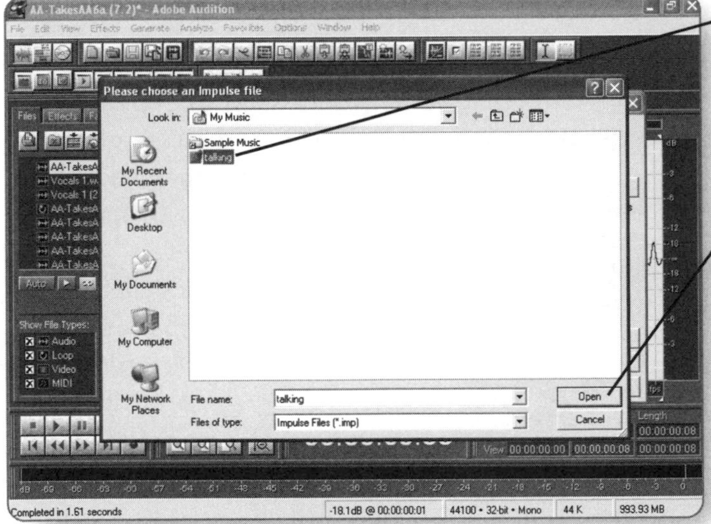

13. Click on the desired **impulse file** to open. This file will be multiplied against your audio.

14. Click on the **Open button**. The impulse file will be loaded and you will be returned to the Digital Convolution dialog box.

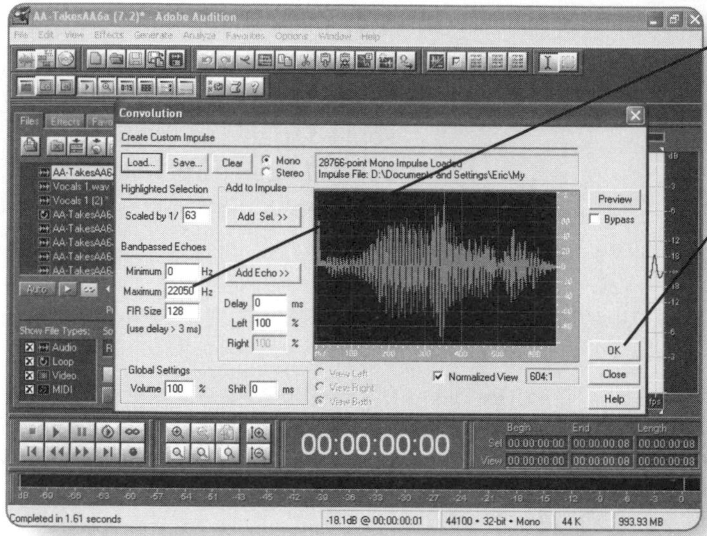

15. Make any other **adjustments** to the settings in the dialog box.

16. Click on the **OK button**. The effect will be applied and the dialog box will close.

Distorting Your Audio

Imagine being so full of anger and rage that you kick in a speaker while it's playing your favorite song. The speaker will somehow still play sound, but it won't sound quite right. That's the type of audio that is mimicked with the Distortion effect. With this effect, you can choose from several muffled presets or adjust the settings to create your own distortion. The Distortion graph provides you with a visual representation of your input and output dB levels.

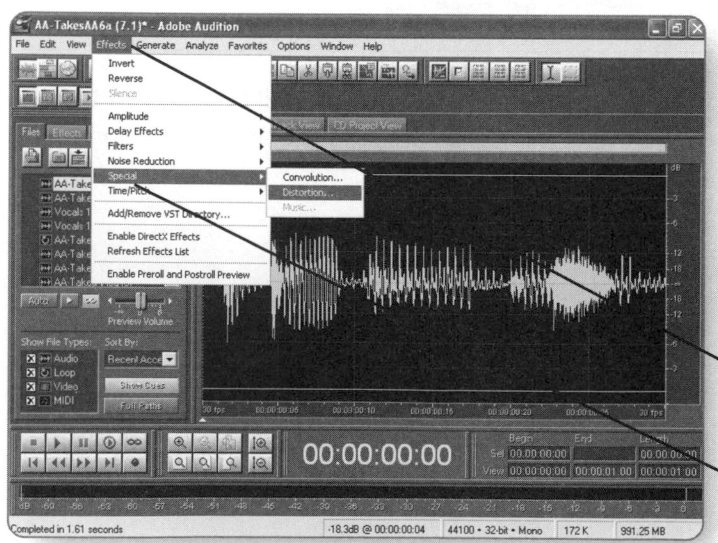

1. Click on **Effects**. The Effects menu will appear.

2. Click on **Special**. A submenu of special effects will appear.

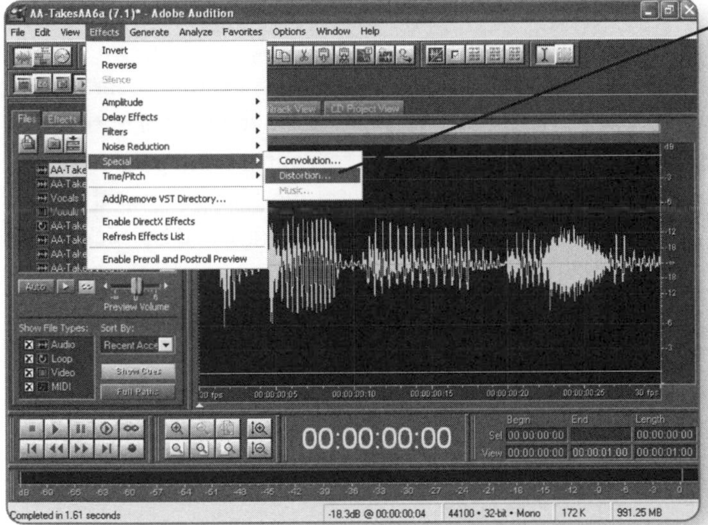

3. Click on **Distortion**. The Distortion dialog box will open, allowing you to apply distortion effects to your audio.

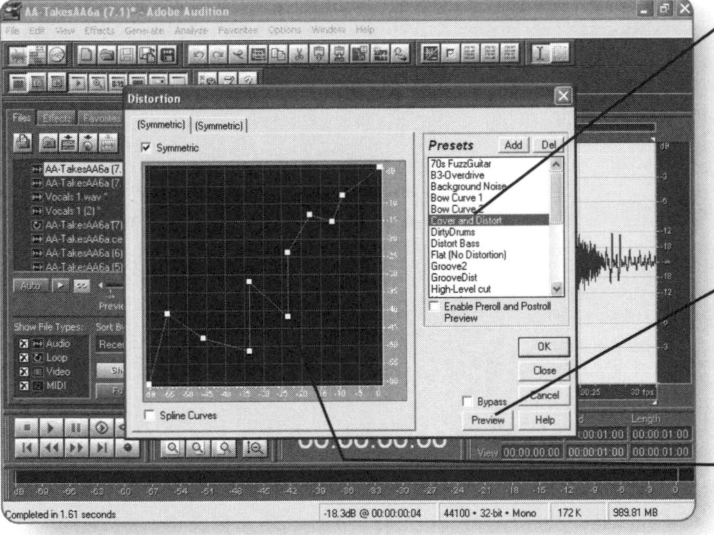

4. Click on a **preset** that most closely matches the effect you are trying to achieve. It will be highlighted. Alternatively, you can skip to Step 6 if you want to manually adjust the settings.

5. Click on the **Preview button**. You will hear how your audio sounds with that effect applied to it.

6. Click and drag anywhere on the graph to adjust the settings. A handle will be created as soon as you click.

7. Click on the **OK button**. The dialog box will close and the effect will be applied.

Composing Your Own Music

The Music effect in Audition is actually a mini composer window in which you can insert and remove musical notes. These note values will be applied to your currently selected audio. Prior to using the Music effect, you have to set the quarter note value by clicking and dragging across the portion of your waveform that will be the quarter note. It may take some time, but you can re-create your favorite songs, replayed by any audio with this effect.

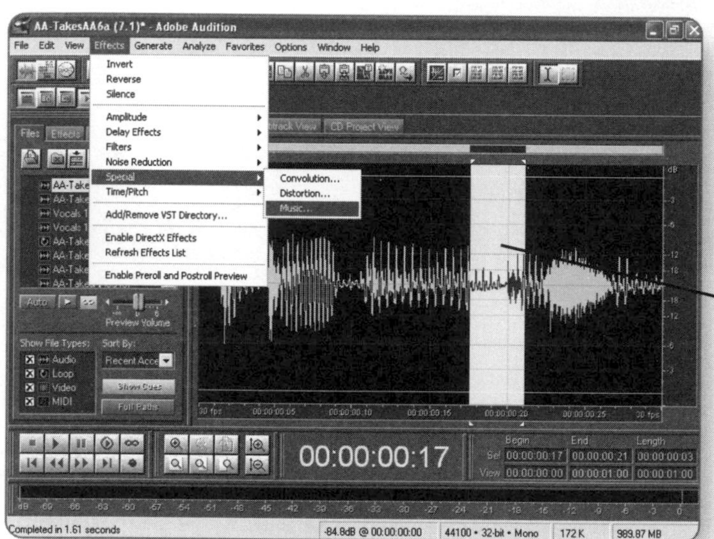

1. **Click and drag across the portion of your waveform** that you would like to represent the quarter note value.

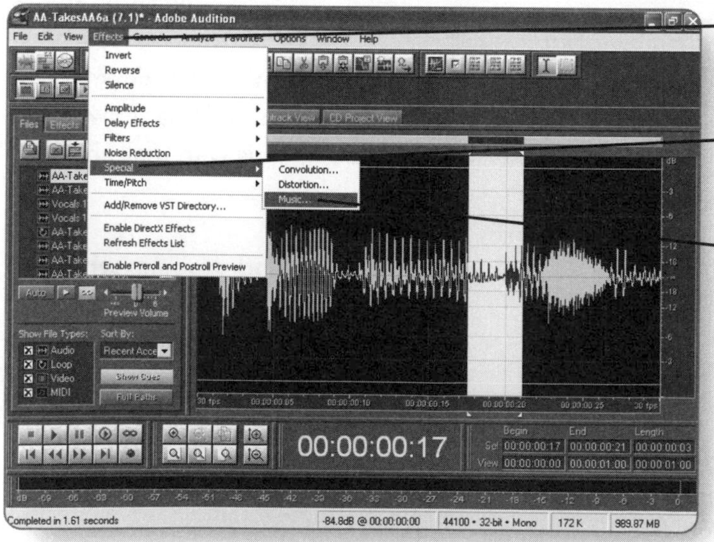

2. **Click** on **Effects**. The Effects menu will appear.

3. **Click** on **Special**. A submenu of special effects will appear.

4. **Click** on **Music**. The Music dialog box will open, allowing you to compose your own music.

5. Type a **name** for your song. You can give it any name you like. The next time you open the Music Effect dialog box, you will be able to select this song by clicking on the down arrow beside this field box.

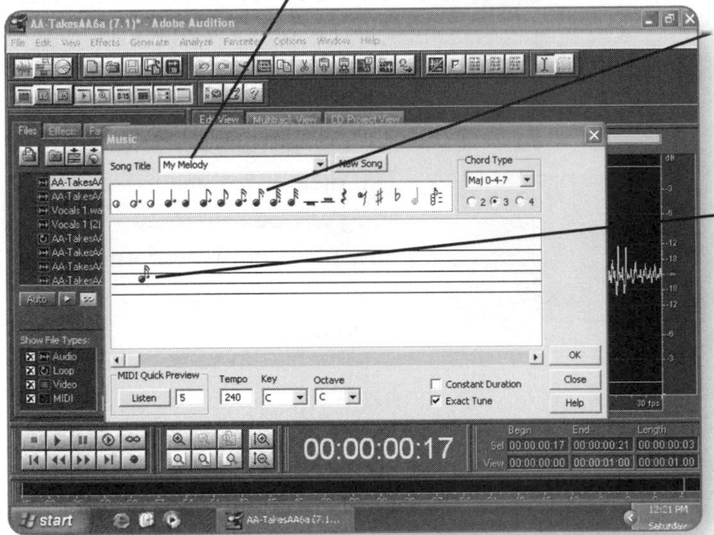

6. Position your **mouse pointer** over the note you would like to insert into the staff.

7. Click and drag the **note** to the staff. You will see a shadow of the note as you drag.

8. Release the **mouse button**. The note will be placed on the staff.

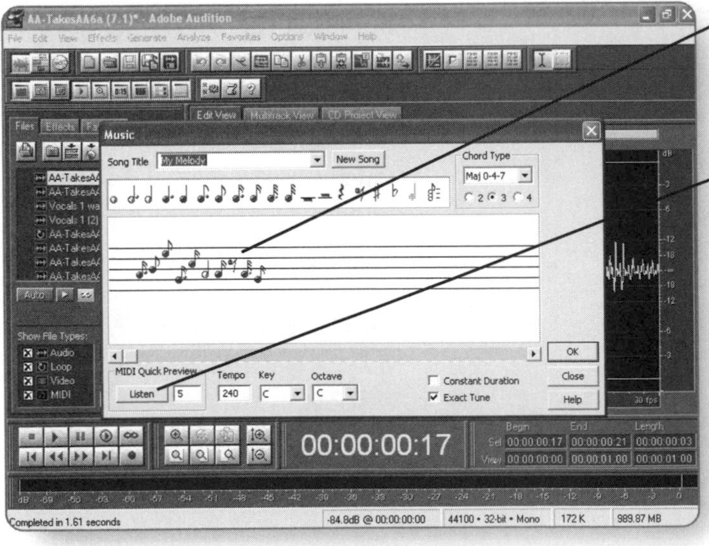

9. Repeat Steps 6-8 for any other notes that you would like to add.

10. Click on the **Listen button**. You will hear the musical value of the notes that you have placed.

11. Make any **adjustments** to the tempo, key, or octave.

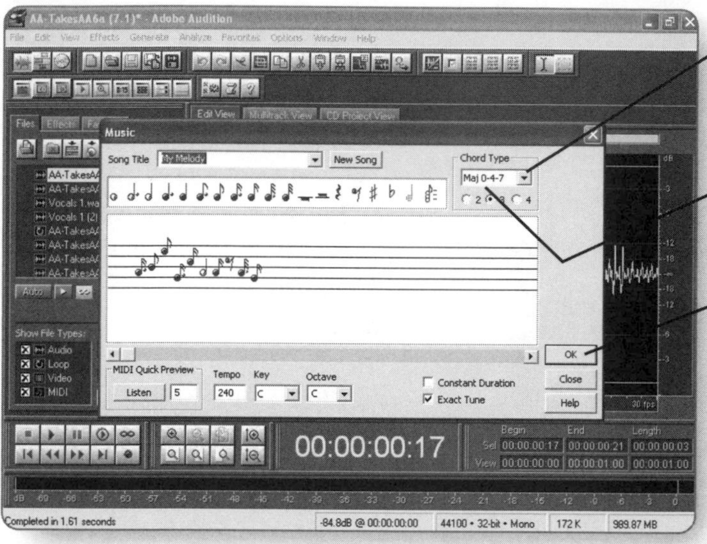

12. Click on the **Chord type down arrow**. A list of different chord types will appear.

13. Click on the desired **chord type**. It will be selected.

14. Click on **OK**. The notes will be applied to your selection. The dialog box will close, your song will be saved, and you can now play your waveform to hear how it sounds against the notes that you have created.

An Easier Way to Apply Effects

I always used to hate it when the math class teacher would make us go through the long way of solving a problem, only to teach us later that there was a much faster way to solve it. Well, I've done that to you here, but I had your best intentions in mind. In the last two chapters, you've learned to access effects from the menu bar. There is a much quicker way of opening effects dialog boxes, by using the Organizer window.

1. Open a **file** in the Waveform view. It will appear in the window.

2. Click on the **Effects tab** in the Organizer window. A list of all of the effect categories will appear.

3. Click on the **+** beside any category to expand its list. All of the effects that fall within that category will appear.

4. Double-click on the **effect** that you would like to apply. Its corresponding dialog box will appear.

Creating and Saving Presets

Almost every effect in Adobe Audition has several useful presets from which you can choose. Presets act as a quick way to apply settings to achieve a specific effect. Adobe Audition allows you to create your own presets so that once you've taken the time to get the settings just right, you can save them so they can be instantly applied in the future.

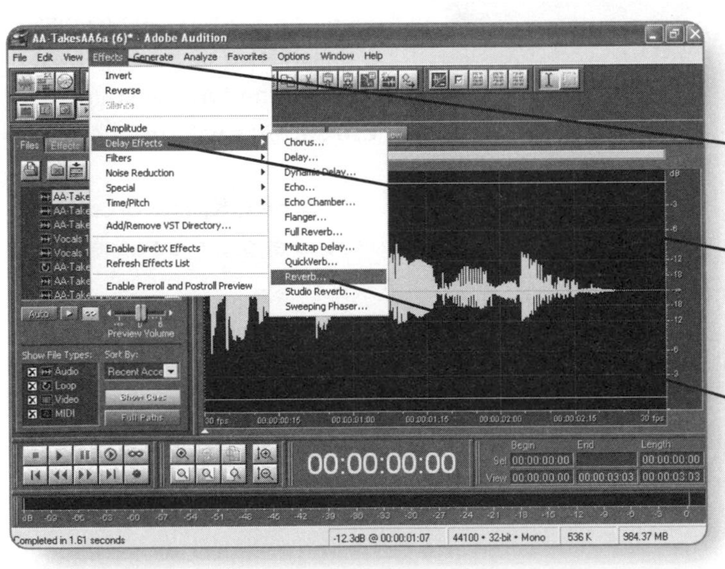

1. Click on **Effects**. The Effects menu will appear.

2. Click on **Delay Effects**. A submenu of different delay effects will appear.

3. Click on **Reverb**. The Reverb dialog box will open, allowing you to adjust the settings for that effect. In this example, we are using the Reverb effect, but you can choose any effect.

4. **Click and drag** any of the **sliders** to make the desired adjustments. These settings will be saved when you create your preset.

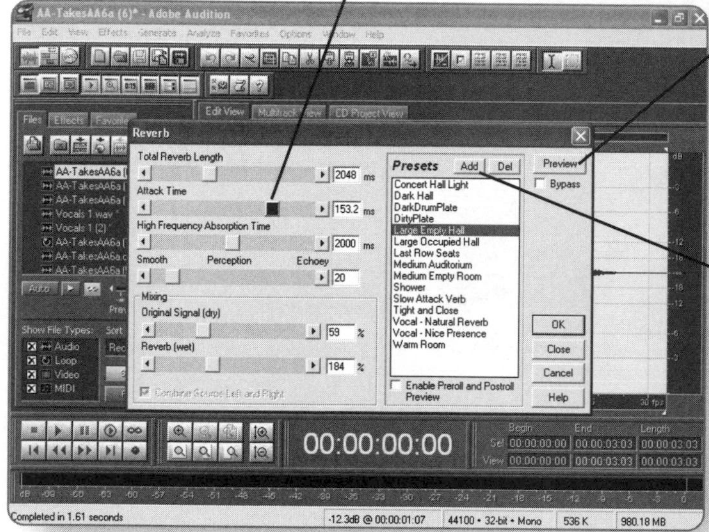

5. **Click** on the **Preview button** to make sure you have the settings as you would like them. You will hear the results. If they don't sound as you would like, go back to Step 4 and readjust.

6. **Click** on the **Add button.** A dialog box will appear in which you can enter a name for your preset.

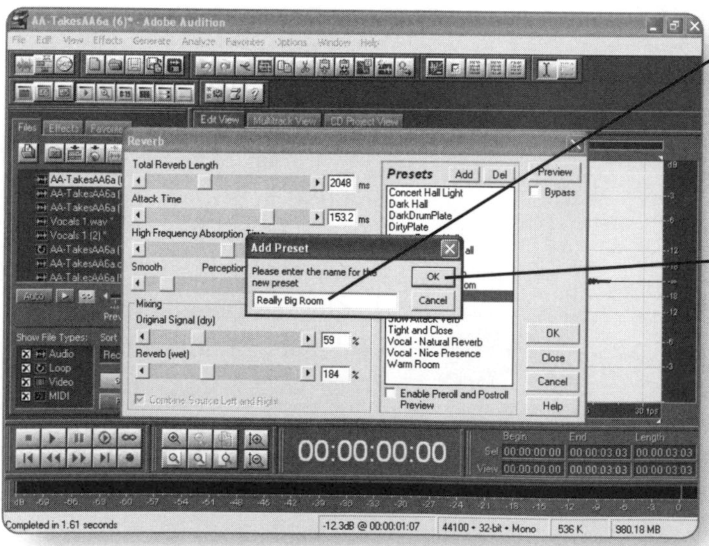

7. **Type** a **name** for your preset. It's a good idea to give it a descriptive name that best describes the type of sound these settings will produce.

8. **Click** on **OK**. The preset will be saved and can be accessed at any time.

11

Scripts and Batch Processing

Nothing is more frustrating than thinking you've finished a job only to find out that something has gone wrong and you must start over again. Imagine you've just recorded a series of audio files only to find out that a fan was running in the background and the noise appears on every track. Rather than individually repairing each audio file, you can correct them all at the same time using the Scripts and Batch Processing feature in Audition. Scripts are similar to macros that you may have worked with in other programs. They allow you to record a series of commands and then play them back at any time. Batch processing allows you to apply scripts to many different files at once.

In this chapter, you'll learn how to:

- Record, play, and edit scripts
- Batch process files
- Use the cue list for batch processing

Scripts

Scripts can be used as a way to speed up the way you work in Audition. If you have to apply the same commands over and over, you can record a script to automate the process. Once the script is recorded, it can be played back at any time.

Creating Scripts

A script will record every command you make during the recording process. To create a script, you simply have to name the script, execute the commands, and then stop recording.

> **NOTE**
>
> Scripts can only be created when you are in Edit view.

1. **Press F12** to toggle to Edit view, if you are not already there. Edit view will appear.

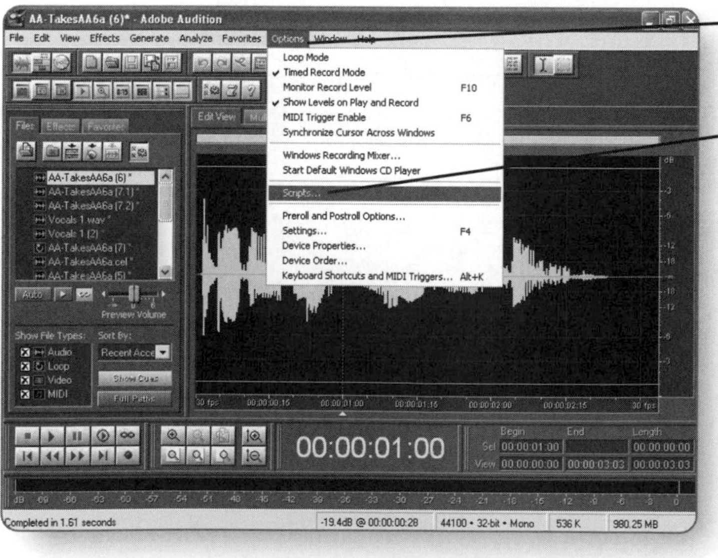

2. **Click** on **Options**. The Options menu will appear.

3. **Click** on **Scripts**. The Scripts dialog box will appear, from which you can create, edit, and run scripts.

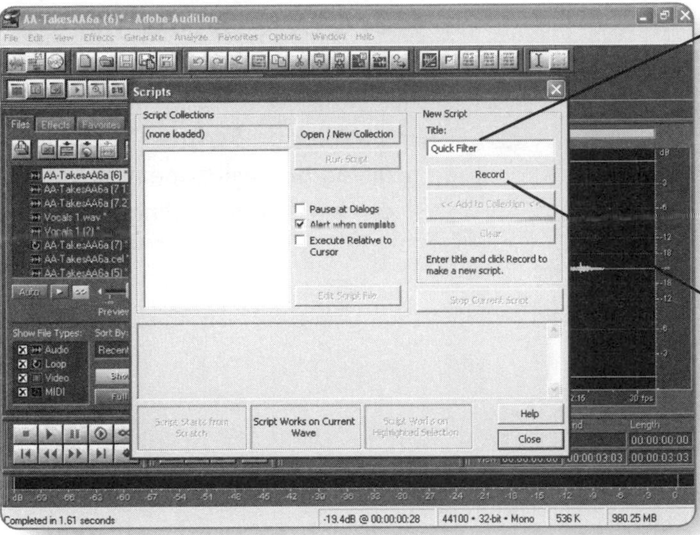

4. Click once in the **Title field box**. You will be able to enter a name for your script here.

5. Type a **name** for your script. It's a good idea to give it a descriptive name.

6. Click on the **Record button**. All of your commands will be recorded until you stop the process.

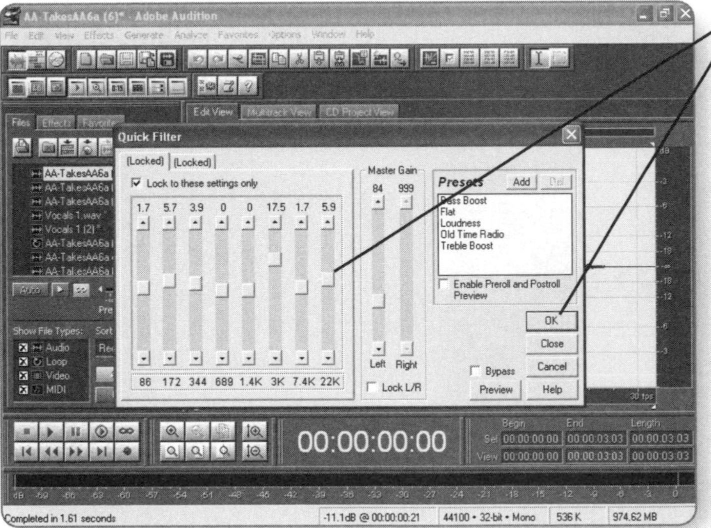

7. Click on the **commands** that you want to record. You will see everything from simple commands like cutting and copying, to apply and adjusting effects. Every command that you execute will be recorded. In this example, we are recording the application of the Quick Filter.

> **CAUTION**
>
> You shouldn't open or save a file when creating a script.

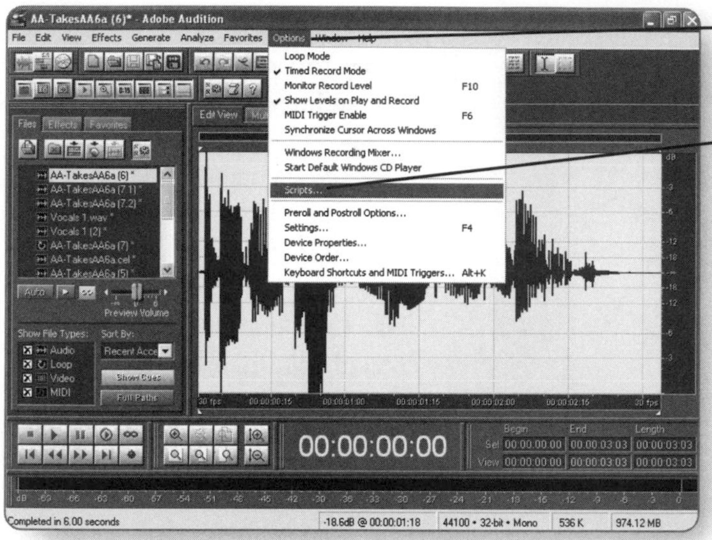

8. Click on **Options**. The Options menu will appear.

9. Click on **Scripts**. The Scripts dialog box will appear so you can end the recording.

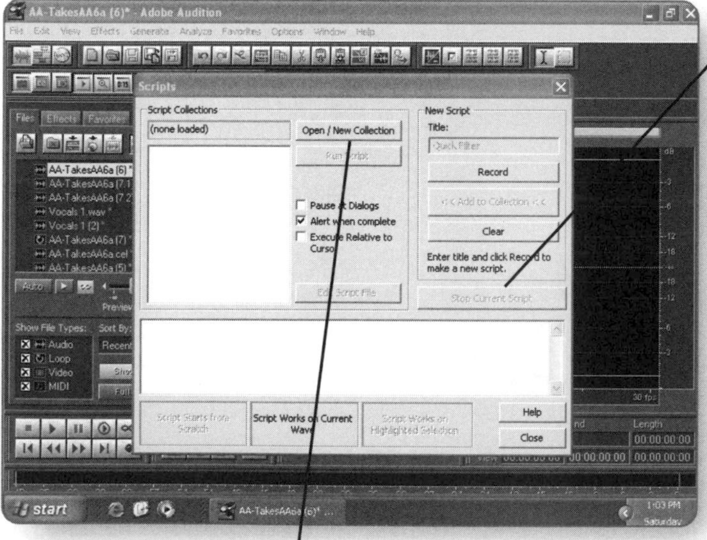

10. Click on the **Stop Current Script button**. The script recording process will end.

11. Click on the **Open/New Collection button** to choose which collection to add this script to.

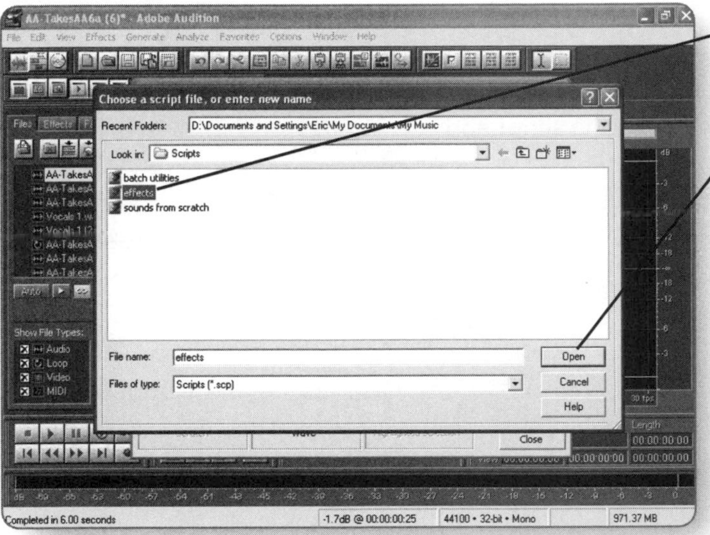

12. Click on the desired **collection**. It will be selected.

13. Click on **Open**. The collection will open and you can add your new script to it.

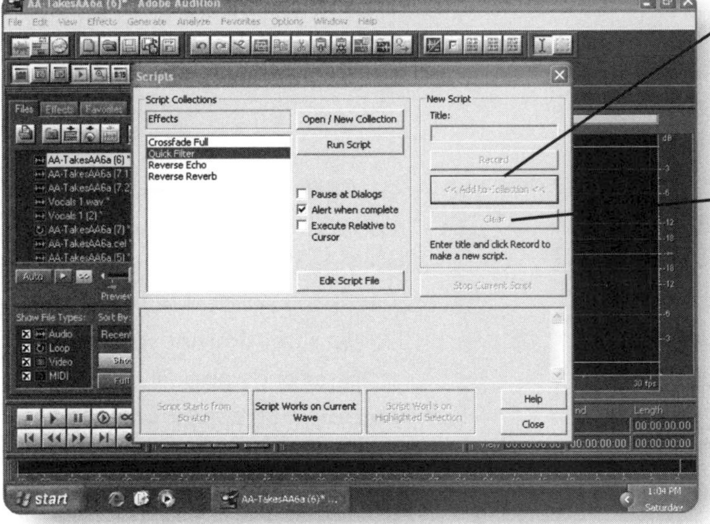

14. Click on the **Add to Collection button**. The script will be added to the Scripts Collection window.

15. Click on the **Close button**. The dialog box will close and you will be returned to your Audition sessions.

Running Scripts

Once you have a script created, playing it is simply a matter of selecting the script and running it.

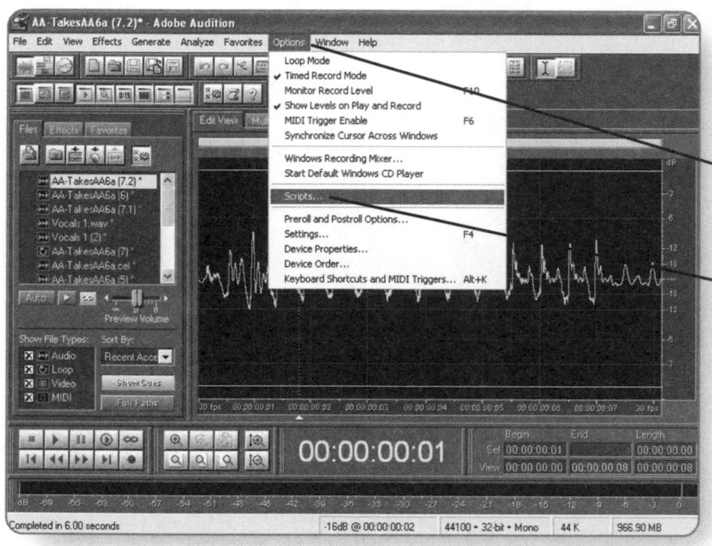

1. **Press F12** to toggle to Edit view, if you are not already there. Edit view will appear.
2. **Click** on **Options**. The Options menu will appear.
3. **Click** on **Scripts**. The Scripts dialog box will appear, from which you can create, edit, and run scripts.

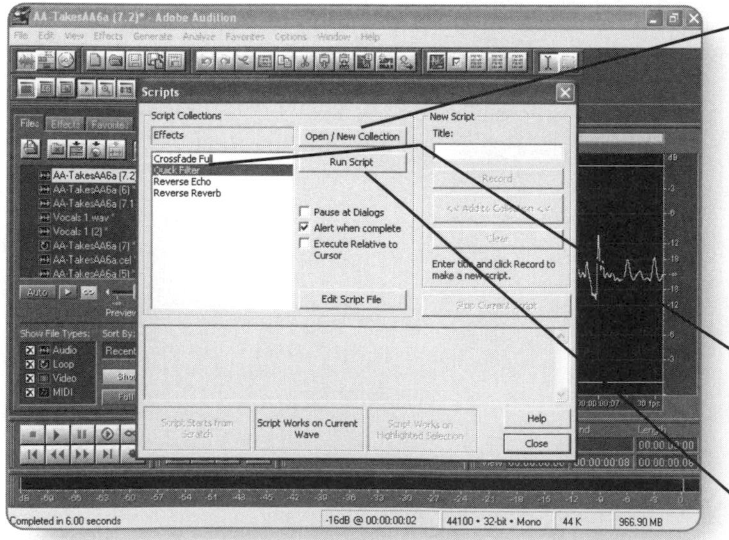

4. **Click** on the **Open/New Collection button**. A dialog box will open from which you can select the script that you would like to run. Alternatively, if the script already appears on the window, you can skip to Step 5 or 6.
5. **Click** on the **script** that you would like to run. It will be highlighted.
6. **Click** on **Run Script**. The script will now be executed.

Editing Scripts

When creating a script, Audition takes the commands that you execute and converts them into a text file. Audition then reads that text file when running the script. Because the script itself is just a text file, it can be easily edited. That being said, beyond changing selection boundaries or removing certain commands, it's a good idea to re-record a script rather then edit it.

1. **Press F12** to toggle to Edit view, if you are not already there. Edit view will appear.

2. **Click** on **Options**. The Options menu will appear.

3. **Click** on **Scripts**. The Scripts dialog box will appear, from which you can create, edit, and run scripts.

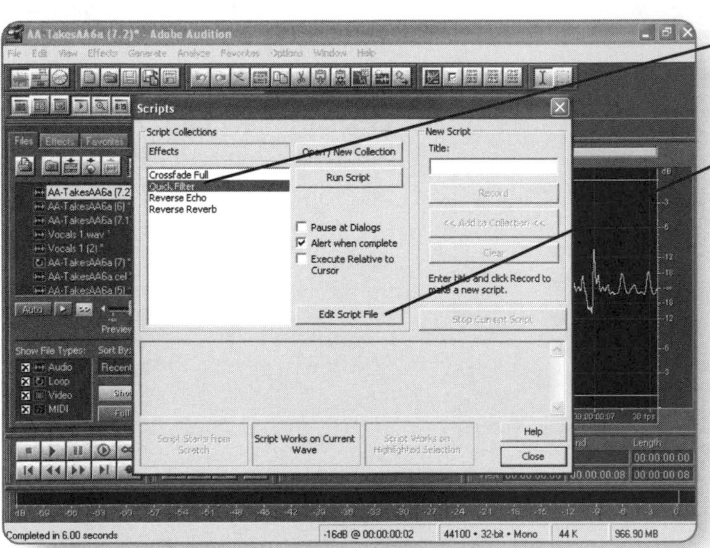

4. **Click** on the desired **script**. It will be highlighted.

5. **Click** on the **Edit Script File button**. Your script will open in the Notepad program.

6. **Click and drag** to **highlight any section** that you would like to delete or change. Once highlighted it can be deleted or changed.

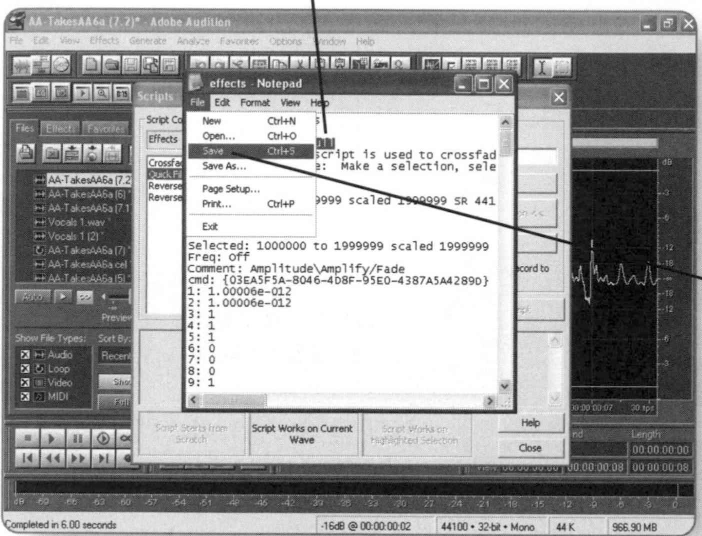

7. **Make** the desired **changes**. They will appear directly on-screen.

8. **Click** on **File**. The File menu will appear.

9. **Click** on **Save**. The changes that you have made to the script will be saved.

10. **Click** on the **X** in the top-right corner to close Notepad. Notepad will close.

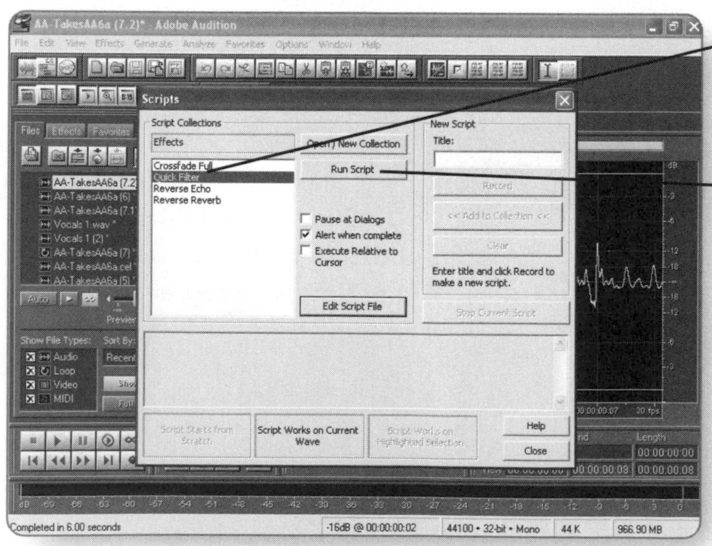

11. **Click** on the **name of the script** you just edited. It will be highlighted.

12. **Click** on **Run Script**. The script that you edited will now run.

Batch Processing

Batch processing gives you the ability to apply a multitude of scripts all at the same time. The benefit of this is that tasks that once would've taken hours to complete can now be done with a few clicks of a button. A good example is if you needed to remove noise from some old recordings. Rather than having to do them one at a time, you can create a script that removes the noise in one of the files and then apply that script to every file you'd like to edit. What's also really cool about batch processing is that you can automatically resample a group of files and change their format. In addition to batch processing with scripts, you can also use cue ranges.

Batch Processing with Scripts

Once you have created a script, you can apply it to many files at the same time.

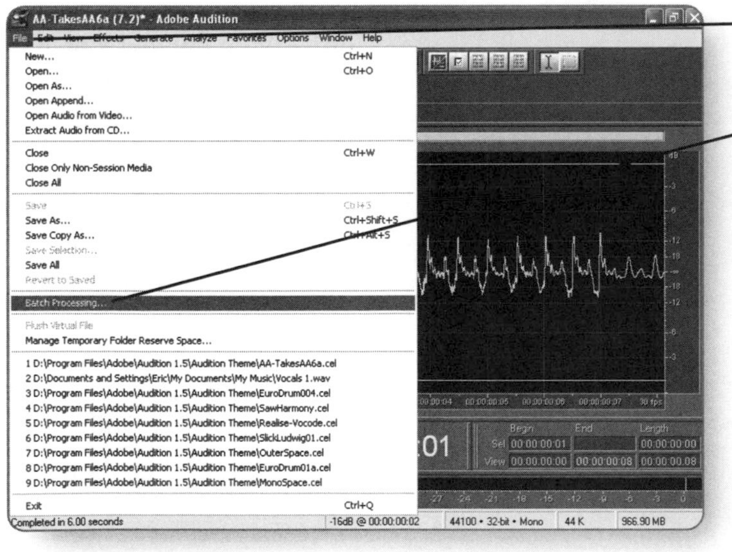

1. **Click** on **File**. The File menu will appear.

2. **Click** on **Batch Processing**. The Batch Processing dialog box will open.

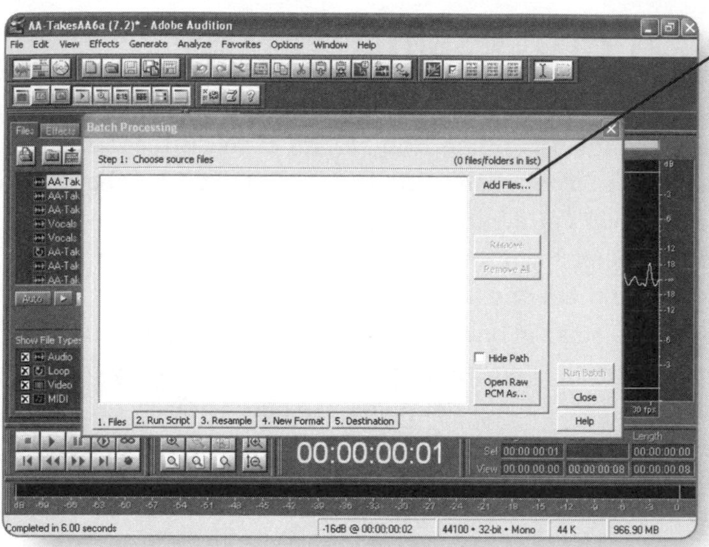

3. Click on the **Add Files button**. A dialog box will appear, from which you can select the files that you'd like batch processed.

4. Navigate to the **folder** that contains the files that you would like to batch process.

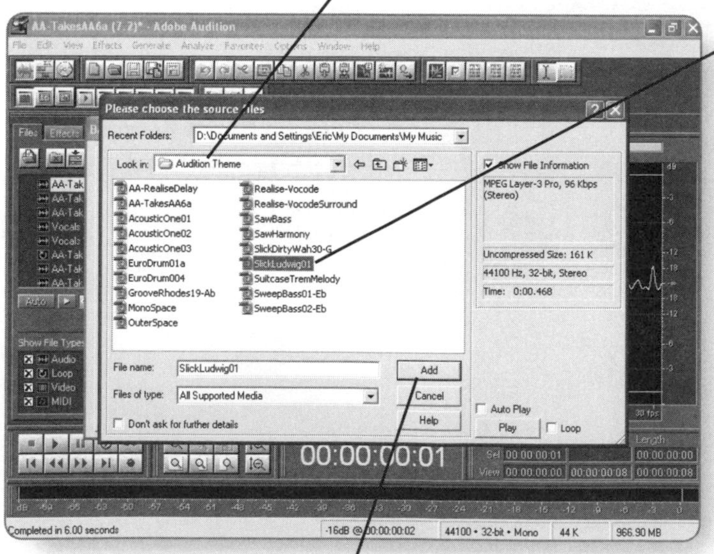

5. Click on the **file** that you would like to add to the list of files to be processed. The file will be highlighted.

> **TIP**
>
> By holding down the Ctrl key, you can select multiple non-contiguous files, and by holding down the Shift key, you can select multiple contiguous files.

6. Click on the **Add button**. The file will be added to the list of files to be processed and the dialog box will close.

7. Repeat Steps 3-5 to add any additional files to be batch processed.

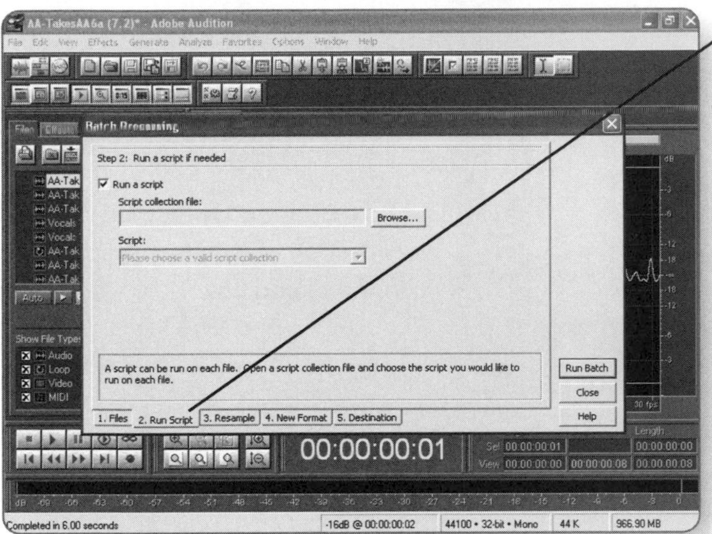

8. Click on the **Run Script tab** at the bottom of the dialog box. You will now be able to select a script to apply to the files.

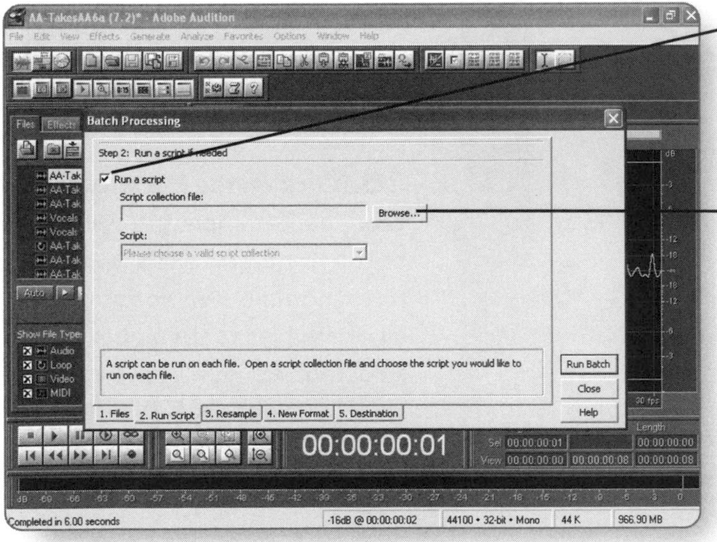

9. Click on the **Run Script check box**, if it is not already selected. A checkmark will appear in the box.

10. Click on the **Browse button**. A dialog box will open, from which you can select the Script collection file that contains the script that you would like to apply to the files.

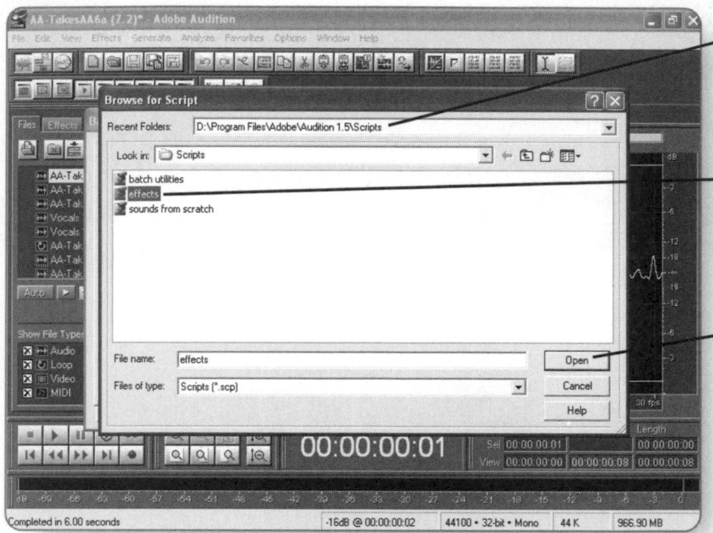

11. Browse to the **folder** that contains the script collection file.

12. Click on the desired **script collection file**. It will be highlighted.

13. Click on **Open**. The collection of scripts will appear in the dialog box.

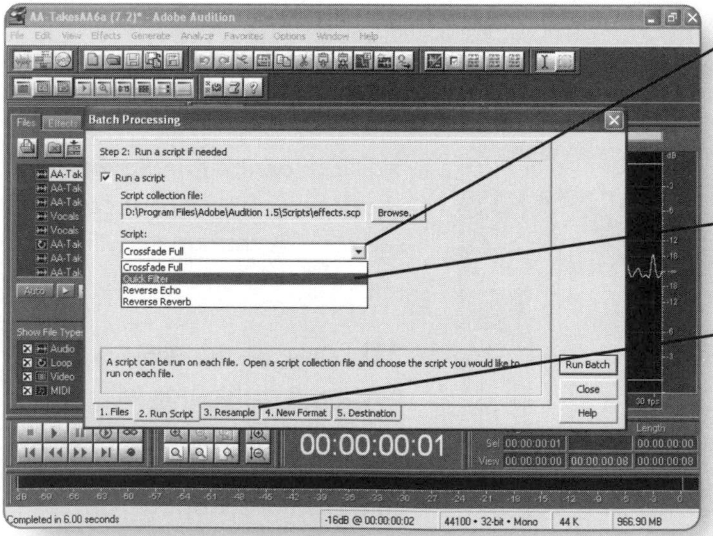

14. Click on the **down arrow** to see a full list of scripts that fall under this collection. The list will appear.

15. Click on the desired **script**. It will be selected.

16. Click on the **Resample tab**. The Resample tab will come to the front. This will allow you to change the sample format for all of the files that you have selected. You don't have to select this option, but it's handy for changing file formats.

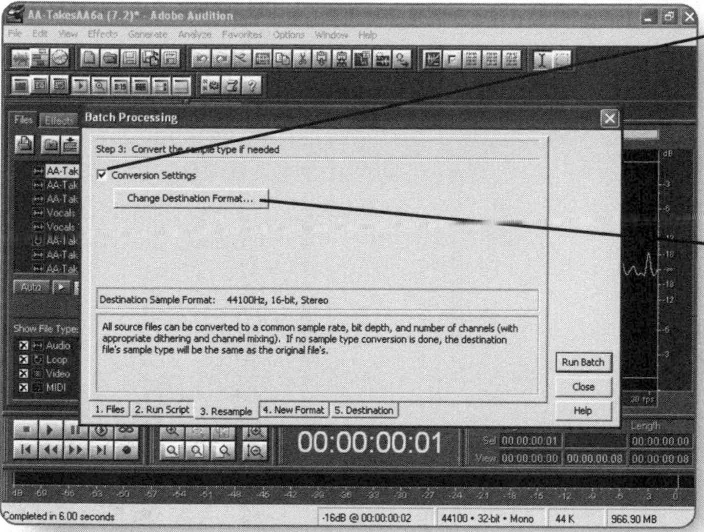

17. Click on the **Conversion Settings check box**, if it is not already selected. Once it is selected, you can specify the type of format for the files.

18. Click on the **Change Destination Format button**. A dialog box will appear, from which you can set the format for the files.

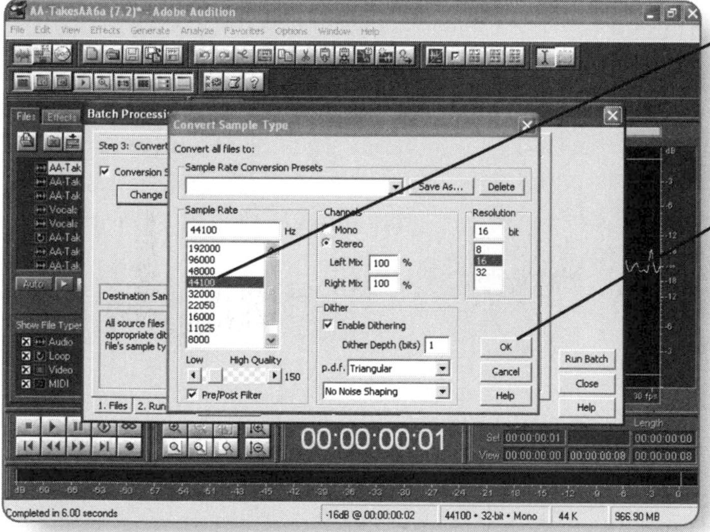

19. Click on the desired **options**. You can select sample rate, channel mix, and resolution settings.

20. Click on **OK**. The settings will be applied to all of the files when you initiate the batch process and the dialog box will close.

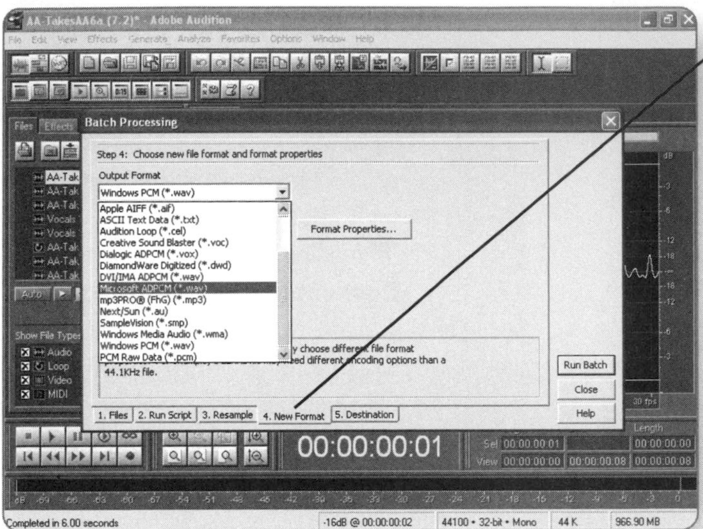

21. Click on the **New Format tab**. The New Format tab will come to the front. This will allow you to change the file format of all the files that have been selected.

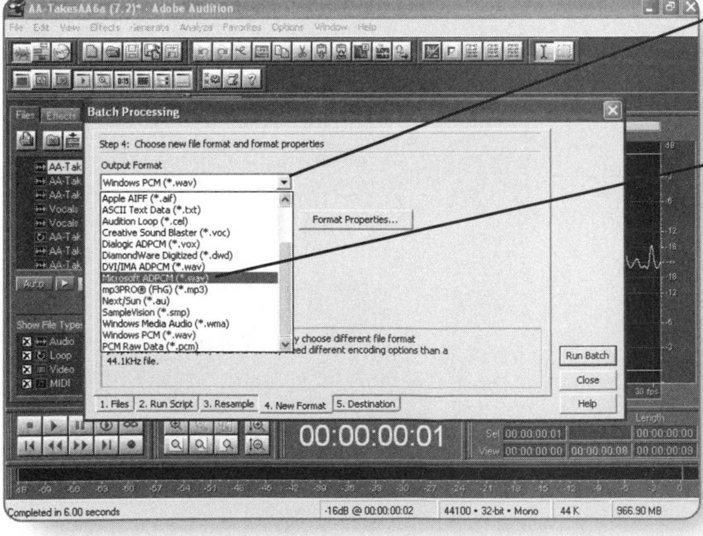

22. Click on the **down arrow** to view the different types of file formats that are available.

23. Click on the desired **file format**. It will be selected.

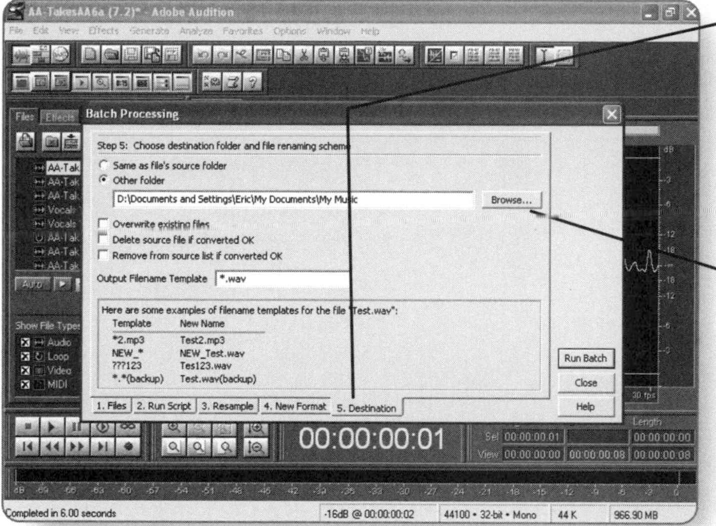

24. Click on the **Destination tab**. The Destination tab will come to the front. You will now be able to determine where you would like to place your files after they've been processed.

25. Click on the **Browse button**. You will be able to select the folder in which you would like to store the files. Alternatively, you can **click** the **circle** beside Same as file's source folder to store the files there.

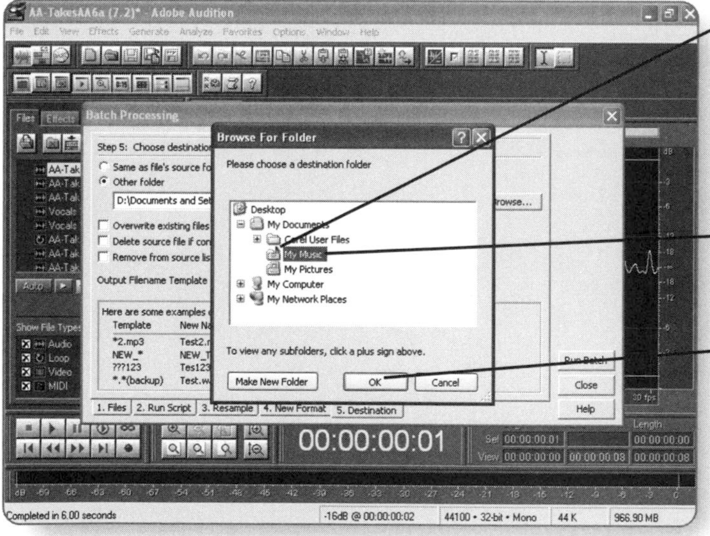

26. Navigate to the desired **folder** in which you would like to store the files after they've been processed. You can **click** the **+** to see any subfolders.

27. Click on the desired **folder**. It will be highlighted.

28. Click on **OK**. The folder will be selected as the repository for your processed files.

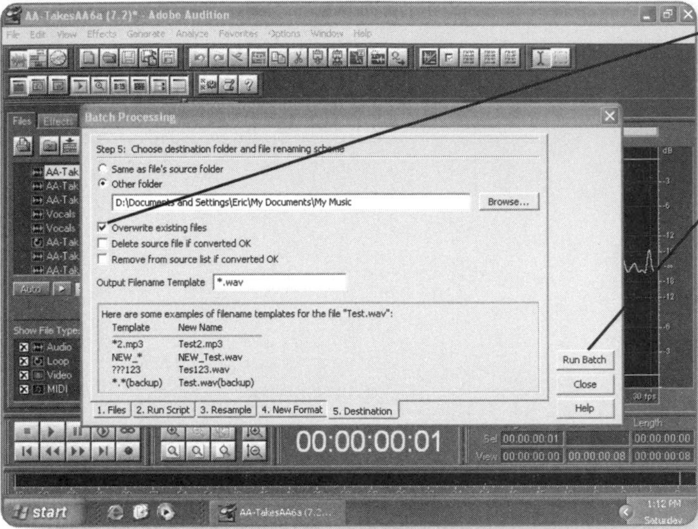

29. Click on the **check boxes** to select options for the file storage.

30. Click on the **Run Batch button**. The files that you selected will be batch processed based on the settings you entered.

12

Working with Video

So why did Adobe acquire Audition from Syntrillium Software? If you take a look at Adobe's product line, they have a strong base in graphics programs and have solid video products, but, at that time, really had nothing for audio. Because video and audio go hand in hand, it makes sense that they would bring in an audio editor to complement their video line. Audition gives you several tools for adding and extracting audio to and from video.

In this chapter, you'll learn how to:

- Extract audio from video
- Import video
- Change the number of video frames
- Add audio to video

Extracting Audio from Video

Audio Audition gives you the ability to extract audio from a video file. Once it is extracted, it can be edited like any other audio file.

1. **Press F12** to toggle to Multitrack view, if you are not already there. Multitrack view will appear.

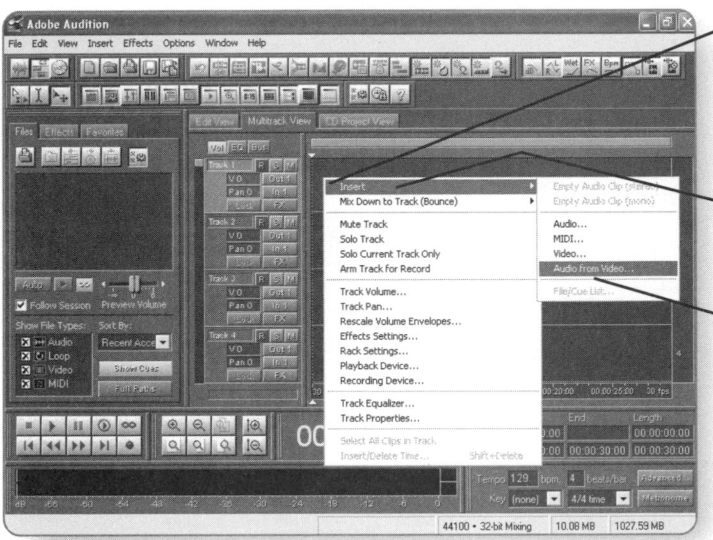

2. **Right-click** on the **track** in which you would like to insert the audio from a video clip. A menu will appear.

3. **Click** on **Insert**. A submenu will appear.

4. **Click** on **Audio from Video**. A dialog box will appear where you can select a video from which the audio will be extracted.

> **NOTE**
>
> You must have DirectX 9.0 installed on your computer to run this feature. If you don't, it can be downloaded from www.microsoft.com.

5. Click on the desired **video**. It will be highlighted.

> **TIP**
>
> Audio Audition allows you to extract video from .avi, .mpg, .mpeg, .wmv, and .asf file types.

6. Click on the **Open button**. The audio will be extracted from the video and will be inserted in the track.

7. Double-click on the **audio clip** to edit it in Edit view. You will now be able to edit it like any other audio file.

Importing Video

You can actually bring video into Audition so that you can create a score for a movie, music video, or home recordings. When you import a video that happens to have sound, the sound is automatically extracted. You have two choices when it comes to importing video, it can be imported directly to a track or it can be inserted into the Files area so that it can be dropped into a track at a later time.

Importing Video Directly to Tracks

Importing a video into a track is a matter of choosing the track where you want to import the video and then choosing the file. Once you have the video imported, it can be viewed frame by frame along side the audio.

1. **Press F12** to toggle to Multitrack view, if you are not already there. Multitrack view will appear.

2. **Right-click** on the **track** in which you would like to insert the audio from a video clip. A menu will appear.

3. **Click** on **Insert**. A submenu will appear.

4. **Click** on **Video**. A dialog box will appear, from which you can select a video to import.

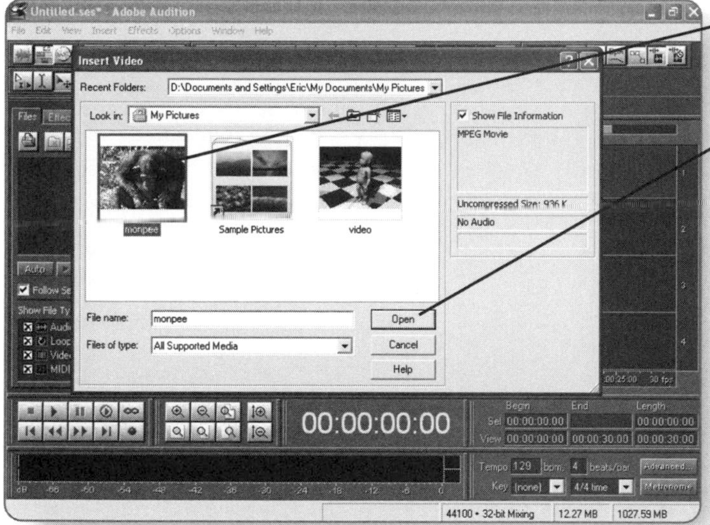

5. Click on the desired **video**. It will be selected.

6. Click on the **Open button**. The video will open in both a separate video and within the track that you selected. If the video also had audio, the audio will open in a separate track.

7. Click on the **X** in the top-right corner of the video window. The video window will close.

> **NOTE**
>
> You can only have one video open per session.

Importing Video to the Organizer Window

You can import video to the Organizer window so that it can be inserted into a track at a later time. When you import a video that contains audio into the Organizer window, the video and audio appear as separate files. You can then edit the audio or insert the video at any time.

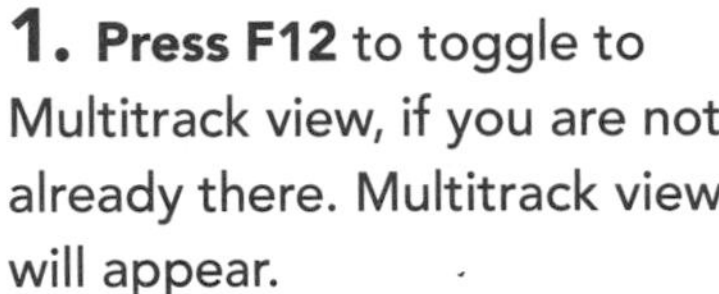

1. **Press F12** to toggle to Multitrack view, if you are not already there. Multitrack view will appear.
2. **Click** on **File**. The File menu will appear.

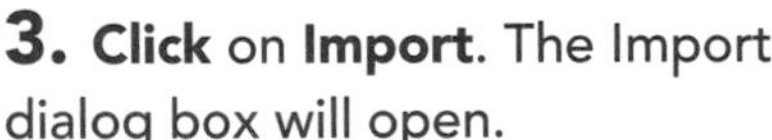

3. **Click** on **Import**. The Import dialog box will open.

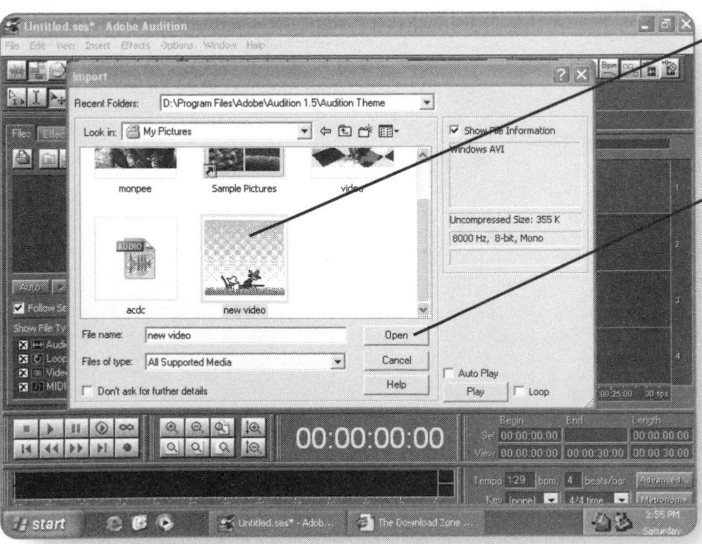

4. **Click** on the **video** that you would like to insert into your session. It will be highlighted.
5. **Click** on the **Open button**. The file will be inserted into the Files area of the Organizer window. If the video contains audio, it will appear as a separate file.

6. Click and drag the **video file or the audio file** from the video into the desired track. Alternatively, you can **double-click** on the **audio file** to edit it in Edit view.

Changing the Number of Video Frames

The number of video frames that you see within the track is dependent on how far you are zoomed in or out of your data. In other words, because when you zoom in or out, you change the values in the time ruler, you can see more or fewer video frames as you change zoom levels.

1. Click on the **Zoom In Horizontally button**. More frames of the video will appear in the window.

2. Click on the **Zoom Out Horizontally button**. Fewer frames will appear in the window.

Adding Audio to Video

Once you have imported an audio file, you can add audio to your session and then resave the video with the new audio attached to it. Using this method, you can create scores for videos, narrate movies, or add sound effects to your videos.

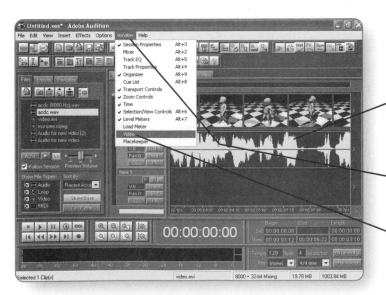

1. Add any **audio tracks** to your session that you would like to be a part of your video.

2. Click on **Window**. The Window menu will appear.

3. Click on **Video**. This will open the video window, if it is not already open.

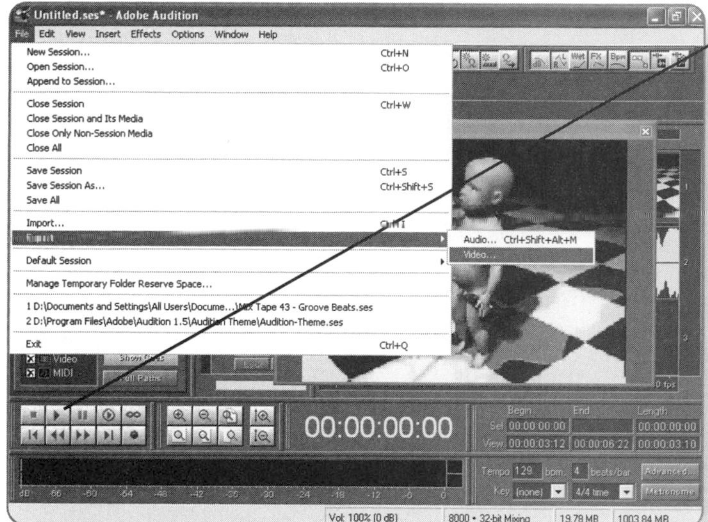

4. **Click** on the **Play button**. The session audio and the video will play so you can preview how the final file will sound and look.

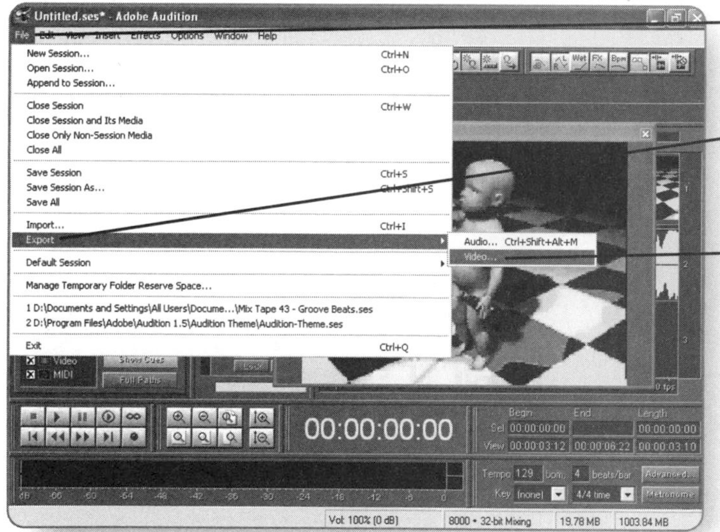

5. **Click** on **File**. The File menu will appear.
6. **Click** on **Export**. A submenu will appear.
7. **Click** on **Video**. A dialog box will open from which you can adjust the settings for saving your video.

> **NOTE**
>
> Adobe Audition can only export to .avi video files.

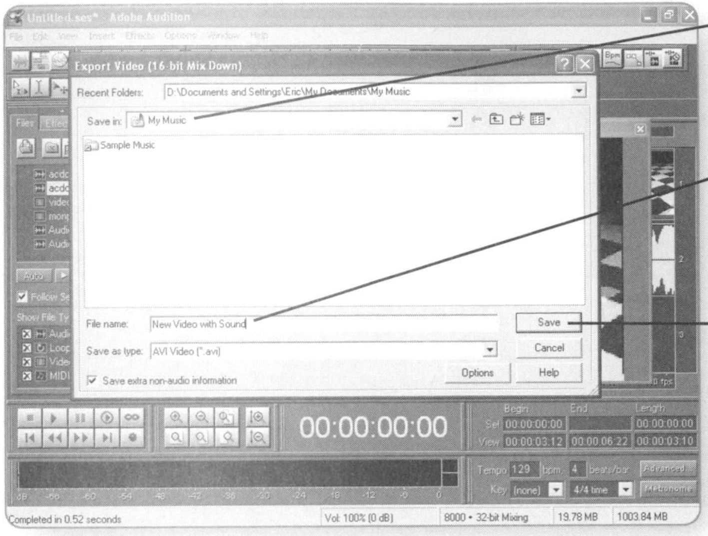

8. **Navigate** to the **location** on your computer where you would like to save your file.

9. **Type** a **name** for your video. You can give it any name you want.

10. **Click** on **Save**. The audio in your session will be saved, along with the video as an .avi file.

13

Creating MP3s and Burning CDs

Your blood, sweat, and tears have paid off, and you finally have the perfect mix. Now what? Once you have completed your project, you have several options when deciding what to do with your music. The most popular option by far is to burn it to CD so that you can distribute it to others. And with the popularity of MP3s as a distribution vehicle for music, you can choose to save your audio as an MP3 and e-mail it to others or place it on a file share.

In this chapter, you'll learn how to:

- Create MP3s
- Import tracks for CDs
- Adjust CD track order
- Write to CDs

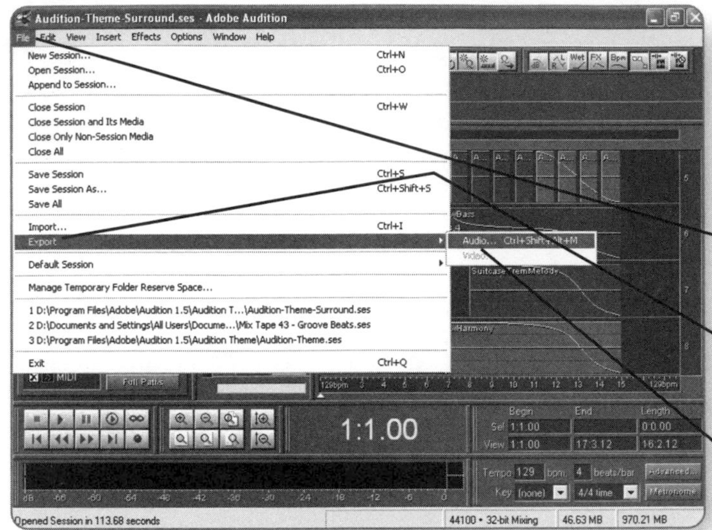

Creating MP3s

The process of creating an MP3 out of an existing project is just a matter of exporting the file.

1. **Click** on **File**. The File menu will appear.

2. **Click** on **Export**. A submenu will appear.

3. **Click** on **Audio**. A dialog box will open from which you can set the parameters for the export.

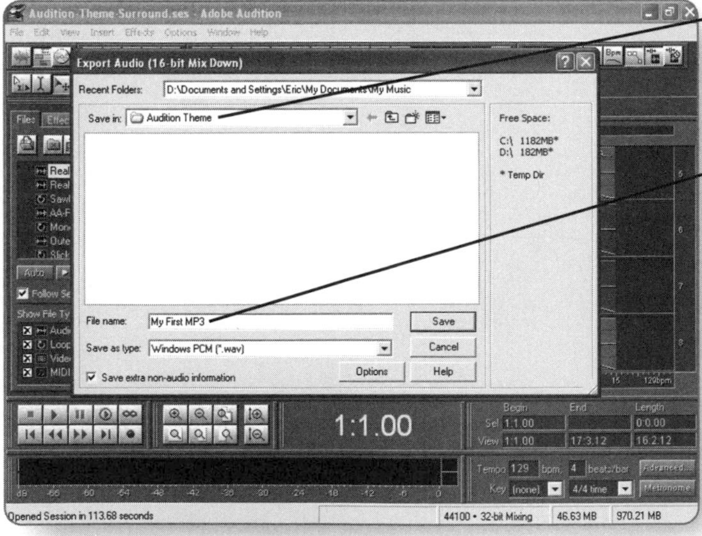

4. **Navigate** to the **folder** in which you want to export the file.

5. **Type** a **name** for your file. You can give it any name that you like.

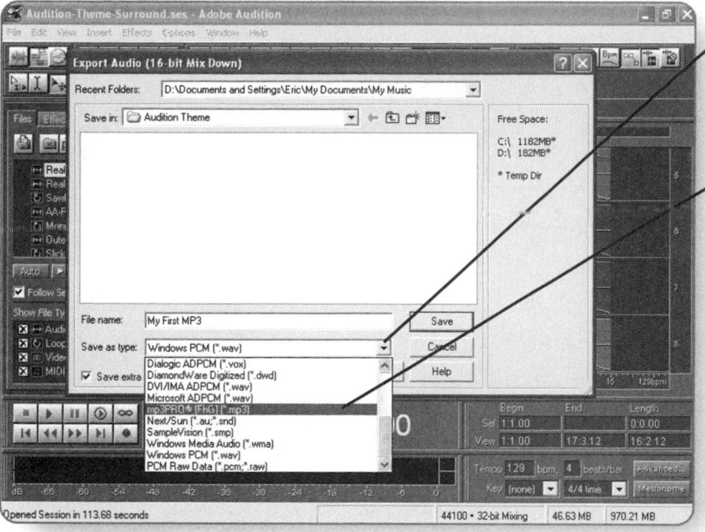

6. Click on the **Save As type down arrow**. A list of different file types will appear.

7. Click on **MP3PRO®(FhG) (*.MP3)**. It will be selected.

> **TIP**
>
> MP3s are just one of over 20 different types of files you can save your audio to.

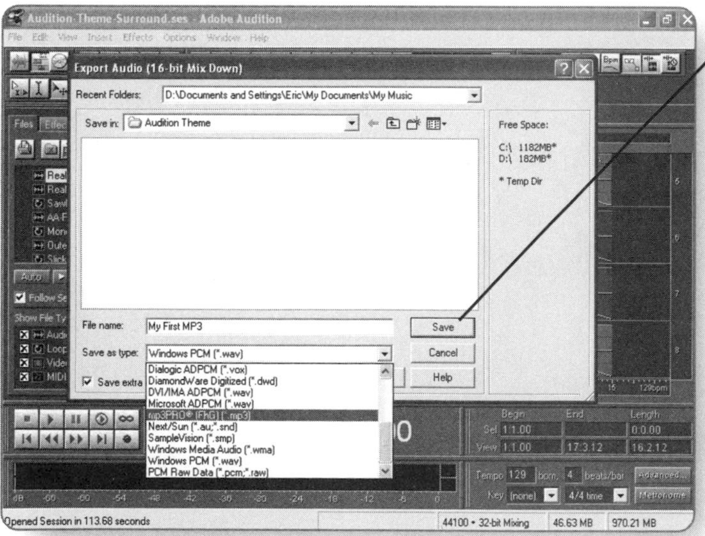

8. Click on **Save**. The file will be saved as an MP3 to the folder that you selected.

Creating CDs with CD Project View

The ultimate location for your audio files is CD. Hopefully it'll find itself on the shelf of nationwide music stores with thousands of adoring fans scrambling to get their copies. The new CD Project View is your one-stop shop for creating CDs from your music. With it you can select tracks, rename them, change their order, see how much space they take up on the CD, and of course, burn the CD.

Adding Tracks

Adding tracks to your CD project is simply a matter of clicking and dragging them into the window.

1. **Click** on **View**. The View menu will appear.

2. **Click** on **CD Project View**. The screen will change to show you the CD Project View.

3. Click on the **Files tab**, if it is not already selected. The Files tab will come to the front.

4. Click on the **Import File button**. A dialog box will appear where you can select your files if they are not already loaded into the session.

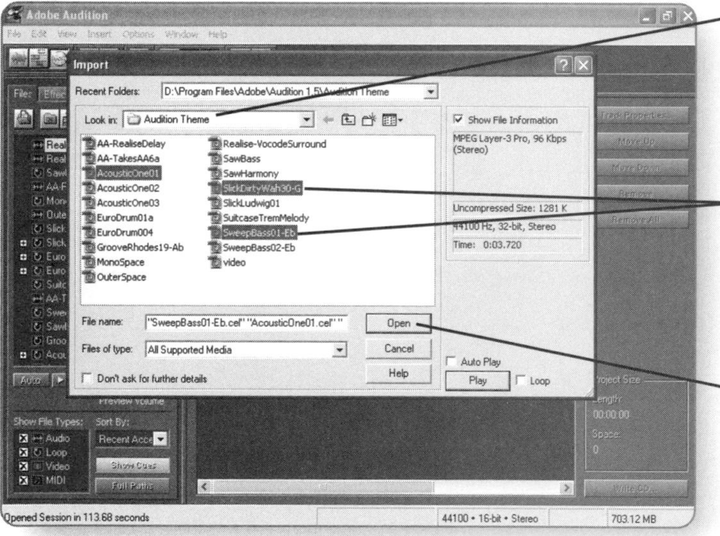

5. Navigate to the **folder** that contains the audio tracks that you would like to add to your CD.

6. Ctrl + **click** on the **audio files** that you would like to add to your CD. The audio files will be highlighted.

7. Click on the **Open button**. The files you selected will be loaded into the files section of the Organizer window.

8. **Click and drag** the **files** from the Organizer window to the CD Project View window.

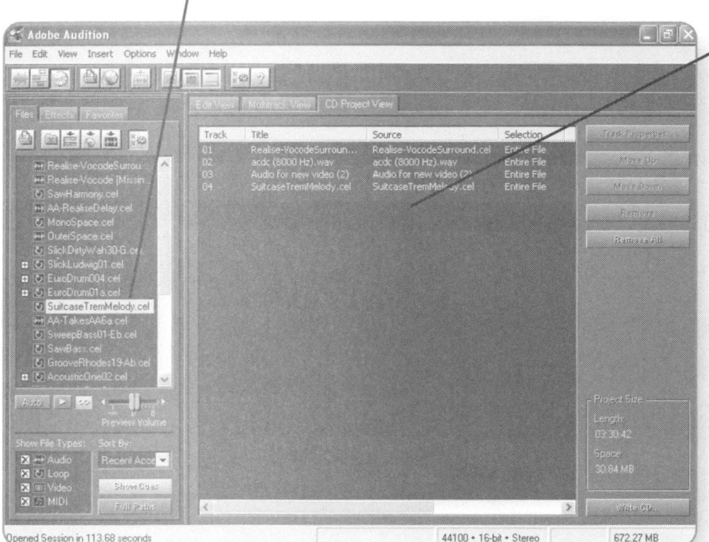

9. **Release** the **mouse**. The file will appear in the window.

10. **Repeat Steps 8 and 9** for the rest of the files that you would like to add.

> **TIP**
>
> Depending on the type of CD you plan on using, you can store anywhere from 60-90 minutes of audio. As you add files to the CD Project View, there is an indicator that will tell you how much room you have used in both minutes and megabytes.

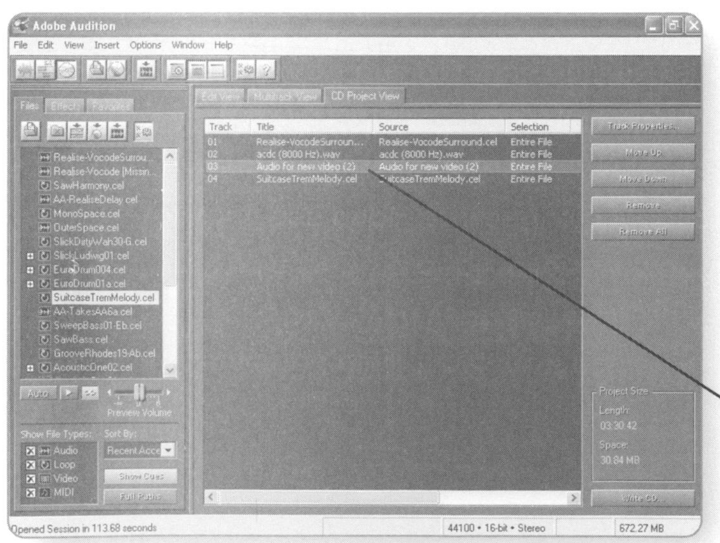

Changing Track Order

You certainly don't want your "B-side material" at the start of your CD, so Audition gives you a quick way to change the order of your tracks.

1. **Click** on the **file** that you would like to move. It will be highlighted.

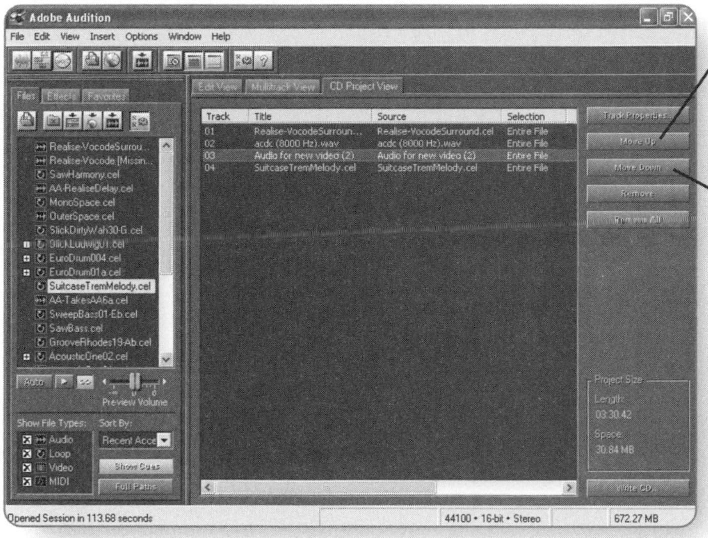

2. Click on the **Move Up or Move Down button**. The file will move up or down by one track.

3. Repeat Step 2 until your file is at the desired location.

4. Repeat Steps 1 to 3 for any other tracks that you would like to move.

Removing Tracks

Getting rid of tracks in the CD Project View is a breeze. You simply select the track and then click the Remove button.

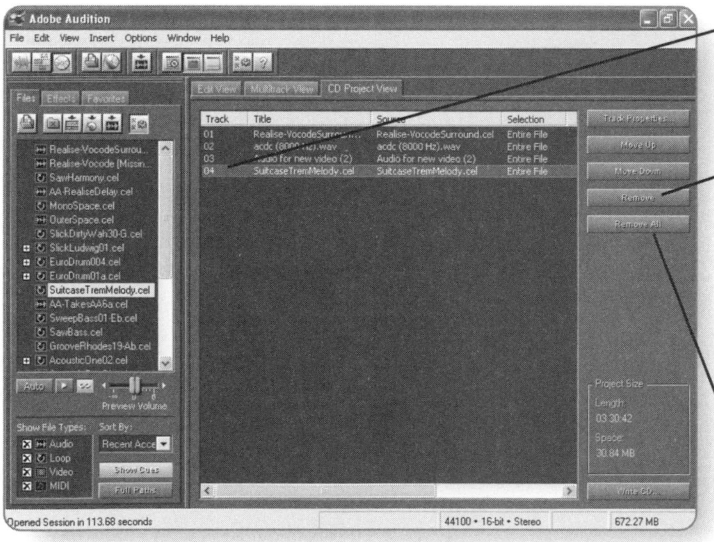

1. Click on the **file** that you would like to remove. It will be highlighted.

2. Click on the **Remove button**. The file will be removed from the CD project.

3. Repeat Step 2 with any other files that you would like to remove.

4. Click on the **Remove All button** if you want to remove all the files from the project and start from scratch. All of the files will be removed.

Changing Track Properties

If the name of your audio file isn't how you'd like it to appear on the CD, you can quickly change the name and other track information by accessing the track properties.

1. **Click** on the **track** whose properties you would like to change. The track will be highlighted.

2. **Click** on the **Track Properties button**. The Track Properties dialog box will open.

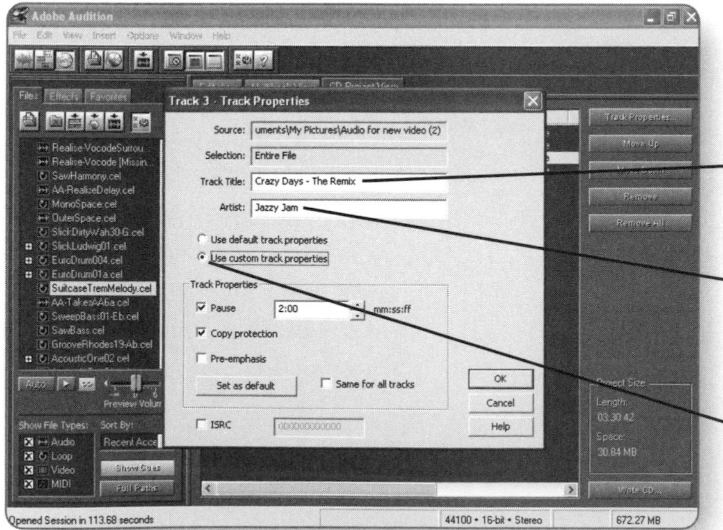

3. **Click and drag across** the **Track Title field box**. The title will be highlighted.

4. **Type** a **new name** for the track. It will appear as you type.

5. **Repeat Steps 3 and 4** for the Artist field box, if you want to enter Artist information.

6. **Click** on the **circle** beside Use custom track properties if you want to manually change some of the track properties.

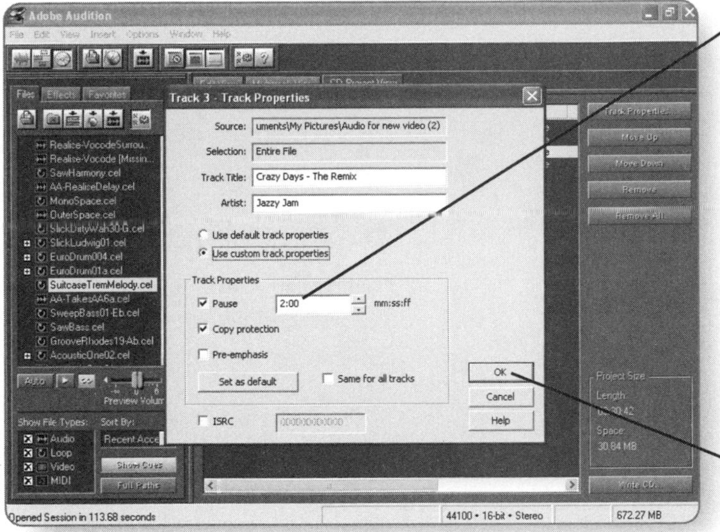

7. Make the desired **adjustments**. You can select check boxes and change the pause time before the track.

> **NOTE**
>
> By default, Audition adds a two-second pause before a track.

8. Click on **OK**. The changes will take effect and the dialog box will close.

Burning the CD

Once you have all the tracks in the right order, with the right names and all the properties set, it's time to burn your CD. Within Audition you can select a burning device and then adjust the settings for that device.

1. Click on the **Write CD button**. A dialog box will appear where you can select your device and enter settings.

2. **Click** on the **Device down arrow**. A list of burning devices on your machine will appear.

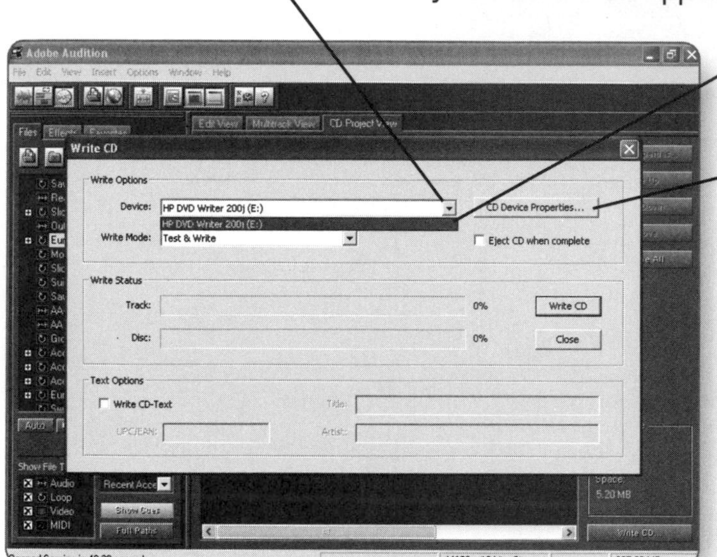

3. **Click** on the desired **device**. It will be selected.

4. **Click** on the **Device Properties button**. Another dialog box will appear where you can adjust settings for your device.

5. **Click** on the **Buffer Size down arrow**. A list of sizes will appear.

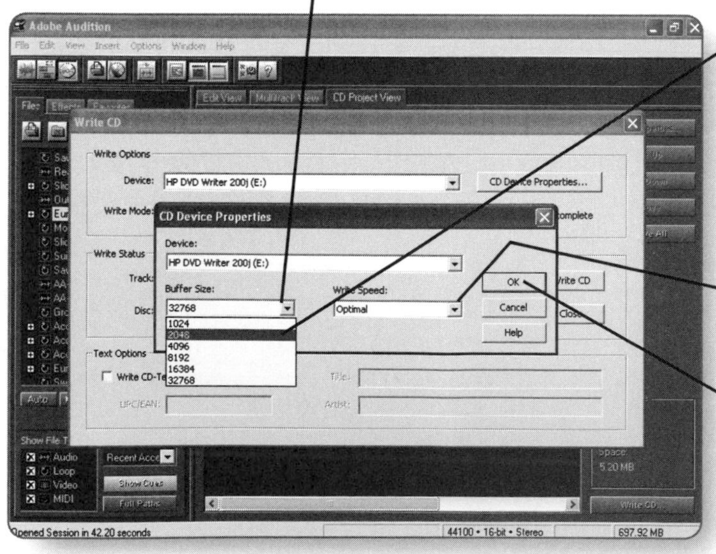

6. **Click** on the desired **buffer size**. It will be selected.

7. **Click** on the **Write Speed down arrow**. A list of write speeds will appear.

8. **Click** on the desired **write speed**. It will be selected.

9. **Click** on **OK**. You will be returned to the Write CD dialog box.

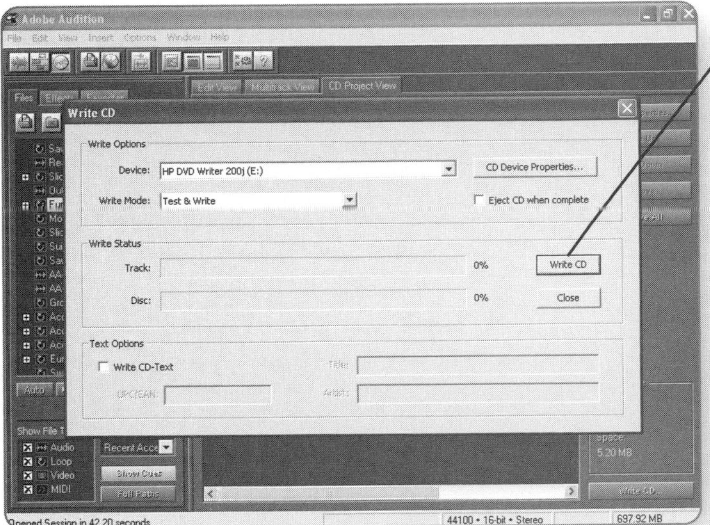

10. Click on **Write CD**. The files will be burned using the selected device.

A

Review Questions and Answers

This appendix includes questions compiled from the chapters of this book. This should serve as a review session to see how well you comprehended the subject matter. Don't worry if you don't know all of the answers off the top of your head. You aren't expected to be an Audition expert. The answers are included for your convenience.

Questions

1. A ________ will record every command you make during the recording process so that it can be played back later.
2. What is the keyboard shortcut to toggle between Edit and Multitrack views?
3. What is the name of the feature that gives you the ability to apply a multitude of scripts all at the same time?
4. What is the name of the view mode that allows you to view both the frequency and the amplitude in the form of a color?
5. What effect is particularly useful for fixing audio that was recorded from old vinyl records?
6. If you want your audio to sound like a turntable losing power, which effect would you apply?
7. The _____ ______ will alter both the pitch and the panning of audio over a period of time.
8. What is the feature that allows you to create the illusion of movement in your audio by providing you with a graph that plots time against degrees?
9. What button do you click to audition an effect before it is applied?
10. What tool would be used for removing vocals from a track?
11. In order to import video, you must be in _________ view.
12. How many videos can you have open per session?
13. Is it possible to import video from a .wmv file?
14. What is the length of the pause that Audition adds before a CD track?
15. When creating a CD, how do you know when you have exceeded the time limit?
16. What do three dots after a menu item indicate?
17. What happens when you right-click on a toolbar?
18. How do you move a toolbar?
19. If you are planning to output your audio to CD, what should the sample rate be?
20. If you want to save your session with a new name, what command should you use?
21. How do you change the speed of Fast Forward?
22. How do you get a selection to play over and over?
23. A ________ allows you to quickly jump to a specific point in your musical sequence.
24. What feature allows you to precisely position a cue?
25. How do you change the time format displayed?

26. If you are recording vocals for a CD, what should the channel setting be?
27. Digitally extracting audio from a CD is called ________.
28. How do you record to multiple tracks at the same time?
29. Under which menu is the Noise feature found?
30. What is white noise?
31. What is a constant tone?
32. A _______ ________ is one whose overtones, frequency, and modulation change over time.
33. What happens if you import an audio file into your session that does not have the same sample rate or other settings as your current session?
34. What feature would you use to re-record a portion of a clip?
35. What tool allows you to set a specific time to start and stop recording, and choose a specific length of time for recording?
36. How is deleting different from trimming?
37. What are the total number of clipboards available to you in Audition?
38. What does the Append command do?
39. How do you set consistent loudness levels for all of your waveforms?
40. When you _______ a wave clip, you create an exact duplicate in a new location.

Answers

1. Script
2. F12
3. Batch processing
4. Spectral view
5. The Click/Pop eliminator
6. Pitch bender
7. Doppler shifter
8. Stereo field rotate
9. Preview
10. The Channel mixer
11. Multitrack
12. One

13. Yes
14. Two seconds
15. The indicator at the bottom of the screen will let you know.
16. A dialog box will open when you select that menu item.
17. A menu will appear from which you can select other toolbars.
18. Click and drag over the double gray bars that appear on the toolbar.
19. 44100 samples per second
20. Save As
21. Right-click on the Fast Forward button and click the desired speed.
22. Click the Play Looped button.
23. Cue
24. Cue List window
25. Double-click on the waveform ruler.
26. Stereo
27. Ripping
28. Enable the tracks you want to record to by pressing the R button.
29. Generate
30. This type of noise produces sound with every frequency in the same amount.
31. A constant tone is one whose overtones and base frequency does not vary from its beginning point to its end point.
32. Varying Tone
33. If the file you are importing does not have the same audio properties as your current session, you will be prompted to have it converted as it is imported.
34. Punch-in recording
35. Timed recordings
36. With deleting you select the area that you would like to remove rather than the area that you would like to keep.
37. Six
38. You can merge two or more waveform files together by using the Append command.
39. Use the Normalize command.
40. Clone

Index

A

D

I

K

L

M

Q

R

S

T

Z

SHARPEN YOUR SKILLS, RELEASE YOUR SOUND with Music Technology titles from Course PTR

SONAR 3 Power!
ISBN: 1-59200-339-7 ■ **$29.99**

Pinnacle Studio 9 Ignite!
ISBN: 1-59200-475-X ■ **$19.99**

Digital Performer 4 Ignite!
ISBN: 1-59200-352-4 ■ **$19.99**

Pro Tools LE 6 Ignite!
ISBN: 1-59200-150-5 ■ **$19.99**

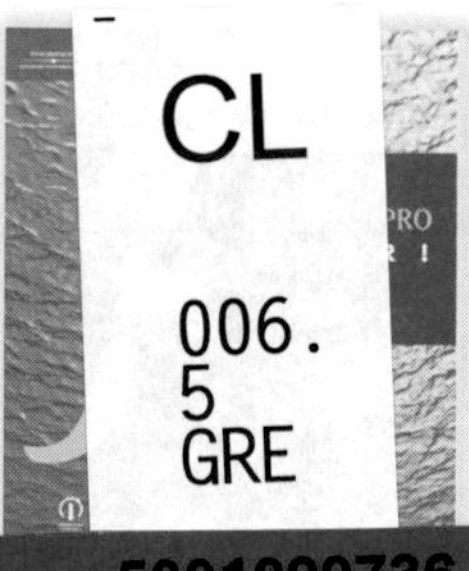

Avid Xpress Pro Power!
ISBN: 1-59200-151-3 ■ **$29.99**

Cubase SX/SL 2 Power!
ISBN: 1-59200-235-8 ■ **$29.99**

Emagic Logic Tips and Tricks
ISBN: 1-59200-135-1 ■ **$24.99**

Soundtrack Ignite!
ISBN: 1-59200-428-8 ■ **$19.99**

GarageBand Ignite!
ISBN: 1-59200-474-1 ■ **$19.99**

THOMSON
COURSE TECHNOLOGY
Professional ■ Trade ■ Reference

Visit our Web site for more information and **FREE** sample chapters.

To order, call **1.800.354.9706**
or order online at **www.courseptr.com**